Longing *for* Connection

OTHER BOOKS BY THE AUTHOR

Democracy's Muse:
How Thomas Jefferson Became an FDR Liberal, a Reagan Republican,
and a Tea Party Fanatic, All the While Being Dead

Lincoln Dreamt He Died:
The Midnight Visions of Remarkable Americans from Colonial Times to Freud

The Original Knickerbocker: The Life of Washington Irving

Jefferson's Secrets: Death and Desire at Monticello

The Passions of Andrew Jackson

Letters from the Head and Heart: Writings of Thomas Jefferson

America's Jubilee: A Generation Remembers the Revolution After Fifty Years of
Independence

Sentimental Democracy: The Evolution of America's Romantic Self-Image

The Inner Jefferson: Portrait of a Grieving Optimist

COAUTHORED WITH NANCY ISENBERG

The Problem of Democracy:
The Presidents Adams Confront the Cult of Personality

Madison and Jefferson

COEDITED WITH NANCY ISENBERG

Rip Van Winkle's Republic: Washington Irving in History and Memory

Mortal Remains: Death in Early America

Longing
for
Connection

*Entangled Memories
and Emotional Loss
in Early America*

ANDREW BURSTEIN

JOHNS HOPKINS UNIVERSITY PRESS ❧ BALTIMORE

This book was published with the generous support of the
J. G. Goellner Endowment

Johns Hopkins University Press
2715 North Charles Street
Baltimore, Maryland 21218
www.press.jhu.edu

Library of Congress Cataloging-in-Publication Data

Names: Burstein, Andrew, author.
Title: Longing for connection : entangled memories and emotional
loss in early America / Andrew Burstein.
Description: Baltimore : Johns Hopkins University Press, [2024] |
Includes bibliographical references and index.
Identifiers: LCCN 2023028035 | ISBN 9781421448305 (hardcover) |
ISBN 9781421448312 (ebook)
Subjects: LCSH: United States—Social life and customs—1783–1865. |
National characteristics, American. | Emotions—Social aspects—
United States. | BISAC: HISTORY / United States / Colonial
Period (1600–1775) | SOCIAL SCIENCE / Ethnic Studies /
American / General Classification: LCC E301 .B84 2024 |
DDC 306.0973/09034—dc23/eng/20231018
LC record available at https://lccn.loc.gov/2023028035

A catalog record for this book is available from the British Library.

Special discounts are available for bulk purchases of this book. For more information,
please contact Special Sales at specialsales@jh.edu.

For Robert and Lois

What seest thou else
In the dark backward and abysm of time?

—William Shakespeare, *The Tempest*

Contents

Longing *for* Connection

A prayerful George Washington. Painting by Joseph Kyle,
engraved by William G. Armstrong, late 1830s.

Courtesy of the American Antiquarian Society.

Introduction

Together let us beat this ample field,
Try what the open, what the covert yield;
The latent tracts, the giddy heights explore
Of all who blindly creep, or sightless soar;
Eye Nature's walks, shoot Folly as it flies,
And catch the manners living as they rise.
—Alexander Pope, *Essay on Man* (1733–34)

❦

Is it reasonable, even for a cultural historian, to think that the inner lives of those long gone are reachable? A way to address the question is to identify prevailing sources of influence. Before the internet and before TV, radio was a hypnotic force in households. And before film, before recorded sounds, before electricity, when the American nation was new, poetry held an immense power over the mind. It spoke the language of emotion, compensating in cases where the Anglo-American vernacular came up short.[1]

Enter Alexander Pope (1688–1744), an Englishman whose name once held magical associations, much as Shakespeare's still does for us. His odd personal story made Pope's words even more alluring. Under five feet tall, physically deformed and wracked with pain, he was nonetheless an extraordinary entertainer, alive with energy and in possession of an open mind. He said he chose poetry as his vehicle for addressing the human condition because of the genre's known capacity for stimulating the mind and the likelihood of his verses being retrievable from memory.

In 1727, a young Bostonian who sent Pope a letter thought the remoteness of his situation had to be explained: "But what corner of the earth is so secret, as not to have heard the fame of Mr. Pope?" he wrote. "You may take the pleasure of an admired name in America." That young man, Mather Byles, became a recognized poet in the colonies and eventually a mentor to the precocious Phillis Wheatley, an enslaved youth who became a sensation on two continents on the eve of the American Revolution. Wheatley, born in West Africa, developed her poetic temper as an eager consumer of Pope's verses, and her name was frequently linked with his once she began publishing.[2]

The world of avid readers that Pope addressed was one marked by a commitment to the "science of humanity" in which popular writers and moral philosophers were alike beguiled by reactive nerves and sublime visions of Nature. Their subjects were mind and spirit, beauty and wonder. Owing to its uplifting effect, Pope's *Essay on Man* would be published and republished up and down the new United States decade after decade. George Washington owned a multivolume set of Pope's works. Benjamin Franklin quoted him in his annual *Poor Richard's Almanack* as early as 1748. The otherwise blank cover of John Adams's diary book for 1765 contains that curious couplet from the opening of *Essay on Man*:

> Eye Nature's walks, Shoot folly as it flys,
> And catch the Manners living as they rise.[3]

Why did so many thousands find emotional sustenance in these words in the eighteenth and early nineteenth centuries?

The epigraph that opens this chapter sets the stage for all that follows. "Let us beat this ample field" is the poet's way of describing the journey of life, one fraught with anxious moments. By deliberately taking firm steps across the nearly measureless ground, the traveler stays alert to the dangers, physical and moral, that lurk.

At this time, readers of poetry looked for sensory cues. Pope first engages the faculty of sight, as he addresses the fleeting character of perception. Embracing "what the open, what the covert yield" means contending with the choices that arise in any life. The "open" choices are the easier ones to navigate; the "covert," being hidden, are no less critical, if harder to reason through. To "blindly creep" is to proceed with little knowledge; the future is unpredictable. These words relate as well to the blindness within, to the transient power of perception and the mind's failure to recognize when some crucial hint is being offered. This not-knowing prevents individuals from seeing into their own heart and from recognizing the emotional cost of passivity.

The phrase "Nature's walks" in the final couplet of the epistle that Adams inserted at the head of his diary urges resistance to artificial wants. Nature's law is an *inner* law, a power of mind that one effects by taking aim at all useless pursuits—that is, by "shoot[ing] folly as it flies." Here suggesting wild game on the wing, the active verb *shoot* makes a forceful impression.

There is an implied social commentary in Pope, adding to his appeal. His oft-quoted lines bespeak an essential understanding of the world that the mind acquires through provocation without forfeiting its attachment to order and balance. The individual cultivates a "mix'd and softened" passion through the study of Nature's endowments. When all life is transitory, the closest one can come to truth is to catch and hold life-sustaining knowledge—"the manners living." *Essay on Man*, in short, is a guide to inner peace.[4]

Each generation needs to be seen in terms of its own backward glance. In the late eighteenth century, Pope was placed beside the even earlier John Dryden, England's first poet laureate, and the comparison went like this: "Dryden is read with frequent astonishment, and Pope with perpetual delight." John Adams purchased Pope's complete works for his son John Quincy Adams when the lad was thirteen. Dr. Benjamin Waterhouse openly borrowed Pope's wit when he described the elder Adams, an old friend, as "a stout polemic, stubborn as a rock."[5]

Anecdotes about Pope appeared frequently in US newspapers in the early decades of the republic. A column of 1797 from a small press in a New Hampshire village suggests that Pope reached beyond an elite audience. It recounts an episode in the crippled man's life when he was helped home one night by a linkboy, as the urchins were known, who, for sixpence or so, held lanterns and lit the way to safety. At his lodging, he asked the lad how much he owed and was told. The poet replied, "God mend me, that will never do," "God mend me" being what he tended to say when something surprised him. The "lighter, unable to ignore Pope's deformed appearance, snapped back, "God mend you[,] Sir! *[H]e had better make a new one.*" And Pope, "so much pleased with the wit," added two shillings to the amount requested. The moral of this anecdote according to the paper's editor was that "a man of true wit is pleased with it, though it be at his own expence."[6]

A quip in a New York paper in 1816 combined Pope's humor with his skepticism about royal prerogative, showing just how he appealed to American sensibilities. After Pope had dined with the young Prince of Wales and paid him compliments, the royal host said, "I wonder[,] Pope, that you who are so severe upon kings, should be so complaisant with me?" The poet retorted with "I like the lion before his claws are grown."[7]

"Pope is always smooth, uniform, and gentle," reads a guide to elocution published in Philadelphia in 1801 that addressed his purity in diction. He is "the most correct of the English poets, and yet entirely an original," a Cincinnati opinion writer judged in 1829. Pope was "too capricious and too independent" to conform to the strictures of a political party, and he embodied a love of liberty, which was part of what endeared him to Americans. A provocateur on the page, he earned himself enemies among conservatives.

Yet another American generation embraced him. The popular antebellum poet-physician Oliver Wendell Holmes Sr., a New Englander, so imbibed him that he could be described as the "Yankee Pope." In an 1859 speech, Abraham Lincoln quoted from epistle 4 of the *Essay on Man*: "Oh, happiness, our being's end and aim!" Pope remains unconsciously present even after all these years in such expressions as "to err is human," "hope springs eternal," "fools rush in where angels fear to tread," and "a little learning is a dangerous thing."[8]

He translated Homer's *Iliad* to great acclaim and "improved" Shakespeare (altering meter and certain vocabulary). His *Essay* was also notable for challenging presumptions of faith and for suggesting that God's power was limited to a display of the grandeur of Nature. He urged readers to explore the sensations and the natural faculties that defined individuality. The markers of culture that operate throughout this book are ones he engages. They are life's fragility, sharp wit and social satire, humanity and inhumanity. Though his life ended when George Washington was yet a child, Pope credibly represents a set of values that was once America.

To open with an extended meditation on the diminutive, pain-ridden Alexander Pope is to warm the reader up for an immersive experience in an unfamiliar world, a vaguely imagined, emotionally distant, routinely falsified American past. The key that unlocks the door to that world is to be found in period vocabulary, in the characteristic language emotion leaned on.

Poets were celebrities on the order of today's athletes and movie stars. They spoke emotion's language best, and helped people give vent to their feelings. The words of poets were anthems, much as popular song lyrics are identified with social movements in more recent times: poems energized in the same way music does. When an emotion was demanded in writing of any kind but the conventions then in place did not provide a way to adequately express it, a poet's words were set down on the page. Secondhand eloquence answered for the incompleteness of the chaste, mannerly Anglo-American idiom that people drew upon in their everyday lives.

Even hate mail invoked the poets. About to complete his first year as president, Thomas Jefferson received a concise letter from New York, written in a stylish hand and cryptically signed "A—X." He saved it, drily listing the subject as "assassination" in his personal records. Mailed to the as-yet-unguarded President's House in Washington, it opened:

> "Read this
> "And then to dinner
> "With what appetite"
> you may
> You are in danger a dreadful plot is
> forming against you—p[oiso]n. the method
> —Julius Caesar was cautioned for the Ides of March
> —I caution you for the last of April

This writer, a disempowered individual whom we today would classify as a "troll," was evidently a reader of both Pope, who popularized the opening taunt, and Shakespeare, who first composed it. Besides making an obvious reference to Caesar's assassination, Jefferson's mysterious correspondent repeats lines from act 3 of *Henry VIII*, in which the king tells the power-hungry Cardinal Wolsey, whose duplicitousness has been exposed, to "read o'er this . . . and then to breakfast with what appetite you have."⁹

It is not acknowledged often enough that post-Revolutionary Americans' cultural references were as much European as home-grown. Their separation from Great Britain was neither as clear-cut nor as comprehensive as most imagine. A majority of British Americans opted for political independence, but they did not have a homespun answer for every concern. Indeed, culturally speaking, they were "embryonic Americans." Adapting British ways to a New World setting and desiring to improve them-selves through literature, the first three million self-styled "freedom-loving" colonists found their performative models across the Atlantic. They were ever eager for acceptance and re-spect from Europe.

The period this book covers has always mattered to students of history and retains an aura of spectacle in the national imag-ination. The American creation myth touts the virtues of its fighting patriots and the collective "genius" of those who forged the federal Constitution. In recent decades, of course, the cor-rective for all narrow forms of ancestor worship has consisted of discovering long-buried stories of the men and women who exposed the lie of a legal system that claimed to ensure indi-vidual liberty but only acted to prop up the entrenched elites who sentenced their human property to lives of forced labor.

Both narratives—that of ennobled statesmen and that of a dignified underclass—are imperfect. They alter the past to serve the present, albeit in ways that cannot be easily proven. They are competing forms of the nostalgic impulse, the longing for connection to a better or more serviceable past through com-memorative ritual, literature, and film, filling a need that is not hard to understand.

As a subgenre of cultural history, emotional history attempts to make sense of the contrast between the present's legitimate desire to right past wrongs and the discriminating historian's desire to access a higher truth. Yet historical objectivity is no more than an ideal, similar to a nation's hope of arriving at a "more perfect union."

An emotional history that aims to tease out psychological states from letters, diaries, and similar texts must reckon with invisible changes that occur with the passage of time. It accepts that preserved history is always a tiny sliver of what was. Historical memory is notoriously fragile and to be distrusted, and the politics of memory can be brutal. Yet historians of all stripes recognize a common enemy in superficiality. The deeper a work of history probes, the more it contends with emotional life. Emotional history fills gaps from a past that will never be more than partially recoverable, imparting a "textured" picture of the human condition.

Narrative Focus: Naming Names

The guiding theme throughout this book is the two-sided coin of *felt connections* and *uncomfortable separations*, sensations of liberation and alienation, and how these contrasting feelings shaped culture. Each of the six chapters centers on public figures in atypical circumstances in order to get under their skin, to get inside their heads. Chapter subtitles (which I've placed in parentheses) give a name to the emotional marker under consideration. Informative opening vignettes display the featured emotion and are followed by accounts of the similarly relatable experiences of less familiar men and women, some of them prominent in their day and now ignored by all but a smattering of scholars. Additional evidence appears in the words of anonymous writers.

As it is impossible to encompass all known emotions, the formula I engage joins American manners to a specific set of emotions that have had a critical impact on historical developments and that, I believe, are translatable. These are categorized under the headings martyrdom, apprehensions, yearnings, laughter, vainglory, and rationalization. Together they take in the unease, wariness, suspense, and expectation that were a part of ordinary life and a cultural inheritance. Individuals face pained absences, express a desire for intimacy, exhibit sociable good humor, offer strained justifications, and confront issues of control versus lack of control. We can sum up their inclinations in one word: longings.[10]

The arrow of time serves as a kind of steering mechanism, a way to segue from one chapter to the next, pointing to consequential connections, some transient, some profound. Most of us have by now heard of "six degrees of separation," the social distancing calculus whereby everyone on the planet has supposedly touched the lives of everyone else. In this book, that stimulating concept is applied cross-generationally. By the concluding chapter, the interconnected names come full circle: six chapters, six degrees of temporal separation. The Revolutionary martyr Nathan Hale (1755–76) is, in this manner, creatively reconnected to an acclaimed grandnephew he would never know, the popular author and minister Edward Everett Hale (1822–1909).

The circle, somewhat loosely drawn, encompasses a number of people who in one way or another crossed paths. Nathan Hale acts at the behest of George Washington; the Washingtons, Martha and George, impart thoughts and feelings to Abigail and John Adams; the Adamses commune with Thomas Jefferson, who familiarizes himself with political satirist and celebrity storyteller Washington Irving. Crossing continents, Irving connects meaningfully with the brothers Alexander and Edward Everett, diplomat-statesmen with a direct Adams connection; the Everetts are in contact with the immensely successful magazine editor Sara Josepha Hale (who was not related to the martyr's family). She, for religious as much as patriotic reasons, presses Abraham Lincoln—who is momentously joined by patriot-orator Edward Everett at the Gettysburg battlefield—to federalize the Thanksgiving holiday, an emotionally framed American tradition.

The first chapter puts the developmental strategy of the book in another frame by investigating words that express romantic truths while telling outright lies. No one and everyone is to blame for the post-Revolutionary projection of America's mythos. Its inspirational foundational narrative rests, of course, on the paternal shoulders of George Washington, icon of courage, man of conviction. He was mourned one way in January 1800, memorialized in print and statuary and in other morally uplifting ways by succeeding generations. He who "sacrificed ease" to lead his people to independence is paired with a young revolutionary in his employ as a spy. Nathan Hale was twenty-one when he sacrificed mortal life for his not-yet-secure country, though, significantly, he did not emerge as a historical actor of any note until the Revolutionaries were disappearing from earth in the mid-1830s.

This chapter takes up the question of how emotionally uplifting legends take the shape they do and why they are accompanied by a need for martyrs and villains when one generation passes them on to the next. Americans honored symbols of solemn virtue who "died before their time," such as Joseph Warren and Nathan Hale, while retaining a lurid fascination with traitors and killers like Benedict Arnold and John Wilkes Booth.

The next chapter tackles an emotion every human being has experienced: the pangs associated with a loved one's absence. John, Abigail, and John Quincy Adams journeyed great distances, more often apart than together, as did members of many other families. In their slow-moving, letter-dependent, seafaring world, defiance of death was constant. The way they saw travel assuredly differs from how people in the age of airplanes view movement through space and across distance. So, this chapter assesses emotional adjustments that an eighteenth- or nineteenth-century terrestrial and maritime consciousness produced.

Human drama takes the stage in the following chapter. Shakespeare's unifying language, beautifully expressing history's soul, resonates across the centuries. Like Pope, he was quoted to improve a thought or amplify an emotion. The first president's witty, accible minister to France, Gouverneur Morris, knowing Washington was fond of Shakespeare, refers to *King Lear* to poke fun at a sycophantic French official, describing him as "a wavering Creature[,] one of those of whom Shakespear says that they 'renege affirm and turn their halcyon Beaks with every Gale and vary of their Masters.'" This chapter testifies to the power of literary authority among people who learned to empathize with the human condition by taking Shakespeare to heart.[11]

It is but a minor detour from Shakespeare to the subject of satire. New Yorkers Washington Irving and James Kirke Paulding, both born before the Treaty of Paris confirmed American independence, made their avid readers think critically as well as laugh at human nature. But how much of the humor that thrilled the masses still lands? Here, the temporal distance is truly felt, because electronic media has overtaken daily life, seizing attention, instantly connecting people to each other, and generating laughs with irreverent and insulting forms of visually direct satire. Just as the emotions associated with long-distance travel in the past have few points of comparison with those of the present, so the humor of the past is disconnected from that of the present.

The unstable politics of memory makes an encore appearance in a chapter that pivots on heroic history and biography. The brothers Everett and their peers, whose pens freely embellished, exemplify mid-nineteenth-century reconceptions of America's prospects. Their generation exploited nostalgia and clung to the idealized concept of e pluribus unum (out of many, one) through the toxic decade that ended in the tragedy of a civil war. It becomes clear in this chapter that attachment to the founders' ideals felt different to a people who related to 1776 from a shorter temporal distance. Meanwhile, US citizens already appeared to outsiders as self-absorbed, effusive in self-praise—qualities still often attributed to Americans today.

The sixth chapter focuses on a nineteenth-century moral calculus in constructions of race. The vehicle here is the once-applauded movement—"colonization"—whose goal was the removal of Black Americans to Africa or elsewhere. Colonization was a blatant act of mass separation that framed its "philanthropy" as a desire to effect a "reunification." A major proponent was the religious author and magazine editor Sarah Josepha Hale, one of the most influential voices, male or female, of the period. The language of Mrs. Hale and the American Colonization Society, a national organization she supported, rationalized their effort as one meant to "improve" life for unwanted freeborn Black Americans by sending them "home" to Africa. James Madison was a confirmed colonizationist. Abraham Lincoln was, too. The question, of course, is how so many white Americans whom history otherwise esteems were co-opted into so obviously cruel a mission.

The concluding chapter recalls Nathan Hale through the long-lived Edward Everett Hale, whose pathos-driven novella *The Man without a Country* was first published during the Civil War and made its minister-author a national figure. Connecting the two Hales makes it possible to conjoin the emotional tales of two kinds of martyrs: the revolutionary Nathan Hale, a noble youth who regrets that he has but one life to lose for his country, and the momentary traitor of *The Man without a Country*, who suffers a life of exile for one impulsive, unpatriotic outburst.

If we take the long view, it becomes painfully clear in the end how martyrdom, betrayal, rationalization, cultural conceit, and unfulfilled longing have coexisted in the grand narrative and, I would argue, in the souls of citizens.

Narrative Focus: Manners, Memory, and Metaphor

In order to learn to present themselves to others or to advance socially, young and aspiring writers of the period often turned to popular guidebooks, a fair number of which existed from the mid-eighteenth century forward. These writing manuals literally dictated the format for a "familiar letter," as it's known, and specified the amount of openness that was appropriate. A writer was taught to affect "gesture" and "intonation" as well as presence of mind in a conversational piece meant to elicit an imaginative response from the letter's recipient. These qualities made for good reading, and so it is no surprise that epistolary novels were among most enchanting as the novel form took hold in England and America.[12]

Writing about the letters of Alexander Pope, the great eighteenth-century wit Samuel Johnson contested the popular assertion that "the true characters of men may be found in their letters." Instead, he insisted that "there is, indeed, no transaction which offers stronger temptations to fallacy and sophistication then epistolary intercourse." While it is true that letters of the time were often performances, that is not all they were. They also reveal what *moved* the generations that came of age between 1775 and 1865. The unfolded pages of rag paper on which letters were written contained intimate language in a familiar handwriting, which made them a prized possession in homes across America.[13]

The manners of a people crystallize in correspondence, where taste, judgment, and traces of unconcealed angst are all on display. The apparent opaqueness in their way of writing is to some degree reflective of shifts in vocabulary over time that camouflage what letter writers were in fact telling each other. When we read these letters discerningly, we see, in often unlooked-for ways, how men and women opened up, seeking solace, confessing to weakness, registering fear, expressing pride, while calculating how to convey assurances that they were in full possession of a healthy, active mind.

The past is always in eclipse, yet the craving to understand it is constant. Memory is flawed, and the brain compensates; it's the same with historical memory. The tendency is to accommodate prevailing ideas when one is part of a community—this is a known function of the brain, which aims to resolve ambiguities. To completely reject a national creation narrative that tells a happy story requires effort, even when the subjugation of Indigenous and dark-skinned people is an undisputed fact. Memory conformity is real science.[14]

People don't bring up memories in the absence of feeling, and they don't believe they know something until it feels like something they know. The five senses, which mediate between the outside world and the human mind, affect manners and memory alike. One way to study something as intangible as the "affective imagination" is to take a cue from sensory history. This is by no means a new field. One of its champions, Mark M. Smith, explains that when Europeans came to North America, they painstakingly described the "gustatory, auditory, visual, and tactile experiences" that greeted them. "So potent were these experiences that the period had a quality of sensory overload, inducing a sort of nervous sensibility from feeling too much."[15]

At present, Americans readily exchange one state for another, even relocating to a job on the opposite coast with a minimum of fuss. That kind of mobility has an intangible but certainly significant impact on the life of the mind, if not the brain's evolution. "Place is no longer felt as the force of destiny," writes social anthropologist Paul Connerton, whose research concerns the impact of the mass production of speed on the human brain and the social imaginary. Living at high speed and amid a certain kind of noise and clutter separates us from the horse-and-buggy past. The commodification of material life has been restructuring imaginations in ways it is too soon to understand.[16]

When data regarding sense experience is not available, metaphorical association becomes one of the most useful tools in writing emotional history. Ever since Aristotle's *Rhetoric* and *Poetics*, metaphor has been understood to relate to emotional states (*pathos*) and to an acuteness of mind in perceiving similarities among different things. Metaphor engages the element of surprise while redescribing reality, revealing the mind's plasticity: we understand how grasping a material object relates to grasping an idea. Connections between body and mind are dynamic, as John Locke's philosophical medicine advertised to the Western world. Think of the convergence of perceptual domains in the "teeth of a comb," how a body part is associated with an object. It has recently been argued that Locke mobilized metaphor for the eighteenth century, resulting in sense and sensation attaining a preeminent position in all aspects of communication. Thus, metaphor is more than a rhetorical choice. Tracing patterns in its use, we make it possible to see (or shed new light on, to double up on the metaphor) distinct elements of a past culture.[17]

An emotional history must be sensitive to ways in which language operated. Think of what a future reader who did not understand the designations "red states" "blue states" or did not know what "grassroots" or "spin" meant would miss about today's political dynamic. A "bleeding heart" exudes emotion; a "heart of stone" is unresponsive. So that's the idea. Language bespeaks an emotional intensity. What would "a sight for sore eyes" convey to someone who lacked "insight" into the nonliteral nuances of dialect? Without a clue to its emotional meaning, "gut feeling" would strike the cultural outsider as a medical observation.[18]

Metaphors in the six chapters are joined to sensations. The martyr tale, with its implication of innocence, sincerity, and a surrender to fate, is a metaphor for the power of historical example that relies on orality (speechmaking), and it is through the sense of hearing that such histories are passed down through the ages. Words of remembrance, memorized and sung by school-children, extend the life of the message.

Physical absence is felt when one contemplates mortal dangers on the road or high seas and aching for a reunion with loved ones. Here, the missing sense of touch must be vicariously sought in letters, in the "hand" of the absent loved one. In many personal communications, the metaphor of the heart beats alongside the metaphor of life as a journey. These connect to fearful evocations of the awesome power of natural phenomena—like the blowing winds of a tempest at sea, signifying both human and beyond-human passions.

The "taste" for humor in popular wit, satire, political ridicule, and racist mockery takes its metaphorical cue from metaphor itself, in how word transposition is used to produce laughter and derision, and the "appetite" for humor is never sated.

Nineteenth-century conceptions of American character, as developed in heroic histories, used words connected with sub-lime natural phenomena to describe George Washington and others. The overt manufacture of "genius," exaggerating feeling for effect, seized on the metaphor of light: the *luster* acquired by virtuous achievement, the *radiance* that continued to illuminate the nation even after the hero's death. The pursuit of light in the production of comforting myths contrasts with the spread of race prejudice through words denigrating darkness. Adjectives such as "coal-black" or "sooty" were stereotypically used to paint Black Americans as unattractively formed beings. The olfactory sense also figured in deprecations of African Americans. Early American medical literature derived diagnoses from offenses to the nose—typhus was "putrid fever"—which indicated a further vilification of Blackness in association with the offense a white person took to an enslaved person's bodily odor. Racist metaphors often indicated the presence of disease. White writers cavalierly identified the proliferation of free Blacks as a "foul infection," their African "blood" a "blot" or a "taint"; on the flip side of the coin, antislavery agitators termed the institution of slavery a "canker," an "affliction."

Scrutinizing Feeling

Emotional history emerged in the 1980s. It is not psychohistory, though it surely aims to reconstitute the life of the mind in earlier contexts: what it felt like to live and love and strive. The voices that speak from what Shakespeare in *The Tempest* refers to as the "abysm of time" are connected by a common thread: the formation of emotional attachments, the human condition.[19]

This book begins when the United States begins. Thirteen states as a single body unit asked the larger world to accept the new entity as a political equal. In declaring independence, they invoked a language that fused the law of nations, moral assertiveness, sentimental attachment, and victimhood. They described an "infant empire" whose governing institutions encouraged civility and decorum, and they claimed innocence and purity for its people—a people intimately connected to Old World culture yet also distinct from it.

From the moment independence was secured, a bright vocabulary appeared in the popular press and published sermons that overlooked imperfections and rationalized white dominion. In 1783, Yale's president Ezra Stiles (among whose achievements was his memorization of all 398 lines of Pope's *Essay on Man*) rhapsodically prayed away the Indigenous population, "whose sparse thin settlement" made it routine to purchase the "right of soil" from them, and he ecstatically predicted that "free citizens" would make sure that wealth was justly apportioned, based on the understanding that "an equitable distribution of property, enters into the foundation of a happy State." The Anglo-American population would diffuse itself across the continent, an "English increase" above all others, making future America a people "high above" the rest and more numerous than the Chinese.[20]

The United States and its overseas friends imagined a fresh start, a wake-up call for Western civilization. At the height of the Cold War, the liberal theologian Reinhold Niebuhr recognized the old claim for what it was in *The Irony of American History* (1952). "We came into existence with the sense of being a 'separated' nation, which God was using to make a new beginning for mankind." Niebuhr saw an "ironic incongruity between our illusions and the realities we experience" in everyday life. Monarchy was the supreme symbol of institutionalized injustice before communism assumed that role in America's self-congratulatory story.[21]

Ideology is a powerful force. Impulse and inertia lead to the substitution of comfort and calm for the destabilizing work of speaking truth. Our feelings persuade us. That is why, to obtain an accurate reading of the past, we must scrutinize feeling in its historical context to see how it inspired exertion, how it explains inactivity.

This book does not claim to cover all emotion. For example, the anger that has incited mobs to rise in opposition to government power in every generation since the founding of the United States is an immense topic that this book does not pretend to do justice to. And although it extracts emotion from published sermons, it does not seek to explain evangelical fervor either. There are historians who specialize in these things. Chapter 6 explores racial prejudice in the colonization movement without arguing the causes of the Civil War. That said, even a selective, episodic reading of the pulse of the past stands to remove fog, repairing damage caused by ideological intransigence and embroidery in standard texts.

Because this book takes the literate public as its focus, it does not treat the poor and unschooled of any ethnicity. It is expected these days that the white male should not overwhelm a narrative that professes to encompass a national community. The presence of women is extensive in this book because women, single as well as married, wrote and published at length in the period covered here. Nonwhite voices appear in the text for the same reason: they were participants in the national community of writers and readers.[22]

Anonymous contributors to newspapers serve as fortuitous intermediaries in this story. They stand with the writers, educators, and politicians who do not necessarily speak for the public at large but nonetheless channel trends. But if my emphasis remains on known individuals, that does not necessarily make my study "exclusive." It would be foolish to insist that the cultural production of emotions is unresponsive to an elite sensibility. We know, for instance, that Black Americans imitated English poets and essayists just as their white American counterparts did. Phillis Wheatley, while enslaved, sought to write in the manner of elite Anglo-American poets, so to treat her voice as solely that of an enslaved woman is an incomplete characterization. History shows elite values repeatedly, disruptively, being imposed on the masses. In this and other ways, *Longing for Connection* confronts the illusion that history is a rational or a controlled process.[23]

Past actors encrypt, modern scholars engage in decryption. The United States is idealized as a community that knits together different cultures, yet everyone knows it as a population torn by disconnections and estrangements, too. It is nostalgic for what may never have existed and ignorant of what it chooses not to see. The twenty-first century, like every preceding century, is a composite of memory and imagination. We say, proverbially, "time heals" without necessarily believing it. Better to say it this way: the past is a silent partner to the present. We may forget it, but that does not mean the past is done with us.

Nathan Hale statue at CIA headquarters, Langley, Virginia.
Courtesy of the CIA.

Chapter 1.

Memorable Words
(Martyrdom)

The legendary origin of events woven into sober
history prepares us to recognise how the imagination has fed the stream of tradition, itself no
mean tributary of that larger stream of history.
—Edward Clodd, *Myths and Dreams* (1885)

᪥

What is the difference between a myth and a lie? Both are
products of the imagination. But the first can be a celebratory
story enlivening the early history of a culture to advance a sense
of moral community or secure a social order, while the second
is a knowing misrepresentation meant to deceive. The English
anthropologist Edward Clodd (1840–1930), a student of Dar-
winism, reviewed the sacred origins of mythic narratives that
had survived and prospered over centuries. According to him,
handed-down myths recording faithfulness, selflessness, and
personal courage did not draw their power from "truth of detail" but from their status as "witnesses" to the comforting belief that civilization was continually raising moral standards.[1]

Clodd's formulation does not vary much from the current assumption that culture is the collection of stories we tell about ourselves whose impact is profound but not always easy to measure. In the United States, myths that attach themselves to the era of the founding have dug their roots deep and remain inspirational. They seek to provide emotional stability by assuming affective control over the national narrative.

America's mythic tale opened with the dramatic dissolution of a marriage, a historical drama worthy of Shakespeare. A freedom-loving people divorced a caretaker-king who had deliberately caused "repeated injury," obliging them to take appropriate measures to insure their safety. Having patiently suffered a "long train of abuses," they at length responded with an equally long train of justifications for why a permanent disconnection had to take place. This was all made public in a decree issued on July 4, 1776.

The "candid world" was on notice. Despite the American colonists' countless appeals to "justice and magnanimity," the document read, the leaders of Britain's government had ignored the well-established rights and concerns of their erstwhile "brethren"; they had turned a blind eye to reason while remaining "deaf to the voice of justice and of consanguinity." The signatories of the world-famous Declaration of Independence gave their total approval to these sensational images of abandonment.

National Creation Stories Don't Die

Creation stories center on firstness and dominance. In America's case, all is owed to a national father who embodied moral courage and nourished in his posterity the sense of an inheritance. George Washington did not sign the Declaration of Independence, but he saw to its realization when he led armies to their eventual victory.

Aspirational individuals and aspirational texts come to symbolize the moral identity of the nation as a community with a common creed. If Jefferson's Declaration has been given a life apart from the words that constitute it and Lincoln has been granted ethereal power as a healer, Washington exists to complete, to bind. While the human being was frustratingly opaque, his selfless devotion and impressive stamina are decisively drawn in countless biographies. From as early as 1775, his image led the way in America's decades-long battle to emerge from Britain's overspreading shadow.

Washington came to embody dignity, duty, and virtue. Even in the abstract, virtue in political action is rarely spoken of anymore, but in 1775, it was widely used to designate one whose concern for the community directed his public and private conduct. From the Revolution to the Civil War, whenever the name of the preeminent founder was uttered it was linked with the word "virtue." In schoolbooks, he was "wise and virtuous Washington."[2]

Early generations of Americans possessed a minimal vocabulary with which to probe the psychology of personality. Freedom and individual rights were translated into impassioned slogans, but "innerness" as we understand it remained conceptually vague. Histories scarcely hint at Washington in his emotional environment. To be sure, at the time of his inauguration as president, the press reported on the emotional surge among the public, at which time Washington experienced "exquisite Sensations" on being welcomed by "Matrons and Young ladies," telling his armed guard that "the affection of his fellow citizens" shielded him from harm. But that's pretty much as far as it goes with respect to the expression of emotion. Concealment was meant to protect both individual and society. Portraitists of this era aimed for emotionally empty facial expressions, as well as to hide bad teeth.[3]

George and Martha Washington resist the emotion-laden descriptions modern consumers of popular history wish to have. While they were social creatures who performed at length for contemporaries, they are not ever represented in dialogue. But pieces of evidence do exist that provide glimpses of private life. The diary of English-born Benjamin Henry Latrobe is one example. In 1796, some years before he was appointed by President Jefferson as the second architect of the US Capitol, Latrobe was in his early thirties and new to America. He had quickly befriended Bushrod Washington (1762–1829), the son of George Washington's younger brother. Bushrod was a very young private at the end of the Revolutionary War; in 1798, he was appointed as an associate justice of the Supreme Court, a position he would hold until his death. He was, less eminently and while he sat on the bench, a proponent of Black removal and first president of the American Colonization Society.

Latrobe visited Mount Vernon in mid-July 1796, in the final year of Washington's presidency. He described the approach to the plantation in considerable detail—the weeping willows and "good fences"—and noted the beveled, sanded wood of the rusticated house. "I introduced myself to Mrs. Washington as a friend of her nephew," he wrote. "She immediately entered into conversation upon the prospect from the lawn, and presently gave me an account of her family in a good-humored free manner that was extremely pleasant and flattering." He added meaningfully: "She has no affectation of superiority in the slightest degree, but acts completely in the character of the mistress of the house of a respectable and opulent country gentleman."

The well-heeled country gentleman was no less agreeable. "He was attired in a plain blue coat, his hair dressed and powdered," Latrobe wrote. "There was a reserve but no hauteur in his manner. He shook me by the hand, said he was glad to see a friend of his nephew's, drew a chair, and desired me to sit down."

Washington then spoke for an hour about land issues and a canal project he had lost faith in.

The next topic Latrobe's diary takes up is domestic life. In the ensuing hours, his host attended to his presidential duties while George Washington Lafayette, son of the celebrated Marquis, lolled about. The French teen was living in exile at Mount Vernon, protected from the radicals who'd imprisoned his parents; this George seemed entirely comfortable as an adoptive member of the first family. At 3:30 pm, as everyone sat down to dinner, the immigrant architect noted that "a few jokes passed between the President and young La Fayette." Other than that, dinner plodded along with solemnity and without noteworthy conversation.

Then, Latrobe synopsizes a private, coffee-accented, after-dinner conversation, during which Washington took up the subject of agriculture. He spoke at length about the Hessian fly that threatened Virginia crops and about a plow that interested him. He detailed an experiment he'd made involving wheat versus corn production and the kinds of bread preferred by those enslaved on his plantation. A man of business—that's the main takeaway.

Latrobe was making preparations to leave when the Washingtons pressed him to spend the night. The next morning, at seven thirty, the president entered the sitting room, "where the latest newspapers were laid out." Matters of business remained on his mind. "He did not at any time speak with very remarkable fluency," Latrobe concluded, though he appeared "intent in thought." The patriarch was "correct" (that is, well mannered), he wrote, yet he added that he "thought there was a slight air of moroseness about him." In other words, he apparently came across as a sullen figure—there was nothing in the outward demeanor of this man who personified virtue to suggest a sympathetic dimension or even a philosophic bent.

This unusual vignette tries, as much as the times allowed, to humanize Washington, but aside from the "few jokes" shared with his namesake, young Lafayette, all we glean is his manner of approaching a first-time guest whose background and education impressed him. He was welcoming, extremely civil, had a live-and-let-live quality about him. He "laughed heartily several times in a very good-humored manner," but it is not clear what caused him to laugh. On one level Latrobe's portrait is compelling, but on another it is bloodless.[4]

A second opportunity to enter the Washingtons' private world comes through a letter written by George to Martha, and it reveals a bit more. At some point after her husband's death in December 1799, she burned their intimate correspondence (or else a close relative did after her death in 1802), a common practice among mourners who retained only what they wanted posterity to see. But one letter lodged in a desk that Martha bequeathed to a granddaughter escaped incineration. The letter, dated June 18, 1775, provides a rare glimpse of their relationship.

George Washington, hard to imagine smiling, posted his note from Philadelphia, saluting "My dear Patcy" and telling her, "I retain an unalterable affection for you, which neither time or distance can change." He was extremely busy with representatives of the "United Colonies," who'd been meeting as a body following the deadly encounters at Lexington and Concord. Only three days prior, delegate John Adams had nominated Washington to lead the new Continental Army. At the time, neither he nor anyone else in the Continental Congress knew that the Battle of Bunker Hill had just taken place in Boston.[5]

We can be sure that Washington's "unalterable affection" for his wife was not a commonplace utterance because he used the phrase sparingly in correspondence, writing in this manner to his younger brother John Augustin Washington (Bushrod's father); to Princeton-educated lawyer Joseph Reed, a trusted aide nine years his junior; and to the French volunteer whom he made a major general in 1777, when he was only nineteen: Gilbert du Motier, the Marquis de Lafayette. "Unalterable affection" was the strongest way Washington and his peers had to indicate "attachment," a loaded term of this era that meant reciprocal devotion, tenderness, and unfeigned commitment. Martha, in turn, referred to her husband unambiguously as "my love."[6]

Martha's treatment of the letter attests to the value of privacy among the privileged set in Revolutionary America. A plantation mistress constantly had an audience, so moments of soul-searching, of spontaneity, held appreciable meaning. One can reasonably infer that she secreted the letter in a special place (forgetting, years later, that she had done so), either because the sentiment in it was pronounced or because it was composed at a historic turning point. Or both.

General Washington was about to travel to the war front and establish headquarters in Cambridge. The Battle of Bunker Hill was the first major engagement between those who styled themselves "provincials" and British "regulars" whose military prowess was known round the world. The two-hour battle witnessed pronounced gallantry and a tremendous loss of life. "Our poor unhappy country!" exclaimed the *Pennsylvania Evening Post* on June 22, as word first trickled in. "What are we to suffer?" When Washington rode off the next day to take command of the militias operating outside occupied Boston, only the barest details of the battle were known. The provincials were outnumbered two to one, yet the regulars lost twice as many men, well over a thousand. Close to half of those who charged up the hill were either killed or wounded before the locals were finally sent scurrying.[7]

Although he answered the call of Congress, Washington was conscious of his wife's desire for repose. He broke the news to her gently: "As it has been a kind of destiny that has thrown me upon this Service, I shall hope that my undertaking of it, is designd to answer some good purpose." For her part, Martha felt she wasn't meant for the scenes he was bound to encounter. "I confess I shudder every time I hear the sound of a gun," she admitted to a Virginia friend as she joined him in Cambridge in the late autumn of 1775. The couple lodged in comfort at a mansion that had been constructed in 1759 and recently confiscated from its Tory owner. Given time, she adapted to camp life, seeing enough of the war to recognize that her role was to bolster morale, to bring refinement and a sense of normalcy in trying circumstances.[8]

After a failed nine-month-long siege of Boston, the British army was forced to evacuate the city in March 1776. The Washingtons spent weeks together in Philadelphia, where he reported back to Congress, and then they traveled (on different days) to New York City, where a fierce new phase of the war would unfold that summer. In late June, as the British armada appeared offshore, Washington directed his wife to return immediately to Philadelphia; he would not risk her safety. As the Declaration of Independence was brought to life in the relative calm of Philadelphia, she was close at hand but entirely uninvolved, while the general, in charge of an increasingly rambunctious army, was holed up in a mixed Patriot-Tory commercial city. The very idea of nationhood was in its gestational period, as was the "idea" of George Washington.[9]

With that, we reach the first connection, that between Washington and Nathan Hale, the first spy to martyr himself in the cause to which they both gave their all.

Nathan Hale and the traitor Benedict Arnold were both from Connecticut. In the historical imagination their names are inextricably linked with that of General Washington and a series of military hostilities that took place in New York.

To frame their story properly and thereby show the long-lasting emotional repercussions of the first year of war, we need to sketch a different general first. Israel Putnam (1718–90) was once a popular subject of Revolutionary biography—a survivor, a folk hero. Like Hale and Arnold, he was a son of the Nutmeg state. In the days following Bunker Hill, before Washington appeared in Cambridge, the American war effort was largely in Putnam's hands. "Old Put" was advanced in years, but he had ample experience leading men into combat. He'd been captured during the French and Indian War, and early biographers describe in detail how he was nearly put to death. After that, he led a charmed life. Known and appreciated for his massive build, plain manners, and a spirited personality, he was a stalwart presence.[10]

Constituted from "the humble walks of life," he was closing in on sixty when he led a party of raw recruits to defend the earthen redoubts at Bunker Hill, a strategically significant prominence overlooking redcoat-infested Boston. "He made a stand," notes his first biographer, a Washington aide named David Humphreys, who gave credit to the death-defying general and his four hundred Connecticut men for arriving on the scene when most needed. "He did every thing that an intrepid and experienced officer could accomplish." Israel Putnam kept going until 1779, when a stroke forced his retirement from active soldiering.[11]

On the eve of the Bunker Hill battle, Putnam conferred with another who'd earned the confidence of Bostonians, a Harvard-schooled physician and patriot orator named Joseph Warren who would become one of the first of many martyrs to the cause. Dr. Warren was a restless and militant (but militarily inexperienced) Son of Liberty who'd dispatched Paul Revere two months earlier on his momentous ride to warn of the British regulars' show of force at Lexington and Concord. Heading the colonists' Committee of Safety, Warren was a newly appointed major general at the time of Bunker Hill. Like General Putnam, he understood the resisters' plight: powder was scarce and had to be expended with care. Both Warren and

Putnam remained in the thick of the action—Warren as a "volunteer" because his formal commission had yet to come through. He was determined to keep on to the bitter end—nothing Putnam could say would dissuade him—voluntarily covering the final retreat and taking a bullet.

Big-boned Israel Putnam was, by all accounts, a force of nature. After the British suddenly withdrew the following spring, Washington sent in the ever-reliable veteran to sniff around and make sure it was safe to reenter Boston. There was good reason to exercise caution. As Washington told the patriarch of a notable local family, Josiah Quincy, who reported on British troop movements, he was little concerned about recognizable "Marauding parties," but he was deeply troubled by officers in disguise and "persons unknown" lurking about town. "There is one evil I dread," wrote Washington, "& that is their Spies," adding "I could wish therefore that the most attentive watch was kept . . . to prevent suspected persons (for I have no doubt but that trusty Soldiers, Sergeants, and even Commissioned Officers in disguise will be sent out) from travelling about." He planned to dispatch a dozen "honest, sensible, and delegent [*sic*] Men" to stop strangers and interrogate anyone who could not "give an acct of themselves in a strait & satisfactory line."[12]

As year one of the war unfolded, Washington called on Putnam again and again, whose "*long Service and Experience*" he trusted through the war's darkest moments. As they prepared for a new phase in combat operations Washington encouraged Putnam to keep his eye on the British in Canada, instructing that he act independently and "*exert* every Nerve to disappoint the enemy's designs." Having by now set up new headquarters in New York City, Washington proceeded to activate an elite intelligence service under Lieutenant Colonel Thomas Knowlton, a veteran of Bunker Hill said to be Israel Putnam's favorite among junior officers. It was Knowlton who would soon after dispatch Captain Nathan Hale on his unpropitious mission behind enemy lines.[13]

Hale, Howe, and Hull

Many Americans mark June 6 each year because it lives in historical memory as D-Day. They think back to the Normandy invasion, when the tide began to turn in World War II. In the adorable town of Coventry, Connecticut, the day is remembered for an additional reason: it is the birthday of native son Nathan Hale, who came into the world in 1755, and died of unnatural causes at the age of twenty-one on September 23, 1776. Hale is known for what were allegedly his last words: "I only regret that I have but one life to lose for my country." But no one in fact knows whether he spoke them.

Like the much older Putnam, Nathan Hale was a Connecticut farm boy, the sixth of twelve children. His paternal line being Hale and his maternal line Strong, his family names suggested descent from a robust people. In tiny Coventry, east of Hartford, family names were far fewer than they'd be in subsequent generations, so it was not that much of a coincidence that one of his instructors at Yale was a cousin also named Nathan Hale. The student Nathan matriculated in 1769, which was no doubt young for college but quite common at this time. His elder brother Enoch was known at school as Hale primus; the sociable Nathan, quaintly, as Hale secundus. The brothers were befriended by, among others, the slightly older Timothy Dwight, class of '69, who remained at Yale to teach. Dwight, a poet and one of the so-called Hartford wits, later spoke to his young friend's martyred spirit. Dwight went on to serve as president of the college from 1795 until his death in 1817.

At eighteen, on graduation from Yale, Nathan Hale found a position as a schoolmaster in New London, Connecticut, a strategic seaport and pivotal communications hub that was to suffer predation a few years later when native son turned traitor Benedict Arnold invaded. Nathan taught there for a year, resigning after Bunker Hill so he could join Washington's army. Encamped on the outskirts of occupied Boston that summer and fall, he rose to the rank of captain, as attested by a document that bears the familiar signature of John Hancock. While there, Hale was often in the immediate company of General Putnam. The following March, British forces abandoned Boston and sailed to Canada to plot their assault on New York City. Anticipating the next phase of war, Washington's army relocated to Manhattan. Hale paused in New London before taking up his new post in the threatened city, near the East River.[14]

As Congress debated independence, Nathan, a week shy of his twentieth birthday, wrote forebodingly to his brother Enoch. The Tory population is numerous and dangerous, he said. "It would grieve every good man to consider what unnatural monsters we have as it were in our bowels. . . . It is really a critical period. America beholds what she never did before." He closed this desperate letter by setting up the drama to come as a British fleet of unknown size neared the area. "Are they not a formidable Foe? Surely they are."[15]

During the spring of 1776, Nathan was on Long Island for a brief assignment and returned to Manhattan prior to the outbreak of fighting in the city. Assigned to build defenses, he was not involved in the catastrophic Battle of Long Island at the end of August, which nearly decimated Washington's army. The young captain had some seventy or eighty men under his command when he was transferred into that specialized unit of New Englanders dubbed "Knowlton's Rangers."[16]

After he volunteered to penetrate enemy lines, Hale either received his orders from General Washington or, more likely, from Colonel Knowlton at Washington's behest. He proceeded with an army companion through Westchester County and into

Connecticut, crossing the Long Island Sound at Norwalk to Huntington Bay, Long Island, where he donned civilian clothes and became a spy, "assuming the character of a Dutch schoolmaster" in British-held territory.[17]

The information Washington hoped to obtain from Hale is obvious: where and when enemy forces would come ashore in Manhattan. Beyond Hale's mission, the commander had a great many other pressing concerns: the recent memory of a Tory conspiracy to assassinate him, a steady number of desertions, significant numbers of his troops plundering the city's residents. As a result, courts-martial were being held regularly. Logistical problems were uppermost in Washington's mind, such as the urgent need for cold-weather clothing and tents.

Hale's departure, supposed to be timely, was in fact hardly more than a week before the British landing on Manhattan Island. That event took place at Kips Bay on September 15, 1776. Washington's army fled north and encamped in Harlem Heights, near present-day Columbia University, where a great battle took place the following day. The Americans held their ground, but at a cost. Among the dead was the very valuable Colonel Knowlton, just thirty-five. The contrived last words attributed to him, unremembered and less beautiful than those of Nathan Hale, went like this: "I do not value my life if we do but get this day."[18]

Tradition has the unlucky Hale captured on Long Island, but it is entirely possible (even probable) that he made his way west and crossed the East River again before falling into enemy hands. Papers in his possession indicated that he had acquired useful intelligence. Tradition also holds that a Tory kinsman named Samuel Hale spotted and unmasked him on Long Island, but this, too, is highly questionable and probably an embellishment designed to add romantic flavor to the story. At any rate, Nathan Hale fell into enemy hands on the night of September 21, in the hours after a series of fires broke out downtown—

some reportedly set by disguised traders who'd sailed in from
Connecticut. British troops and their local allies took matters
into their own hands and immediately put to death an unspeci-
fied number of the arsonists. Whether or not he knew anything
about the fires, Nathan Hale was captured at a moment when
extreme actions were being taken. He was hanged as a spy on
the twenty-second, shortly before noon, on direct orders from
the commanding general of British forces.[19]

A confidant of Hale's, Yale classmate William Hull, reported (years later) that the brave captain consulted with him
in advance of the mission and that he duly warned him about
the dishonor that befell captured spies, who tended to be seen
less as brave men than deceivers. Hull's posthumous memoir recounts his words of warning to Hale. His daughter (and aman-
uensis) explains: "In the chapter concerning Captain Hale, I
have more fully unfolded sentiments expressed by my father
with that noble young man. In the work generally, I have introduced remarks not found in the MS., but which were familiar to my recollection from our frequent interchange of thought."
This is not the definition of verbatim language, of course. The
conflation of verbatim and approximate language is likewise evident in her noting that "few persons were around [Hale], yet
his characteristic dying words were remembered. He said, 'I only
regret, that I have but one life to lose for my country.'" "Characteristic" words are not exact words, and no one in particular
is named as among the "few persons" who were around him.
We cannot know with any degree of certainty that the final sentence Hale is said to have spoken is an accurate memory.[20]

We get Hull's testimony for the first time in 1799, courtesy
of the modest Hannah Adams (1755–1831), a distant relative of
the two Adamses who served as president. That year, she self-
funded a well-received book titled *A Summary History of New-
England*. The book contains specific language provided to her
by Hull. In relating Hale's "dying observation, 'that he only

lamented, that he had but one life to lose for his country,'" she credits Hull for conveying the "interesting account" of a martyred comrade. We should note that Adams refers to herself as the "compiler" of a history and does not overstate her credentials as a historian.[21]

A British deputy adjutant-general named Frederick Mackenzie penned in his diary in 1776 that Hale addressed those present at his execution, saying that it was "the duty of every good Officer to obey any order given to him by his Commander in Chief"—a direct reference to General Washington—and that anyone in his situation "should be prepared to meet death in whatever shape it might appear." Presumably a paraphrase of what Hale conveyed to his captors, these words lack the smoothness of what history tells us he said at the end. Let us bear that in mind, because the Mackenzie account is the most objective evidence we possess that dates from 1776 (far fresher than Hull's memory twenty-odd years later).[22]

Under a flag of truce, John Montresor, captain in the British Engineers, informed a party that included General Putnam and Captain William Hull and Captain Alexander Hamilton of Hale's execution. After Mackenzie, Montresor is a second witness, present when Hale was taken to the gallows, who is deemed credible. Montresor delivered the official news of Hale's fate and is presumably the source for Hull's statement to Hannah Adams. He has nothing more direct to say to history about Nathan Hale, though we do know that his own life was mired in controversy: Montresor had a reputation for arrogance and eventually died in prison in England.[23]

Montresor reported that Captain Hale acknowledged his rank and confessed to his mission before Lord Howe himself. Howe had commanded Britain's costly victory at Bunker Hill as well as the largely successful Battle of Long Island. As the sentence was read, a villain entered the Nathan Hale story: William Cunningham, Howe's provost marshal, who loomed over proceedings and willfully destroyed two letters the prisoner wrote as his final testament to family and friends, which poses a problem for history: lack of firsthand knowledge of Nathan Hale's state of mind as he faced the hangman's noose.

Hull would have been familiar with Joseph Addison's well-rehearsed play *Cato*, a tragedy written in 1712 and set in ancient Rome, that was performed at Valley Forge at Washington's request, in 1778. Its subject, Cato the Younger, was an enemy of Julius Caesar, a republican hero, a symbol of virtuous sacrifice. In act 4, Cato states, "What a pity it is that we can die once to serve our country." Did Hull willfully adapt Montresor's statement to make Nathan Hale a latter-day Cato? Or did Hale borrow Addison's vocabulary at the gallows? One can only speculate.[24]

Another more relevant factor in assessing Hull's testimony is the fact that he tried to warn off his comrade lest Hale succumb to a death less noble than one earned on the field of battle. It comes across as a bit self-serving for Hull to loom large as a sage advisor, spokesperson for the military ethos, cautioning Hale about the loss of military glory (and standing) if one were caught spying, given that secrecy was the very watchword of the colonial resisters in advance of the opening assault at Lexington and Concord and that disguise protected participants during the destruction of East India Company tea in Boston Harbor. Paul Revere gamely spied on the activities of the redcoats stationed in Boston in 1775.

Indeed, the word "spy" was proudly featured in the title of newspapers in both London and America. The *Massachusetts Spy* was a premier outlet for Revolutionary speech in 1775–76, borrowing the concept of "observing" society from the *London Spy* (1698), the *Universal Spy* (London, 1730s), the *Spy* at Oxford and Cambridge (1744), and others. "Spy" was a term of public amusement, metaphorically applied when not used in a military mode.

And a gentleman officer could take on a spying capacity. The British army hired scouts and mapmakers who functioned as intelligence gatherers. For the purpose of coordination, both sides had to locate armies—the enemy's, and quite often, their own. Deserters and escaped prisoners of war provided useful information, and in the case of the British effort, this included runaway slaves. Commanders needed to gauge an enemy's strength and detect movements, which was precisely why Washington needed a Nathan Hale.[25]

Distinguishing friend from foe was a constant concern, and we have already seen how it weighed on Washington's mind until it was proven to him that British withdrawal from Boston in March 1776 was complete and irreversible. In June 1776, leading up to the formation of Knowlton's Rangers in Manhattan, he urged creation of a "Committee on Detecting and Defeating Conspiracies." The chief instigator in that operation, John Jay, would become the secretary for foreign affairs in Congress after war's end and a trusted associate of President Washington upon his appointment as the first chief justice of the Supreme Court. Indeed, Washington was so intent on chipping away at the enemy's obvious advantage in money and manpower that he underwrote as much "silent" intelligence gathering as he could. We are left, then, wondering exactly why Hull thought it important to minimize the value of serving as Washington's spy when Washington himself saw no dishonor in removing one's uniform when one was penetrating enemy lines. Hull's cautionary advice to Hale reads as a dramatic flourish after the fact rather than an accurate recollection of a decisive conversation.[26]

Ironically, Hull was moved to write a spirited defense of his own less-than-heroic actions in the War of 1812, when he faced execution for dereliction of duty and worse. At the start of that unwished-for war, Major General Hull was governor of Michigan Territory. He lost Detroit to the British without firing a shot. "Weak, indecisive, pusillanimous," growled Revolutionary

War veteran and future president James Monroe. Thomas Jefferson, who as president appointed Hull to the position, rued the day, communicating to his successor, President Madison, that "we can tell by his plumage whether a cock is dunghill or game. With us, cowardice and courage wear the same plume." Comparing the general to animal excrement, Jefferson was saying he had no way of knowing that Hull would turn coward when he did.

After his court-martial and until Madison pardoned him, Hull was under orders to be shot. But as the dust settled, the discredited general received numerous testimonials from knowledgeable individuals, including a son of the late Israel Putnam, who disputed the official view of Hull's conduct and represented him as a sacrificial lamb offered up to divert attention from bad government planning. With no previous black mark on his record, his reputation remained mixed.[27]

In 1901, Henry Phelps Johnston (1842–1923) produced a limited private printing of *Nathan Hale, 1776*, carefully wrought and rich in documents. Johnston graduated Yale in 1862 and rose to the rank of second lieutenant in the Connecticut Volunteer Cavalry during the Civil War. He became, in turn, a lawyer, a newspaperman, and then a history professor at the City College of New York, a position he held the longest and with distinction. His sources are strong, and he makes clear where the earlier record is tainted, indulging only occasionally in unwarranted speculation about Hale's motives. That said, he buys into Hull's account completely.[28]

All we really know is that Nathan Hale's end came at Artillery Park. Two so-named parks existed in Manhattan at the time, one in the vicinity of UN Plaza at First Avenue and 45th Street and the other at a site near East 65th Street. In 1844, the first complete chronicler of the Nathan Hale story, James Babcock of Hale's hometown of Coventry, lamented the absence of a known site where patriots could enact a commemorate ritual.

"The fatal tree has been cut away, the ground desecrated," Babcock wrote. "Footsteps of thoughtless men trample it day by day." Like so many others martyred for the same cause, "the soil for which he lived and died" does not remember Nathan Hale. The only avenue in remembrance of Hale is paved with romantic truths that remain resistant to historical truth.[29]

Martyrs, Plural

Other than Captain Hale, the Revolution's chief martyrs were Dr. Joseph Warren and General Richard Montgomery, an associate of Benedict Arnold (before he committed treason). Montgomery fell on the last day of 1775 in the unsuccessful campaign to conquer Canada for America.

As the youngest of three Revolutionary martyrs, the least accomplished professionally, Hale is the one who has most conspicuously retained his place in the American imagination, despite the fact that his entire legacy is a single memorable sentence. Modern statues of him stand in places that exude cultural power. Two of these are located in the nation's capital: outside the US Justice Department and CIA headquarters. But in the first half century after independence, Warren and Montgomery loomed larger than Hale in histories of the Revolution, they having died in battle, while Hale did not see any combat at all.

Warren and Montgomery were mourned in annual public ceremonies, while Hale remained a local figure, evidently forgotten outside the walls of his alma mater and select Connecticut towns. If we are to judge by his appearance in books in print, Hale finally came to eclipse Montgomery in 1846, the year his granite memorial was erected in Coventry. Warren is another story: it was only during the period from 1900 to 1940, when a kind of cult emerged around Hale, that the captain-spy garnered more attention than the physician who fell at Bunker Hill. In 1924, Hale was one of the "Founders of America" in a book included in the Colonial Press's Famous Leaders' Series. What qualified one as a "founder" had changed: without having fired a shot or signed an important document, Nathan Hale had made a sacrifice that was enough to class him with Washington, Adams, Jefferson, et al.[30]

And yet, perversely, none of these three martyred patriots ever came close to matching popular interest in John André or Benedict Arnold. Until the Americans captured him, Major André was the accomplished British gentleman spy, an acquaintance of General Arnold's young wife, who arranged for Arnold to come over to the British side—presumably for riches. André and Arnold, one a cultured gentleman able to prevail upon a disillusioned general officer, the other a proven field commander-turned-murderous traitor. Stories sell.[31]

André's story surpassed Arnold's. Nineteenth-century writers plumbed carefully catalogued records to tell and retell his adventures both as history and as historical fiction. Each time an effort was made to publicly resuscitate the name of Nathan Hale, it was cast in comparative terms, defensively, Hale being presented as "the equal of André."[32]

Warren unquestionably earned his immortality. At Bunker Hill, he bade General Putnam direct him to where he could be "most useful." He died, out of powder, sword upraised, his body recovered from a shallow grave only after the British gave up Boston to Washington's army, when he was reinterred with all appropriate honors. Abigail Adams, who tended to the physician's young children the day he died, conveyed the tragic news to her husband, who was at Congress in Philadelphia: "My bursting Heart must find vent at my pen."[33]

In his postcorporeal life as a Revolutionary martyr, Warren made a greater impression on the collective consciousness than the Irish-born Montgomery, who was honorably buried by the British, a sign of respect both Hale and Warren were denied. Yet both Warren and Montgomery received their due in post-Revolutionary remembrances at home. In 1786, the Connecticut artist John Trumbull, whose scenes grace the Capitol Rotunda, completed magnificent paintings of both men's final moments. *The Death of General Montgomery in the Attack on Quebec* and *The Death of General Warren at the Battle of Bunker's Hill* were clearly designed to tug at the emotions. The Montgomery canvas features his comrades recoiling in shock, the expiring general in a contorted pose. In the painting of Warren, the martyred figure's glazed eyes give an impression of his dying realization when the last light departs. In both paintings, men mass together, unable to escape unfolding horror. Smoke envelops the scene.[34] And in the most famous of all ritual mourning pieces of the period, David Edwin's engraving, *Apotheosis of Washington* (1800), Warren and Montgomery appear as angelic figures, side by side inside their heavenly cloud, serenely awaiting the recently deceased father of his country.[35]

As the nineteenth century progressed, only Warren was given the "what if" treatment. Writer-diplomat Alexander Hill Everett wrote: "Had it been his fortune to live out the usual term of human existence, . . . we should have seen him, like his contemporaries and fellow patriots, Washington, Adams, and Jefferson, sustaining the highest magistracies at home." In juvenile literature, the fallen patriot was ennobled with ready dialogue, à la Washington and the cherry tree. The frontispiece to an 1835 volume pictures Joseph Warren's frail mother entreating him to stay home after he'd dispatched Paul Revere to Lexington and Concord. "I will either see my country free," he insists, "or shed my last drop of blood to make her so."[36]

Historical context is needed in order understand how Warren, Montgomery, and eventually Hale earned their reputations as martyrs. Back when the Revolution was building up steam, one event in particular captured the public's imagination: the "horrid massacre" of 1770, as it was immediately labeled in the *Boston Gazette*. The death of five young protesters made martyrdom a cause célèbre. Bostonians memorialized the "fatal fifth of March" on each anniversary from 1771 to 1775. Overflowing crowds listened as a distinguished speaker reminded the masses never to forget "when our ears were wounded by the groans of the dying, and our eyes were tormented with the sight of the mangled bodies of the dead." These tortured sounds belonged to the day's orator in 1772, none other than the ill-fated Warren. He was twice selected as the man best suited to tug at the heartstrings; the second occasion was in 1775, three months before his own martyrdom was sealed in blood.[37]

In a way, the representation of Warren, Montgomery, and Hale is foreordained in the representation of the five who fell in 1770. The pathos expressed in the patriot press from that point in time until the Battle of Bunker Hill emphasized the "raging soldiery" and its callous disregard for the dignity of their victims. One unsigned effort, joined to Warren's 1772 oration, was deemed important enough that it was reprinted sixteen years later, after the Constitutional Convention. In a dirge-like cadence, James Allen, a Harvard dropout and Warren's friend, took aim at the "impious hand" of the "remotest" king and "bid ruffian murder drink the dregs of life." Allen's speech was a fantasy, bringing justice to the dead by way of shaming those who would forget. It is important to underscore that the American side is "modest but firm" in its bearing before a dismissive and brutal opponent: "When first thy mandate shew the shameless plan,/To rank our race beneath the class of man." The accusatory tone of the Declaration of Independence is prefigured.[38]

In newspapers of 1775–76, the word "martyr" was rarely used in a nonreligious context, but by the end of the war, that began to change. In 1783, artillery was set off to honor those who fell at the opening Battle of Lexington in April 1775. Newspapers hailed "the first victims of the oppressor's cruelty, and martyrs in the cause of liberty, America, and mankind."

American martyrdom was born, never to disappear—neither would the corresponding need for villains in retelling the martyrs' noble stories. The enemy's disgrace, or sadism, amplified the meaning of the tragedy.

At the start of 1784, a New York paper recalled the practice of the ancient Greeks and Romans stamping the likenesses of their "heroes and patriots" on coinage and suggested the new American republic follow their example. Three coins were proposed: the first featuring "WASHINGTON the FATHER of his COUNTRY," with a wreath around his head; the second, a hero scaling the walls of a city with the inscription "MONTGOMERY SOUGHT and FOUND the GOAL of HONOUR"; the third, "a warriour with his sword drawn, standing near a slight fortification, from which might rise clouds of smoke; just before it the enemy flying, and some lying dead" with the inscription "WARREN, AMERICA'S FIRST MARTYR."[39]

Thanks to those who knew him personally, who searched for ways to keep his memory alive, Connecticut rediscovered the misplaced volunteer Hale in the 1820s. That is when he first became the subject of dramatic odes. The post-Revolutionary generation had become aware of the penurious circumstances into which thousands of war vets had fallen. A dilatory Congress awoke to the federal government's hallowed duty to tend to the nation's "hoary-headed" heroes. Unsung Revolutionary heroes were back in the headlines.

An original poem titled "On the Memory of Capt. Nathan Hale" was published in the Hartford *Connecticut Mirror* in 1820. It begins: "Lamented warrior!—young in life's career,/But old in glory—." At the conclusion of the opening section, the poet expresses remorse, not over Hale's life having been cut short but over his having been denied the funereal rites a gentleman who had made such a sacrifice deserved: "Long thy name/Shall be rever'd by patriots, tho' no tear/Hallowed thy obsequies."

The unnamed poet goes on to compare Hale to the Roman general Marcus Atilius Regulus, who was thought to have been captured in war, brought to Carthage, and then released on parole as a negotiator. Proud but unwise, Regulus returned to Carthage, was reincarcerated, and eventually tortured to death. The deserving Hale, ignominiously treated by his captors, hanged too soon, was a symbol of an enemy's rashness and brutality.

> Firm as Regulus,
> Thou didst endure for thy country's sake,
> 'Mid scoffs and insults, the strong speechless pang
> That mark'd thee for a martyr.[40]

Though the allusion went unremembered, the first to memorialize Hale in print was his friend and teacher at Yale, Timothy Dwight. His biblically wrought *Conquest of Canaan* (1785), dedicated to Washington ("the Saviour of the Country"), is considered America's first attempt at epic poetry. It was long enough in preparation that Hale himself, while alive, received a request from Dwight (in early 1776) for help in acquiring subscribers to the earliest iteration of the work. His tributary lines to Nathan Hale come early in book 1:

> Thus, while fond Virtue wish'd in vain to save,
> Hale, bright and generous, found a hapless grave.
> With genius' living flame his bosom glow'd,
> And science charm'd him to her sweet abode:
> In worth's fair path his feet adventured far;
> The pride of peace, the rising grace of war;
> In duty firm, in danger calm and even,
> To friends unchanging, and sincere to heaven.[41]

In a footnote to the phrase "Hale, bright," the poet explains that he will not, henceforth, be lamenting individual sacrifices over the course of his metered tale, given the numbers that had fallen over seven years of war; his reference to Hale (first name unmentioned), he notes, is special, "annexed to the poem to indulge the Author's own emotions."

Dwight immediately proceeds to make the same comparison as many later memoirists, citing the different treatment accorded to the British spy John André, who "bowed to war's barbarian laws" and suffered the same penalty of death. But there was one clear distinction: instead of a summary execution, André faced a military tribunal, properly convened, and was not put to death until the exchange demanded by Washington—André for Arnold—was explicitly rejected by André's forlorn admirer, the British commander. There was enough drama to go around.[42]

The Contrast in Depictions

Hale's end remains a mystery. We don't know the precise form his spy mission took, where he was at the moment of capture, or where he is interred. We have only a limited idea of what he was carrying on his person that tilted the scale and made his hanging inevitable. Far greater certainty attaches to André, who was, in fact, twice captured by the Americans. The first time, in October 1775, he was taken prisoner by General Montgomery at a garrison outside Montreal. This was two months before the American invasion collapsed at Quebec City.

André was returned to the British army in a prisoner exchange at the end of 1776. Well-traveled and adept at several languages, he lived a carefree life as a noted raconteur during the period of Philadelphia's occupation, attaining the rank of major in 1778. Even in the company of American generals who, under the laws and practices of war, felt bound to pronounce a sentence of death, André commanded respect. (In the category of tales that seem unlikely but are true, André lived at length at the home of Philadelphia's number one celebrity, Benjamin Franklin, who was then in Paris.) Once the British abandoned the City of

Brotherly Love and solidified their control of New York City, André took charge of the secret service and engineered Arnold's attempt at surrendering the strategic overlook of West Point. The thirty-year-old major went up the Hudson River in September 1780, met with Arnold, and was captured by a small party of militia as he moved south through the American lines in Tarrytown. He was eventually placed in the custody of Benjamin Tallmadge, who had been coordinating General Washington's intelligence operations in the New York area since 1778.

This leads to yet another ironic twist in the story. Tallmadge had been Nathan Hale's close friend at Yale. From the town of Tappan, New York, as André awaited his fate, Tallmadge wrote sensitively to a Connecticut friend: "He has unbosomed his heart to me, so fully . . . that he has endeared me to him exceedingly. Unfortunate man!" But by the close of his letter, he recanted: "But enough of poor Andre, who tho' he dies lamented, falls justly." Adding to the drama, captor and captive discussed the sad fate of Nathan Hale directly. It was almost four years to the day since Hale had been hanged when, in response to Tallmadge's query, Major André allowed that his case and Hale's were very similar. That name may have been on few lips by 1780, but André certainly knew Hale's story.[43]

In his second novel, *The Spy* (1821), which takes place in 1780, James Fenimore Cooper addresses the difference in the way André and Hale were treated. There appears a single but notable reference to Hale late in the book when a spy is captured in a manner akin to the way Hale was, in disguise, crossing enemy lines. In deciding the fate of the spy (in this case, British), Hale's precedent is invoked: "The royal officers gave Hale* but an hour," Cooper's soldier observes. The asterisk, inserted in the 1849 edition, is explained at the bottom of the page: "An American officer of this name was detected within the British lines, in disguise, in search of military information. He was tried and convicted, as stated in the text, as soon as the preparations could be made. It is said that he was reproached under the gallows." Upon which, according to Cooper, Hale remarked: "Gentlemen, any death is honourable when a man dies in a cause like that of America." Cooper then draws the key contrast: "André was executed amid the tears of his enemies; Hale died unpitied, and with reproaches in his ears. . . . Posterity will do justice between them." This ends the chapter.[44]

Washington Irving's multivolume biography of his gloried namesake, published in the years immediately preceding the Civil War, digresses from General Washington's military activities to engage at length with Arnold's treason and André's life story. Irving repeats the conversation between Tallmadge and André, elsewhere recorded by this time, and follows up with a long footnote that starts by noting that "the fate of the heroic youth here alluded to [Hale] deserves a more ample notice." The note goes on at some length, recounting Hale's educational background and military career and his attachment to Knowlton's Rangers. It concludes with "his patriot spirit shone forth in his dying words," which are then set forth as Hull and Hannah Adams rendered them.

Hale in this way gets considerable treatment in two separate texts by the best known of post-Revolutionary era authors, Cooper and Irving, even if in the case of Irving, it is a literal footnote woven into the much embellished story of "the gallant" André. The footnote was necessary because Irving passes over Hale in the first volume of his *Life of Washington*. He sees to it that Israel Putnam looms large, that Montresor is introduced, and that Knowlton's death at Harlem Heights is covered, but he does not mention the intelligence operation tying Washington and Knowlton to Nathan Hale. So it is left for Tallmadge to query his prisoner in a footnote several hundred pages later, "Do you remember the sequel of the story?" and for André to exclaim of Hale, "Yes, he was hanged as a spy!"[45]

James Thacher was a twenty-six-year-old army surgeon from Massachusetts who witnessed the execution of André as it unfolded: "I was so near during the solemn march to the fatal spot as to . . . participate in every emotion which the melancholy scene was calculated to produce." He tells us that André breakfasted, shaved, and announced to his guards that he was "ready at any moment" "to wait" on them. The journal continues: "He betrayed no want of fortitude, but retained a complacent smile on his countenance, and politely bowed to several gentlemen whom he knew, which was respectfully returned." Alexander Hamilton met with the condemned man as well and came away with "an exalted opinion of his character." Hamilton flatly disagreed with Washington's decision to hang André.[46]

The British spy secured a legacy by maintaining his poise to the end, going so far as to place the noose around his own neck in a gesture of acceptance of military justice at a time of war. When the dashing major dropped, General Lafayette, in attendance, broke down and cried (or so it was said). This was high pageantry, performed—"calculated," in the parlance of the time—to write itself into history. Hale's final moments, his comparable exhibition of eighteenth-century decorum, by contrast, could only be loosely surmised. At the time of his execution, Hale's comrades were about a mile from the British lines; they did not learn of his capture until he was already dead. The lack of information made it hard for all who came later to reconstruct the scene of martyrdom as was done with André. All that Nathan Hale gives us is one line of uncertain provenance, while every gesture of the British major was recorded, moment by moment, and preserved.[47]

Of greater embarrassment to the memory of Nathan Hale is the symbolic treatment of his corpse. The patriot's body was unceremoniously disposed of and lost, while André's remains were disinterred at Tappan, delivered into the hands of the British consul, and returned to England in 1821. André came to rest in Westminster Abbey. Three years before André's exhumation, the remains of Montgomery were ceremoniously returned in a well-publicized processional that ended in Manhattan with his reinterment at St. Paul's Chapel, at Broadway and Fulton streets.[48]

Hale does not appear in Jared Sparks's highly regarded Washington biography of 1839 nor in Edward Everett's, published in 1860. In his treatment of the Arnold-André affair, Everett (the younger brother of senior diplomat Alexander Hill Everett) focuses on a different facet of the sober reckoning, seeking to justify Washington's decision to send the "unfortunate" André to his death. Everett combats posthumous "reproaches" against the commanding general for his refusal to spare the life of the worthy spy, for not employing his veto after a court of thirteen officers ("some of them the most intelligent in the service") rendered their verdict. "Personally General Washington was the most humane of men," Everett claims, "and it is well known that it cost him a painful struggle with his feelings, to allow the sentence of the court to be executed on the accomplished prisoner."[49]

The people of Coventry, Connecticut, didn't give a hoot about the ennobled spy André. But they were disturbed by the fact that their hometown hero "should sleep in an undistinguished grave, unpitied and unknown," while the other, a "willing agent of the most cruel tyranny," was treated almost as an American icon. Those who could not forget the slight formed an association aimed at memorializing Hale. The shaft that stands to this day is made of granite, forty-five feet in height. It was erected in 1846 under the supervision of the same man who was responsible for the Bunker Hill Monument two decades earlier. On one side of the marker is the line Nathan Hale is famous for having spoken before the gallows. As his star continued its rise, as his story was more widely disseminated, a bronze statue of Hale was placed in the Capitol building in Hartford in 1887. Subsequently, the Sons of the Revolution funded the bronze statue that was installed in New York's City Hall Park in 1893. Presiding at that ceremony to honor Hale was a grandson of Benjamin Tallmadge.[50]

Dramatizations

But did anything change with the rediscovery of Nathan Hale in the nineteenth century? One way to answer this question is to compare the case of another Revolutionary, who was neither a hero nor a martyr but an undistinguished shoemaker, the oddly named George Robert Twelves Hewes, whose rise to fame in the nineteenth century suggests that something did indeed change with the discovery of previously unknown Revolutionary War participants and demonstrates the significant role patriotic biography assumed during this period. Alfred F. Young did the history profession a giant service when he reexamined the Boston Tea Party and announced that it didn't get its performative name until the 1830s. Before that, it was uniformly referred to, without the least flourish, as "the destruction of the tea in Boston harbor" or "the action against the tea." It was something that happened in the lead-up to war but had left no great impression on students of American history. Until Hewes came into the picture.

Hewes was "discovered" when he was upwards of ninety years old. In December 1773, age thirty, he had joined in the destruction of 342 chests of tea. This collective act of civil disobedience resulted in the imposition of the Coercive Acts and further militarization of Boston, which in turn led directly to the outbreak of war in 1775. Interviewed in 1833, he offered a detailed account of the tea party that made him special. And it took. The newest American celebrity had his portrait painted and became the subject of two biographies. Both authors attested to a memory that was "extraordinary." It was a moment when writers were bent on dignifying the common man, and in Hewes they found a kind of mascot. Old newspaper stories verified his active participation in the Revolutionary movement; it emerged that the noted radicals who took part in hoarding British vessels and tossing tea overboard wanted some leaders of the event drawn from the "lower ranks" to obscure the participation of elites in a mob action. But Hewes made claims that challenge credulity, too: he reportedly saw Warren "fall" at Bunker Hill and met one-on-one with General Washington at the Cambridge headquarters in 1775, where he took a meal and "Madame Washington" waited on him.[51]

A host of opinion makers in the nineteenth century found it increasingly important to fortify the national creation story and saw patriotic biography, a genre meant to promote good character in a rising generation, as a means to achieve that goal. Newspapers, magazines, and books aimed at youth grew apace with standard biographies. Documentary history took a major step forward in 1824, when Jared Sparks began collecting and publishing Washington's papers. The "life and letters" hybrid form, like biblical exegesis, allowed readers to become immersed in the details of a great moral life. Biographies were also folded into long public eulogies, which tended to present the subject almost as a perfect being.

Washington was, of course, a standout. An immense number of works were dedicated to him while he lived, and full-length narratives attesting to his singularity emerged in the years immediately following his death. Most notable of the early Washington biographies was a five-volume cradle-to-grave treatment by long-serving chief justice of the United States John Marshall, published between 1804 and 1807. Marshall's work became a model of thoroughness and control and remained unrivaled until the 1830s.

Wherever Washington went, vigor, innate reasoning ability, and masterful reserve were on display. A French minister remarked, "I have had many conversations with General Washington, some have lasted three hours. It is impossible for me briefly to communicate the fund of intelligence which I have derived from him." The irreproachable Washington deserved power because he sincerely did not seek it. And though not a man of erudition, there was in Washington "a genius of political and military skill; of social influence, of personal ascendancy," and, of course, "a moral genius of true heroism, of unselfish patriotism, and of stern public integrity."[52]

During the War of 1812, biographies of living military heroes were particularly well received by the public, but nothing had quite the staying power of dramatic episodes dating back to the Revolution. From the 1820s on, printed tracts of all kinds announced that nation-building required men of inner fortitude with survival skills, such as William Cutter's *Life of Israel Putnam*, which was published just as the Hale biographies began to appear and which conflated history with romance while pretending otherwise.

A typical vignette in Cutter's book recounts a dark moment in the French and Indian War when our hero is crossing the Hudson River near dreaded rapids with Indians in hot pursuit. Then Major Putnam, at the helm of his bateau, offers "an astonishing spectacle of serenity." The contrast between his men and him is stark: they, "with a mixture of terror, admiration, and wonder, saw him incessantly changing his course to avoid the jaws of ruin that seemed to expand to swallow the whirling boat." Description feeds the legend: "With no less amazement, the gazing savages beheld him sometimes mounting the billows, then plunging abruptly down." Though masters of the wild themselves, these "rude sons of nature" looked on the undaunted one with "superstitious veneration" that Europeans of the Dark Ages reserved for their "valiant champions." Putnam, unhurried and heroic, behaved with steely confidence.

At this, the author takes a step back, half acknowledging the problem with this genre: Putnam, he says, had already been "made the subject of a series of adventures and perils, which seem, in many particulars, more like romance than a sober tale of real life." What the patriotic painting style of John Trumbull or Emanuel Leutze's *Washington Crossing the Delaware* (1851) has done for that medium, a host of nineteenth-century biographies did for the cause of founder sainthood. In books like Cutter's, the quasifictional element is fortified with extensive but unlikely dialogue meant to have taken place in crucial situations: at Bunker Hill, for instance, Cutter represents Putnam and Dr. Warren as wrapped in conversation.[53]

It is not entirely clear whether the nineteenth-century reader was meant to accept this sort of thing as verbatim conversation or rather meant to recognize the imposture of literary license. In a powerful 1842 address given before the Capitol Hill Institute titled "On the Uncertainties of History," Levi Woodbury trenchantly pointed out that it was not even known "who commanded at Bunker Hill." Historical truth was, he said, "frequently discolored, when not suppressed" and such "exaggerations being emblazoned, and additions and inventions heaped up without end" have had the effect of misleading Americans about their past. Woodbury was not no one: he was a former New Hampshire governor and US senator who had already held two cabinet positions and would shortly become a Supreme Court justice.[54]

In such times, with celebrity biography coming up fast, Hale fit the new mold for appreciative dramatization. When he leapt from obscurity onto landmark acreage and statuary, he joined a pantheon of spirited adventurers who doubled as moral exemplars. Hale was special because his contribution had sublime elements: the reader opened the book knowing of his noble last words and worked backward to find out why someone so young, with so much to lose, risked honor (not just life) by embracing the morally ambivalent role of secret agent. Only General Washington, who sanctioned his man's fateful mission, could be trusted to keep the whole truth (his spy's identity) in his sacred breast. By a sheer act of deliverance, stage-managed by Washington, a spy was no longer an equivocal creature.[55]

Once it went from "the destruction of the tea in Boston harbor" to "the Boston Tea Party," a new storyline became possible. Once he went from victim to hero, Nathan Hale became an essential moral subject in America's chosen self-creation narrative. There was something magnificent in rescuing in story one who could not be rescued in life.

Famous Lines

George Washington left behind few famous lines and no beautiful words—the apocryphal cherry tree incident notwithstanding. If words are recalled that relate to his essential value, they are those spoken eulogistically, such as the grand trio "first in war, first in peace, and first in the hearts of his countrymen," authored by General Henry "Light-Horse Harry" Lee (father of Robert E. Lee). The language is succinct, unlike the sentence that follows, weighed down by wearisome phraseology that could hardly be avoided in the eulogy of one so favored: "When nations now existing shall be no more; when even our young and far-spreading empire shall have perished, still our Washington's glory unfaded shine, and die not."[56]

The words most remembered from this era are Jefferson's trio, "life, liberty, and the pursuit of happiness," spoken aloud by town officials and read by that rational readership he termed "a candid world." Jefferson never meant for the phrase to sound like something he had thought up on his own. In John Locke's

Essay on the Human Understanding, a work well thumbed by Jefferson's intellectual peers, the phrase "pursuit of happiness," which speaks to the idea of a moral community at peace with its government, appears in two different sections. All Jefferson intended was to convey the consensus of his colleagues in the several "United Colonies" represented in the Continental Congress. The phrase "pursuit of happiness" was then incorporated into a number of new state constitutions between 1776 and 1784.

Why does the phrase resonate so? It's in the preamble of the Declaration of Independence, yes. But perhaps it's also the way it sounds: the cadence, the consonance. The Scottish authority on eloquence Hugh Blair, whose 1784 *Lectures on Rhetoric and Belles Lettres* was taught at American universities up to the Civil War, wrote that a "musical sentence" can be "artfully arranged": "Vowels give softness, consonants strength." Of the qualities that contribute to sublime writing, he proposed that "rapid conciseness" will "strike the mind with greatest force," while "the grandeur of the object" naturally feeds the imagination. So, when we contemplate the manner of thinking that produced Jefferson's talent, "We hold these truths . . ." is a reminder, as Blair explains, that "music has naturally a great power over all men, to prompt and facilitate certain emotions."[57]

At the Battle of Bunker Hill, where militiamen were short on powder and the redcoats kept charging, "Don't fire until you see the whites of their eyes" was the compact call that went out to the troops. It is alternately attributed to Israel Putnam and Colonel William Prescott. Both were well-built farmers with previous fighting experience. Both were known to have inspired the men under their command. But it is also possible that the order to conserve ammunition was spoken by many on that hill, under tense battle conditions, and was inherited from an older generation of warriors. No one can say for sure who coined it. But we understand why it's memorable. Perhaps history remains uncertain as to who "commanded" on June 17, 1775, as Justice Woodbury reminded us, but at least we can say that the memorable line is not fiction: it was spoken, and under duress.

Then there is Patrick Henry's taunt of 1775, "Give me liberty or give me death," which first appears in the 1817 biography by William Wirt and existed nowhere on paper before that year. Indeed, the mesmerizing courtroom pleader Henry—elected Virginia's first governor in 1776—left precious little for posterity to quote that had staying power. He was certainly not a writer of significance; to his staunch critic Thomas Jefferson, Henry was "all tongue without either head or heart."[58]

Wirt constantly beats around the bush when he's not apologizing outright, finding a multitude of ways to marvel at the orator's magic while bemoaning the lack of documentary evidence. Poor Henry, his early years "wasted in idleness," was "celebrated as an orator before he had learned to compose"; "when withdrawn from the kindling presence of a crowd, he was called upon for the first time to take the pen, all the spirit and flare of his genius were extinguished." Wirt then circles back, bidding readers recall that it was 1775, an incipient moment of revolutionary fervor, when "the people seem to have admired him the more for his want of discipline."[59]

The biographer quotes extensive passages of Henry speaking, based in large measure on the faded memories of the old men he interviewed. Wirt, himself a widely respected expert on oratory, attempts to ventriloquize Henry with a rising crescendo, pulling out all the stops for the great man's greatest moment:

> ". . . We shall not fight our battles alone. There is a just God who presides over the destinies of nations. . . . There is no retreat but in submission and slavery! Our chains are forged. Their clanking may be heard on the plains of Boston! The war is inevitable—and let it come!! . . .

. . . Is life so dear, or peace so sweet, as to be purchased at the price of chains and slavery? Forbid it, Almighty God—I know not what course others may take; but for me," cried he, marked with both arms extended aloft, his brows knit, every feature with the resolute purpose of his soul, and his voice swelled to its boldest note of exclamation— "give me liberty or give me death!"[60]

Nothing of the preceding had been written down. Henry died in 1799. Wirt began researching his book in 1805 and completed it ten years later. Were these Patrick Henry's words? Were they even close? The answer is, "Extremely doubtful."

Henry's seven immortal words live on in patriotic lore, beside Nathan Hale's fourteen. It is the attempt to establish provenance that ultimately reminds us to pay attention to what is really going on: a culture's longing for consummation through iconic words of moral import.

We can take comfort in the knowledge that didactic history fell out of fashion once modern historians began dissecting ideologies. But let us not imagine ourselves immune to creative appropriation when "celebrity" authors, often TV pundits, hire on researchers and ghostwriters to help package an "accessible" product that substitutes catchy phrasing for careful analysis. Like Wirt's *Life of Patrick Henry*, our popular history is shallow, aphoristic, bathed in a false familiarity, feigning insight into past lives and cultural practices. The triumph of style over substance for which we fault extravagant histories of an earlier age still plagues us.

Washington Knew

It is entirely likely that George Washington would have recognized Nathan Hale. They'd seen one another. On June 16, 1776, the general showed he was aware of the young officer's role when preparing orders to cover the court-martial of "Lieut: Chapman of Capt: Hale's company," an issue of real concern to Washington: "The General approves of the sentence of the Court Martial, against Lieut: Chapman, and orders that he be dismissed from the service, and depart the camp." By that August, with the formation of Knowlton's Rangers, Washington must have known young Hale well enough to expect a debriefing upon his hoped-for return from Long Island. According to a witness who accompanied Hale as he marched off from the American camp, Sergeant Stephen Hempstead, Washington personally gave Hale guidance. The Rangers were a select group of men who acted on orders from the general. An officer and a Yale graduate who'd volunteered for a secret mission that Washington had urgently requested was not going to escape notice with the impending invasion of New York City preying on the leader's mind.[61]

Washington knew who his spies were. If Hull did not speak to him about Hale's hanging, then either Putnam or Hamilton filled him in on the details they'd learned from Montresor. So, in 1780, when he sought to exchange André for Arnold, it is hard to imagine that Washington would have forgotten the first of his operatives to forfeit his life in the service of the United States—indeed, the first man executed in the War for Independence. Given how well-documented Washington's daily accounts were and how directly involved in the Arnold-André business he was, it could be expected that he would have commented for the record, expressed outrage, or demanded an explanation from his British counterpart when Hale was hanged, and so it is odd that he appears not to have.[62]

Its provenance is obscure, its composer unknown, but during the war, it is said, a tune was sung that came to be known in later years as "Hale in the Bush." This fanciful ballad, thirteen stanzas long, refers to the "brave captain" by his surname alone, while depicting the loneliness of his sacrifice in ominous echoes. "The guards in the camp on that dark, dreary night / Had a murderous will, had a murderous will." Absent the consolation of a friend, he acted the hero: "In his heart all was well, in his heart all was well." Resolution accompanied resignation: "For he must soon die; for he must soon die." We can only guess how widely known "Hale in the Bush" was and whether those who sang it were aware of the events it depicted. After all, it took no time at all for Captain Hale to retreat into the shadow of Major André.[63]

Control over Memory

Finally, it seems unlikely that George Washington knew the words spoken from the gallows that seduced later generations. Hale's actual words may have been "massaged" by Montresor; more plausibly it was Hull who supplied the well-tailored version most accept as the captain's original. And Hull, we must remember, did not make the words public for a good two decades. Distinguished though they may once have been, William Wirt and William Hull are merely stage managers in a long-running show: the ritual of reframing historical memory. They contributed sound bites that proved hard to resist. They elicited calls for statues that symbolize pride and glory—and affective control.

In our century, alert activists showed how the war for control over memory is waged when they noted, and media outlets began reporting, that men who seceded from the federal Union were still memorialized on Capitol Hill and across the South. The eyesore of monuments cast on behalf of a racist ideology in the form of Confederate "heroes" and "statesmen" brought awareness to modern Americans of what public symbols have always meant. For as many years as they look upon visitors, statues are unchallenged statements of power over the mind, and as such they retain an edifying function. They can oppress or they can clarify. Along with the written word and the loop of voice and image in electronic media, statues, polished or weathered, broadcast the past's message to the future. They are who we once thought we would always be.

Emotional history is very much at play in all of this. From 1775 forward, Massachusetts, Connecticut, New York, Pennsylvania, and Virginia engaged in a decades-long competition over the primacy of their citizens in the Revolutionary cause. Every state had to boast at least one people's hero: an embodiment of patriotic selflessness, nobility of purpose, rectitude in conduct. All the better if they could be joined to sublime oratory or a single memorable phrase and even better if enveloped in martyrdom.

The first-line patriots weren't just national symbols, then; they were local symbols first. Yale, in a sense, needed Nathan Hale to divert attention from the taint of Connecticut native son Benedict Arnold. Harvard had it easier with its martyr, Joseph Warren, along with Son of Liberty Samuel Adams and the unsung heroes of the Boston Tea Party. Princetonians formed General Montgomery's inner circle and were placed in the foreground of Trumbull's Capitol Rotunda painting that froze the moment of martyring. Right beside Montgomery lie captains Jacob Cheeseman and John MacPherson, both of them only twenty-five. It should not be lost that martyrdom is tenderest when the sacrifice is of youth: Montgomery was thirty-seven; Knowlton was thirty-five; Warren was thirty-four; Hale was twenty-one.

The ties that bind are easily observed. Yale grads all by themselves urged on the public the emotional symbol of their fellow alumnus Hale. Impassioned promotion, beginning with them, gave this one young man, his life cut short in an act of violent retribution, a kind of untouchability. In Hale's and similar cases, promoters recur to a Christ-like iconography that gives the torn physical body new mystical power. The tragic hero, eulogized, mourned on successive anniversaries, is invariably recalled as socially popular and physically attractive (a saving grace of André, the dignified enemy spy). The martyr's virtues earn him divine favor through which he is spiritually purified.

Though they practiced the Christian faith, when they constituted their pet narratives, elite Americans immersed themselves in the poetic tradition of tragedy. The nation's educated consciously borrowed mythological identities (and statuary) from the ancient Greeks whom they adored, whose beautiful words and stories endured, whose monuments used the strength of the human body to harness the power of supernatural forces.

The Greeks, along with Roman lawgivers, imprinted on Revolution-era American writers and orators many of their convictions and conjectures on the meanings that ought to attach to life and death. Reputation was often decided, they noted repeatedly, at the moment of undoing. The Theban general Epaminondas was asked to compare himself to two Athenian generals of his day and responded: "You must see us die before you can decide." To become a celebrated martyr was to achieve in death what could not be experienced by the individual in life. Nathan Hale's tortured soul became an instrument of reconditioned memory.[64]

To keep a memory alive typically requires embellishment that tugs at the heartstrings. School texts, patriotic paintings, public statues, the ceremonial naming of buildings, streets, and cities are all formal ways of remembering and sacralizing. Monuments to the mythologized and the martyred are overt attempts at persuasion. Here is recorded "our history"—or, to be more accurate—something less than history until properly vetted.

"The First Parting." Lithograph by M. E. D. Brown, 1832.
Courtesy of the Library of Congress.

Chapter 2.

Great Distances
(Apprehensions)

O absence, what a torment wouldst thou prove,
Were it not thy sour leisure gave sweet leave
To entertain the time with thoughts of love,
Which time and thoughts so sweetly doth deceive.
—William Shakespeare, Sonnet 39

❧

Thy Vessel that yon Ocean sails,
Tho' favour'd now with prosp'rous Gales,
Her Cargo which has Thousands cost,
All in a Tempest may be lost.
—Benjamin Franklin, *Poor Richard Improved* (1750)

❧

The threads that tie Washington to his martyred spy are thin, and no direct commiseration was expressed by Washington or his adjutants to the Hale family that we know of. Nevertheless, we can safely say that nothing is more potently conveyed in wartime correspondence than the matter of missing loved ones. Enoch Hale traveled to New York to seek the truth about his brother's fate, holding on to a faint hope that he would discover a case of mistaken identity; that Nathan lived.

Similar emotion applied to journeys overland and, especially, overseas. Communications were slow and unreliable even in the best of times. Weather events and infectious disease were but two rampant causes of anxiety and apprehension. Weighing the impact of these and related forces, the present chapter demonstrates anew the determined, unceasing power, in any culture, of a language of emotion.

In early America, sensitive pens performed the duty of transmitting solace. We have a good example in a letter from Martha Washington to Abigail Adams during the summer of 1794, midway through the second term of the first presidency (and first vice presidency). Economic insecurity at home was matched by strained foreign relations, as Abigail's twenty-seven-year-old son John Quincy was about to embark on an overseas mission at the behest of President Washington. He would be assuming the very post his father had held in wartime: US minister to the Netherlands.

In response to a note that had been handed to her by John Quincy the day before, Mrs. Washington wrote to the young man's mother, saying she appreciated the stakes when anyone ventured out on the high seas for any length of time. Here is how the first First Lady expressed empathy: "That parental feelings should be put to the test at a seperation (perhaps for years) from a dutyful, and meritorious son, is not to be wondered at; but as there is no trial bereft of consolation, so in the one before you, you have a flattering view of his future welfare. . . . This I know is the opinion of my Husband."[1]

"No trial bereft of consolation." Abigail Adams appreciated the test before her, probably better than anyone else in their world. She was about to reenact a seemingly unbearable drama that she had endured on several prior occasions. Her husband was absent in Philadelphia more than he was at home outside Boston during two Continental Congresses, from 1774 to 1776. He and a very young John Quincy made two separate voyages to Europe: in 1778 (they were gone for a year); and again from 1779 to 1785, when Abigail and her one daughter finally took their lives in their hands and sailed the Atlantic unaccompanied by a male protector. They were met in London by John Quincy, a child of ten when she'd last seen him, largely independent at sixteen.

The wait was no easier in 1794 than it had been before. "We have flatterd ourselves that you had a prosperous voyage, as the Winds from shore were favourable for a long time," she wrote to John Quincy ten weeks after he sailed. "I hope you will not omit any opportunity of writing to her whose happiness is so intimately blended with your prosperity, and who at all times is your/ever affectionate Mother." From London, the son wrote soon after arrival, "It is the second time I have been to Sea in a crazy Ship, I think I shall beware of the third." Their letters crossed on the gaping ocean, as was to be expected.[2]

Months passed between letters, and Mrs. Adams responded effusively whenever one arrived. "My Dear son," she penned in early 1796 after more than half a year without word from him, "the very sight of a Letter exilirates my Spirits." Recalling precious days they'd spent in each other's company in Europe a decade before, she gushed: "Those Scenes have all past as a Dream." Repeating her appreciation for the personal sacrifice he'd made in accepting the appointment his father urged upon him, she quoted a major poet, Alexander Pope: "'When Stern prudence quenchd the unwilling flame,' only virtuous souls are capable of true attachments."

What might appear to be a common specimen of moral encouragement was something far less innocent. Her evocation of Pope was a clear allusion to a sore point between them, which he would have immediately recognized: the last time she intervened in her adult son's romantic life. She had leaned on him to sever a passionate relationship she felt was ill-advised. Assuming that he was waiting until his recall to find a proper mate back home, she sighed, "Do not despair." And indeed, he did not. He circumvented his mother's plan for him and married in London.

Maintaining expectations of him that we would judge unreasonable, Abigail willfully ignored what a massive change in circumstances might bring with it. No doubt perturbed by his actions, she could do little from so great a distance, continuing to answer his infrequent letters with some form of "it gave me pleasure to see your Hand writing addrest to me, after a painfull interval of three months."[3]

The Adams papers are easy to turn to, a rich repository for heartfelt correspondence, because of the unusual amount of travel family members conducted. The Washingtons are not known for emotionally wrought correspondence, of course, but this is not only because such letters were incinerated: the absences the general's wife bore were of more supportable length.

Soldiering was a grim occupation. Their privileged position allowed the Washingtons far greater freedom of movement than the average Continental soldier enjoyed. Most of the volunteers in 1775–76 had scarcely strayed from home at the time they joined up—no more than twenty miles in many cases. "My separation from you and my dear little one becomes daily more Intolerable," wrote Long Island-based army surgeon Samuel Kennedy to his wife, not long before the British descended from Canada and Nathan Hale set out on his mission. The pain he felt echoed a few days later: "I apprehend myself declining in flesh, which must undoubtedly arise from local separation from you. How time and a greater distance may operate I know not, but at present I feel as much as my constitution will bear." At Valley Forge, another complained in military-speak while affecting lightheartedness: "I shall be home sick again.—Muses

attend!—File off to the right grim melancholly." Homesickness
was a new concept, akin to depression and medicalized before
it became a common, neutral expression of emotion. In his self-
mockery, this Connecticut man showed no less sentimental a
spirit than Abigail Adams.[4]

"Complacency"

To understand how they coped with absence, we must appreciate their emotional vocabulary in full measure. At the Washingtons' Cambridge residence in July 1775, Mrs. Adams paid a
call on the general and was "struck" by his good qualities. To
her husband, off conducting the United Colonies' business in
Philadelphia, she observed: "You had prepaired me to entertain a favorable opinion of him, but I thought the one half was
not told me. Dignity with ease, and complacency, the Gentleman and Soldier look agreably blended in him." The Adamses'
close friend Mercy Otis Warren of Medford, Massachusetts, a
politician's wife soon to be celebrated for her satirical theatrical
productions, expressed her view of Martha Washington to Abigail as a durable presence at her husband's side: "I was
Receiv'd with that politeness and Respect shewn in a first in-
terveiw [sic] among the well bred. . . . Complacency of her Manners speaks at once the Benevolence of her Heart." The word
"complacency" that both women separately used to describe the
two Washingtons conveyed a message no longer recognized.
"Complacency" meant that Martha exuded a pleasing moral
character, not that she was smug or self-satisfied.

In her multivolume history of the Revolution, published in
less unsettled times (1805), the same Mercy Warren, no longer
writing defiant plays, described George Washington as one
"of a polite, but not learned education . . . with some considerable knowledge of mankind."[5] She intended no humbling of the
great man. A "knowledge of mankind" was as monumental a

compliment as a man of this time might earn. It meant that he could stand above crassness and deal with his fellows diplomatically, with no offending ego. As "complacency" was a synonym for the combination of "civility" and "gratifying manners," a "knowledge of mankind" disclosed one's social status and general refinement, one's judgment and level of compassion. Gentility was superior to intellectual pretension; self-knowledge opened up the path to worldly knowledge. To put it another way, the sharpest arrow in any eighteenth-century writer's quiver was the faculty of mind that spoke to one's ability to discern character. If dubbed the "Age of Reason" for the philosophic bent of its leaders, it could as well have been the "Age of Self-Cultivation."

By the same principle, restraint was expected in modes of communication. Reason and emotion had to balance each other; compassion had to stop short of maudlin excitement. In 1789, writing to her sister, Abigail Adams said of Washington's admirable bearing: "our August Pressident [*sic*] is a singular example of modesty and diffidence. He has a dignity which forbids Familiarity mixed with an easy affibility which creates Love and Reverence."[6] This, too, signified complacency. For an aspiring gentleman or gentlewoman, everything that held meaning in life was reflected in that self-consciousness which directed the development of good character. The quality that defined Washington's "genius" was not the conventional inspiration of the poet or scholar but his heroic example of selflessness, of integrity, that manifested in his ability to resist unwarranted power. The justice and humanity evident in his conduct was thought intrinsic but also cultivated and fine-tuned.

On another level, of course, Washington simply filled an emotional need. Those who wrote of him in his time all cited his disinterested character, his moderation. The paragon of reason and judgment was emotionally available to the public through a manufactured image; private emotion had to be masked, tempered by the exigencies of command. To be America's protector, Washington had to be protected from any appearance of vulnerability beyond the softness that bespoke the masculine ideal of the age.[7]

Though remote and ostensibly untouchable, Washington had to appear close enough to inspire attachment. The social logic of this era allowed for a kind of personal "dignity" (poise) that "forbids Familiarity" to accord with "an easy affibility"; the result of this blend of emotional traits was "Love." The formula only reads as contradictory to us. It was effectively the same in familiar letter writing more broadly. A pen bridged distance. The letter's recipient was meant not only to acquire information but also, and especially, to discover joy.

Sensory Language Calls Forth Feeling

The familiar letter was a primary means for thoughtful people to do all that society asked of them: establish reputation, reveal character, demonstrate authenticity, and express the heart. Alexander Pope offered his appreciation for the medium in his poem about two historic lovers, "Eloisa and Abelard":

> Soon as thy letters trembling I unclose,
> That well-known name awakens all my woes

There was hardly a more commonplace verb to describe active emotion in literary life than "tremble." Pope carries his message forward:

> Yet write, oh write me all, that I may join
> Griefs to my griefs, and echo sighs to thine.[8]

In 1809, an Ohio newspaper appealed to readers to cherish letters as immortal artifacts of "the noblest feelings," exclaiming with Pope from the same poem:

They live, they speak, what love inspires,
Warm from the soul, and faithful to its fires.[9]

Nothing so marks the post-Revolutionary decades as the power of print and the enduring value of familiar letters. Communicating with those they most trusted, correspondents wrote with vigor and excelled as observers. In friendly correspondence, sympathy was expressed in the opening or closing paragraph of a letter mingling family news with a discussion of financial concerns. Everyone at this time witnessed an amount of suffering we can scarcely conceive. Their religion demanded acquiescence. The medicine available to them was mostly ineffective; sudden death was common, and tragic news rarely came as a surprise. A thirteen-year-old Samuel F. B. Morse wrote to his two older brothers who were away at school: "Mama had a baby, but it was born dead & has just been buried. Now you have three brothers & three sisters in heaven & I hope you and I will meet them there at our death. It is uncertain when we shall die, but we ought to be prepared." This lesson was inculcated from an early age and repeated in countless letters: death was expected and "domestic grief," as it was commonly termed, had no bounds.[10]

Consolation was found in comforting letters. When gossipy reports of James Madison's demise made their way into the press, soon proven false, Dolley Madison's cousin expressed relief as she hoped for a better night's sleep: "Good night, my more than Friend, may I behold you in the 'dreams of my rest' as I was wont to do, radiant with smiles of joy and happiness." In a year when yellow fever resulted in countless thousands of deaths across cities and towns of the United States, Abigail Adams's sister Elizabeth Smith Shaw of Haverhill, Massachusetts, wrote to her, breathing a sigh. Their families had escaped the scourge. Mrs. Shaw acknowledged, in their customary manner of communicating news, how this devastation wrought upon humanity by nature had "torn so many Mothers from the arms of their clinging infants." There was no dearth of description of brokenness in letters, along with gratitude in being among those who escaped harm.[11]

Martha Washington and Abigail Adams provide a window into the kind of outreach that genteel people were taught to perform through letters. The two families remained exceedingly cordial through two presidential terms, though one would not say that John Adams, bright and combative, was an influential advisor to Washington. As the vice presidency held little allure for him, their correspondence during these years is formal and inconsequential. Fortunately for us, the women were less constrained; they at least communicated about matters of personal health in a doubtful disease environment, displaying greater personal warmth.

The spring of 1791 provides an example. As Martha went about her daily routine in the crowded capital of Philadelphia her husband conducted an official tour of the South. The plantation mistress, out of her element, pooh-poohed the "fashionable world" that surrounded her and envied the "salubrious" air of New England where Mrs. Adams lived months on end. Responding from her quieter community, Abigail wrote of how life's daily struggles were met. She announced the deaths that had occurred in the neighborhood, complaining of a "vile Ague" that was dragging her down. Mrs. Adams entered into such detail that she had to acknowledge the burden she had put upon Mrs. Washington: "To a Heart less benevolent I should apologize for relating my Grief, but I know that you Madam can sympathize with those who mourn as well as rejoice in their felicity."[12]

The language these letter writers drew on, it should be clear by now, was not formulaic. It revealed reading habits, literary and epistolary conventions, but also the range of choices that "compassionating" (an eighteenth-century term for solicitous concern) provided. The language available to them activated (in their idiom, "excited") the sensory system that governed sympathy. A considerable amount of research has been done on the language of sensation and all-consuming culture of sensibility. Take the young science of hot air ballooning, in which experiment gave rise to more than a gas-filled globe. A Virginia newspaper reported that a man testing out his balloon produced ripe "sensations" among spectators when it appeared that he was about to plunge to his death. "There was a general shriek among the women, and several fainted away; the men seemed fully to participate in their feelings, though few exhibited such strong symptoms of emotion."[13]

Sensibility was ascribed a decidedly feminine character. When Benedict Arnold escaped capture in 1780, leaving his young wife behind to face the music, she was represented as exhibiting every expected female weakness, affecting a pained, nervous, almost crazed suspicion of the soldiers who approached her, "the most genuine and agonizing affection," in the telling of witnesses. "Exhausted by the fatigue and tumults of her spirits, her phrenzy subsided towards evening and she sunk into all the sadness of distress. It was impossible not to have been touched with her situation." Novels of sensibility bathed in this script—it was mindlessly invoked. Yet at the same time, *novelty* itself was designated as dangerous, connotating possible impropriety in challenging social norms. This medicalizing of language conveyed a bittersweet message: sensible behavior delighted in genuine feeling while "nervous irritability" yielded to "torpor" or worse.[14]

John Quincy Adams's betrothed, Louisa Catherine (née Johnson), evoked several of the requisite expressions of feminine sensibility at the end of 1796, when he was in the Netherlands, and she, living with her parents in London (her father was US consul), exhibited "delicacy" by resisting the urge to join him. "You tell me you are to remain at the Hague," she wrote, "and that you hope a greater distance, and longer time of seperation than we had contemplated, will have no effect upon my affection—I am almost angry when I read that part of your letter, as it implies a sort of doubt which I am sure I cannot have merited. No my beloved friend e're my affection ceases I shall cease to breathe." Her language was precisely that of the novels of sensibility then current. "I am apprehensive upon reflection," the apology continued, "that all your fears proceed from my conduct before you quitted England—perhaps I appeared too anxious to go with you, but your Louisa was so little guided by reason, and so much by the impulse of the moment, that she thought not of impropriety untill too late." She attributed her indecisiveness to a confused sensibility and bore full responsibility for their extended separation. "People tell me I am much altered, I believe I am and sometimes am inclined to think that when we meet you will cease to love me."[15]

Ten years later, as the mother of his children and living in Boston while her husband was in Washington, Louisa received from John Quincy a handwritten copy of a tender poem, eighty lines in length, that he'd written for Louisa's sister Nancy, at that moment the grief-stricken mother of a lost child. "Oh! Nancy! be that solace thine:/Let Hope her healing charm impart/And soothe with melodies divine/The Anguish of a Mother's Heart." His original verse assured the distraught survivor that, in death, "the soul's perennial flower/Expands in never-fading bloom." A spate of deadly disease was taking children right and left, causing, he said, an "increase of sensibility" among parents. At the same time, he lamented to his wife that his own "inattention" to the "graces" expected from a man of his caliber and distinction gave others (including her extended family) the impression that he was cold and withdrawn: "It has perhaps been natural that my deficiency should be imputed to a deeper, and more inexcusable Cause—to a want of proper sensibility—to an unfeeling heart."

On reading the poem, Louisa replied with astonishment, in a stream of consciousness, to the lyrical power of his "very beautiful lines," telling him that they revealed who he truly was:

My best beloved friend you have more than answerd my every wish and evidently proved how little trouble it costs you to gain the hearts of all those you wish to please you may smile mon ami but a fond and tender Mother of every human being who possesses real sensibility must feel affection for a man whose heart so truly sympathizes in the afflictions of his fellow creatures.[16]

To feel "sensibly" in a society dominated by physical suffering and loss meant a lot. Sensible women governed affective exchange and excelled at sympathetic understanding. "Low" women did not rise to this level of awareness, though it was said that all women shared a natural susceptibility to a range of nervous disorders ("convulsions," "hysteria") that was greater than what strong-willed, publicly active men typically experienced. Nevertheless, while among the female protagonists of most novels the discovery of sensation had to model passivity, real life allowed for a wider spectrum of self-expression. Women resisted the trap laid by mechanistic rules. They had a pronounced antipathy for "dullness," whether it was to be found in company or at home. They desired "amusement" (as they employed the term) to lift spirits. They cultivated the imagination in the reading done in solitude or the reading aloud that took place before the hearth.

A feminine consciousness, enhanced by sensibility, was apparent in some men in greater abundance than was prescribed, revealing itself in passionate gestures and unpleasant emotional breakdowns. To appeal, a man was taught to exhibit some of the sensibility of a woman, but it had to be less pronounced and better managed if he was to be "effective" (their term) in public.

He needed no more of sensibility than led him to feel the optimal amount of sympathy for others' suffering.

Despite this gendering of sympathy, men resorted no less to "affectionate" language—as they constantly styled the generous impulse they claimed to feel. There was "affectionate attachment," "affectionate respect," "affectionate sentiments," and as sign-offs to their familiar correspondence, "my affectionate assurances" or "from your affectionate friend." Gentlemen, it seemed, never tired of this word. In retirement, John Adams famously attributed the motive power underlying the American Revolution to "radical Changes" that took place not just in the rejection of British forms of privilege, but also in the felt "Sentiments" and "Affection" among people. An "habitual Affection" for Britain dissolved with the arousal of new attachments.[17]

To judge by the press it received, the days-long processional in 1789 as Washington marched to Philadelphia to assume the presidency was marked by one "affecting moment" after another, and the sturdy statesman himself was said to experience "exquisite sensations" in his encounters with the admirers who came out to catch a glimpse of him. At one stop, a nineteen-year-old was engaged to speak words of welcome but was so overwhelmed that his voice failed him. As a man of feeling, Washington acknowledged the moment of fraught sensibility with a bow and a handshake. The awestruck youth, who grew up to be a university president, recorded in his autobiography that "marks of feeling" apparent in the great man's countenance when he performed his bow and handshake transferred the power of feeling to all members of the welcoming party: men otherwise noted for their "firmness" were at once on the verge of tears. The combination of a tactile connection and invisible sensations caused by Washington's sublime act epitomized for them (and us) the culture of sensibility.[18]

It was de rigueur in eulogies of 1800, as in that of Boston minister Oliver Everett, to credit the late president with "an heart of keen sensibility." Speaking on what would have been Washington's sixty-eighth birthday, the father of future statesmen Alexander and Edward Everett made certain to blend Washington's masculine sensibility with a "strong energetic mind," a "temper formed to the most perfect order," and, at the risk of repetition, "humanity ever conspicuous." Sensibility, while prized, rarely stood alone in a tribute given to any honored gentleman.[19]

According to the cultural historian Constance Classen, "in their world of sensations, impressions" of all kinds mattered. "Image fixed in the mind" was Samuel Johnson's dictionary definition of "impression," in addition to the more literal, physically imprinted, "mark made by pressure." Over the course of the eighteenth century, tactile measures of home were magnified as the importance of comfort was tacked on to the already persuasive idea that a home should *impress* visitors. Members of the working classes, too, felt an impetus to treat home as something greater than shelter. Feminine touches were applied to interior design in embroidered crafts, scissor work, and *pressed* flowers between the pages of a book. John Locke and other thinkers, professionally trained as physicians, stimulated a transformative discourse when they accepted sensation as the starting point of human knowledge. For Locke, crucially, an impression resulted in "some perception in the understanding." In novelistic prose, we have the telling example of a kiss: "my heart rising to my lips, stamp'd with its warmest impression."[20]

The emotive power of metaphor was *impressed* on them early in their education. With the far-reaching passion for poetry that they acquired, which drew heavily on metaphor, writers learned to manage absence and distance. Writing "to the moment" in lofty language shaped their ideas about intimacy and confidentiality—ideas that differ from those of the present day and yet are not so remote as to be indecipherable.

Privacy

"One wonders," the cognitive scientist Antonio Damasio writes, "how the world would have evolved if humanity had dawned with a population deprived of the ability to respond toward others with sympathy, attachment, embarrassment and other social emotions." He makes the point that memory is associated with emotion, that feelings are never passive; a body reacts to stimulation and produces emotion. The nervous sensibility literate people "spoke" in 1800 took the same path to discovery as Damasio, who tracks the microbiological origins of feeling.[21]

Like sympathy and social attachment, the related history of privacy (of both body and thought) connects inner sense to outer world. Early Americans lived under conditions that made privacy hard to find and maintain. Those who traveled from place to place were routinely obliged to share their bed with a stranger—a bed that would not have been clean, let alone disinfected. Yet this does not at all mean that they failed to value privacy in the manner we do. "Sorrow rarely suffers its tears to be seen," went a typical essay that showed how solace was obtained in private meditation. Similarly, the mirror, or "looking glass," an object designed for self-discovery, sat on a lady's dressing table, where she could prepare herself to be seen by others—to show herself only as much as she cared to.[22] Further, while when a sociable woman went "abroad" (out in public) she often had an escort, she spent more of her life on her own maintaining the domestic world, guarding the health of children, managing property—enduring nights alone when the men of the household traveled. The secret world of a woman of respectability existed in her "closet," a physical site meant to represent privacy. To "retire into" oneself was to acknowledge the power of that interior world, where the life of the mind was vulnerable.[23]

In early Americans' literary lexicon, there was the physical "privacy of a dwelling-house" and, figuratively speaking, a call for "modest privacy" (i.e., modesty) in comportment; privacy whose goal was retirement assured that "genius" could be nurtured in quiet study—an earned respite from public exposure. On the other hand, privacy whose purpose was mysterious was suspect and could lead to the speculation that one was plotting in secret to subvert another's interest. In short, anxieties that arose in one's daily life made seclusion a valuable purchase and made protection from intrusion necessary, lest prying eyes spread the kind of information that damaged a reputation.

Privacy as a state of mind found its way beyond polite expression for one reason above all others: reading. Reading lay at the heart of the late eighteenth century's understanding of the self and explains the explosion of friendly correspondence and the accompanying penchant for personal writing in diaries. It joined solitude to solicitude, providing a way to deal with the psychological forces of agitation, disturbance, unbalance, disruption; it served as a primary stimulus in the deepening of religious feeling.

Readers, especially of poetry, often responded to their reading by making penciled notes in their texts as a means of engaging in virtual conversations with absent or lost loved ones or with themselves. This distinctive mode of "reading in action," or "nostalgic revisitation," as one scholar has recently described the process, continued in full force through to the end of the nineteenth century.[24]

A reading habit informed, enlightened, and encouraged morality, but as an *indulgence* it was said to pose a grave threat in the eyes of men who took it upon themselves to govern female behavior. Sincere guides and a slew of newspaper pieces confidently asserted that the wrong kinds of novels implanted in young women's impressionable minds a more glamorous, more amorous life than "decorum" prescribed. The "age of trembling nerves" led the charge against frivolous and dangerously seductive reading material, promoting in its place awe-inspiring poetry in the mode of John Milton's seventeenth-century epic *Paradise Lost* and Edward Young's heart-pounding *Night Thoughts* (1742–45), readings bound to bolster a virtuous disposition.

This brand of poetry condemned pride and extravagance. Young undercut the expectation that a terrestrial lifetime should contain more enjoyment than pain. "We push Time from us and wish him back," he versifies in *Night Thoughts*. "All-sensual man" needed humility to see that what is called time is "cut off" from eternity just long enough to toy with his conceits. Young was a hugely popular poet with a flair for melancholy expression that held appeal into the next century among romantics. In the era preceding romanticism, his message was received instructively: it was folly to neglect life's impermanence; to love beauty was subsistence enough. Because fantasy bred confusion, eyes and thoughts wafted toward the hereafter, as young Samuel F. B. Morse had been taught.[25]

Lessons in humility were especially directed toward the female of the defective species. Women's desires were tightly controlled, and female letter writers could allude to the physical only when the reference was mediated by the social requirement of modesty. The introspective state could be discussed openly, and personal idiosyncrasies could be readily admitted to, allowing one to "unbosom" oneself. Openness was reconciled with privacy.[26]

Imagination

"Of all the figures of speech," wrote Hugh Blair, the era's master rhetorician, "none comes so near to painting as the metaphor. Its peculiar effect is to give light and strength to description; to make intellectual ideas, in some sort, visible to the eye, by giving them colour, and substance, and sensible qualities." Well-chosen words magnified the sensations that joined to sensibility.[27]

Impressed or painted, a writer's strength derived from his or her ability to deploy metaphor. "Spirited and dignified" are two of Blair's adjectives for a superior metaphor. If productive, it left "a strong and full *impression* of his subject on the reader's mind." Modern specialists in linguistics agree: metaphor—seeing one thing in terms of another—adds a dimension to all that the mind needs help in understanding, "an imaginative rationality." We say someone's imagination "ignited" or "caught fire," to express its generative principle or impulsive "spark." Metaphors of heat were then, as now, illustrative of a range of personality traits. Fear and fire go together: "a hot temper," "heated rhetoric," "burning with emotion," "in the heat of passion." Meaning is granted to a simple word: we see gray as a color (fact) and as an emotion (gloom, sorrow). Language is a forensic tool in emotional history, one that recorded the emotional rhythms of everyday life.[28]

During America's post-Revolutionary growth spurt, metaphor took conventional knowledge and put it to work creatively. Metaphorical associations drawn from a medicalized environment came to symbolize the intensity of eighteenth-century Americans' exertions. Food consumption was measured in its "lightness" and "heaviness"; one became "dull" from excessive intake or "phlegmatic" (apathetic) from a lack of proper nourishment. The sensitive gut came into play in the adjectival application of "intestine" to mean "innate," "internal," or "coming from within," as in "intestine broils," which meant a "state of unrest" within a community. Their emotional concepts easily crossed over from visceral concerns to a psychologically directed idiom. Male or female, one found lodged in the corporeal "breast" or "bosom" an interiority that likened inmost thoughts and feelings to the pages of a life "impressed" in ink.

Effusive poetry spoke to the moral imagination. But "imagination" remained a loaded term and not a simple concept. It described a volatile form of energy. In gendered terms, this meant that cultivated women with superior taste, while regarded as the near equals of male poets, were, in a way, compromised by naturally endowed feelings of affection. They were still to be protected from the rough and tumble of public venues, lest deep "affection" be converted into unwanted "passion." Imaginations had to be properly channeled.

Phillis Wheatley's was. Before the Revolution, the precocious poet acquired a unique reputation: her enslaved status caused jaws to drop as her powerfully wrought poems were read. Her "On Imagination" bids "the subject-passions bow" before Imagination's "throne." When "Fancy," a synonym for the imagination, roamed about, its "silken fetters all the senses bind / And soft captivity involves the mind." These images do not go unnoticed: "fetters" and "captivity" state the obvious, that the poet is freest in *her* imagination.

The imagery is even clearer in Wheatley's "To Maecenas," which self-consciously imitates the Augustan poet Horace, whose first-century BC "To Maecenas" calls attention to his patron, Gaius Maecenas, a promoter of literary genius known for his humanity. As a poet, Horace critically mulled Roman slavery, and as Wheatley scholar David Waldstreicher notes, Wheatley "didn't have to tell eighteenth-century readers directly why she would imitate and elaborate on the most self-conscious and slave-conscious of poets. . . . She could be direct through indirection, *through* Horace." In her version of "To Maecenas," praising the soul-soaring "notes" of the ancient poets, she engages Homer as well as Horace before bringing up *"Afric's* sable race" and remarking on the even older African-born slave-turned-playwright, Terence, whose Roman comedies are said to have influenced Shakespeare.[29]

Another early American poet, New Yorker Ann Eliza Bleecker, wrote in the convention of her time of "the soften'd heart," "the dropping tear," taking up classical subjects and paying homage to Pope's style. Her familiar letters show a daring personality: she mocks the pretensions of men in her "polite circle" as "mechanical, artificial sons of ceremony" and enjoins a friend to recall their "laughing, indolent hours . . . where we chatted with impertinent caution."

Descended from Dutch American merchants, Bleecker had an equally inspired daughter, Margaretta Faugeres, notable as both poet and playwright and an early antislavery proponent. In her 1795 tragedy *Bellisarius*, Faugeres adopts a recognizably Shakespearean cadence. In 1797, she composed a poem contesting the death penalty. She had a deep connection to the upper reaches of the "mighty Hudson," near her family seat, and offers glimpses of the romantic mood yet to come in her description of this locale: "Where in thy verdant glooms the fleet deer play,/And the hale tenants of the desert stray." Faugeres's promising voice was lost early, when she died at twenty-nine, in 1801. Her obituary alludes to a desperately unhappy marriage that estranged her from her father—an unsung American story featuring the union of unstable talent and emotional frailty.[30]

The post-Revolutionary reader found consolation in a surprisingly wide variety of texts. So in her letter to Abigail Adams after she and her family survived the year of yellow fever, Elizabeth Smith Shaw found better words than her own to express the emotions she felt by quoting three different poets. First, she took a stanza from Isaac Watts, the Congregational minister who in the early years of their century wrote hymns and heartfelt poetry: "Nor let thine eyed too greedily drink in/The frightful prospect when untimely death/Shall make wild inroads on a parent's heart." Next, reporting on "a nervous putrid fever" that had "carried off" a young husband and father, she drew on Homer's *Iliad* to express the sentiment: "Lamented youth! In life's first bloom he fell." The deceased, in this case, was a Harvard-trained minister, "meek—& serious, with out affectation—cheerful, with out Levity." Finally, relying again on a religious model, Shaw invoked Anne Steele, an English Baptist who wrote under the name Theodosia: "In Sorrow, may I never want a friend,/Nor, when others mourn, a Tear to lend."³¹

Letter writers cited novels nearly as much as poetry when conversing with an intimate. These included the picaresque: Miguel de Cervantes's *Don Quixote*, Alain René Lesage's *Gil Blas*, Henry Fielding's *Tom Jones*, and Laurence Sterne's wild, anarchic *Tristram Shandy*. Men and women alike expressed their appreciation for irony and comic, even absurd, scenarios. Yet these works also imparted their share of humanity. When she lay dying after a difficult childbirth in 1782, Martha Wayles Jefferson and her husband, Thomas, copied out lines from one of the latter chapters of *Tristram Shandy*, creating a precious relic by mingling their handwriting on a small, square scrap of paper: "Time wastes too fast," she wrote. "Every letter I trace tells me with what rapidity life follows my pen." He continued the quote: "—and every time I kiss thy hand to bid adieu."³²

As with "impressions," one could, of course, be "touched" nonphysically. In an earlier period, "touched" was used primarily in religious contexts, but as the age of "trembling nerves" found its mooring in sentimental literature, the word was more frequently summoned. "Touching" readers was Sterne's superpower in both of his illustrative works of the 1760s, *Tristram Shandy* and *A Sentimental Journey*. Long after his death, the controversial Anglican minister retained a reputation for using lewdness as a way to generate outlandish humor. The compiler of a thirteenth edition of his choicest vignettes, *Beauties of Sterne* (George Washington's library contained a copy), combined the suave and the sensory, addressing the "propriety" of the text by insisting that it was necessary to take the edge off "too serious a system of grave morality" and to include "those sprightlier sallies of fancy" that the late author had scattered through his writings. The Sternean imagination could not be dour.[33]

While men could afford to possess a healthy degree of imagination, it had to resist airiness or overly experimental "projection," or what in the late eighteenth century was known alternatively as "morbid melancholy" or "morbid imagination." An agitated mind put an inquisitive society on notice.[34]

Excess regularly came under metaphorical fire in this age of "trembling nerves." We know what "unbridled" means. The metaphor is still in use. An old word with literal reference to a horse gone wild, it was metaphorically invoked in early America to condemn unrestrained or ungoverned conduct. There was the danger to the female population from the "unbridled rage, rapine, and lust" of privateering sailors and enemy invaders, and one had to beware "unbridled ambition." Other common combinations were "unbridled passion," "unbridled tongue," and "unbridled fury." Men who ranged about the vulgar world were little constrained, and the strictly guarded "fair" were cautioned against conduct that might provoke "insult" to her dignity, or the accusation of "folly" that might result in "scandal." Women faced "ridicule" for an excess interest in political issues. Such limits were well understood. An unbridled imagination might wreak havoc.[35]

The double-edged sword of the imagination was a constant subject of analysis and debate during the final decades of the eighteenth century. The English writer Hester Chapone (1727–1801) was one such practical-minded critic. She was a friend of the most notable champion of gender equality, Mary Wollstonecraft, and her conduct books were well received in America. In *Letters on the Improvement of the Mind*, Chapone outlined the slippery slope that led from "sullenness, or obstinacy" to fatal error. She warned that "resentment . . . , nursed in secret," and "aggravated by the imagination, will in time become the ruling passion." Once affection was "swallowed up" by tormenting thoughts, base instincts prevailed. Resentment, she decided, was an overreaction that a "heated imagination" made worse.[36]

A survey of words modifying "imagination" in published and unpublished writings of the late eighteenth century shows that worries over loss of control were more common than creative optimism. "Imagination," as often as not emotionally neutral as a noun, was mostly negative when preceded by an adjective: "vivid," "lively," "excited," "wild," "untamed," "distempered," "deluded," and "disordered" were far more frequent than "fond" or "pleasing," which serves to implicate the imagination in the undoing of hopes and plans. The connotation of "imagination" as departure from the calm of ordinary reality makes even more sense if one goes back a century, when the verb "to imagine" meant to conspire against the king or other high authority: to "imagine a plot" was to anticipate a violent outcome.

In popular literature, the imagination misled more often than it guided one toward clarity, recognition, or accomplishment. In *Wieland*, a haunting tale published in 1798, Philadelphian Charles Brockden Brown allows for moments of genial mystery in a vignette where metaphors abound: "An awe, the sweetest and most solemn that imagination can conceive, pervaded my whole frame. . . . An impulse was given to my spirits. . . . I passed the night wakeful and full of meditation. I was impressed with the belief of mysterious, but not of malignant agency." The author sets up his reader for an emotional crash, the imminent exposé of a tortured mind that is "impressed" with a powerful belief, nerves agitated.

Similarly framed psychological effects feature in William Godwin's popular novel *Caleb Williams* (1794). His characters' imaginations are "rich, but undisciplined," "ingenious in torment," the result of "exuberant sallies," and only every so often "purged" by the counteracting medicine of "philosophy." True to his mistrustful character, cautious John Adams sandwiched "imagination" between "prejudice" and "enthusiasm" (meaning excess) in a letter he wrote to Thomas Jefferson at the time of the Constitutional Convention. Political pieces dismissed "imaginary evils" when the writer's design was to urge readers to let down their guard and accept the proffered reality. If the imagination in later generations was fertile territory for a better understanding of humanity, this was not so much the case in 1800.[37]

"The Greatest of Human Evils Is the Seperation {sic} of Dearest Friends"

One might imagine that the matter of distance stabilized as the United States found its footing. But in emotional terms, small progress occurred until after steamboats, railroads, and the telegraph stretched across the land. In 1840, letters continued to provide the only solace: "At last, my dear husband, after the lapse of more than three weeks, I have had the gratification of receiving a letter from you." He was an army captain, on assignment four hundred miles from the fort where his young family huddled in barracks on the Maine-Canada border. The letter contained news that was (predictably) meant to reassure him that life went on—"our darling child has been spared to us"—and (as predictably) that some new contagion lay at every turn: "there has been a great deal of sickness and many deaths among the children here."[38]

We say, lightly, "the suspense is killing me," but these generations waited in suspense in ways most of us will never know. They "surrendered" loved ones to an early grave—at war, metaphorically, with death. The anxious days and months that absence produced were an extreme version of the everyday concern about letters expected or overdue. Louisa Catherine and John Quincy Adams disappointed one another by committing words to paper that caused days or weeks of alarmed imaginations; often it was simply the impression that the other wasn't paying attention when in fact successive letters were lost or un-delivered for entirely innocent reasons.[39]

To allay the concerns of loved ones, travelers wrote imme-diately upon reaching their destination, even if it were only two days' ride from home. "I arrived without incident" put a family member at ease. But the months of anticipating the same news from overseas demanded a different kind of adjustment; some-times it was a newspaper story that told of a public figure's ar-rival or the sinking of a vessel. During the War of 1812, the otherwise resilient wife of secretary of the treasury Albert Gall-atin appealed to her friend Dolley Madison, as she waited for word that her husband, sent as a peace negotiator, had arrived safely in Europe: "At the time I am all anxiety to hear of the safe arrival of our dear *Voyagers*," Hannah Nicholson Gallatin wrote. "I have been so miserable about my dear husband that I think I did very wrong not to accompany him, and if it pleases Heaven ever to restore him to me, I think it must be the last time of separation." Recounting the torments of recently be-reaved neighbors, she closed with: "Write to me again soon, my dear friend. I love to receive your letters, they comfort me."[40]

In a case of unintended irony, the young attorney Joseph Story, addressing a classmate, quoted one of the maxims re-corded by the seventeenth-century wit François de la Roche-foucauld: "Absence destroys trifling intimacies, but invigorates strong ones." Within days of this potent statement, his wife fell ill and died suddenly at the tender age of twenty-two. It was not unusual for sorrows to pile on unmercifully, and a short time later his father met a similar fate. Then, after three months of mourning his two losses, Story wrote to another friend: "I have been solitary and closeted, unknowing and un-known in the world." He sought one thing only, he said: "tran-quility." The future Supreme Court justice later reflected on this dark period: "I was new to grief, with an ardent enthusiasm and an almost romantic fervor of imagination." In their emotional register, "tranquility" and "imagination" were near opposites: the first was a synonym for untroubled repose, the ideal emotional balance, while the second was so "ductile" (plastic) that it manifested most often as edginess and inner disturbance.[41]

Preindustrial generations of Americans prized material abundance less than emotional coherence. They aimed for a cultivated "cheerfulness," one of their favorite words. Happiness was measured by how much of life was spent in "tranquil" enjoyment, a message contained in countless odes from amateur poets as well as renowned ones. Just as Story urged upon himself, men and women made "tranquility" the counterpoint to "anxiety" in looking ahead. The calming effect of a walk through a public garden, the loving description of a venerable someone who enjoyed an untroubled old age—these were defining images of life-saving self-government. Letter writers variously praised "tranquil reflection," a "tranquil mind," a "tranquil spirit," or took pleasure in being a "tranquil spectator" to public bustle. Mourners tried to find the silver lining by attesting that the loved one "died as she lived, tranquil and resigned."[42]

Tranquility was earned over time. The novelist Catherine Maria Sedgwick described an aging Chief Justice John Marshall: "His face has a fine union of intellect and tranquility, the seal of a well-spent life." The final metaphor was drawn either from the "seal of authority" (stamped on an official legal document) or from the personalized wax impression that turned a thrice-folded page into an envelope; either way, it suggests the satisfactory completion of a life that the "union of intellect and tranquility" actualized.

Sedgwick is an exemplar of epistolary prowess, knowing when to deploy emotional language and when it would be perceived as overwrought. She teased her brother during one of her short-term absences, when he confessed how much he missed her. "I admire, dear Robert, the admirable adroitness with which you insinuate your grief at my departure," she chastised, but "even 'Temps le Consolateur' [Time the Comforter] will not get a monument this time." Between intimates, writerly wit was adequate to raise a smile. "I care not how much those who are as my own soul value my presence," she went on, hitting all the right notes, "but I do not desire they should mourn my absence. Life is quite too short for useless regrets. Our present duties need all the life they can get from the leaven of cheerfulness." Her felicitous pen marked the difference between intermittent separations and the kind of absence that provoked rational fears for a traveler's safety.[43]

Absence threatened the loss of ready memory, whether the absence was caused by the death of a loved one or a loved one's embarking on a death-defying voyage. Nothing eased the pain of this loss more than a miniature painting held in a locket, a letter in the absent person's handwriting, or some other tactile object. Just as husband and dying wife copied out a precious quote from *Tristram Shandy* onto a scrap of paper that was subsequently folded and unfolded repeatedly, Thomas Jefferson daily wound his pocket watch with a small golden key that had his wife's birth and death dates engraved into it. The reverse side contained, under quartz crystal, what is believed to be a woven lock of her hair, a further indicator of a tactile thing bearing an emotional message.[44] Memory was sustained by other tangible means such as birth and death dates recorded in family bibles, names passed down from one generation to the next, and the materials of household production including samplers and quilts and other items produced by sewing needle and spinning wheel or a tall clock or other handcrafted cabinetry.[45]

Painting was both a production of tremendous emotional power before the advent of photography and a popular metaphor in the hands of expressive writers. In the latter mode, imagination's hazy contours were "painted"—creatively but imperfectly accomplished. Eliza Pinckney of South Carolina, who managed her family's South Carolina plantation, was a particularly affectionate correspondent. To her absent grandson, she wrote that "yr. sister . . . paints you to her imagination with every perfection. You are almost dayly subject of her conversation." To her overseas younger brother after no word arrived from London "by the last ship" to dock at Charleston, she was moved to write "I was much concerned at not hearing from my Dear brother. . . . I have now more reason to be so since my Cousin B informs me of a dangerous illness which you have hardly over-come." Meditating on the inevitability of death at some length—"Surely one of the greatest of human evils is the seperation [*sic*] of dearest friends"—she remarked on her inability to put aside "a scene that has been often acted over in my imagination."[46]

Imagination reached far on the wings of letters, and these tangible symbols of absent friends like other mementos were retained, typically bound by ribbon in a stack, and carefully tucked away. Appreciated as a literary form, unmatched as symbols of intimacy, letters performed a number of emotional services, from grief counseling to outright drollery. It is not wrong to accord the familiar letter a position of seniority among the arts. When one could not "paint" pictures from the imagination, a letter did almost as much, conveying "sensations of extraordinary pleasure" or "sensations too painful to be described." Twenty-year-old Phoebe Morris, a Madison White House favorite, addressed the First Lady:

> My affection for you is a sensation new to my heart. It differs from that love I feel for many of my young Friends, it is more pure, it is more refined. . . . [O]h never can this sentiment be enfeebled, I feel that absence will add new force to an attachment so ardent & so tender; and you will I know indulge me in expressing it . . . as the compensation for an absence, which must, I fear be permanent.[47]

The sound of Phoebe's voice transferred to the page in her own hand strikes today's reader as perhaps something less than sincere. But feelings were, in fact, mutual. She had lost her mother and looked to Mrs. Madison for poignant reminders of maternal affection. Her letter typifies a population's persistent reflection on the power of distance on memory.

cAngst in the cAge of Sail

What slow-motion travelers in the age of sail felt more intensely than any cell-phone-equipped traveler today were the physical shocks, sudden interruptions, and ravages of the natural world that the open road or open seas presented. The intrepid Alexander Mackenzie, exploring Canada's Indian country in the early 1790s in search of a northwest passage, described what it was like to take on the endless emptiness of land and sea. "I was animated by the desire, to undertake the perilous enterprize," he wrote, embracing his fate. Still, "perplexity" and "disappointment" constantly dogged him: the words he chose cast discovery in less propitious terms than adventure fiction has since provided.

The voyages Mackenzie undertook offered little variety in scenery: "dreary waste, and wide-spreading forest, the lakes and rivers succeed each other in general description." In consequence, "my thoughts were anxiously employed in making provision for the day that was passing over me. I had to encounter perils by land and perils by water. . . . I had also the passions and fears of others to control and subdue." While determined to press on, each time he did his party exhibited "fainting spirits" and "rising discontents" as the risks mounted. Unpredictable weather over wide waters along with hostile earth made it all worse for the unprotected souls whose emotions were daily tested by such extremes.[48]

Once travelers had gone more than ten or twenty miles from home, they began to feel unease. It's why so many letters contained the words "longing for," followed by "your letter," "your return," "the happy day," "the moment when . . . ," or a similar construction. And because so many letters miscarried, writers traveling abroad often numbered each one sent to a regular correspondent: they began by confirming receipt of "yours of the 16th" before entering the body of the letter.

Because traveling by sea was the only way to get to many other parts of the world, it is not surprising that in early American letters, sea metaphors were as common as sports metaphors are today. In his defense of the soldiers on trial for their actions in the Boston Massacre of 1770, trial attorney Josiah Quincy cautioned: "How careful, lest borne away by a torrent of passion, we make shipwreck of conscience." Thomas Jefferson inveigled against the "boisterous ocean" of politics, where the better statesman had to "steer with safety the vessel in which we are all embarked." To her wandering twelve-year-old son, Abigail Adams wrote in 1780: "Ungoverned passions have aptly been compaired to the Boisterous ocean which is known to produce the most terible Effects." The same John Quincy Adams, as a grim ex-president, would later say that history itself was "a narrative of a few prosperous voyages and multitudes of shipwrecks."[49]

Pope drew on the metaphor to argue that reasoned judgment was guided by a navigation chart while passion moved the vessel:

> The rising tempest puts in act the soul,
> Parts it may ravage, but preserves the whole.
> On life's vast ocean diversely we sail,
> Reason the card, but passion is the gale.[50]

Letter writers regularly expressed a fear of having their hopes "shipwrecked." A Philadelphia physician observed American slavery through a mariner's eyes: "There appears to have been much sensibility awakened in the national legislature by the question affecting Slavery," he wrote in 1820. "It looks like a distant rock, whose head is hardly above the waves, on which we are in danger of suffering a sanguinary shipwreck at no very distant day."[51]

The boisterous sea could be abstracted in ways that other phenomena could not. Whereas moral character was "engraved" or indelibly "impressed upon" a person, the uncontrollable sea resembled the "savage state" in taxonomic science, an untamable force that could not be related to anything wrought or manipulated by human hands. The sea was an outward, not an inward, phenomenon, a sign of the cruelest of passions: random, erratic, wreaking havoc wherever humans ventured. Few seafarers lacked for horror stories.

When her husband and son ventured to Europe for the first time, Abigail Adams, moored to home, expressed the most common fear of those who waited for news from one who had braved a transatlantic crossing. The Revolutionary War was being waged at sea. In 1778, as she wrote, ships that were not taking prizes were being taken: "I have waited with great patience, restraining as much as posible every anxious Idea for 3 Months. But now every Vessel which arrives sits my expectation upon the wing, and I pray my Gaurdian Genious to waft me the happy tidings of your Safety and Welfare." Today's analogue to the shipwreck is the airline tragedy. Everyone knows where the imagination goes on hearing of the loss of hundreds in an instant, swallowed up by the earth or the sea. Shock is captured on the faces of those who wait at the gate—in early America, who wait at the dock—for loved ones who won't be arriving.

In the left-behind's letters, as in seagoing memoirs, anxiety was palpable. The creaking wood of a large vessel, its moaning heard in the darkness and blending with the emptiness of the high seas—what was the imaginer to do to stay the nerves? Abigail Adams revisited the Homeric epic:

Hitherto my wandering Ideas Rove like the Son of Ulissis from Sea to Sea, and from Shore to Shore, not knowing where to find you. Sometimes I fancy'd you upon the Mighty Waters, sometimes at your desired Haven; sometimes upon the ungratefull and Hostile Shore of Britain.[52]

If a transatlantic odyssey, which could take anywhere from four to seven weeks to complete, fed the frightened imaginations of loved ones left behind, seasickness onboard sometimes lasted for the majority of a journey. Abigail found this out when she herself traveled to England. Sailing ships were not designed for comfort but for cargo-hauling profit. Rooms in the wing of the captain's cabin were the only ones supplying any amount of personal freedom. The hold was crowded day and night, and captive passengers huddled close with scant privacy. Bodily cleanliness was not possible. Illness spread through the foul air, wafting on human stench. Rats were everywhere on board.

Countless diarists recorded their struggles. As the winter of 1779–80 approached, John Adams embarked on his second voyage to Europe. *La Sensible*, which had carried him safely home from France only weeks before, would nearly shipwreck this time and deposit him and his young sons at a Spanish port far from their intended destination, requiring an agonizing mule trek across the Pyrenees. In 1784, another storm-tossed voyage from England to the Netherlands landed John and John Quincy in the right country but on "a desolate shore, we knew not where." After braving the North Sea, the elder Adams languished under a "wasting sickness" and later described his seaborne trial: "a tremulous, undulating, turbulent kind of irregular tumbling sea that disposes men more to the mal de mer." The restless language half tells the story.[53]

The French exile Moreau de St. Méry kept a diary over a treacherous, nearly four-month passage aboard an American vessel in the winter of 1793–94, during which he shed fifty

pounds. To go by his report, American sailors had their pecu-
liarities. "They fear neither fatigue nor danger," he said, yet they
had a disturbing "lack of foresight," lighting fires without adequate safety precaution. St. Méry provided numerous examples
of their "shortsightedness" that resulted from their "mania" for
boasting of a superiority to French sailors. The captain's harsh
punishments for a crewman's misbehavior struck him as "unusual in a free people."

The deadly events that transpired next were not to be laid
at the feet of Americans. For ten days in January, all aboard
St. Méry's ship were "playthings of a tempest." As if hunger,
fetid odors, and bad drinking water were not trial enough, he
was "attacked by bedbugs, those hideous insects," before unpredictable winds very nearly blew him overboard. After they
came ashore, the American captain praised St. Méry for his
"cheerful endurance" and "strength of mind" throughout their
hellish passage.[54]

On his return voyage from England, Carolina-born,
Philadelphia-trained physician Charles Caldwell wrote of the
"ominous" changes he faced at the halfway point in the
mid-Atlantic:

> We were assailed by a furious tempest of three days' con-
> tinuance, during which all the rage and power of the ele-
> ments of air and water, embodied and embattled, appeared
> to be poured on our devoted ship. Terror and despair, such
> as I had never previously witnessed or fancied, overwhelmed
> the passengers, who were numerous. The screams and sob-
> bings of women were unspeakably distressing; and those of
> some men, more spiritless than women, though contempt-
> ible, were frightful.[55]

It was the captain's twenty-seventh voyage and, he informed
Caldwell, "the most annoying." That sounds like an understate-
ment, given that the fifty-two-day passage was "little else than

an unbroken series of head-winds, cross-winds, squalls, tempests, and no winds at all." To hear him tell it, the proud Dr. Caldwell asked to join the crew during the worst of it, addressing the captain: "My good sir, I am neither frightened nor weakened, and some incident may occur in which I can be useful." But the captain ordered him below, upon which "a stupendous wave struck and deeply overwhelmed the ship, . . . washing overboard the best sailor." Caldwell then rushed to the deck "against the current of water that was still pouring in on us" in time to save a crewman "clinging to the end of a piece of wrecked timber." The valiant one congratulated himself on his resistance to "unmanning fear" in the face of the tempest. He considered that strength of mind a gift of nature, the bequest of hardy ancestors.[56]

Others likewise used their escape from a tempest to assert a personal power. After crisscrossing the Equator and rounding the Cape of Good Hope, a veteran English traveler en route to Philadelphia smugly contrasted his bearing with that of his squirming shipmates as they dropped to the deck. "The cabin was by no means an envious place," he recounted in his 1803 memoir. "To the roll of the vessel I was fully accustomed, but my companions not having got their sea legs on board, tumbled grievously." Knowing what to expect, he carried his own hanging cot shipboard but still found sleeping difficult: "In the wake of the hatchway, the breeze from the deck made my situation very unpleasant." He unhooked his cot and sought a corner where he might stay dry until the seas cooperated.[57]

Tales of woe compounded. In 1801, Aaron Burr's only child, Theodosia, married wealthy South Carolina rice planter Joseph Alston. The couple's young son, the only child they had, was born the next year but succumbed to illness soon after his tenth birthday: "My child is gone forever," the grieving mother informed her father. (She was ten herself when she lost her mother.) One month later, she lamented, "Alas! my dear father, I do live, but how does it happen?" The loss of an only child shattered hopes. "Of what service can I be in this world," she mourned, "either to you or anyone else with . . . a mind enfeebled and bewildered?" After more tearful strains, she noted, "I think Omnipotence could give me no equivalent for my boy."[58]

The Burrs, father and daughter, were especially close. At the insistence of her remaining parent, Theodosia received the elaborate education given to elite young men. His infamy as the duelist who slew Alexander Hamilton had no impact on their relationship. At the end of 1812, after a European exile that lasted years, Burr, back in New York, dearly wished to be reunited with his daughter. Father, daughter, and son-in-law all weighed whether she should travel north by land or sea to visit him. They opted for the latter. It was the end of 1812, the war underway, and Joseph Alston, as the newly named governor of his state, had been commissioned a brigadier general.

Weeks after what should have been a journey of mere days, Joseph had not heard from Theodosia and was beside himself. From Charleston, he communed with his father-in-law, writing of what his life had been like before: "With my wife on one side and my boy on the other; I felt myself superior to depression." Loss of their son was sorrow enough: "My own hand surrendered him to the grave." He sought to redirect himself from dwelling on the worst-case scenario and went so far as to write to his wife, in care of her father: "All I have left of heart is yours. All my prayers are for your safety and well-being."[59]

The prospect of her falling into enemy hands on the water route north was the lesser of his worries. Having heard "rumours of a gale off Cape Hatteras," he feared Theodosia may have been lost in a shipwreck. "Forebodings!" he exclaimed. "My mind is tortured." Joseph recounted what he had done to insure a safe passage while apprehending that nothing in their world was ever truly safe. The *Patriot*'s "reputed swiftness in sailing inspired such confidence of a voyage of not more than five or six days." The captain and crew were reputable. "Gracious God! Is my wife, too, taken from me? I know not why I write, but I feel that I am miserable." One month having passed from the day the *Patriot* set sail, there was only one possible conclusion to be drawn: "What a destiny is mine!"[60]

The mourner wrote one more time to his father-in-law, the only individual who could truly share in his anguish, the political pariah he knew as a firm friend. Summing up his inner state, Alston alluded to the tortured mind of Hamlet: "He is a poor actor who cannot sustain his little hour upon the stage, be his part what it may. But the man who has been deemed worthy of the heart of *Theodosia Burr*, and who has felt what it was to be blessed with such a woman's, will never forget his elevation."[61]

The brooding Joseph Alston survived his wife by a scant three years. "I feel too much alone, too entirely unconnected to the world, to take much interest in anything," he wrote in 1816, in his final letter to Aaron Burr. Illness worsened the depression and he died, as his own words of foreboding testified, a "miserable remnant" of his former self. He was thirty-six.[62]

The North American coast was particularly susceptible to shipwreck due to navigational errors attributed to the currents and waters that became suddenly shallow. In 1817, Betsey Champlain's twenty-year-old daughter Eliza, chaperoned by relatives, sailed from New London, Connecticut, to lower Manhattan to visit her aunt. After a close call, she informed her family: "We got here alive. If you had been with us you would have had forty thousand fits. Our vessle took in water at a great rate but we were so sick we did not mind it. We are now taking all the comfort in the world." Her mother replied: "Hearing of your safe arrival in New York has deliver'd me from considerable anxiety."

But that was not the end of it. After a pause in Eliza's regular flow of letters, Betsey wrote again: "Your unexpected long silence is quite alarming." With Eliza's brother conducting business in disease-ridden Natchez, Mississippi, their mother was already on edge. "Suspence is one of my heaviest troubles," Betsey bewailed, but "I find I can bear every trial and affliction in life that is laid up on me better than formerly." So she moved on to another worry that would not go away: her young and single daughter lived in a dangerous environment. Did Eliza know how to steer clear of the city's social ills? Mothering from a distance, Betsey urged her to suppress "any imaginary want." Once again, the threat of undoing lies in imagination. "I desire," she finished up, "that you will write me if but one line as soon as possible to let me know if you are well." Knowing that a loved one had survived the perils of a journey did not put an end to the apprehensions of those at home.[63]

Time at sea could be a letdown amid calm, too. Onboard meals were repetitive. On an ocean-going ship, vegetables could not be preserved, and the smell of fish was constant. When storms weren't sending shock waves through the cabin or hurricanes weren't tearing apart masts and jarring everyone's nerves, windless days added the frustration of tedium. Many vessels reached their destination only after hobbling their way to shore, fearfully disabled, with passengers and crew gaunt and traumatized. As paradoxical as it might seem, an ocean voyage was believed the only known remedy for any who suffered from a lung ailment—which was the announced reason for why Washington Irving was sent by his family to Europe in 1805.[64]

The sailor's lot gave rise to an encyclopedic array of coping mechanisms. Jack Tar's journals were replete with sketches of women (some respectable, others not). Men were known for rough language, and the ditties they sang were often lewd. But not all. Richard Henry Dana wrote in *Two Years Before the Mast* that "a song is as necessary to sailors as drum and fife to a soldier. They can't pull in time or pull with a wheel without it."

From at least the time of Daniel Defoe's *Robinson Crusoe* (1719), maritime literature fixated on survival skills.[65]

Lord Byron's beloved *Childe Harold's Pilgrimage* (1812–18) recollects the journeys of a ruminative young man. Told in three epic cantos, it captures the seaborne spirit of the era:

> Once more upon the waters! yet once more!
> And the waves bound neath me as a steed
> That knows his rider. Welcome to their roar!
> Swift be their guidance, wheresoe'er it lead!
> Though the strained mast should quiver as a reed
> And the rent canvas fluttering strew the gale,
> Still must I on; for I am as a weed,
> Flung from the rock on Ocean's foam, to sail
> Where'er the surge may sweep, the tempest's
>   breath prevail.[66]

Fate cannot be turned away, so the passenger accepts his lot. The one grace, deferring the descent into melancholy, is the reflective act of admiring the guiding power of Nature: with strained mast quivering, humanity lay at the mercy of wind and wave. Sea disasters were a fact of life.

"The Voyage" (from New York to Liverpool) is the opening meditation in Washington Irving's sensation-causing *Sketch Book* (1819). The passenger-author relates the story of a young Englishman, deathly ill and hanging on to life just long enough to catch a glimpse of his beloved, who waits at the dock to welcome him.

Irving's power as a writer derived from his ability to address mortal concerns without the doom and gloom. Though not every life can be saved, in "The Voyage" he never abandons hope: "When the ship is decked out in all of her canvass, every sail swelled, and careering gaily over the curling waves, how gallant she appears—how she seems to lord it over the deep."

But later "thunders bellowed over the wild waste of waters. . . . I saw the ship staggering and plunging." Pathos is often his instrument, as when the dying sailor whom the narrator cannot turn from, stays alive just long enough to sight land. Dockside in Liverpool, his "countenance so wasted, so pale, so ghastly," he meets the eye of his love and faintly calls her name. Finally, "at the sound of his voice her eye darted on his features—it read at once a whole volume of sorrow—she clasped her hands, uttered a faint shriek and stood wringing them in silent agony."

In the nautically drawn metaphors in eighteenth-century American English, the word "tempest" was routinely invoked in referring to the real and imagined pressures people felt. "Tempest" could describe a tax revolt, a civil war, or politics in general. "I cannot wean myself from the Subjects of politicks," wrote Mrs. Adams in 1800, as her husband faced a difficult reelection fight. "If tempests threaten us, we look for judgement prudence calmness and intrepidity in the commander—but Rocks & Shoals are before us—Heaven knows where we Shall be landed we see as yet but in part; I was loth to believe that we Should be Set afloat."[67]

Retrospectively, we see the final decade of the eighteenth century as nothing short of tempestuous. The possibility of French Revolutionary violence bleeding into American political life embroiled the United States in a "quasi-war" with France, tax revolts brought federal troops into the Pennsylvania backcountry, newspaper writers and publishers were locked up for criticizing the sitting president. Hyperpartisanship nearly shipwrecked "mild government," the stated intent of republicans.

That is the framework in which the popular Shakespearean drama *The Tempest* was understood in these years. The play's opening scene presents howling winds and a tempest-tossed vessel that appears to be sinking. The unnerving sounds of roaring seas loomed as large in the imagination of post-Revolutionary

Americans as they had in that of the early-seventeenth-century English.

Yet *The Tempest* is about more than its catastrophic contours. On the surface it concerns the restoration of Prospero, exiled Duke of Milan, who was left to die at sea by his grasping brother Antonio, in league with others. Prospero uses magic powers derived from books to bring about a tempest, shipwreck the conspirators, and fight back. The plot contains disguise and ventriloquism, undertones of racist enslavement (as represented by the monster-like Caliban), and while Prospero is ostensibly the hero, he has a cruel streak. It all ends with a love match, forgiveness, and reconciliation, and Prospero's enjoyment of a peaceful retirement. In early republican America, *The Tempest* was not just read as a commentary on political deception among the highborn but as a morality tale encouraging the confronting of errors and the making of amends.

The play was also, notably, about America's founding as a British colony. It was written in or about 1611, as the tormented beginnings of the colony of Jamestown were rattling around the playwright's head. The entire premise of *The Tempest* is a mix of ancient tales of treacherous voyages (Aeneus, Odysseus, Jason and the Argonauts) and a Virginia-bound shipwreck that was just then grabbing attention in London. Sailing from England, the colony's new governor did not arrive and was presumed drowned. Stranded for a year in the Bermudas, he miraculously appeared in Jamestown. Back in England, his deliverance formed a topic of Anglican sermons. Because all who came to America from elsewhere braved open waters, the example lived on.[68]

"Our passage through time makes us all leaky vessels, incapable of holding on to our experiences," writes Philip Weinstein, a scholar of modernist fiction. History and literature abound in lessons that command broad acceptance of human infirmities. Some of these stories spring from leaky memories. For the generations that could not depend on medical intervention to extend life at any age, and the tempest-tossed who faced internal struggles and high seas, acquiescence was demanded.[69]

THE PLAYS OF

WILLIAM SHAKSPEARE

ILLUSTRATED WITH ENGRAVINGS,

BY

George B. Ellis

FROM THE DESIGNS OF

R. Smirk R.A.

TEMPEST.

PHILADELPHIA.

PUBLISHED BY M^C CARTY & DAVIS,

& H.C. CAREY & I. LEA.

1824.

Title page of an early US printing of
The Tempest from *The Dramatic Works and Poems of William Shakespeare*, vol. 1
(Philadelphia: McCarty and Davis and H. C. Carey and I. Lea, 1824).

Courtesy of Special Collections, University of Virginia Library.

Chapter 3.

Shakespearean Recitals
(Yearnings)

Shakespeare, that great Master of every Affection of the Heart and every Sentiment of the
Mind as well as of all the Powers of Expression,
is sometimes fond of a certain pointed Oddity
of Language, a certain Quaintness of Style.
                            —John Adams, 1772
                            ❧

And what do we not owe to Shakespear for
the enrichment of the language by his free and
magical creation of words?
                            —Thomas Jefferson, 1816
                            ❧

According to the 1821 *Dictionary of Arts and Sciences*, published in New York, the goal of every dramatist was to capture
an audience by capturing character. Shakespeare's achievement
lay in having succeeded at this above all others: "To construct a

truly dramatic fable is no easy task. The author has to provide sources of constantly augmenting interest, to present characters, to suggest situations capable of extorting from the spectators an active participation in the scene." Shakespeare was able to "transmit the impression of every feeling" that could possibly be portrayed. (Here, "impression" and "feeling" align yet again.) Even Shakespeare's prose was deemed poetic excellence. The philosophically inclined regularly consulted the works of the bard in their considerations of what moved the human heart.[1]

One such was Abigail Adams. "Your kind and friendly letter found me in great affliction," she wrote an old friend in September 1813, as she mourned the loss of her only daughter. Abigail Adams Smith (known as Nabby) had succumbed to breast cancer several weeks earlier, at the age of forty-eight. Her correspondent was Thomas Jefferson, who had lost both his wife and an adult daughter from childbirth complications. "You sir, who have been called to seperations [*sic*] of a similar kind, can sympathize with your bereaved Friend."

He had written to her, unknowingly, just as a family tragedy was unfolding, innocently asking after Abigail's health. They had not exchanged letters in years, and he was unaware of Nabby's illness. "I will now take time to ask you how you do," he prodded gently, "and to express the interest I take in whatever affects your happiness." All he knew was that she, like he, suffered from rheumatism.

In response, Abigail half apologized for dwelling on the details of the grief that afflicted her, just as she had done in her 1797 letter to Martha Washington ("To a Heart less benevolent I should apologize for relating my Grief," she'd written), saying, "The full Heart loves to pour out its sorrows, into the Bosom of sympathizing Friendship." Before closing, she inserted three affecting lines from Shakespeare's *A Comedy of Errors* (5.1.1736–39), slightly misquoting:

Greif has changed me since you saw me last,
And carefull hours, with times deformed hand
Hath written strange defections o'er my face.

For good measure, above her signature, she reminded him of the complicated history between Jefferson and the Adamses with another Shakespeare reference, this one from *Measure for Measure* (3.2.1694), writing that "although, time has changed the outward form, and political 'Back wounding calumny' for a period interrupted the Friendly intercourse and harmony which subsisted, it is again renewed, purified from the dross." She'd quoted the same passage more extensively sixteen years earlier, during her husband's presidency, railing against the pro-Jefferson press in a letter to her nephew William Cranch, a distinguished jurist. Notably, the plot of *Measure for Measure* exposes how politics is poisoned by ill will, greed, and jealousy.[2]

Mrs. Adams and Mr. Jefferson had been fond of each other during overlapping months in Paris in the mid-1780s. But she became downright antagonistic following Jefferson's electoral defeat of her husband in the presidential contest of 1800. Indeed, of the two Adamses, Abigail was the more offended by the outwardly placid, covertly calculating Virginian. It was John Adams who, in 1811, reopened what grew into a flourishing correspondence with his successor, but she solidified its repair when she inserted a postscript in one of John's letters to Jefferson soon after their daughter came home to die.

Never one to mince words or hide emotions for long, Abigail deployed Shakespeare in a variety of contexts over the course of her epistolary career. With little formal education, she drew on the comedies, tragedies, and histories, always with the object of stirring the spirit. In at least thirty letters written to close family members during the last quarter of the eighteenth century, she underscored an emotion by including a meaningful quote from one of the bard's plays.

The American Revolution was destined to evoke comparisons to one dramatic text or another for years to come. Writing to John in April 1776, by which time the British had departed Boston, Abigail contemplated the fate of family friend Joseph Warren, whose remains were dug up at Bunker Hill and reinterred with military honors. The event led her to cite the scene of pathos in *Julius Caesar* when Romans filed past Caesar's body (3.1.1487–93). Again she slightly misremembers certain lines while deliberately changing others (writing "Britton" in the place of "Italy"):

> Woe to the hands that shed this costly blood
>
> . . . .
>
> A curse shall light upon their line;
> Domestic fury and fi[e]rce civil strife
> Shall cumber all the parts of Italy.[3]

In another letter, this one to her sister Mary Smith Cranch in 1786, she found a Shakespearean allusion that applied to the romantic life of her daughter. Nabby was weighing the character of Royall Tyler, a charming Harvard graduate whose fondness for her was obvious to all but whose reputation was spotty. In this instance, Abigail quoted from notes Nabby had taken as she made her way through *Two Gentlemen of Verona*. The verses her daughter had copied out spoke to the mother as well:

> I am sorry I must never trust thee more
> But Count the World a stranger for thy sake
> The private wound is deepest; oh time most curst
> Mongst all foes, that a friend should be the worst.
> (5.4.2222–25)[4]

As a mother who leaned into whatever situation affected her children, Abigail judged the character of men and judged from the gut. It was *her* doubt of Tyler's "strickt honour" that convinced daughter Nabby to break with him. She went on to marry her father's personal secretary, Colonel William Stephens Smith, in 1786, one whose known character, according to Mrs. Adams, was "fair and unblemished." Smith was a Revolutionary War veteran with a good conduct record who'd served on the staffs of two generals, that of the Marquis de Lafayette and that of Washington himself. Despite these signs, the noble colonel would prove a wretched choice for son-in-law, revealing himself over time to be a faithless schemer and cad.

In 1786, as Colonel Smith won the trust of mother and daughter alike, Tyler nevertheless maintained his hold on the family. "Let the memory of former attachments . . . sleep in oblivion," the mother wrote to son John Quincy of Nabby's emotional confusion, adding that "a Heart agitated with a former passion is most susceptable [*sic*] of a new one." She was thinking, again, of lines from *Two Gentlemen of Verona*: "Even as one heat another heat expels,/Or as one nail by strength drives out another,/So the remembrance of my former love/Is by a newer object quite forgotten" (2.4.854–57). She paired this line with a second Shakespeare quote (lifted from *The Tempest* [4.1.1882]) in stating her hope that the memory of Tyler would soon disappear from all of their minds like the "baseless fabric of a vision," one of the most often deployed of Shakespearean metaphors.

Adopted by many in a wide variety of contexts across decades, "baseless fabric of a vision" invariably referred to an unfounded notion or any plan that seemed doomed to fail. Washington used it in a wartime letter and again as president in a letter to a close female friend, contesting groundless criticisms in a political pamphlet, while disgraced general James Wilkinson claimed that the charges he faced were "as insubstantial as the 'baseless fabric of a vision.'" Jefferson favored it, too. What makes any metaphor memorable is its hold on the imagination. This one made the rounds among political insiders.[5]

In another letter to John in May 1794, Abigail issued a complaint about back-stabbing politicians, salting the page with allegations of "abuse," "malice," and a looming "judas." Adapting lines from *Julius Caesar*, she went after the main target of the letter, Alexander Hamilton, her husband's chief antagonist within his own political party: "I have ever thought with respect to that Man, 'beware of that spair Cassius'" (1.2.293).[6]

In letters to her husband over the years, Mrs. Adams variously quoted from *Julius Caesar, Hamlet, Richard III*, and *Cymbeline*. As for John, he began reading Shakespeare a decade before their marriage, and in a lengthy diary entry of 1758 he took stock of the playwright's portrayal of tragic characters, male and female alike: "Shakespeare, in the Character of Lady Mackbeth, and of Gertrude, the Wife of old Hamlet, and afterwards of King Claudius, and in the Character of Lady Anne in King Richard, has shewn a sense of the Weakness of Woman's Reason, and strength of their Passions." It was Macbeth who caught his special interest: "His imagination created 100 things, a Voice crying, Sleep no more, Mackbeth doth Murder Sleep; the innocent Sleep. Sleep is the Idea now. What Thoughts does this call up. Sleep that knits up the ravelled sleeve of Care, the Death of each days Life. As Death is to a mans whole Life, so is each night's Sleep." The virtue-signaling diarist, age twenty-three, was especially taken with the "sound and fury" monologue and with how guilty minds operated.

Fifteen years later, as the Revolution incubated, John Adams commended Shakespeare for his insights into public ambition, the "Passions and Prejudices, the Follies and Vices of great Men." How the public could be seduced by "the Will of a dishonest Master" was a problem the playwright had inspired him to examine early, and a concern that he would repeatedly bring up in detailing his personal philosophy. In retirement, he informed his son, then a newly elected US senator, that he was once again "uncommonly engaged and interested in reading Shakespeare, and particularly the historical Drama's." For his part, John Quincy Adams was already familiar with Shake-

speare's colorful characters by the age of ten when he traveled
with his father to Europe for the first time. In a diary entry years
later, an amazed New York City mayor gushed that John Q.
Adams knew "every line of Shakespeare."[7]

The Adamses were an extraordinary family, wary students
of human psychology, obsessed by those passions that led to
folly. But they were far from unique in their attachment to
Shakespeare. As the founding generation's children came of age
and the glories of their Revolutionary parents were pressed into
pages, bound in cloth or calf, they enlisted the Elizabethan bard
to help amplify the emotion contained in their histories. In his
long-researched, if deeply flawed, biography of Patrick Henry,
William Wirt apparently drew on *Julius Caesar* to adorn the
"Give Me Liberty or Give Me Death" speech. Wirt imagined
that Henry was keenly attuned to the story of the Roman's rise
and fall—known Henry speeches revealed as much, and indeed,
according to his son-in-law, Henry was decidedly a Shakespeare
fan. Thus, a version of Cassius's speech in act 1, scene 2 (an appeal to Brutus to oppose Caesar's monarchical ambition) made
its way into Wirt's dramatization of Henry's signature appeal
to the colonies. In the lead-up to Revolution, the threat of "Cae-
sarism" was in the letters and on the tongues of a number of
America's leaders.[8]

Shakespeare's authority was exceeded only by Shakespeare's
emotional drawing power. Recall from the previous chapter the
shipwreck that made South Carolina Governor Joseph Alston
a widower at the start of 1813. The mourner revealed his inner
state to his father-in-law, Aaron Burr, the only individual who
could truly share in his anguish, by alluding to the tortured
mind of Hamlet: "He is a poor actor who cannot sustain his
little hour upon the stage, be his part what it may. But the man
who has been deemed worthy of the heart of *Theodosia Burr*, and
who has felt what it was to be blessed with such a woman's, will
never forget his elevation."[9]

Until her son's death altered the tone of their communications, Aaron and Theodosia Burr punctuated their playful letters with French phrases and philosophical challenges. In her twenty-first year, he wrote: "When any thing amuses me, my first thought is whether it would also amuse you; and the pleasure is but half enjoyed until it is communicated." The following year, ever focused on the importance of mental exercise, Burr urged her: "Read over Shakespeare critically, marking the passages which are beautiful, absurd, or obscure. I will do the same, and one of these days we will compare."[10]

"Every reader of feeling and sentiment"

Prior to 1795, as well developed as the print trade was in the United States, the only way an American could acquire Shakespeare's works was by importing them. The Boston Public Library has preserved the London (1748) and Edinburgh (1761) editions of *The Works of Shakespear* that were owned by the Adams family. Jefferson's private library contained Shakespeare in both octavo and duodecimo sizes as well as the London (1766) four-volume version with twenty plays and its ten-volume successor (1778–80).

During and after college, Jefferson kept a commonplace book with notations from books as he was reading. He copied fifteen distinct passages from Shakespeare, drawing from a 1744 edition of the works selected lines from *Julius Caesar, Coriolanus*, and three of the histories. In 1786, at the same time his friend Abigail was fretting about her daughter's love life, Jefferson visited the family in London. He saw a live performance of *The Merchant of Venice* at the Drury Lane Theatre and together with John Adams paid a visit to Shakespeare's birthplace in Stratford-on-Avon.[11]

Despite the abundance of his letters—some eighteen thousand extant—Jefferson quotes Shakespeare far less than his regular correspondents John and Abigail Adams. Nevertheless, his fondness for the bard is clear. Before the Revolution, in a letter to a young Virginia lawyer (a relative by marriage), he recommended "must own" books for any library and spoke to the power of Shakespeare: "We never reflect whether the story we read be truth or fiction. If the painting be lively and a tolerable picture of nature, we are thrown into a reverie, from which if we awaken it is the fault of the writer. I appeal to every reader of feeling and sentiment whether the fictitious murther of Duncan by Macbeth in Shakespeare does not excite in him as great horror of villainy, as the real one of Henry IV by Ravaillac. . . . A lively and lasting sense of filial duty is more effectually impressed on the mind of a son or daughter by reading King Lear, than by all the dry volumes of ethics and divinity that ever were written." Like the Adamses and countless others, Jefferson valued Shakespeare as a moral physician.[12]

From estate inventories, we learn that planters, lawyers, physicians, and others across the states owned copies of Shakespeare. There were several to choose from, but the one Jefferson recommended, indeed the most accurate, was that of Edward Capell (1713–81). Multivolume editions were advertised in newspapers up and down the Atlantic coast from the 1760s onward. In the early 1790s, when future congressman John Randolph, another Virginia planter, read the law with his second cousin, George Washington's attorney general Edmund Randolph, he was assigned, in addition to standard law texts, David Hume's *Treatise on Human Nature* plus the works of Shakespeare. He was told that this was how one acquired "metaphysical reasoning."[13]

A Maryland attorney named John H. Thomas delivered a Fourth of July oration in 1807, at the Washington Society of Alexandria, Virginia, citing Shakespearean lines by the barrelful to awe those who packed the pews. He apparently felt that British criminality was best conveyed through the bard's idiom, quoting "hell itself breathes out contagion to this world" from

Hamlet (3.2.2264–65) and "revel the night, rob, murder, and commit/The oldest sins the newest kind of ways?" from *Henry IV, Part II* (4.5.3021–22). Thomas railed that "poor old England had no Cordelia among all her daughters," with reference to the faithful, persecuted one in *King Lear*.[14]

Misrule of the colonies brought out "the meteors of a troubled heaven," the anniversary speaker continued, no doubt with prodigious feeling. This line from *Henry IV, Part I* (1.1.11) would have been familiar to his audience: it was in the first speech of that well-known play, after the opening lines: "So shaken as we are, so wan with care/Find we a time for frighted peace to pant" (1.1.1–2). In 1807, America did not want another war with Britain, though, of course, it would have one soon enough. Thomas was trying to say that his countrymen were possessed of sufficient hardiness and valor to meet any challenge. British power was "not a tempest," nor was America's "a wild Utopian voyage . . . and all 'such stuff as dreams are made of'" (*The Tempest* [4.1.1887–88]). If forced to sail on Hamlet's "sea of troubles" (3.1.1752), America would fight against indignity, for dignity.[15]

Shakespeare's plays take up the same emotion-laden subjects that affected those Americans who were so keen to imbibe eighteenth-century poetry. Throughout the plays, leave takings are constant: farewell glances as a ship sails, fearful disappearances, and dramatic separations (Juliet's "parting is such sweet sorrow" [2.2.1049–50]) frame the plots. In *All's Well that Ends Well*, before Bartram disobeys the king and steals away to war in Italy, he sees off a lordly compatriot with "I grow to you, and our parting is a tortured body" (2.1.633). In *Cymbeline*, Princess Imogen learns of her secret lover's sailing and paints a picture of her pain at being interrupted by the king (who had other plans for her) before she could "give him that parting kiss which I had set betwixt two charming words" (1.3.310–11). "What store of parting tears were shed?" asks Richard II in the eponymous tragedy (1.4.619).[16]

Shakespeare came up in unusual contexts, too. In 1807, in New Orleans, some soldiers were playing cards when another was invited in. "He declined, with a quotation from Shakespear." Somehow, this led quickly to an argument, a duel, a dead man, and a remorseful killer—unfortunately, the newspaper did not say what Shakespeare quote had caused the dispute. A few years later, Captain Gilbert Longstreet of Augusta, Georgia, reported an attempt on his life, occurring as he sat reading a now-forgotten novel at home and opened to an epigraph from Shakespeare's *Henry VI, Part 2*. Scanning the lines, "Deep night, dark night . . . That time best fits the work we have in hand" (1.4.643–47), he got the shock of his life. "A musket, loaded with bullets and buckshot, was discharged at his head thro' the window. . . . No discovery has yet been made as to the perpetrator of this foul deed."[17]

It is difficult to pinpoint a year, or even a decade, when Shakespeare can first be referred to as fashionable among Americans. A dozen lines from one of the histories might be cited in a newspaper of the 1730s or 1750s, assigned to Shakespeare but without their precise source, suggesting that few if any readers had access. When any of the plays were performed in late colonial times, they were more often than not in episodic form and by actors who used imprecise language.

Fifteen Shakespeare plays were acted across the colonies on 166 occasions from 1750 to 1774. The most popular among these were *Romeo and Juliet*, *Richard III*, *Hamlet*, and an adaptation of *Taming of the Shrew*. In 1774, the Continental Congress recommended against theater in general, denoting it a "Species of Extravagance and Dissipation," somehow lumping plays together with horse racing and cockfights. But as the British monarchy came to stand for a threat to Americans' idea of their moral identity, the tragedy of *Richard III*, in particular, attained tremendous popularity. The deformed, pretentious King Richard, a quintessential villain, created a poisonous atmosphere

at court, and the analogy was irresistible. Soldiers in the Continental Army, whose commander was a great fan of theater, were
treated to performances of *Richard III.* General Washington saw
The Tempest performed in Philadelphia during the 1787 Constitutional Convention and remained a lover of theater even as major US cities were encountering harsh criticism from moralists
far and wide over the unseemly social gatherings that staged
dramas tended to invite.[18]

The inventory of Washington's books at the time of his death
shows only a single-volume edition of Shakespeare. But even
though Washington was not a pronounced lover of literature, he
ordered "a bust of the immortal Shakespear," as he denoted it,
from England and displayed it at his Mount Vernon home.[19]

The Penetration of Privacy

In 1795, in the temporary national capital of Philadelphia, Shakespeare's complete works rolled off an American press for the first
time. The editor touted them for their uplifting content. Over the
next twenty-five years, as New York City eclipsed Philadelphia as
the center of American theater, eight more American editions of
the complete works appeared. Anglo-American cultural competition soon reached the point where American commentators were
claiming a closer kinship with "pure" Shakespearean language
than England itself could boast.[20]

The preeminent dramatist of the Western world was many
things, but to the people of 1800, he was first an exemplar of
moral struggles and next an interpreter of states of mind and
human motives. He shied from no subject and his cautionary
voice appealed to women as much as to men. Then as now, it
was said of Shakespeare that his art touches on timeless truths.
The resentments and presentiments in their world, grounded in
their experience of war and exposure to repeated plots to un-

dermine authority, compared easily to those expressed in Shakespeare's plays. The tricks of his trade had clear resonance. Means and motive came to life.

We need not look very far for analogues. Patriot rebels were captured by Tories who pretended to be sympathetic to the cause, and wartime spies like Nathan Hale and John André were taken while dressed in civilian disguise. Shakespearean plots are filled with examples of cross-dressing, substitutions, and tricks played to obtain advantage in love and war. Best known, perhaps, is the cross-dressing Viola in *Twelfth Night*. Americans of 1800 knew the story of the cross-dressing Revolutionary soldier Deborah Sampson, who enlisted as "Robert," strapped a bandage over her breasts to disguise her sex and was made into a battlefield heroine in a somewhat embellished biography designed to help her family supplement the small pension she received as a veteran.[21]

Then there is Shakespeare's Portia, the powerful, self-taught lawyer in *Merchant of Venice*, author of the sublime "quality of mercy" speech. She passes as a man in order to accomplish her noble aims. And until she marries the good Benedick and embraces convention at the end of the play, Beatrice in *Much Ado about Nothing*, like the Shakespeare-quoting Abigail Adams, is a strong-minded female whose pronounced wit and wordplay give her an irresistible appeal. In *Love's Labour's Lost*, a group of men attempt to fool the women by donning disguises, but the ladies do the same and outwit them. So for every Gertrude who marries her husband's murderous brother, for every devious Lady Macbeth or victimized Desdemona, there is a woman who knows her worth.[22]

Politics in republican America created new alignments that produced strenuous arguments and blatant antipathies. In Washington's cabinet, Jefferson perceived the cagey Hamilton as an Iago-like presence, whispering dangerous, unrepublican ideas into Washington's ear. Fear and desperation magnified as the two-party system took hold. Federalists appeared as "monarchists" to their enemies (Jefferson coined the term "monocrat"), ready to sell their souls to a British regime from which the United States had only recently freed itself. Republicans became "terrorists" by sucking up to the destabilizing French Revolutionary regime. What could be more Shakespearean than court intrigue and the whispers of would-be usurpers?

As in Shakespeare, intercepted and doctored letters framed personal dramas with state implications; innocent mistakes could cause irreparable harm to a public figure. Washington's loyal (Republican-leaning) attorney general, Edmund Randolph, was falsely accused of conspiring with the French and was hounded out of office by arch-Federalists. The publicity given to a private letter Jefferson sent to Philip Mazzei, an old friend of America's who had returned to Italy, caused Washington, in retirement, to see Jefferson as a betrayer. In this case, language imperfectly translated from English to Italian to French and back to English, was used by his political detractors as proof of Jefferson's belief that George Washington had been reduced to a pawn of London.

References to private conversations and private emotions enrich Shakespeare's plays.: "He desires some private speech with you" (*All's Well That Ends Well* [2.5.1320]); "a private whisper" (*Coriolanus* [5.3.3947]); "What infinite heart's ease / Must kings neglect that private men enjoy!" (*Henry V* [4.1.2083–84]); "In private will I talk with thee apart" (*Henry VI, Part 1* [1.2.266]). In *Henry VIII*, there are many: "private chamber" (3.1.1665) "private malice" (3.2.2161), "private conscience" (5.3.3098), and the unmistakable "How dare you thrust yourselves / Into my private meditations?" (2.2.1093–94). In *Julius Caesar*, after the title character offers an explanation to the Senate for his failure to appear, he gives an honest explanation to his aide: "for your private satisfaction / Because I love you I will let you know"

(2.2.1054–55) In the same play, as he delivers his famous "Friends, Romans, Countrymen" speech, Antony says: "They that have done this deed are honorable:/What private griefs they have, alas, I know not" (3.2.1756–57).[23]

Throughout history, the penetration of privacy has been at the heart of most memorable stories. In the literature that was popular among Americans in the late eighteenth and early nineteenth centuries, as in the plays of Shakespeare, secrets are spilled, impostures are exposed, deceptions abound. Characters in these works hide from view and spy on conversations: female domestics lurk, seeing and hearing. Readers could easily relate to all such scenarios because American households were still units of production where itinerant laborers mingled with servants and other permanent residents. All understood the adage that appearances are deceiving, that an interloper can cause trouble by pretending to be one thing when he or she is just the opposite. Everyone knew a troublemaker.

In *The Adventures of Peregrine Pickle*, a staple in home libraries first published in 1751, Tobias Smollett's scene-stealing misanthrope states:

I now appear in the world, not as a member of any community, or what is called a social creature, but merely as a spectator, who entertains himself . . . in beholding his enemies at loggerheads. That I may enjoy this disposition, abstracted from all interruption, danger, and participation, I feign myself deaf; an expedient by which I not only avoid all disputes and their consequences, but also become master of a thousand little secrets, which are every day whispered in my presence, without any suspicion of their being overheard.[24]

Inside spaces were a familiar site of mischief, but it did not stop there. The inviolability of private property was adjudicated in colonial courtrooms from the outset of settlement, and the Constitution's Fourth Amendment guaranteed "the right of the people to be secure in their persons, houses"; yet no such warrant applied in the outside world, and in public taverns, scandal grew from whispers. Fierce editorial rivalries and the desire to sell more newspapers than one's competitors made malicious publication a daily reality. As "secret histories" spread, reputations were never completely safe. In the same newspapers, the pseudonymous authors of high-minded articles argued against human nature, urging readers to exercise agency, to resist temptation, and practice self-control. Middle- and upper-class parents instructed their daughters to be wary of the vice-ridden world: outside the home was "deceit and falsehood," as a representative guide warned, a world "where few persons or things appear in their true character." That was what Eliza Champlain's family worried about when she, a young single woman, left New London, Connecticut, for Manhattan, to make her way in the art world. One was supposed to hide behind a mask of bland contentment, to practice the "art of pleasing," to conceal the personality that was only meant to be known within the trusted domestic circle. Concerns over privacy were accompanied by fears of betrayal.[25]

"*All the world's a stage*"

Sexual passion, a mainstay of Shakespearean drama, was not a taboo subject in the eighteenth and nineteenth centuries, though it was exclusively the male of the species that had permission to engage in public discussions of physical desire. In an 1817 letter, Dr. Benjamin Waterhouse (1754–1846), who taught medicine at Harvard, spoke his heart to John Adams. The two bonded in 1780, when they boarded together in the Netherlands; they'd remained close ever since. The physician's wife died when he was sixty. It was not uncommon for a man of that age to remarry, but two years later he was still single and unfulfilled. "I am curious to know what such old folks as you can feel & know

& judge of affairs of the heart, or what may be called sexual affection," he wrote his eighty-year-old friend. "The wise people
round about me ridicule all such feelings of the heart in me. . . .
I have been blundering about alone, heartless—cheerless &
comfortless." Before she died, his wife had urged him to find
someone else. The children were grown and gone. "To a man of
my sociable turn, & cheerful disposition, & affectionate constitution, this is dreadful!" The one woman he desired, a widow
still in her thirties, was opposed by his children, because she
bore those "endowments that are calculated to make a fool of an
old man."

He asked John and Abigail for advice. "I wish to know of
you & madam if the warm affections of the heart cool at 60;
become quite cold at 66; and are frozen up by 70; and at 80
cannot hardly be remembered." He felt confident in what the
late Benjamin Franklin, "old pump-thunder" (a bawdy nickname, to be sure), would say to him: join with the young widow
and remain sexually active. The question Dr. Waterhouse
wanted answered—"the plain naked fact"—was whether at his
age, the obliging widow and he should unite, come what may.
"They shudder '*at the world's dread laugh*,'" he reported in the
third person, paraphrasing the poet James Thomson. "They
wish to act right; they fear to act wrong." Should they allow his
children to dissuade them?

He'd written the same letter to his intimate friends the Adamses months earlier but had tossed it in the fire, out of embarrassment. "A man, or woman may think too little; or they
may think too much. The line of true wisdom lies *somewhere* in
between." And the big takeaway: "I have never until lately recognized the wisdom of Providence in making young people *in
love*;—that is, giving them an almost blind impetus that ex-
cludes deep reflection."[26]

Not only are the foregoing maxims Shakespearean in
tone, but whether he knew it or not, Waterhouse had laid out a

Shakespearean comic plot for himself. In *As You Like It*, for instance, the play in which the immortal words "all the world's a stage" are spoken, Orlando and Rosalind are in love, but they are both, separately, driven into exile. Eventually, though, the family relents, and they find their way to marry.

John Adams's response to his distraught friend was true to form. The letter "touched my feelings," he wrote, playing on the irony that an esteemed doctor was "deeply infected with a dangerous distemper" and somehow asking a lawyer's advice to mend his heart. Adams considered first the remedy of "jocularity," having anecdotes at hand that would serve. But, he averred, "your Malady is too inveterate" to be cured through humor. His answer, then: "If the Lady is legally a Widow I advise you to follow your own ultimate deliberation Judgment and Inclination."[27]

In life as it is staged, everyone gives everyone else advice. In *Hamlet*, Laertes warns his sister Ophelia not to succumb to the allure of the amorous prince of Denmark. But Adams, rather more like Shakespeare in his comedies, values life for the contest of wits it provides in each social engagement (as mirrored in epistolary engagement). As a character in Dr. Waterhouse's comedy, he'll go only so far—like Friar Francis in *Much Ado about Nothing*, who asks the reticent Claudio and his betrothed, Hero, "if either of you know any inward impediment why you should not be conjoined." (4.1.1652–53). The "inward impediment" for Adams's friend has nothing to do with manners or morals; it is, rather, his humanity, his embarrassment, his concern with what others think.

But this, too, is part and parcel of Shakespeare's appeal to post-Revolutionary Americans. He takes on human nature unabashedly—it was in this sense that Harold Bloom anointed him "inventor" of the human. The "benign nihilism" at the heart of *Much Ado about Nothing*, to quote Bloom paradoxically, is present in Adams's impulsive jocularity. Yet Adams also knows what Shakespeare so beautifully expresses across his plays and sonnets: that the unsaid can be a rich source of individual contentment but only when coolly monitored. Go inward, is what this old friend instructs in the curious case of Benjamin Waterhouse.

Shakespeare, likewise, peers out at his creation from an inward place, shadowy, generally reserving judgment. As he does so, early Americans who saw him as an authority on the human condition regarded him as elemental, almost as a form of consciousness.[28]

"An extreme sensibility of mind"

Ways of silent communication were important to both eighteenth-century Americans and Elizabethans. Shakespeare addresses this mode of relaying information in sonnet 24.

> Mine eye hath play'd the painter and hath steel'd,
> Thy beauty's form in table of my heart;
> My body is the frame wherein 'tis held,
> And perspective it is best painter's art.
> For through the painter must you see his skill,
> To find where your true image pictur'd lies,
> Which in my bosom's shop is hanging still,
> That hath his windows glazed with thine eyes.
> Now see what good turns eyes for eyes have done:
> Mine eyes have drawn thy shape, and thine for me
> Are windows to my breast, where-through the sun
> Delights to peep, to gaze therein on thee;
> Yet eyes this cunning want to grace their art,
> They draw but what they see, know not the heart.[29]

Body and feeling are at once engaged. Post-Revolutionary Americans had been taught to see, by way of a painter's ability to capture likeness, the metaphorical window to the soul; the eye to beating breast; light transmitted from eyes to heart. The educated (and self-educated) could read and understand what Shakespeare the poet meant: the heart wanting to come alive in the artist's studio ("my bosom's shop"), the windows penetrated by all-seeing eyes. However, the eyes' "cunning" achieved only an imperfect amount of discernment, for even with the sun's illumination, the heart is never quite seen.[30]

In the late eighteenth century, this interest in nonverbal indicators of character took shape in the "science" of physiognomy. Educated Americans found Johann Caspar Lavater's method of discerning good faces and ferreting out malevolent ones to be entirely credible. The innovative Swiss clergyman-criminologist had authored an illustrated physiognomy guide in the 1770s suggesting that the detection of human motives was possible through an examination of facial formations, such as indelible features in the forehead, eyes, nose, mouth, and chin.

Prominent Americans sought evidence of their republican character by associating physiognomy with political values. The nationally renowned portraitist Charles Willson Peale (1741–1827), a Revolutionary patriot and physiognomy devotee, applied his imagination to Lavater's facial science when he put the native genius of America's principal founders on display in his Philadelphia natural history museum. He fully expected visitors to the "Gallery of Distinguished Personages" to identify wisdom immediately: in the profiles of their leaders, citizens would recognize character worth emulating.

The constant republication of Lavater's guide through the third decade of the nineteenth century kept his name and ideas in the public eye. His system of identification suggested that one could rest easier in the presence of a stranger whose face expressed tranquility and good intentions, as Henry Mackenzie's protagonist Harley in *A Man of Feeling* believes. One chapter in his emblematic novel is titled "His Skill in Physiognomy," in which Harley, "too apt to forget the caution" against judging by appearance, encounters a benevolent-looking elderly gentleman whose generosity of spirit is confirmed. Harley's stagecoach companion tells of a youth who "pawned his great-coat for an edition of Shakespeare." The connection hardly seems coincidental. Over the course of the novel, Harley meets a variety of physiognomic types and never "lost his attachment to that science."[31]

Conversely, dissimulation and untrustworthiness left indelible marks. One's "fascinating manners" could be penetrated and the "inmost recesses" of the heart exposed. In the words of the New York editor of *The Pocket Lavater*: "Physiognomy is the very soul of wisdom, since it elevates the mutual pleasures of intercourse, and whispers to the heart when it is necessary to speak." A universal curiosity about human nature led to eager experimental probes of the human imagination.[32]

It is not a coincidence that in 1770, the year before *The Man of Feeling* was published, Mackenzie called Hamlet representative of enlightened masculinity. "The basis of Hamlet's character seems to be an extreme sensibility of mind," he wrote. For Mackenzie, doubt and irresolution were a natural outgrowth of melancholia caused by trauma. Hamlet reaches the pinnacle (or depths) of introspective capacity; there is vastness in his self-probing and in his demand for hard truths.[33]

Shakespeare lavished much attention on the joys and perils of imagination. "He waxes desperate with imagination," says Horatio to Marcellus when Hamlet disobeys his friends and follows the ghost of his father. Later in the same play, the Danish prince announces, "My imaginations are as foul as Vulcan's stithy" (3.2.1962–63)—that is, the forge worked by the god of fire. Viola, in *Twelfth Night*, implores: "Prove true, imagination, O, prove true" (3.4.1930). When Gloucester in *King Lear* bewails Lear's madness, it is put powerfully that "woes by wrong imagination lose / the knowledge of themselves" (4.6.2903–4). Shakespeare associates imagination with destabilizing effects and unevenness of emotional needs: Hamlet's inwardness is directly tied to his fate.[34]

As demonstrated in the previous chapter, Americans were similarly inclined to see the imagination as double edged. The most gruesome example, perhaps, is Philadelphia novelist Charles Brockden Brown's *Wieland*, published in 1798, in which a man's out-of-control imagination leads him to murder his own family. During a single week in Philadelphia, at the time *Wieland* appeared, amid debate of a bill in Congress, a representative predicted that his opinion would be treated as "the mere wanderings of a heated imagination." Another's bad idea came from "a fertile imagination." The point of honor that led a hotheaded man into a deadly duel was, likewise, "a creature of the imagination." Few periodicals were emotionally neutral, but they resorted to passive constructions ("general anxiety was immediately excited") and a vernacular that, consciously or unconsciously, dodged the emotion that classic poetry and daring literature delivered.[35]

The protoromantic consciousness built on Shakespearean precedent. The year 1798 saw the publication of *Lyrical Ballads*, a joint production of William Wordsworth (1770–1850) and Samuel Taylor Coleridge (1772–1834), which added intensity to the imagination's cause and represented something of a revolution in English poetry. *Lyrical Ballads* began to make its way through the United States in 1801, elegantly bound and sold alongside earlier British classics. Wordsworth and Coleridge conscientiously did away with artificiality in poetic diction, engaged more intimately with nature, and presented memories as honest autobiography. Wordsworth's "Ode on Intimations of Immortality" returned to his childhood and famously suggested birth as "but a sleep and a forgetting:/The Soul that rises with us, our life's Star,/Hath but elsewhere its setting/And cometh from afar."

Coleridge, for his part, was early recognized for his vivid imagination. Before *Lyrical Ballads*, he'd conceived a strategy to plant a community of poets and philosophers in America. If

Charles Brockden Brown inaugurated the American horror story, the extravagant Coleridge promoted enchantment. Saying that Shakespeare came as close as any human mind to understanding nature, Coleridge credited the playwright's "vitality which grows and evolves from within." Coleridge biographer Walter Jackson Bate puts it well: "It is because he so habitually turns to Shakespeare as the grand exposition of his entire aesthetic theory that we begin to feel, in reading Coleridge's criticism, that Shakespeare is almost the only poet, and Coleridge is his prophet."[36]

The Battle over Neology

Shakespeare introduced many words and phrases into the language that are colloquially spoken without our recognizing their source, such as "Knock, knock! Who's there?" (*Macbeth*), "green-eyed monster" (spoken by Iago, in *Othello*), "green-eyed jealousy" (*The Merchant of Venice*), and "fair play" (*The Tempest*). The most oft-repeated metaphor from a Shakespeare play may be "love is blind" (*The Merchant of Venice*). Among its relatives are "do thy worst, blind Cupid!" (*King Lear*) and the couplet "love looks not with the eyes but with the mind / And therefore is wing'd Cupid painted blind" (*A Midsummer Night's Dream*). Lastly, from the star-crossed lovers' tragedy, good Mercutio references the arrow of Cupid thus: "If love be blind, love cannot hit the mark" (*Romeo and Juliet*). As a neologist, Shakespeare does not have a lot of competition.

According to the authoritative *Oxford English Dictionary*, the word "neology" (generally interchangeable with "neologism") did not exactly enjoy acceptance among imperial English speakers. The first is found in two separate pieces in the London *Monthly Magazine* in 1797, where it is defined as "the coining or use of new words or phrases." Such coinage is represented as decidedly negative in the second piece, an article in which the author is describing the philology of one M. le Brigant. He reports on Brigant's account of Celtic, which Brigant asserted was the single language used by all people in the past, noting that it had been "disfigured by neology, corruption, and barbarous modes of speech." One of the most quoted sources in the *OED*, *Transactions of the Royal Society*, lodged this complaint: "Neologisms are often so troublesome, and sometimes so arbitrarily introduced into languages." Fearing "the imputation of neologism," the author of a 1796 scientific treatise even apologized for being "obliged to form some new words" in expressing chemical processes.[37]

Conversely, America's tastemakers saw invention in its every manifestation as a means to add honor and reputation to an inchoate identity. If the Revolution represented a metaphorical divorce from Old England, new words would be liberating, too, accompanying a new set of manners and values. On the ground, the United States was reconstituting itself, developing its cultural "brand" in new settlements on new land as it expanded west. Language, too, was property. Language, too, was a construction project.

American newspapers carried as much intelligence about European affairs as they did their own. For all who wanted England to notice the "U. States," as the new nation was sometimes abbreviated, words had to count—that is, conversation only worked when both sides were listening. The U. States were longing to connect with the former mother country, to be noticed and credited. Yet London's elect stubbornly refused to look their way other than to scoff. The problem simmered for years, becoming more overt in the decade following the War of 1812.

Typical of the culture clash that retarded efforts to improve US-British relations is the *Times* of London critiquing the performance of "Mr. Pelby, from the New York and Boston theatres" who took on the title role in *Hamlet* at the celebrated Drury Lane Theatre. Pelby was "far, far removed" from the known (British) portrayers of the Prince of Denmark, "rather to blame for attempting with his slender powers" so famous a character. The reviewer pulled no punches: "Mr. Pelby's qualifications for the stage are of an ordinary and common-place kind," his voice "exceedingly objectionable," his elocution "drawling and affected," and his delivery at the most dramatic moments expressive only of "apathy." But what more could one expect from an American?[38]

Despite its attainment of political independence, the Old World consistently doubted America's self-sufficiency. The United States was generally regarded as culturally backward and financially weak, a logical deduction when the accepted center of world knowledge and international banking was in European capitals. Theirs was a world of ranks, and America ranked far below the competition. Decades would pass before that changed. Updating literary language was one option available to Americans who sought to rebalance the relationship with England.

The primary impact of a cultural idiom is the confirmation of affinities among those who learn it. Language is a resource to be managed. It expresses control over perceptual experience and is in this way prescriptive. It is a bond that can also intensify a separation: the Declaration of Independence voices Americans' deep disappointment over their "British brethren" being "deaf to the voice of justice and consanguinity"—in other words, deliberately not respecting their American kin, who yielded, reluctantly, to the "necessity, which denounces our Separation."

Americans displayed national pride in unmistakable ways. But they barely constituted a nation. Pride without status meant there was plenty of room for the United States to grow its own character. "National character" was a term that frequently appeared in patriotic speeches and texts. The word "character" in this context was not neutral. It connoted both moral character as it related to republican government and collective character as a well-defined identity. Noah Webster's *American Dictionary* would not be published until 1828, and even then, the job would not be done.

Words are heard, not just written, of course. They are also sung. Patriotic tunes were a popular genre that developed as popular participation in politics enlarged. Thomas Jefferson, a technically proficient violinist, sheet music collector, and life-long music lover, did not compose, but he possessed a sonorous gift in phrasing his thoughts and opinions. The popular song when he assumed the presidency in 1801, "Jefferson and Liberty," gave credence to the substance of change. Liberty (whether real or imagined) demanded its own style of linguistic expression, along with public pageantry.[39]

Jefferson was an active proponent of linguistic development, eager to welcome new words and usages into American English. In 1813, he declared to John Waldo, the author of an English grammar and one of Webster's acquaintances, that he was "no friend . . . to what is called Purism; but a zealous one to the Neology [introduced] without the authority of any dictionary." Nor was this a one-time, offhand comment. Seven years later, at the age of seventy-seven, he reached out to eighty-six-year-old John Adams, offering an assertive defense of neology by defending the word "neologism": "If Dictionaries are to be the Arbitors of language," he asked, "in which of them shall we find *neologism?* No matter. It is a good word, well sounding, obvious, and expresses an idea which would otherwise require circumlocution. . . . I am a friend to *neology.* It is the only way to give to a language copiousness & euphony." Whether or not influenced by Jefferson, one early nineteenth-century periodical featured a semiweekly series, penned by a member of the rising generation and titled "the Neologist," which delivered "learned criticism" by way of "chaste composition."[40]

Adams took Jefferson's letter to Edward Everett (1794–1865), a young scholar of ancient Greek and newly appointed editor of the *North American Review*, a Boston-based journal concerned with social commentary and literary merit. Everett was responsible for critiquing the report on education authored by Jefferson and his compatriot James Madison that had prompted Jefferson's latest defense of word creation. Everett was a proud scholar recently returned from studies in Europe, where, among his other adventures, he'd communed with the gifted wordsmith Lord Byron. In his review of the Jefferson-Madison study, Everett had duly noted the inclusion of, as he put it, "a little *neologism* in the language, and a few unauthorized words."

Rather than pursue a "disrespectful discussion" with the estimable Jefferson over his criticisms, the young editor drew on his own linguistic background: "I beg leave," Everett told Adams, "merely to say of the word *neologism* [that I had it] printed in *Italics* expressly to indicate it to be a foreign [French] word. For the rest, I doubt not I should agree with Mr. J. in his theoretical views of the necessity of enriching a language by the adoption of New terms: the difficulty is, in practice, to put a barrier to the licence of private innovation." New words should happen naturally, in his view, and not even one as entrusted as "Mr. J." was in his knowledge of the American character should have a license to debut linguistic forms independently.[41]

Tempest in a teapot? It is hard to fathom why any of this should matter, but the point is that it did matter to the literati of this era. Young Everett appears a nitpicker (that's a mid-twentieth-century neologism), the kind of purist Jefferson repeatedly admonished. In fact, some of the words in the education report Everett placed under his linguistic microscope were not Jefferson's innovations at all and can be found in the same context in previous years in congressional oratory and elsewhere.

The late nineteenth century had an implied comeback for Everett, a doctor of philosophy who became a politician. According to college president Henry Shepherd, the author of the compendious *History of the English Language* (1874), Jefferson's "philological recreation" during "the last great period of transition in English" showed "remarkably clear and accurate views of the invigorating influences which dialects exert upon a language," revealing that he "looked upon language as the minister and not as the mere drapery of thought." Shepherd regarded Jefferson, in this way, as a worthy successor to Shakespeare. If the English idiom reached "the full meridian of its splendour" with Shakespeare, yielding a vocabulary "as comprehensive and varied as his conceptions of humanity," then republican America's embrace of beautiful language was at once lively and retrospective, which was no contradiction at all.[42] Still it was an uphill battle for the Americans. A fair number of them continued to idolize Dr. Samuel Johnson, whose English language dictionary had been circling the globe since 1755. Webster's *Dictionary* did not sell well until some years after its author had died.

Transatlantic language battles were a persistent feature of Anglo-American competition from the early years after America won its independence. In 1787, when Jefferson, then a senior diplomat in Paris, published his encyclopedic *Notes on the State of Virginia* in London, he took heat from the *London Review* for having coined the word "belittle" in one notable passage. "For shame, Mr. Jefferson!" the reactive Englishman exclaimed. The American could almost be forgiven for "trampling upon the honour of our country" in 1776, but "for the future, spare—O spare, we beseech you, our *mother-tongue!*"[43]

In the cited passage, Jefferson defended the strength and size of species native to the North American continent against charges by the French zoologist Comte de Buffon who insisted everything was of a smaller scale and less potent in the United States. The American referred to "this new theory of the tendency of nature to *belittle* her productions on [the American] side of the Atlantic." The Abbé de Raynal, a natural historian who agreed with Buffon's theory of degeneration, piled on, demanding evidence of a world-class American poet or mathematician, artist or scientist. Jefferson had pert answers for both French intellectuals. To Raynal, it was look how long it took the French to produce their Voltaire, or the Greeks their Homer, or the English their Milton and Shakespeare. While young as a people, Americans had already given to the cause of scientific discovery a Benjamin Franklin, who had "enriched philosophy" besides. Above the rest stood General George Washington, "whose memory shall be adored while liberty shall have votaries."

With Monsieur Buffon, the more formidable of America's detractors, Jefferson employed a kind of wit he did not often make public, expressing doubt "whether nature has enlisted herself as a Cis- or Trans-Atlantic partisan." Our champion of New World creatures attributed to the French thinker a "vivid imagination and bewitching language" but also insufficient reasoning. Note that Buffon's "imagination" is cast as a shortcoming, twisted rather than healthy.[44]

Thanks to *Notes on Virginia*, Jefferson's one major book, the belittlement of Buffon lives on among Jefferson scholars. So does its nationalistic author's coinage of "belittle" and, for that matter, the verb "neologize." Webster accepted Jefferson's "belittle" into his dictionary, and the larger English-speaking world in time followed suit. Jefferson has been variously credited with at least a hundred neologisms.

In 1817, Joseph Milligan, the third president's favored Washington, DC, bookseller, advertised *A Treatise on Political Economy*, by Destutt de Tracy. Jefferson had arranged for its English translation, and personally, though anonymously, authored its foreword. Milligan's ad quotes from Jefferson's foreword on the ticklish issue of word creation, whose purpose was to clarify translation difficulties:

> Some Gallicisms have therefore been admitted, where a single word gives an idea which would require a whole phrase of Dictionary English; indeed the horrors of neologism, which startle the purist[,] have given no alarm in the trans-

lator, where brevity, perspicacity, and even euphony can be promoted by the introduction of a new word, it is an improvement in the language. . . . And what do we not owe to Shakespeare for the enrichment of the language by his free and magical creation of words? In giving loose to neologism, indeed, uncouth words will sometimes be offered; but the public will judge them, and receive or reject.

Jefferson's nonconformist view of language translated into a committed effort to boost the wider (democratic) adoption of an America vernacular.[45]

Wherever Jefferson praises neology, he credits euphony. Euphony is everywhere in his own emotive writing style, which is one reason why he remains most quotable among the founders, save, perhaps, for Ben Franklin. "Euphony" means "sweet-voiced" in Greek. The sound of Jefferson's words resonate in distinctive ways, occasionally with alliterative affect. He coordinates "vulgar vehicles of passion" with "insults and injuries"; he writes to his adult daughter of harmonious social prospects absent of "jarring or jealousies" to upset "future fortunes." Note how "jarring" is sensually endowed with sudden motion (as are the "j" words "jerk," "jitter," "jumble," and "jump"); elsewhere Jefferson pairs "harangued and jostled." He touchingly tells a French liberal that Dr. Franklin "listened with all the glow of a tender interest" to that gentleman's news—"glow," like other "gl" words ("glare," "gleam," "glimmer") sheds beneficent light on a subject. As an expositor of the Enlightenment, Jefferson smoothly contrasted "glaring falsehood" with "a glimpse of truth" and also expressed a "glimmer of hope" in numerous of his letters.[46]

In subsequent correspondence with Edward Everett, Jefferson reiterated what he'd said to others: "I readily sacrifice the niceties of syntax to euphony and strength." He used the word "euphony" in familiar letters on several occasions, but it only ever concerned two subjects: the power of the ancient Greek language

and the soundness of neology. Euphony gave language more freedom to grow. At the same time, it is striking that Jefferson did
not show generosity toward Native American languages. Enno-
bling Indigenous peoples in other respects when he wrote *Notes
on Virginia*, especially in their courage and capacity for friendship, he was incurious about the construction of Cherokee, which
he believed formed from dull combinations. He chose to defend
American species (nature) against Buffon's belittling project
while belittling Indian languages (culture) as primitive.[47]

By the early nineteenth century, it had been generally accepted in the English-speaking world, and in no small measure
owing to Jefferson's urging, that American English was going
its own way. A British essayist explained in an 1821 piece republished in Boston that "amongst all the mutable things of
earth, language is perhaps the most unstable. Governments,
manners, fashions, rise, flourish, and fade, but they rise again,
the same in form or mould: a language once changed or perished, can never resume its original character. . . . The Americans have accordingly thought proper to exercise their ingenuity in this manner."[48]

Final Touches

In 1988, the historian Lawrence Levine wrote: "The profound
and long-standing nineteenth-century American experience
with Shakespeare . . . was neither accidental nor aberrant. It was
based upon the language and eloquence, the artistry and humor,
the excitement and action, the moral sense and worldview, that
Americans found in Shakespearean drama." We can take that
one step further and state that Shakespeare's pre-Revolutionary
appeal grew exponentially after independence because of an affective power that began to mean more as the years went by.[49]

Shakespeare's suppleness attracted those Americans who
opened to the sensations of interior life in their familiar letter

writing. His appeal was gut-level, with bawd and bluster and
double meanings, excavating the human heart from the parched
page. They also related to the interior experiences of unconventional, unconstrained characters in episodic adventure novels
and as eagerly read Cervantes, Sterne, Fielding, and Smollett.
As his education in the ways of the world was barely underway,
twenty-three-year-old John Adams recorded in his diary: "Let
me search for the Clue, which Led great Shakespeare into the
Labyrinth of mental Nature." Not every reader was as articu-
late as Adams, of course, but he was far from alone in desiring
literary guidance in introspective hours.[50] While the percentage of Americans who were literate was higher than that of the
British, those who had access to libraries or could afford to own
more than a few books were a minority. They read poets and
novelists when young, and many would return to the same authors again and again. For them, Shakespeare continued to heat
up the English language.

The American press held that Shakespeare belonged to
the entire world. In 1818, the *Alexandria Gazette* published
"The Fidelity of Shakespeare," declaring the playwright's
"excellence . . . as an instructor in history and political science."
Honoring Shakespeare's birthday a decade later in a piece titled
"Poet of all Nature," the *Raleigh Register* likened the bard to a
"wild garden" where a variety of fruit grew, "some crude, some
sour" but the rest "incomparable." He was a rushing "cataract"
to Milton's "enchanting" river, "preserving the accuracy of facts
without any sacrifice of the charms of poetry." Several mentions
of the bard noted that dry history did not have to be force-fed
when Shakespeare was around to convey its authenticity. Above
all, he taught each rising generation "the direful consequences
of pride and ambition." The nuances in his plays were so publicly discussed that two widely circulating newspapers got into
an argument over whether certain lines from *Hamlet* were actually misprinted stage directions. To speak of Shakespeare as

a great genius in the early and mid-nineteenth century was as much of a cliché as to speak of Washington's virtue.[51]

Histories and tragedies etched a vision of humanity onto imperial fields of battle where awe-inspiring figures were allowed to triumph or condemned to suffer. Americans read history for its grandeur, and Shakespeare's historical methods did not seem unreliable to them. David Hume's discursive, multi-volume *History of England* chronicled Shakespearean times, but the only "theatre" he covered was the that of war. Nevertheless, his work had an epic quality and was regarded as another expansive study of the human character. The other great work of history that sold in these years, Edward Gibbon's *Rise and Fall of the Roman Empire*, decried ancient militarism, "lust and luxury," in larger-than-life scenarios. Both Gibbon and Hume considered it the function of the ostensibly dispassionate historian to contribute to political stability and an upholding of the moral order. This was what all literature (other than comedic) was meant to do. Hume, of the generation for whom sensibility mattered, dressed Queen Elizabeth in requisite language: she was "touched with compassion," "touched with more tender sympathy." Her successor, James I, was creditably endowed with "an affectionate temper;" and the Irish insurrectionists of 1641, being devoid of compassion, were able to "steel their hearts against every movement of human or social sympathy." It was the same with Shakespeare's heroes and villains. In his very influential *Theory of Moral Sentiments*, published as Hume's volumes on the Tudors and Stuarts were emerging, Adam Smith wrote: "We detest Iago as much as we esteem Othello."[52]

Shakespeare's reputation in America rested on both the entertainment he provided and the productivity and purpose he gave to the language. Language had to breathe to be emotionally mobile, to have an affective life. Those who quoted him in their letters did not just memorize famous lines; they found whatever operated on thought and feeling at the moment of writing. They felt impelled to understand the human condition as Shakespeare did, writing of men's "envious looks" and "envious tongues." They knew what "discord bred" and what it felt like to suffer "ingrateful injury." While John Adams's pre-Revolutionary diary entry that serves as one of the epigraphs to this chapter may convey the sense that Shakespeare was merely charming, Shakespeare did not feel at all quaint to them.

American letter writers used words in the ways Shakespeare did because they could do so without appearing pretentious. We have long since replaced those words with those better suited to fast-changing times. The people of the early 1800s still detected "malice," "perfidy," and "inhumanity" in speech and especially in writing. They selectively judged when old language struck harder than new language. Today, "malice" is more likely to have a legal implication, and "perfidy" is rare; we'd probably use "evil intent" or the simpler "hatred."[53]

Shakespeare and young America alike warned of "plots" and spoke of "reckonings" and "retribution" and things that "portended" other things. They could still appreciate "Fortune" as a goddess; they "bade" someone come. The sensations he invoked, they invoked. In Shakespeare there is the "bitter touch," "touch of modesty," "touch of love"; and "heavenly touches." A single stanza in *Venus and Adonis*, an early poem of Shakespeare's, takes up four of the five senses:

> Say, that the sense of feeling were bereft me,
> And that I could not see, nor hear, nor touch,
> And nothing but the very smell were left me,
> Yet would my love to thee be still as much.

In Shakespeare's day, touchstone was a fine black marble used to construct monuments and against which gold or silver could be rubbed to determine its purity. It had already acquired its figurative meaning of anything that could be tested for its value or correctness as a principle. In *As You Like It*, he named the court jester "Touchstone." Already in Shakespearean English, a heart was "touched." So we have "How dearly would it touch thee to the quick" (*Comedy of Errors* [2.2.519]) and "when his soaring insolence/shall touch the people" (*Coriolanus* [2.1.1202–3]). In American English after the Revolution, political writers addressed "the touchstone of our virtue" and "touchstone of the people's feelings"; others wrote, "No honor has more tenderly touch'd me." Then again, one could be "touch'd in the head" if mentally compromised or downright mad. The usage now current, "to be in touch with someone" (by direct communication), only arose in living memory.[54]

Shakespeare's characters touch more than they smell or taste, though the five senses are strategically employed in virtually every plot. The characters speak to their "apprehensive senses" (*All's Well That Ends Well* [1.2.302]) or their attempts to reestablish a "true sense" (*Comedy of Errors* [4.4.1228]). King Lear complains: "The tempest in my mind/Doth from my senses take all feeling else" (3.4.1814–15). There are "knaves that smell of sweat" in *Antony and Cleopatra* (1.4.445), and in his soliloquy in *Hamlet*, when he admits to the murder of his own brother, Claudius states, "O my offense is rank, it smells to heaven" (2.3.2318). Elizabethan England was nearly ready for the science of the nerves that attained its full power over language and culture in the eighteenth century.[55]

During the nineteenth century, Shakespeare never lost his honored position in American popular culture. In 1875, Mark Twain pointed out that Americans accounted for three-quarters of the pilgrims who traveled to Stratford-on-Avon and paid their respects at Shakespeare's tomb, and he reminded his readers of the attempt made three decades earlier by the showman P. T. Barnum to buy, uproot, and transport across the Atlantic the house where Shakespeare was born. The famed huckster quite nearly succeeded. In that regard, not a lot has changed. It was recently discovered that the Folger Library in Washington,

DC, and other American archives own no less than 145 copies of the precious 1623 edition of Shakespeare's first folio, while only 43 remain in England.[56]

* *

In 1807, a newspaper in Brooklyn related the story of an Irish actor playing Othello who'd exited the theater between acts and pinched "a brace of partridges" from the shop next door. A dog belonging to an audience member leapt to the stage, interrupting the performance in act 3 by accosting the "gallant Moor." The actor all at once gave up his prize, shouting, "Take them and be damned." Then, without missing a beat, he continued: "He that is robb'd, not knowing what is stole, let him not know't, and he's not robb'd at all" (3.3.2019–20).[57]

Now, that's acting! It also gives us a good idea what an American newspaper editor in the so-called Age of Jefferson took for humor, which is the subject of chapter 4.

In the absurdist serial *Salmagundi*, a collaborative effort of New Yorkers James Kirke
Paulding, Washington Irving, and William Irving, Christopher Cockloft decides to raise
his children the way he grows vegetables, but his "whimwham" is proven ill advised on
discovery that watering infants and leaving them out in the sun tends to deprive them of
life. *Salmagundi* was first published in 1807. The engraving dates to the 1850s.

Chapter 4.

Explosive Satire
(Laughter)

A couple of politicians will quarrel, with the most vociferous pertinacity, about the character of a bum-bailiff whom nobody cares for; or for the deportment of a little great man whom nobody knows; and this is called talking politics.
—*Salmagundi*, 1807

❦

A man can now play the Scoundrel in Politics with perfect impunity, provided he only talks sufficiently loud about his Conscience.
—James Kirke Paulding, 1826

❦

Thomas Jefferson's interest in language and literature was well known to his intimate friend and immediate successor as president. But when Madison recommended a work of political satire in an 1812 letter to Jefferson, he apparently was not too concerned about getting the name of the author correct. He not only misattributed the work but also misspelled the name of the author he ascribed the work to. "You will be amused," he told Jefferson, "with the little work of the Author of several humorous publications. Irvine of N. York. It sinks occasionally into low & local phrases, and sometimes forgets the allegorical character. But is in general a good painting on substantial Canvas."

The allegory, *The Diverting History of John Bull and Brother Jonathan*, was a parody of the long lead-up to war—a war President Madison was now prosecuting. It portrayed Great Britain and its former colonies as estranged family members fighting across a little millpond. Madison took to the format so well that he imitated it in a lampoon he wrote eight years later (but dared not publish) that tackled the anything-but-funny debate over slavery.[1]

Although *The Diverting History of John Bull and Brother Jonathan* was not the brainchild of Washington Irving (1783–1859) as Madison believed when he wrote "Irvine," he wasn't far off: it was that of a companion of Irving's youth, his lifelong friend and occasional literary collaborator who in the late 1790s introduced him to the tranquil scenes of Sleepy Hollow, New York. The sickly teen had been sent twenty miles north of the city owing to a yellow fever panic. With this older friend, he enjoyed a gambol he would not forget once he'd abandoned the law and turned to storytelling. Madison soon came to know this other gentleman, James Kirke Paulding (1778–1860), a lot better. He was a first cousin of the celebrated militiaman John Paulding (1758–1818), recipient of a Congressional medal for his featured role in the capture of the British spy Major John André in 1780.

For twelve months beginning in January 1807, Paulding and Irving teamed up to publish the comical *Salmagundi* papers. A salmagundi was a meal of chopped meat and pickled vegetables or, in this case, a mishmash of absurdist chatter and social satire.

To aid in their antics, the two conscripted the eldest Irving brother, William (1766–1821), a former fur trader who ranged about the wilds of upstate New York and who was married to Paulding's sister Julia. In 1813, William Irving would enter Congress as a pro-Madison New York City Republican. Connections weren't that hard to come by in early American society.

The Paulding and Irving families effectively merged. James K. Paulding's eldest brother, another William (1770–1854), was a lawyer, brigadier general during the War of 1812, and mayor of New York City for multiple terms in the 1820s. In the 1790s, William Irving and William Paulding both belonged to a respectable, long-running literary club, the Calliopean Society. A generation later, after Washington Irving's death, the son of James Kirke Paulding—William Irving Paulding no less—conferred with Pierre M. Irving, a son of William Irving, with regard to their common interest in the republication of *Salmagundi*, artifact of a beautiful, edgy fraternity.[2]

As for *The Diverting History of John Bull and Brother Jonathan*, the War of 1812 lampoon, Madison's misattribution of its authorship makes more sense in view of the fact that Washington Irving was the author of the widely read faux history of American settlement, *A History of New-York* (1809), popularly known as "Knickerbocker's History." Irving did a fair bit of research when he created the mock-historian "Diedrich Knickerbocker," whose legend would attract such a following that New Yorkers en masse came to be known as "Knickerbockers," a nickname so well respected and enduring that in 1947 it was adopted by the city's professional basketball franchise, later shortened to "the Knicks." Irving's evocation in *Salmagundi* of his hometown as "Gotham" (after an English town of questionable repute) stuck, though branding its people as "Gothamites" did not survive the era. Paulding would keep the nickname alive in satirical productions with his later *Chronicles of the City of Gotham*.

Washington Irving was the youngest child in a large merchant family. He was born the year independence was acknowledged by treaty, when his namesake, the victorious general, marched down Broadway and the British formally, officially, departed. Paulding grew up north of the city, in the Hudson River–fronting village of Tarrytown. His father had seen the world as the commander of several oceangoing vessels, supplying food to Washington's army during the war and sacrificing his personal fortune in the process. Young James heard stories of the Revolution told by active participants; young Washington had the advantage of four well-read older brothers. Neither Washington Irving nor James K. Paulding attended college (though some of Washington's brothers did). Their backgrounds spelled middle-class respectability, not upper-class privilege.

Paulding was a moderately successful author in his own right but nothing like his co-conspirator in satire, who had the distinction of becoming America's first true celebrity author. After "Knickerbocker's History," Irving took a hiatus from fiction, editing the *Analectic* magazine during the War of 1812 and printing straightforward minibiographies of US naval heroes. After authoring *The Diverting History of John Bull and Brother Jonathan,* Paulding, who was a staunch advocate for a strong navy, contributed to his younger friend's magazine. The pair lodged together with Commodore Stephen Decatur, a hero of both the Barbary Wars and the War of 1812, in a residence near Manhattan's Battery. Decatur, along with first-term congressman William Irving, kept Paulding's name in circulation in Washington. In January 1815, President Madison named Paulding secretary of the Board of Navy Commissioners. From that moment on, in addition to profiting from his experiments in literature, Paulding enjoyed a salaried position in government.

As Paulding removed to war-defiled Washington, where once-stately government buildings lay in ruins after an invasion force had put them to the torch, his writing pal Irving sailed to

England to try to help save his family's dying import business. There he made the acquaintances of writers and publishers and found unimaginable commercial success. The transatlantic publication in 1819–20 of *The Sketch Book of Geoffrey Crayon*, which contained the two enduring tales "Rip Van Winkle" and "The Legend of Sleepy Hollow," launched a career in short stories, history, and biography. Irving popularized Shakespeare tourism in *The Sketch Book*, writing at length about "the immortal bard," "whom we behold defying the encroachments of time." An entire *Sketch Book* essay is devoted to the author's "poetical pilgrimage" to Stratford-on-Avon, where he beheld the sword that was allegedly Shakespeare's model in *Hamlet*. There, too, Irving tested the chair in which the poet-playwright was alleged to have sat. In another essay he took in Boar's Head Tavern, the hangout of Falstaff in *Henry IV, Part I*.[3]

The difference between Irving and Paulding was tonal. In his career as a lighthearted critic, Irving mocked with an exuberant wit, half pensive, half present, always depicting quirks of personality in the human subjects he chose to toy with. Paulding struck more heavily with his satire, taking a bite out of a victim whenever he thought he needed to. Irving was speculative, Paulding less so. Irving wrote to captivate—that was his means of convincing. Paulding was not a magician but a wrestler, hands-on with his barbs. Irving's words were sewn together by diaphanous threads, Paulding's (even when he composed verse) were connected by a taut rope.

The allegorical work that Madison so enjoyed, *The Diverting History of John Bull and Brother Jonathan*, isn't interested in sweet talk. America's "Jonathan" (symbolizing its hardy young population) is an axe-wielding son of nature who builds himself *"thirteen good farms"* and in no time grows into a "tall, stout, double-jointed, broad-footed cub of a fellow" bearing an unmistakable likeness to the elder John Bull (long the personification of England). Jonathan, like Bull, "was apt to be blustering and saucy, but in the main, was a peaceable sort of careless fellow that would quarrel with nobody, if you only let him alone." But Bull kept "picking his pockets of every penny" and made the youth so angry that he seized a "TEA KETTLE" and threw it at the "choleric" squire, who turned on the "rebellious rascal" and "seized him by the collar," and "forthwith a furious scuffle ensued." Jonathan got the better of Bull and "made him sign a paper, giving up all claims to the farms." That's how we go from the 1773 Boston Tea Party to the 1783 Treaty of Paris.[4]

Readers would have known instantly who Paulding's Jonathan was. "Brother Jonathan" *was* the United States before Uncle Sam took over as the official national mascot. Jonathan was a good-natured fellow, slightly comical, mostly Yankee, countrified, near innocent. He dressed plainly and looked homely. If, as the average American, he was not quite the politico Uncle Sam was, he still had a patriotic persona: under the heading, "ANECDOTES," a newspaper of 1800 recalled an instance just after the Revolution ended, when a British soldier called from the shore to a US vessel that was anchored along the Thames: "From whence came ye, Brother Jonathan?" The answer from a boatswain was swift: "Straight from Bunker's Hill." In a similar vein, an American jokebook recounted a purported conversation between an English diplomat and his French counterpart at the Hague, not long after the French joined the colonists' side in the Revolution. "You have been guilty of a dishonourable act that is unpardonable—no less than debauching our daughter," said the indignant Brit, in the guise of the rebellious colonies' political parent. "I am sorry (replied the French ambassador) that your excellency should put such a severe construction, upon the matter: She made the first advances, and absolutely threw herself into our arms; but rather than forfeit your friendship, if matrimony will make any atonement, we are ready to act honourably, and marry her."[5]

In Paulding's treatment of the Anglo-American contest, Jonathan is a good egg. With the death of "Lewis Baboon" (the executed Bourbon king Louis XVI), he exhibits a "sneaking kindness" toward the overproud "Beau Napperty of Frogmore" (i.e., Napoleonic France). Yet Jonathan remains "the very best customer Bull ever had." Envious of the other's abundance of land, the irritable squire "could not bear to see Jonathan enjoying the fruits of his peaceable disposition"—by which was meant free trade, which continued even among belligerents during the ongoing Anglo-French war. Discontent reigned as Bull, whose motto was "once a tenant always a tenant" (i.e., colony), took revenge on Jonathan for giving succor to "poor runaways" (defecting or impressed seamen). Here we have, in essence, the proximate cause of the War of 1812—"Free Trade and Sailors' Rights," as the American slogan went. The patriot Paulding no doubt chuckled in imagining Squire Bull as Jonathan struck at his boastful pride: "Several of his boats, on trying to seize Jonathan's, had got most bitterly bethumped."[6]

Though he got the author wrong, Madison was right when he made his recommendation. Jefferson got a kick out of Paulding's spoof, lent it to a neighbor "who loves to laugh," who in turn sent it to friends who sent it to other friends. When it finally found its way back to him, Jefferson sent the book to his onetime Philadelphia landlady and dear friend Eliza House Trist. "If it diverts you for an hour or two, I shall be gratified," he wrote. "I was myself amused by it's [sic] humor."[7]

Jim Paulding (as he was known to intimates) flattered the sitting president further when he published *The United States and England*, a biting treatment of the same subject that he completed as the War of 1812 reached its undramatic conclusion. With that effort, Paulding took aim at the violent language used by British critics of American manners and morals, in the process denying England its monopoly on their common language. "Shakespeare belongs to the world," he states in the middle of his tirade. Repeatedly invoking America's "patient if not silent endurance" of arrogant pronouncements and "persecutions," he echoes Jefferson's determined complaint in the Declaration of Independence against the "long train of abuses" inflicted by London, and he upholds the sunny prediction by "Mr. Jefferson and Mr. Madison" of the nation's future greatness. Congressman William Irving made a point of telling Madison that Paulding "possesses that independence of spirit, that ever accompanies men of lofty minds." Thus, it was a combination of his satirical bent and polemical talent that put Paulding in good stead with the fourth president and launched him on a career that would culminate in his tenure as secretary of the navy under future president (and fellow New Yorker) Martin Van Buren.[8]

In 1817, at the end of his second term, Madison left Washington, DC, and was accompanied home to Orange, Virginia, by Paulding, by now a fond friend. "He was as playful as a child," Paulding recorded of the president's attitude as he slid into retirement. Writing down his reflections in later years, Paulding expanded on the portrait: "He was a capital story teller—he would relate anecdotes highly amusing as well as interesting. He was a man of wit, relished wit in others, & his small bright blue eyes would twinkle most wickedly, when lighted up by some whimsical conception." Though it's not how history prefers to think of Madison, that is, in fact, how those who knew him best described him.[9]

At the start of their literary careers, Paulding and Irving were as inseparable as the political alter egos Jefferson and Madison. What drew them to each other was not straight-up politics but their appreciation of social satire within a political universe. While the playful *Salmagundi* papers were written in the voice of Jeffersonian-era freedom, Paulding always preferred Madison to Jefferson. Irving, for his part, was not a fan of either

Jefferson's pose as a "man of the people" or his erudite style. Writing to a friend as the twenty-part series was proceeding, he coyly critiqued his own nonsensical "effusions" on the page, comparing himself to "the illustrious Jefferson who after toiling all day, in deciding the fates of a nation, retires to his closet and amuses himself with impaling a tadpole." Reducing great men to caricatures was the American satirist's specialty—as was poking fun at erratic, emotion-laden reactions to the world at large, no matter the subject.[10]

While Irving came from a political family and interacted personally with several US presidents, he never seemed to care deeply about the results of ongoing political campaigns. The one exception was his active show of support in the spring of 1807 for a man he admired and whose daughter he adored: Judge Josiah Ogden Hoffman. "I was as deep in mud & politics as ever a moderate gentleman would wish to be," Irving told a female friend at that time. Quoting from *Henry IV, Part I*, he said, "I can drink with any tinker in his own language." He had a field day with the carnivalesque performances that partisan electioneering brought about, tackling "that great political Puppet-show—an Election" in an issue of *Salmagundi* printed soon thereafter. Fun was had in these absurdist sketches.

Irving spent several weeks in Washington, DC in 1807, and in one letter home, he satirically compared politicians to asses: "The only great personages I saw there were two Jackasses in a field, kicking at each other—Metempsychosis [reincarnation] forever! thought I—here are the souls of two of our illustrious Congressmen transfused into the bodies of Kindred animals, and they are engaged in the presidential experiment of 'trying which shall do each other the most harm.'" Tauntingly, Irving opened this letter with the line "There is a tide in the affairs of men" from *Julius Caesar*, as if he were about to make a serious disclosure. But then he made hay with the planter-led Virginia of Jefferson and Madison, "that land famous for grog drinking, horse racing and cockfighting; where every man is a colonel a captain or a Negro, the first title being conferred on any who has killed a rattle snake—where indolence is the true (& often the only) mark of gentility."[11]

Unlike Paulding, who admired southerners and would take their side in the 1850s, Irving held northern prejudices, which showed in his humor. He generally displayed indifference to nonwhites, but his feeling for humanity grew along with his extensive travels. Prior to *Salmagundi*, prior to "Knickerbocker," having traipsed about Europe when barely out of his teens, he acquired expansive ideas about writing. From Messina, in southern Italy, he'd penned a letter to a New York chum, combining phrases from Shakespeare's *Henry IV, Part 1* and Addison's "A Letter from Italy," to describe his excitement in hastening "to those 'poetic fields' where fiction has shed its charms over every scene." Like the British writers he channeled, he seized on local customs to paint precious scenes and enduring characters; he arranged to make his characters speak for the world at large. What he, Paulding, and other American satirists of the time had in common as humorists was not style so much as judgment: they shared an intense dislike for smallness and malevolence. Irving had little quarrel with the world he burlesqued. His success was due to his air of joviality, even when he satirized the so-called great.[12]

Before there was a Paulding and an Irving or two, there was Francis Hopkinson (1737–91), a Philadelphian who had signed the Declaration of Independence and loved to concoct clever satires. *A Pretty Story*, written on the eve of the Revolution, is the likeliest model for Paulding's *The Diverting History of John Bull and Brother Jonathan*, which he conceived as a second war with England loomed. Using a method typical of eighteenth-century satirists, Hopkinson twists his words and meanings and relies heavily on metaphor and allegory. The preface begins: "A Book without a Preface is like a Face without a Nose. Let the other Features be ever so agreeable and well proportioned, it is looked on with Detestation and Horror if this material Ornament be wanting." Then he starts over, exchanging metaphors: "A Book is like a House," which makes him a "clumsy Carpenter." The preface functions as a front door in this construction, a "grand Staircase" at the entryway encouraging readers to "set [their] Imagination to work."

The title page of *A Pretty Story* gives the author's name as "Peter Grievous, Esquire." It is, naturally, a tale of grievances, carried by a narrative that is naïve and unsubtle. Hopkinson prefigures Paulding's millpond residents in his representation of Great Britain as "a very valuable Farm" whose "Nobleman" owner had acquired "an immense Tract of a wild uncultivated Country at a vast Distance from his Mansion House" (the American colonies). His children are "Adventurers" who go off to settle it, enduring hardships while maintaining "a constant Correspondence with their Father's Family." In time, the settlers grow "very fond of a particular Kind of Cyder," this referring to the drama of the Boston Tea Party. The Nobleman "began to neglect" the "Inhabitants of the new Farm," at which point he cedes authority to his cunning "Steward" (Parliament). *A Pretty Story*, composed in 1774, ends abruptly, punctuated with a Latin motto that translates as "the rest is missing," which is to say that the impending Revolution leaves the future unsettled.[13]

Aspects of Early American Humor

Anglo-American jokesters went after easy marks like swindlers, debtors, and drunks. They were quite bullish on ethnic humor, indulging at length in stereotyping—from representations of an endearing rivalry (Frenchmen) to cheap displays of domestic debasement (servants and slaves). *The Youthful Jester* (1800) contains a typical example of a made-up slave's mangled speech and childlike logic. A white master instructs him to wake at sunrise, and the slave replies: "But suppose, massa, the sun rise before day-light—What I do den, sir?"

Native Americans were treated differently. Even before James Fenimore Cooper's popular re-creation of the noble Indian who was master of the forest, the aboriginal had earned a reputation for fearlessness as well as for being able to effectively contest his people's depressed status in the land of their ancestors. Thus, in printed anecdotes, Indians got the better of the white man unless they were being mocked for drinking themselves into a stupor. Indians were therefore slightly less obviously the butt of a joke than "Paddy," the easily confused, low-class, hard-drinking Irishman. The long-accepted notion that women lie about their age joined this species of humor. On being asked her age, a woman claims to be forty and turns to her male cousin for confirmation: "I am sure, madam, replied he, I ought not to dispute it; for I have constantly heard you say so for above these *ten years*."[14]

Newspaper and magazine editors showed little restraint when highlighting the battle of the sexes. "The Eye of a Woman" (1824) is fairly typical: "The glare, the stare, the leer, the sneer, the invitation, the defiance, the denial, the consent, the glance of love, the flash of rage, the sparkling of hope, the languishment of softness, the squint of suspicion, the fire of jealousy, and the lustre of pleasure." It was commonplace to categorize females as beauty-obsessed shopping addicts: "Mrs. W, walking on one of the wharves in New York, jocosely asked a sailor why a ship was always called *she*? 'Oh, faith,' says the son of Neptune, 'because the rigging costs more than the hull." Some gendered jokes were straight puns. On entering the theater one evening, a lady was "so roughly justled by the crowd that her ruffles were torn off." At her box, the gentleman sought to put her at ease with a compliment: "that notwithstanding the rude usage she had met with, she was *unruffled!*"

While women were regularly reproached for their pride and vanity in serious essays as much as in facetious commentaries, an equal number of gender-specific gags made the rounds that avoided any feint in the direction of misogyny: "A gentleman, at a tea-party, happening to offend the Lady next him, had a piece of toast thrown him by the affronted fair. He cooly took it up, and threw it in the face of the next person to him, desiring that Miss A's *toast* might go round."[15]

Many jokes of the era, tame to us, played on the double entendre or mistaken hearing: A man hid his fortune "in a bank of earth under a hedge," only to find it gone when he tried digging it up. "A wag, who had more wit than feeling," evinced surprise because the money was, after all, "put into the *Bank*." A famous punster was confronted with the opinion that punning was "the *lowest* sort of wit." He answered: "It is so, and therefore the *foundation* of all wit." When a pair of punsters communed and one failed to watch where he was going, this happened: "Why, Sam, you have *kicked the bucket*." "Oh no," replied the other. "I have only turned *a little pale*." Another joke indulged in gallows humor, quite literally. A country carpenter had not received payment the last time the court ordered him to construct a "gibbet," so he refused to act on the next such request. When the circuit judge returned to town, he asked the carpenter: "Fellow! How came you to neglect making the gibbet that was ordered on my account?" "I humbly beg your pardon, (said the carpenter) had I known it had been *for your Lordship*, it should have been done immediately." (Editors often used italics to make sure a joke landed.) Similar wordplay was deployed in gags about sleep-inducing sermons: "A gentleman dined one day with a dull preacher. Dinner was scarcely over before the gentleman fell asleep but was awakened by the divine and invited to go and hear him preach. 'I beseech you, sir,' said he, 'to excuse me, *I can sleep very well where I am*.'"[16]

The Salmagundians found their own special way to embarrass an inveterate punster, creating a scenario in which the habitual offender, in the company of partygoers, is "sitting silent on the watch for an hour together, until some luckless wight . . . dropped a phrase susceptible of a double meaning; when—pop, our punster would dart out like a veteran mouser from her covert, seize the unlucky word, and after worrying and mumbling at it until it was capable of no further marring, relapse again into silent watchfulness, and lie in wait for another opportunity." The humorists' father-figure, "Pindar Cockloft" (William Irving), posed aloud whether a punster could at the same time be a good Christian—while testifying that the fall of the Roman Empire was owing to a pun.[17]

Satirists of the higher order distinguished their work from low humor. They hoped their depictions of human foibles would command hearts, instruct in humility, and illustrate affinities. Many city and village newspapers went in a different direction as vehicles for light humor, accepting less sophisticated quips as fill-ins at the end of articles, for instance, taking the low road with gibes at Irish drunks: "Two blades [dashing young men] came home late from a grog shop . . ." "Jemmy, and why don't you come to bed!" the one asks. "'Faith, Paddy,' said he, "'*let it come round again and I'll try.*'"[18]

Newspapers throughout the country thrived on witticisms, and more than a few editors tried to distinguish themselves by declaring war on the "scribbling boobies" who butchered the language in pursuit of a cheap laugh. It was vulgar and hackneyed "to a nauseous extreme," when a writer took the easy route to a laugh by substituting complex language for a simple proverb: "A rolling stone gathers no moss" thus became "a petrification in a state of progressive revolution is not augmented by herbaceous increments." This was "hardworking facetiousness," making for "doubtful amusement" (draining language of emotion), which could be "executed by any clown who can hunt for synonyms in a dictionary."

On the other hand, a good many ordinary folks were made into antiheroes, being assigned special talents in scoring points.

A "wag" looking out from a stagecoach that was passing by poor but still fenced-in property called out to the fellow who farmed it: "I say, mister, what are you fencing that pasture for? It would take forty acres on't to starve a middle-sized cow." "Jusso," the man replied. "I'm fencing of it to keep eour kettle out." The two were meant to represent rural Yankee dialect, the passenger and the farmer staging a vintage class-accented battle of wits.

Keenly conscious of what they might do to promote the fraternal causes of dry wit and generous laughter, editors periodically felt inclined to define the differences between wit and humor or wit and satire. Wit, it was generally thought, required imagination, humor did no one any harm, satire alone was "biting," and the best humorists tended to be those most prone to melancholy: "The higher class of writers, who have indulged in the quips and sports of the pen—the wild riot of wit, and exaggeration of fun—have made humor the safety-valve of a sad, earnest heart." Their talent bore marks of intelligence and subtlety arising from the "contests of life" they'd endured.[19]

A favorite resort of humorists was the versified witticism that those with a common education could appreciate. Pope's translations of the Homeric epics provided fodder for this genre:

> On the bankruptcy of a person by the name of Homer
> "That *Homer* should a bankrupt be
> Is not so very *Odd-d'ye-see*
> If it be true, as I'm instructed,
> So *Ill-he-had* his books conducted."[20]

Sometimes the joke was visual, dependent on the uniqueness of the moment. *Niles' Weekly Register*, the popular national news digest out of Baltimore, could not resist a father-son courtroom exchange, where each was testifying about his Revolutionary War service in an attempt to secure a pension. The father, ninety-four, kept correcting the son, who was seventy: "Tut, boy, you are mistaken. . . . You are wrong, boy." The son's "whitened locks and wrinkled visage" didn't mean he wouldn't still answer to "boy." In this vignette, one catches a glimpse of the hardest history to resurrect: nonlinguistic symbols of emotional life. That's the thing about laughter: it's personal and it's social; it erupts when one is home alone (stimulated by a thought) but occurs more frequently in company (mirroring intimacy). It's a regular reminder that eccentricity, excitability, and imperfection combine in the human species and make us self-aware.[21]

Public entertainment was a valued part of civic life. In 1823, one paper decided to take issue with the spoilsports who showed up at the performances of magicians and interrupted sleight-of-hand shows. Apparently, this happened a lot: "We have never been present at an exhibition of *leger de main*, without being disgusted with the conduct and observations of some *knowing ones*, among the audience, who display their *wit* and *wisdom* by attempting to *balk* the performer, and destroy the pleasing illusion." The humorless were not appreciated.[22]

Slang-Whangers of the Logocracy

In the gestational phase of *Salmagundi*, the Paulding-Irving cohort dubbed themselves "Lads of Kilkenny." Why they chose Kilkenny, Ireland, as their club moniker is unclear: the place was a source of black marble, rarely mentioned in newspapers otherwise, though Sir John Carr's *The Stranger in Ireland* (1806) did find its way to the United States, and Sir John did note the singular attractiveness of the local peasant population. That was the sort of fodder Paulding and Irving might have drawn on; more likely, though, they just liked the sound of it: "Lads of Kilkenny."

Irving, Paulding, and their circle wrote for educated commoners like themselves. They palled around with their intellectual peers, some of whom lived on family wealth and occupied an inherited property. The Lads of Kilkenny represented such a mix of middle class and privileged young men. There seems not to have existed any envy among them: social distinctions were a fact of life and financial insecurity was fairly universal. The freedom to poke fun at the habits of those above and below meant that authority increasingly belonged to the middle ranks, which swelled over the first half of the nineteenth century.

In his private journal, Washington Irving jotted notes on humor-driven, hard-living Irish fellow travelers. To one of the lads, while the gang was scattered, he jocularly complained that "the riotous, roaring, rattle-brained orgies at Dyde's, succeeds the placid, picnic, picturesque pleasures of the tea-table." Dyde's was the upscale pub adjoining Manhattan's eminent Park Theater. This was how *Salmagundi* came to life.[23]

The three Salmagundians—two Irvings and one Paulding— gave loving attention to the names of their pseudonymous selves and fellow travelers: the crew included Anthony Evergreen (Washington Irving), Pindar Cockloft (the fur trader turned poet William Irving), artistic Will Wizard, and the regularly discomfited Launcelot Langstaff (generally Paulding), who railed at the weather and concluded that Nature would have been more reasonable if gendered male rather than female. Occasional characters in *Salmagundi* include "Hook'em Snivey, the famous fortune-teller," the social climbing "Timothy Giblet," and the mysterious sage of yore, "Linkum Fidelius."[24]

We never can truly know Fidelius because he is infinitely obscure. His pedantic pose is all that attaches to him, so he wafts over memory, the muse of nothing-knowledge, as his aphorisms prove: "How Gotham city conquered was, and how the folks turned apes—because." A few Linkum-isms strike existential notes: "Habit," he says, "is second nature." Thus, Linkum Fidelius rules sublimely—if by rumor alone—and remains as hard to pin down as Irving's actual political affiliation. These are reminders of the eighteenth-century British authors of satire who established a tradition of disguising their names on a title page, no doubt enjoying the thought that readers had to guess at their identity.[25]

In the essay "On Style," Paulding made fun of rhetorical studies along with class pretensions. "Style," he held, was "an arrant little humorist of a word, and full of whim-whams"; it "assumes to itself more contradictions, and significations, and eccentricities, than any monosyllable in the language is legitimately entitled to." Having achieved style, a man turned down his nose on "honest people" who aimed for the same height: "Each one looks down upon his neighbor below, and makes no scruple of shaking the dust off his shoes and into his eyes. . . . A family that once required two or three servants for convenience, now employs half a dozen for style." America was a probationary republic that was consumed with status, which explains the sly drollery that came easily, that was at times unmannerly and that told significant truths.[26]

The Salmagundians' specialty was "whim-whams," a term for "odd fancies." Poking fun at such fancies was not new; the practice went back two centuries within comedic circles, but the Salmagundians took it to a new level. It was a "whim-wham" of one of the Cockloft genealogy to follow a "quack" childrearing philosophy taken from botany: "He sprinkled them every day with water, laid them out in the sun as he did his geraniums." The purpose of a good portion of *Salmagundi* was to have a field day with eccentricities in New York State politics—the baronial Livingston family being the apparent model for the Cocklofts. Satire did not have to provide answers to serious questions but only had to lend them sparkle.[27]

The Salmagundians' brand of humor was gentle, however, in an age when humor occupied a conspicuous place in public life and could turn nasty quite easily. A prime example concerns James Ogilvie, a Scottish-born celebrity orator and former schoolmaster patronized by President Jefferson and befriended by Washington Irving. During a swing through the Northeast, Ogilvie was lampooned by an anonymous author, subsequently identified as John Rodman, a New York shopkeeper with ties to Irving's circle. *Fragment of a Journal of a Sentimental Philosopher* cast the orator (unnamed in the pamphlet) as a self-absorbed phony, a pretender, a seducer. Rodman's work bleeds sarcasm, as when he has his philosopher-diarist convince himself that his pathetic dance moves at a gathering are superior to the graceful style of the others who surround him: "was awkward—so much the better—good dancing quite common here—my bear-like movements more interesting—imputed to genius and uncontrolled sensibility—the girls all enraptured with me." *Salmagundi* made light of dancing but in the form of good-humored comments about elite families who marveled at their dance instructor or an upwardly mobile make-believe family called the Giblets who "made a prodigious splash in their own opinion" as they aimed at the "tip-top of style" by enlisting "every paper-hanger, every piano-teacher, and every dancing-master in the city" to help them advance in society.[28]

This well-disposed approach to humor was reflected in the way Irving related to the press. Newspapers were having a growth spurt as never before, having become since Washington's presidency an instrument of social power that teased and tantalized when and where it could. Irving appreciated the possibilities. Part of his charm lay in the fact that he never burned bridges. So, for example, once his brother Peter's Burrite *Morning Chronicle* folded, he continued to recognize the authority of William Coleman's *New-York Evening Post*, a Hamiltonian Federalist organ. He maintained ties as well to James Cheetham's pro-Jefferson *American Citizen*, which supported positions taken by New York's powerful Clinton family. The point here is that *Salmagundi*—best compared to the *Onion* of today—did no damage to anyone's reputations and received favorable notice in papers across the United States.

Salmagundi declared the nation a "logocracy," or government of words, while it presented long-tongued newspaper editors as unapologetic "slang-whangers" who remained eternally at war with one another. It was William, the eldest of the Irvings, who coined the term "logocracy": a logocrat was transpartisan, positively cranky, and quintessentially American.

In a logocracy, the future three-term congressman wrote ironically, "a great man" need not be "wise or valiant, upright or honorable." Such qualities only served to "impede his preferment." Logocracy undercut the Washington myth: a "candidate for greatness" need only be supple, insect-like: "He buries himself in the mob; labors in dirt and oblivion, and makes unto himself the rudiments of a popular name." Political democracy converted an able man into a useful tool, serving only to uplift the rogues of society. The cynicism embedded in this *Salmagundian* message is eminently relatable in the twenty-first century.[29]

While the "slang-whanging" of politicians and their scribbling minions came in for a good drubbing, the three *Salmagundi* authors also—and repeatedly—mocked non-Western peoples, stereotyping practicing Muslims along with Africans and Chinese. In a digressive, absurdist review of *Othello*, the title character, "most ignominiously henpecked," was not black enough for Will Wizard's taste, though the performance itself was sufficiently dark: "I like frowning in tragedy; and if a man but keeps his forehead in proper wrinkle, talks big, and takes long strides on the stage, I always set him down as a great tragedian." In "On Style," Paulding observes that "a Chinese lady is thought prodigal of her charms if she exposes the tip of her nose" and that "in Egypt, or at Constantinople, style consists in the quantity of fur and fine clothes a lady can put on without danger of suffocation."[30]

Cross-cultural gaffes were as satisfying to the laugh-seeking public as class vengeance dished out in caricatures of pompous rich folk putting on airs. Paulding doubled down in a story he wrote much later called "The Azure Hose" (code for "bluestocking") that mocked a right honorable family of the South, whose patriarch, the priggish Lightfoot Lee, cares about inconsequential things and constantly misses the big picture, devoting excessive attention, for example, to the art of boiling an egg, which in his view required particular "discretion." His daughter Lucia, meanwhile, cares for a poet named Goshawk who had "written much, thought little, and spoken a great deal." Dressing up the insult, Paulding added of the swaggering Goshawk that "it was impossible for him to say the simplest thing without rising into a lofty enthusiasm, flinging his metaphors about like sky rockets." The high-flying leisure class was always fair (and easy) game. For her part, Lucia is not enough grounded: "She was not exactly blue, but she certainly inhabited that circle of the rainbow, and when reflected on by the bright rays of Mr. Fitzgiles Goshawk, was sometimes of the deepest shade of indigo." A society that assumed access to higher education would produce morals and judgment along with book knowledge assumed too much. Yet while such is the conclusion Paulding arrives at in this story, in his correspondence with South Carolina politicos he expressed more compassion for the high-toned proslavery element than for the downtrodden. He walked a fine line.[31]

A popular form in satirizing manners was the traveler's journal. Oliver Goldsmith's 1762 *Citizen of the World* was the acknowledged model in *Salmagundi* for nine ironic pieces by a pretend visitor to Manhattan named Mustapha Rub-a-dub Keli Khan, modeled on an actual Tripolitan ship captain, a prisoner taken during the Barbary Wars who'd been transported to New York not long before. In Goldsmith's original the traveler was a Chinese philosopher residing in London. Numerous reviews of *Salmagundi* made the obvious connection: "The Letters from the Tunisian prisoner contain a specimen of satire in the style of 'Citizen of the World.'"[32]

Paulding introduced Mustapha, and the brothers Irving took their turns with him as well. The "infidel nations" Mustapha spied on in his travels exhibited traits he found curious: the Spaniards "sleep upon every affair of importance"; the French "dance upon everything"; Germans "smoke upon everything"; Britons "eat upon everything"; and "the windy subjects of the American logocracy talk upon everything."[33]

In another episode, Mustapha learns from a knowing tailor that wars were "considered very useless and expensive" in America and that it was believed that a "philosophic nation" needed its military only for show and "regimental parade." Militancy having been banished from the military mindset, only the sartorial effects remained.[34]

Everything connected with *Salmagundi* had an unconventional quality about it, down to its publisher. "Dusky Davy" Longworth, an original "Lad of Kilkenny," presented himself as something of an eccentric. The owner of Shakespeare-related engravings, he stretched a gigantic banner across the entrance to his home celebrating the "crowning" of the playwright as a genius. His printing house was known as "the Shakespeare Gallery," where he republished a London edition of Shakespeare's works. For laughs, he advertised his bookshop as "the sentimental epicure's ordinary," playfully giving it a name identified with tavern life.[35]

As satire soared, those who wrote about it who were not practitioners credited the genre for serving moral ends. In earnest strains, newspaper contributors at the time of *Salmagundi* rendered such judgments as "general satire is one of the most successful weapons for combating the vices and follies of the age." Less generous critics fell to dismissing the form as "transitory" and a poor substitute for actual virtue. These commenters blasted American satire as rude and irrelevant, as a flawed species of ridicule designed to "magnify petty accidents and trifling vexations . . . into intolerable grievances," with unforgivable exaggerations and "effusions" too "unwieldy" to reach their target. When an author's "indignation is impotent," nothing is to be achieved. "The arrows of satire shall be shot at vice and folly," countered an 1807 prospectus announcing a new literary journal.[36]

Reviewers, at least, knew what they were getting in *Salmagundi*. It was "that kind of satire which tickles rather than cuts," declared the *People's Friend*, a short-lived New York periodical. The Philadelphia *Aurora* claimed that the Irving-Paulding effort, "although not wholly original, contains genuine wit and well-directed satire, in abundance." In the same year as *Salmagundi's* run, another Philadelphia paper, the *Tickler*, sought help from the ancients to lay out definitions and inform the public: "Satire extends the victim on the bed of *Procrustes*, but *Ridicule* is the executioner of his vices." Procrustes, in a thoroughly gruesome tale taken from Greek mythology, invited travelers to spend the night, and when they did not fit the bed provided, he stretched their bodies or otherwise cut off their legs till they did. In Massachusetts, one columnist philosophized: "While folly remains in the world, the word of satire need not rust by disuse; while vice and depravity inhabit the globe, there will be employment for the pen of the moralist." Such scripted statements, attempts at cleverness, show a limited imagination and an overall inability to appreciate satire for its own sake. They "got" *Salmagundi*, and they didn't.[37]

Diedrich Knickerbocker Discharges His Debts

Jefferson's policies as president came in for a concerted lampooning in 1809 with Washington Irving's single-authored parody, *A History of New-York*, aka "Knickerbocker's History." The third president was recast as a splenetic ruler of the defunct Dutch colony of New Amsterdam, "armed with pronouncements" and opposed to military expenditures—which was a common critique of Jefferson's foreign policy at this time. Irving largely disregards chronology in his satire, creating characters whose shadowy identities survive best in timelessness.

Jefferson held no grudge against Irving. They never met or corresponded. But Irving did encounter James and Dolley Madison in (as he put it) the "blazing splendour" of a social gathering at the President's House in Washington, just after New Year's Day in 1811, by which time his mock history had found favor far and wide. He left posterity a precious one-liner on President Madison's dry appearance: "Poor Jemmy! he is but a withered little apple-John." (The worn and delicate applejohn, a fruity morsel no longer consumed, belonged, in fact, to the age of Shakespeare.)

The friendly and effusive First Lady completely won over the author: "Mrs. Madison is a fine, portly, buxom dame—who has a smile and a pleasant word for every body." Her two sisters, in attendance, were, Irving wrote, "like the two Merry Wives of Windsor"—Shakespearean characters of deviousness and charm. Invited back the following month, he was giddy when the "withered little apple-John" advanced the idea of a foreign appointment for him and the "buxom dame" approved. "The President . . . said some very handsome things of me," he told his brother William. "Mrs. Madison is a sworn friend of mine." It was during these days of merriment up and down Pennsylvania Avenue that the patriotically named Washington Irving finally met the namesake and apparent inspiration for his mock historian, the very real Herman Knickerbocker (1779–1855), a congressman from upstate New York, who became, henceforth, "my cousin Knickerbocker." On the surface, "Knickerbocker's History" was a romp through the seventeenth century, though readers had no difficulty making a direct connection between the imperfect Dutch governor, "William the Testy," and President Jefferson.[38]

The stage management of "Knickerbocker" was brilliant. Some months after the seamless transition between Jefferson and Madison administrations, and with Jim Paulding's help, Irving lured in potential readers with a shrewd publicity campaign. The two Salmagundians clandestinely invaded the pages of William Coleman's upstanding *Evening-Post* to get their man's name before readers. A one-word headline, "DISTRESSSING," was followed by a short squib that announced the disappearance of "a small elderly gentleman, dressed in an old black coat and cocked hat," who went by the name of "KNICKERBOCKER." At this point, nothing was disclosed about his occupation. Two beguiling *Evening-Post* updates later, Irving's publisher announced the release of the two-volume masterpiece, described as having been "found in the chamber of Mr. Diedrich Knickerbocker," a historian heretofore obscure, which was being published in order to "discharge certain debts he left behind."[39]

The well-researched, pseudohistorical tome draws on the little-studied Dutch colonial past. Its power lies in its merging the fruits of the archive with outlandish situations. Being a narrowly focused history of seventeenth-century New York, it has to open, of course, with a primordial Earth and a complete cosmology. "Knickerbocker" privileged esoteric theories from obscure corners of the Near East on the nature of the heavens, the composition of the sun, and "this rotatory planet." In book 1, the reader enters the classroom of the learned "Professor Puddinghead" (Von Poddingcroft in the original Dutch). The philosophic gentleman's clothes are drenched by a bucket of ocean as he is demonstrating how gravity works, the mishap owing to his having indulged a pesky student, "one of those vagrant geniuses, who seem sent into the world merely to annoy worthy men of the puddinghead order."

In his extensively footnoted, systematically confounding history, Knickerbocker invokes Pythagoras, Socrates, Plato, and "Mohawk philosophers" before irreligiously avowing that he will make do "with the account handed down by Moses," adding that in so doing he is merely "follow[ing] the example of our ingenious neighbors in Connecticut; who in their first settlement proclaimed, that the colony should be governed by the laws of God—until they had time to make better." Irving thrived on this sort of irony.[40]

In book 4, we arrive at the moment in Dutch colonial government when Wilhelmus Kieft (William the Testy, the Jefferson stand-in) assumes office. The real Governor Kieft was a merchant who got promoted and opted to make war on area Indians in the 1640s. But in Irving's version, rather than build a formidable armada to protect the land, William the Testy flings pronouncements: it's the "cheap mode of fighting," he says. A "potentate" armed with "speeches, messages, and bulletins" has a clear monopoly on talk—just like a democratic politician.

Testy is credibly Jefferson-like in his "brisk, waspish" appearance, but at six-foot-two-and-a-half inches Jefferson was hardly the "withered" (applejohn-like) "little old gentlemen" Irving sketches. The ironist shuns meanness and bile—the partisan strife that offends him. He wants to convert history into something dreamlike, a world where no one actually gets hurt.[41]

In spite of his harmless intent, Irving could not avoid irritating a smattering of Dutch-descended New Yorkers who interpreted "Knickerbocker" as an enfeebling portrayal of their culture. In 1819, a full decade after the book's publication, the author's close friend Gulian Verplanck (they'd trained in law in the same office) let people know what he thought about ethnic humor. About to spend the next decade and a half representing New York City in the state assembly and then in Congress, Verplanck described Irving's as a talent wasted in "coarse caricature." Irving, by then living in London, found the timing of Verplanck's address quaint: he read it just as he was "finish[ing] the little story of Rip Van Winkle." Diedrich Knickerbocker was about to resurface as the professed source of Rip's crazy memoir, a tale of discombobulated memory wherein a simple, good-natured villager disappears into the mountains for twenty years, though for him it feels like a single night's sleep.[42]

"Rip Van Winkle" resonated. It pleased audiences first as an endearing tale and as a touring theatrical production in later decades. One reason the story worked was because readers immediately recognized memory as an imperfect endowment and fodder for jokes. Even modern neuroscience acknowledges that we do not know, and may never know, why our feeling for times past reshapes many former experiences into something brighter and occasionally magical. Emotive response fashions and refashions the stories that comprise culture. Irving, more than any other early humorist, popularized a magical, timeless America. Not until Mark Twain came along would he have any real competition in that realm of literary craftsmanship.

Old-School Rules and Modern Chivalry

On one of his trips to Philadelphia, Irving made the acquaintance of a fellow satirist named Joseph Dennie (1768–1812). Unlike Irving, Dennie was naturally antagonistic on the page. An inveterate Federalist, he ran the hard-hitting Jefferson-hating periodical *Port-Folio*.

Immediately after the democratic icon Jefferson wrested government from its respectable Federalist guardians of order, Dennie took the name Oliver Oldschool. Distrusting popular opinion, Oldschool insisted that "the clear and harmonious voice of the good and wise" should always outrank it. This was in 1800. When he took up his quill two years later at the age of twenty, Irving chose the pen name "Jonathan Oldstyle." That made the two of them pseudonymous cousins.

Dennie bore the distinction of being prosecuted by President Jefferson for seditious libel after publishing a piece that asserted that "a democracy is scarcely tolerable" because "its omens are always sinister, and its powers are unpropitious." The editor had prophesied that "civil war, desolation, and anarchy" would be the result of democracy. With this ostensible affront to the chief executive, Dennie was forced to stand trial and was found not guilty.[43]

But that was not all he was known for. In *The Lay Preacher*, an early offering, he opted "to turn gay subjects to moral purposes." Here he affected "an ardent thirst for knowledge" so as to pursue all possible beauty in literary expression. Amid his "rambles," he happened on creative word combinations: "the shrinking vegetable of irritableness," "the hurry of dissipation, the agitation of play," "the couch of anguish, or the gripe of indigence," a "gust of adversity," and "pleasure [that] may flash before the giddy eyes." Like the Salmagundians of New York, Dennie romanced language from his comfortable "elbow chair." Adopting poses, the satirist proved to the republic of letters that he could do more than one thing: cut down a man he didn't respect and still preserve the plain-spoken flavor of a forthright humorist with a taste for neology.[44]

His stinging brand of political humor occasionally found inspiration in Shakespearean imagery. Dennie taunted Aaron Burr, no stranger to sexualized satire, when the sitting vice president was estranged from the Jefferson-Madison circle and resting his bones in New York. Quoting from *Henry VI, Part 3*, the editor took liberties with the widowed statesman's personal reputation:

> I'll make my heaven in a lady's lap
> And deck my body in gay ornaments
> And witch sweet ladies with my words and looks.
> (3.2.1637–39)

It wasn't an entirely inaccurate picture: one of Burr's claims to fame as a trial attorney was his ability to deliver an eyeful of personal power. When accused of treason in 1807, he was brought to Richmond, Virginia, where Washington Irving captured a dramatic moment in the courtroom as the defendant heard the name of his overfed accuser, General James Wilkinson, announced. As the soldier "strutted into Court" and stood "swelling like a turkey cock," bracing for the encounter, "Burr turned his head, looked him full in the face with one of his piercing regards, swept his eye over his whole person from head to foot, as if to scan its dimensions, and then coolly resumed his former position, and went on conversing with his counsel as tranquilly as ever." Journalistic pathos met unadulterated satire in this letter from Irving to Paulding.[45]

Humor publications appeared in the new republic with sprightly regularity. Though they routinely struggled to stay afloat, America's satire-based periodicals kept on coming. The *Tickler*'s editor, writing under the name "Toby Scratch 'Em," used a verse from Alexander Pope's 1734 "Epistle to Dr. Arbuthnot" as its salacious motto: "Give virtue scandal, innocence a fear, / Or from the soft-eyed virgin steal a tear." As a six-foot diameter "mammoth cheese," a gift from a Baptist congregation in Massachusetts, was wheeled and floated to President Jefferson's Executive Mansion in 1801, Joseph Dennie's *Port-Folio* quoted Pope in order to reduce the great cheese to "a mere white curd of asses' milk."

The *Trangram, or Fashionable Trifler*, was launched in Philadelphia in 1809 by an editor and a team that introduced themselves as "Christopher Crag, Esq., his Grandmother and Uncle." One of the people it took aim at was Dennie, whom it referred to as "Oliver Crank." Two years later came the *Cynick*, "by Growler Gruff, Esquire, aided by a Confederacy of Lettered Dogs." Its motto had teeth: "We'll snarl, and bite, and play the dog, / For dogs are honest." Despite its assertiveness, the paper wore out its welcome and quickly disappeared but not before making the important point in its sixth issue that "the satirist must be a lover of his kind, but a greater lover of truth" who exposed in order to clarify, to vindicate—as a duty to the public.

The weekly *Independent Balance* began its run in 1817 under the watchful eye of the *Tickler's* previous editor, who was now designated "Democritus the Younger, a lineal descendant of the Laughing Philosopher." In 1820, the *Critic*, under the youthful eye of Geoffrey Juvenile, Esq., made its debut just as Washington Irving's "Geoffrey Crayon" began making transatlantic waves as *The Sketch Book's* ostensible narrator. The *Critic's* Mr. Juvenile made it a particular point of recalling "the Salmagundi school," while at the same time targeting new work by Paulding for its "bathos and silliness." Like America's partisan political press, champions of satire paid close attention to their competition, met in clubs and ran ideas by one another, and sometimes got into surprisingly bitter feuds.[46]

Between 1792 and 1815, the western Pennsylvanian Hugh Henry Brackenridge (1748–1816), produced in several installments the picaresque *Modern Chivalry*, a digressive, American-inflected *Don Quixote*. While Brackenridge's politics were middle of the road, his satire was anything but. The desultory adventures of its two main characters, a mature republican gentleman and his devious sidekick, prop up American-style democracy in one sense only: granting it a future. For the moment it's mostly about making noise and upsetting norms.

Having seen his share of political upheaval in the Pennsylvania backcountry, Brackenridge well understood how language could disguise intent and dictate perception. "Language," he wrote with some weightiness, "is the highest glory of our species." Yet its built-in deceptions obliged him not to take it too seriously. In one chapter, as narrator, Brackenridge addresses the reader directly regarding the properties of language. Initially confessing that in spinning this yarn he is merely amusing himself in "abstract composition," he digresses further, recommending to the several heads of executive departments that they plop down money and buy his work. He does not guarantee that they'll see the brilliance of his writing style, for he only counts on the "delicately discerning" to "discover its beauties." (This was a lighthearted dig at the "harmless nonsense" that issued from the pens of government officials.)

The self-infatuated narrator proceeds to quote an imaginary critic's favorable review of his work:

> The author of the work before us, is well known in the literary world for his treatise on the Economy of Rats, a satirical composition, in which, under the veil of allegory, he designates the measures of the federal government; as also for his History of Weasels, in which the same strokes are given. . . . In the present work, which he entitles Modern Chivalry, he disowns the idea of any moral or sentiment whatsoever.[47]

Deliberate confusion in maintaining a distance between the author and the story was the calling card of many early American parodists, and no one deployed the technique quite so brilliantly as Brackenridge. *Modern Chivalry* is quixotic, but as an exercise in spoofing public ambition it is unlike the satires of Irving or Paulding. Brackenridge sees himself as a truth teller, closer to a philosopher than the other two. As they matured as authors, the New Yorkers were more invested in the life of the story.

Nevertheless, Brackenridge's decades-spanning saga is important for two reasons. First, it is of value to an understanding of America's developmental experience because it reveals how grating, if overlooked, class tensions have always been, Second, the colorful, often ridiculous portrait of the western frontier character that it offers would become a mainstay of American writing. The buffoonish costar of the novel, the con artist Teague O'Regan, is unself-conscious and way too proud for a person of his modest talents. He is the author's vehicle for the political statement he feels a need to make, over and over, in reproaching the masses for their outstanding ignorance. In the book's later installments, the satire fades. Brackenridge proves, in his creative decline, that satire and didacticism do not mesh well.[48]

American satire did not come about in a vacuum. Eighteenth-century English satire was its acknowledged model. The United States was still a socially underdeveloped country that was built on the distinct personalities of its mutually jealous states and regions. They were brought together, in a real way, by their common connection to literary models in England and Scotland. The satirist in Britain relished his freedom as much as any American democrat. By 1800, he already had a proud history of exposing pretenders to knowledge and unseemly modes of behavior (in the category of minor vices), effectively defining the boundary between sensibility (modesty) and acceptable ridicule. As the satirist and literary critic T. J. Mathias, a fellow of the Royal Society, noted in 1794, "All publick men, however distinguished, must in their turns submit to [satire], if necessary to the welfare of the state." British satirists toyed with the notion that polite society could not quite agree on the amount of control required when a man or woman was brought to laugh.[49]

American satire found common cause with British satire in poking fun at the world of ladies' fashions, both cultures being at the mercy of French designers. Irving early on used French dancing masters to symbolize Americans' pathetic effort to copy European markers of refinement. The United States was still wearing hand-me-downs by consciously and unconsciously imitating without doing much to improve its chances of obtaining acceptance abroad.[50]

American readers not only enjoyed Shakespeare but also followed the mock-heroic threads woven through Jonathan Swift's *Gulliver's Travels* (1726). That author's mockery of fools, his scorn for pettiness, struck a chord. Daniel Defoe's even earlier *Robinson Crusoe*, a novelistic offshoot of *The Tempest*, spoke to Americans' taste for adventure, while Henry Fielding's comedy of manners *Tom Jones* (1749) reaffirmed their antiestablishmentarianism. Roguish characters and generous irony appealed, as the enduring popularity of Rip Van Winkle and Huckleberry Finn bears out. Familiar letter writers quoted from these works, namedropping characters without any need to elaborate: to mention an incident was to call up a complete image.

Aside from the poetry for which he was best known, Alexander Pope was a particular favorite for other reasons. His translation of the *Iliad* received warm accolades in America. His edition of Shakespeare's works, while controversial at home, was widely appreciated in America during the Revolutionary era. But it was his *Dunciad* (first published in 1728) that cemented Pope's reputation for mock-heroic satire. This was a tale about British ruling circles; those he cast as dunces lived in the land of "Dulness." This was an obvious spoof of the reigning monarch, George II, and his queen. Pope's masterpiece exercised clear influence on Irving's *A History of New-York*.

Then there was Laurence Sterne's frantically brilliant collision between pen and consciousness, *Tristram Shandy* (1759–67). The absurdist element in *Salmagundi* as well as *A History of New-York* owed much to Shandean irrationality. All of these early novels aimed to display something new to literature: natural emotions. That set them at odds with Samuel Richardson's successful female-directed literature of the same period: prim, sentimentally enriched tales of virtue imperiled told through letters. Richardson's interpretation of emotion was morally rigid, whereas Sterne, a rascal of a clergyman, joined episodic mischief to a masculine humanity that rejected hypocrisy.

Of Irish writers, none did so well with Americans as Oliver Goldsmith, who combined humor and realism in his two classics, *Vicar of Wakefield* and *Citizen of the World*. According to his reverential later biographer Washington Irving, Goldsmith injected a loveable personality into all he wrote. A lowborn,

wandering boy, he scrounged for work for years, remaining un-
discovered until midlife. For Irving, this exemplary author exhibited an "artless benevolence that beams throughout his works;
the whimsical, yet amiable views of human life and human nature; the unforced humor, blending so happily with good feeling
and good sense."[51]

The genial method employed by the masters of social criticism, Joseph Addison and Richard Steele, exerted an incalcu-
lable force on American readers and writers. Their "familiar essays" in a compilation known as the *Spectator* (1711–12) were
absorbed by every up-and-coming American male into the nineteenth century. In the expressive art of English prose writing,
no one surpassed Addison.

As reports from Europe continued to dominate their pages
into the nineteenth century, American newspapers and magazines published poetry and stories that imitated the British
mode. American writers were not yet the equals of their transatlantic brethren, nor did they claim they were. Nor were their
efforts acknowledged outside the states until after Washington
Irving made his way to England in 1815 and took up writing in
Liverpool. As with their appropriation of Shakespeare, American writers' opportunistic embrace of the "mind" behind English
literature helped provide a claim to worldliness. It is worth noting that those most prized in America tended to be outsiders
like themselves: the scrappy journalist-observers Addison and
Steele, the Irishman Goldsmith, the iconoclastic clergyman
Sterne. According to his modern biographer, Addison distinguished misdirected laughter (false humor) from honest mirth,
associating real wit with good sense and truth while finding
fault in "Pedantry, Dulness, and Ill-Nature." All of these writers were, in some way, ahead of their time.[52]

Over the next few decades, American satire migrated west
in a rusticated dialect that culminated in the successful career of
Mark Twain. Once the distinction between British and American

English was no longer perceived as a sign of cultural weakness or provinciality, the joke could be told in countrified dialect. Paulding himself helped to inaugurate this tradition with his 1830 play, *Lion of the West*, a whimsical farce whose hero, Nimrod Wildfire, was a thinly veiled version of Davy Crockett, the Tennessee congressman whose tall tales about frontier exploits loomed larger than his positions on national issues.[53]

When it did no harm, and often, even when it did, almost everyone appreciated satire. Sometimes the manner or affect was benign: tired of blundering attempts to pass bills of little consequence, frustrated members of Maine's legislature introduced one "to define the length of comets' tails." (The headline in the *National Intelligencer* read "Legitimate Satire.") At other times, the joke dwelled on regional stereotypes and might be racially tinged. A New Orleans scribbler who signed himself "Brother Jonathan" pretended to be a northern peddler come south to ply his trade: "Ye fair Creoles and pretty quatroon misses / I greet ye all, I come here to retail / My Yankee notions— cheese, wit, verse, codfishes." Buried in this doggerel is a debate over which to fear more: the swampland's sticky climate or the "bad habits of the Louis–an–ers."[54]

Starkly racist language that the modern conscience cannot stomach could appear unapologetically in a temperance periodical that specialized in religious homilies and sold itself to the public as "a family companion devoted to pure literature, temperance, morality, education, and general intelligence." Attributing this morsel to an Ohio source, the *New-York Organ* told of an older woman impatient with the neighbor family's repeated requests to borrow food items—in this case, cornmeal, known colloquially as Indian corn. "Mother sent me over to see of you couldn't lend us a little *Injun*," said the neighbor girl. The woman, "raising her spectacles, and pretending not to know" what was meant, replied, "I should like to oblige your mother, but we haint got no *little Injun*. Tell her, however, she can have our ni**er boy any time she wants to borrow him." Diminishing the humanity and the value to society of Blacks and Indians was so ordinary that no sensitivity or self-censorship was required by editor John W. Oliver. Yet the same newspaper could print, on another occasion, a story about a man's encounter with a wren's nest, "The Sympathy of Birds." It contained this plea: "Respect for ourselves guides our morals, and deference for others governs our manner." When robins, bluebirds, sparrows, and doves assembled as a "mob" on nearby branches to protect a threatened nest, nature exhibited a sublime form of communion, but races of humans apparently felt less of nature's spirit.[55]

"*Diverting History*": *An Encore Performance*

The first quarter of the nineteenth century saw significant developments in magazine culture. In 1801, the first year of publication of Dennie's *Port-Folio*, politics felt momentous. The incoming president, Thomas Jefferson, called for "harmony and affection" across the Union, and Dennie, unconvinced, raised the more likely prospect of separation, "dissolution," in America's future. "Quarrels, of which the seeds are too thickly sown, will shoot up, like weeds in a rank soil," he held. He figured that increasing militarization among the disunited states was inevitable and that war was a foregone conclusion. Oliver Oldschool's realpolitik dictated against the Enlightenment promise of peace and mutual improvement, taking aim at "the flood of philosophy, which poured upon that self-conceited dupe, the eighteenth century." Invoking Shakespeare's *Measure for Measure*, Dennie branded America's democracy "a grub, a 'poor beetle that we tread upon'" (3.1.1308) while commending absolute monarchy as "a higher order of the tribe, than a democratic rhetorician is willing to allow." In 1802, he reprinted a piece from the *Anti-Democrat* that arrived at a similar conclusion, noting New

England's unwillingness to be "a colony of Virginia." Increasingly, "the manners, habits, customs, principles, and ways of thinking" differed so much between northern and southern states that an "amicable dissolution" was the best way to bring "general advantage" to all parts of a shaky union.[56]

Before long, though, *Port-Folio* lost its potency. A few years after Dennie's death in 1812, one of his early contributors, John E. Hall (1783–1829) took over as editor. *Port-Folio* regained steam, reimagined book reviews, and posted sincere poetry, and while it still peppered its issues with a modest amount of political snark, Federalism had gone quiet and the tone of the magazine softened in turn. Hall made *Port-Folio* a family business, enlisting both his mother and his younger brother James (1793–1868) as contributing writers.

The United States was a prouder nation than it had been a quarter century earlier. In 1825, no less an authority than John Quincy Adams, a man who greatly admired and even wrote for Dennie's *Port-Folio*, became the first chief executive to describe the American nation as a "representative democracy." *Port-Folio* reflected this new rhetoric. James Hall was now writing that "the same American character" existed no matter where one traveled and that citizens of the North, South, and West were observably compatible. He had served honorably in the War of 1812, in which he was wounded, and assumed the editorship of an Illinois newspaper in 1827, when his nationalistic creed, serialized in *Port-Folio* over three years, was published as *Letters from the West*.

The older brother, John Hall, retained some British sympathies, recognizing the problems inherent in blind nationalism. An otherwise serious piece he published in 1821 veered into satire. Fictional "Letters from an Englishman in the United States" included the traveler's characterization of New Yorkers: "The first peculiarity that forcibly struck me was the great number of persons to be met with in every street, smoking cigars.

In passing along, you are assailed by those fragrant perfumers, for this being a *free country*, they puff and spit, to the right and left." Not everything Americans did was admirable.[57]

Sometimes, satire practically wrote itself. A few years before his "Letters from an Englishman," another Manhattan event caught the attention of *Port-Folio*'s editor when a rather odd case was presented to a New York jury. In 1818, the New York State legislature proposed a quality inspection system for fish oil that included a penalty for noncompliance, and the case centered on whether whale oil, which was used in lamps for illumination and as a lubricant in machinery, counted as fish oil. The case featured the testimony of the most esteemed scientific authority in the community, Dr. Samuel L. Mitchill (1764–1831), who had done about everything a man of erudition could do in his life: it was, in fact, his compendious work (*A Picture of New-York*) that Washington Irving took on directly, and in utter jest, when he conceived his version of the same—so it's no wonder he titled the Dutchified satire *A History of New-York*. Mitchill had earned a degree in medicine at the prestigious University of Edinburgh, directed the program in natural history (specializing in botany and chemistry) at Columbia, and served as founding editor of the nation's first medical journal. As if these were not sufficient credentials, by 1809, he had represented the city in the state assembly, the US House of Representatives, and the US Senate.

Dr. Mitchill testified on behalf of the defendant. He insisted in his most authoritative voice that a whale was not a fish. "There are many strange fish in New-York," the story began, anticipating the fun. Called to the stand, Mitchill covered every possible angle, showing that he was conversant with the business of whaling as much as he had studied gills, lungs, the rearing of sea animals' young and the warm-blooded creature's every conceivable trait: "As far as human discoveries have gone, and human research penetrated, it is received as an incontestable fact in zoology, that a whale is no fish." He hammered his point home. "As a man of science I can say positively that a whale is no more a fish than a man; nobody pretends to the contrary now-a-days, but lawyers and politicians."

A back-and-forth ensued between the smarm of the opposing attorney and the healthy ego of the testifying scientist. Under cross-examination, Dr. Mitchill was obliged to contend with popular opinion on the subject of fish versus mammal. "The legislature," he stated as a Jeffersonian Republican, "to the honour of our democracy, consists of all classes of men. It is one of the felicities of our form of government." But the freedom for varieties of opinion to coexist did not obviate the fact that cetaceous beings "suckle their young," and "fish do not give suck." The argument devolved from here to Greek and Latin roots and whether the first chapter of Genesis proved that God created whales and fish on different days. Pressed as to the proper interpretation of what happened on that critical fifth day of terrestrial and aquatic existence, Mitchill averred, "The word fish may not be used, but the inference is obvious." Along with everything else under the sun (recall Irving's "Professor Puddinghead"), biblical exegesis fell within the scholar's reach. And thus, cleverly excerpted, an arcane courtroom conversation needed little adjustment to make for a delicious satire. In the end, the law established that a whale was indeed a fish, "Doctor Mitchill to the contrary notwithstanding."[58]

In 1827, shortly before *Port-Folio* folded, Hall reprinted a piece from the *London Magazine* that went after all such happy talk as his brother's nationalistic *Letters from the West* indulged. "The most ignorant and barbarous people are the most national, or the most attached to themselves, and the most contemptuous of others," the author proclaimed. He had found, by observation, that the Irish were ornery, the Spanish "sulkey," the French bright in temperament and downright "gay," and England, of course, was the most troublesome of all: "Bull land is surly . . . [and] perfectly, utterly, and entirely ignorant of all other lands, things, people, institutions." In this construction, national pride and national distemper were equally inheritable. "And that," went the *London Magazine*, "is ignorance enough for our theory." As travelogues became ever more fashionable as literature, satirizing national character grew into something of an art form.[59]

A most glorious illustration of the satirical imagination manifested in real life during the election of a US senator on the floor of the Ohio House of Representatives. (State legislators voted in their senators until the popular vote was introduced in the twentieth century.) As rival views were aired, the violence of language resulted in one member challenging his colleague to a fight. At the next session, the aggressor appeared wearing a "dirk" at his side, its "glittering hilt . . . projecting ostentatiously from the folds of his waistcoat." Observing this performance, another member of the elected body "rigged himself out with an immense wooden dagger," fashioning a corncob as its makeshift hilt. With an air of mock gravity, he paraded before the gallant one and laid down his weapon, causing the entire hall to erupt in laughter. The would-be duelist, shamed, gave up his bloody crusade on the spot.[60]

Which takes us, finally, to ex-president Madison and his little satire on the contest between slave and free states represented as an interracial marriage. In 1819, Missouri, the first of the territories acquired in the Louisiana Purchase to join the Atlantic-facing states, was sufficiently populated to apply for statehood. Congress heatedly debated whether the federal government had any right to dictate a new state's laws regarding the institution of slavery. In 1821, the presidency behind him, Madison, at sixty-six, recalled Paulding's *The Diverting History of John Bull and Brother Jonathan*. In view of his growing appreciation for the federal appointee, stylist of language, and occasional companion, he now tried his hand at an imitative political satire. Without veering much from his friend's earlier effort, he titled it *Jonathan Bull and Mary Bull*. In it, Jonathan is the North, Mary the South.

The piece begins by referencing the ancient connection between the married Bulls and "old Mr. Bull," who is no longer in the picture. Next, Madison addresses the fertile couple's offspring, each of whom had been provided with "a good farm," which passed to the child "on its attaining the age of manhood" (thus meeting the requirements for statehood). Mary, alas, had a "stain" on her arm, caused by "a certain African dye," of which Jonathan was perfectly aware at the time of their marriage but that had detracted little from her "comely form." Over time, however, he became obsessed with the "black arm" and goaded her to "tear off the skin from the flesh or cut off the limb." Obviously, such an operation was a painful prospect.

The onus was thus placed on Jonathan. Madison singles out the husband's ultimatum to his wife: "I can no longer consort with one marked with such a deformity as the blot on your person." Mary, after a stunned silence, reminds him that at the time of their nuptial, he, too, had "spots & specks" of blackness on his person. And did he not appreciate the danger to his lawful companion? The surgery, if tried, might prove fatal to her—"a mortification or bleeding to death."

In the story's conclusion, Jonathan is "touched with this tender and conciliatory language of Mary," and the couple find their way to a reconciliation. In Madison's telling, the reader is expected to accept their tiff as a common feature of marital union. That said, if the Bulls made up in this one instance, they do not appear to have done so with much enthusiasm.[61]

The ex-president refrained from sharing his satire with the public for another fourteen years. The year before his death, he agreed to its release when the editor of the *Southern Literary Messenger* requested something—anything—from Madison's pen. This new literary review, headquartered in Richmond, went ahead and published it anonymously in March 1835. Possibly uninformed as to the identity of its hidden author, the *Richmond Enquirer* newspaper complimented the writing by comparing it to the treasured style of Joseph Addison. *Jonathan Bull and Mary Bull* was "a beautiful allegory, enforced by powers of reasoning, which betoken a master mind." Furthermore, "the argument used by Mary Bull, cannot but arrest attention."[62]

Emotions were bubbling up as the salmagundi of America's cultural politics stewed. A language of harmony versus separation, of union and disunion, had become a more or less permanent idiom in a gothic drama. Jonathan and Mary Bull were not going to be happy. As heavier clouds formed, the increasingly untouchable spirits of America's gloried founders wagged arthritic fingers at those responsible for the faithless future that beckoned.

THE LAYING OF THE CABLE—JOHN AND JONATHAN JOINING HANDS.

The representative American Brother Jonathan finds common ground with longtime nemesis John Bull, symbol of Great Britain, as the first transatlantic telegraph cable unites the two continents. Jonathan is emboldened enough to feel himself England's equal: "May our hearts always beat together; and with one pulse . . . we yet shall see ALL NATIONS speaking our Language, blessed with our Liberty." John Bull agrees: "You have grown to be a tall and sturdy man—quite as big as your Father!" The engraving was published by Baker and Godwin of New York in 1858.

Courtesy of the Library of Congress.

Chapter 5.

Historical Sensibilities
(Vainglory)

If the citizens of the United States were indeed
the devoted patriots they call themselves, they
would surely not thus incrust themselves in the
hard, dry, stubborn persuasion, that they are the
first and best of the human race, that nothing is
to be learned but what they are able to teach.
—Frances Trollope, *Domestic Manners
of the Americans* (1832)

❧

As they seized the advantage, Americans did damage to
themselves by failing to be sufficiently introspective. While they
pursued land ownership and cultural distinctiveness, European
commentators took potshots at them in published opinions that
newspapers across the United States masochistically reprinted.
One of the most notable among these carpers was a very proper
Englishwoman, Frances Trollope. In her commercially successful book, *Domestic Manners of the Americans,* she punctuated

lively vignettes with repeated instances of men spitting in public.

The novelist James Fenimore Cooper had lived abroad, and he sought to tone things down. The former midshipman described how the two sides each boasted that their seaworthy vessels were the fastest, and his thought was that neither side came out particularly well: the English routinely resorted to "bigoted" language when discussing the habits of Americans, while his fellow Americans failed to adequately control themselves, lacking the overall steadiness of their British cousins. He felt "a national character somewhere between the two would be preferable to either." One thing he really didn't like about the American scene was the uncertainty of popular opinion, which he characterized as "the *unresisted* force of ignorance and cupidity." Some nineteenth-century grievances as to the gullibility of the masses and their total faith in the free market economy sound shockingly similar to those heard in the present century.[1]

Like the better-known Frenchman Alexis de Tocqueville, newspaper editor Michel Chevalier wrote of the America he toured in the early 1830s. The "multitude," Chevalier found at the end of his two years abroad, lived far better than their counterparts in Europe, but they lacked the "greatness of soul" of the poorest Parisian and the "gleams of taste and poetical genius" found in the most downcast of Neapolitans. They were energetic and manifestly self-assured but culturally untutored.

While Chevalier's exposition is disparaging in places, he did not approve of the aristocratic hauteur that characterized British travelers' accounts either; he was closer in perspective to the many American critics who took pleasure in disproving published observations they assigned to English writers' "sheer spirit of falsehood." Chevalier's goal was to understand what made Anglo-Americans distinctive as a people. "The American democracy is imperious and overbearing toward foreign people," he said, while allowing that "an enterprising, active, vigorous nation" eyeing the "miserable lethargy" of the sprawling provinces to the south and west of its borders, planted so long ago by Spain, could be forgiven for assuming such an attitude. Were the States to rob Mexico of territory in support of an "egoistic . . . national ambition," it would be a pardonable act, just as the Romans' imperial policy was seen to be justified when the land seized "flourished in their hands." An expansionist United States would convince posterity, as Rome did, that arrogance in the service of collective enrichment was acceptable. Success was what mattered.[2]

Harriet Martineau (1802–76) spent five weeks in Washington, DC, in 1835 and found a dizzying array of personality types and conflicting manners reflecting the country's parochial divisions; there were "pert newspaper reporters," "heaps of newspapers" at breakfast time, and such clamor about politics that privacy was hard to come by. According to her, the city was only a place for persons "who love dissipation, persons who love to watch the game of politics, and those who make a study of strong minds under strong excitements." In private, she found, conversation was usually intelligent, thoughtful, and genuine; in public, life was boisterous and tiring. Political arguments were rarely resolved. This critique, too, sounds strangely familiar.[3]

Not all British-authored books on the United States were negative in their assessments. There were converts, notable among these John Bristed (1778–1855), who arrived on American shores when he was in his late twenties, having already published several works in his native land. During the War of 1812, he ecstatically praised the people of the United States as "the legitimate offspring of the most enlightened nation in the elder world," "with the best blood of Europe flowing along all their veins." His book *America and Her Resources*, published in London in 1818, compared the governments of England and the United States at length, finding the latter "daily and hourly acquiring strength," its institutions increasingly stable. The "child and rival" of Britain was "rapidly emerging into unparalleled national greatness." Bristed went on to marry a widowed daughter of the German-born fur-trading millionaire John Jacob Astor and practiced law in New York before entering the clergy in New England.[4]

"The Height and Consummation of Mortal Glory"

From 1815 to 1832, Washington Irving traveled in the opposite direction as Trollope, Chevalier, Martineau, and Bristed, composing tales that came to his mind in England, Scotland, France, and Germany, and, most passionately, in dusty corners of mystery-laden Spain, where lines could be drawn from the Old World to the New. No matter what genre he wrote in—satirical, sentimental, gothic, or straightforward biography—he specialized in reconstituting bygone eras. What he seemed to realize before others was that nostalgic feeling could be infused into multiple genres. Writing history and biography, he influenced the way his fellow Americans reassessed their composite character. Remarkably, he did most of this work in Europe.

Irving's closest confidant back in Manhattan, the financially comfortable Henry Brevoort, asked him in 1821 if he planned to return home in the near future. From Paris, the author answered that life abroad had brought him luck. "I have," he wrote, "by catching the gleams of sunshine in my cloudy mind, managed to open to myself an avenue to some degree of profit & reputation." After the appearance of his instant classic, *The Sketch Book of Geoffrey Crayon*, with its immortal myths "Rip Van Winkle" and "Legend of Sleepy Hollow," he was enjoying a transatlantic reputation unsurpassed by any living American writer, and yet he was still anxious about finances. A professional author could not rest on his laurels for long. Relying on his busi-

nessman brother Ebenezer and the well-heeled Brevoort to ne-
gotiate with New York publishers, he went wherever stories
could be plucked from local history. He had to keep writing.[5]

In 1825, Irving was asked by the Scottish publisher John
Constable to write a biography of his namesake, George Washington. It no doubt would have been a financially remunerative
undertaking, as Washington's birthday was celebrated every year
with well-attended military parades. But while nearer the end
of his life Irving would do as Constable asked, producing a five-
volume record of Washington's life, at this early date he de-
murred, saying that he felt "incapable of executing" such a work.
"I stand in too great awe of it." But the very next year, he crossed
the Pyrenees and found himself writing a biography that was
nothing if not ambitious; one could argue that it changed the
way most Americans viewed their past. Irving's subject was a
fifteenth-century mariner from Genoa, Italy, who, in Irving's
hands, came off as uncannily Washington-esque.[6]

Cristoforo Colombo's Anglicized name of Columbus had
been woven into the new nation's sense of its history from the
start, though the discoverer was known only in an abbreviated
way. Noah Webster's 1791 *The Little Reader's Assistant* supposed
a patriotic education should include "the story of Columbus."
Irving's 1828 *Life and Voyages of Christopher Columbus* was the
first English-language life of the explorer and the first publication in which the name Washington Irving (rather than one of
his choice pseudonyms) appeared on the title page. The author
had lived among the beau monde of Genoa for two months
when he visited Italy nearly a quarter-century earlier. Accorded
carte blanche in Madrid in 1826, the now forty-three-year-old
author enjoyed unprecedented access to Spanish government
archives, which enabled him to transform the explorer into a
symbol of conspicuous courage, consummate leadership, calm
confidence, and unbroken determination—everything George
Washington was thought to be. It was not an accident.[7]

The man behind Irving's biography of Columbus was a career diplomat and native of Boston, Alexander Hill Everett (1790–1847), the older brother of Edward Everett. Late chargé d'affaires in the Netherlands, he had only recently accepted the upgrade to US minister to Spain, an honor conferred on him by his longtime patron, now the sixth president, John Quincy Adams.

Everett's 1822 book on European politics earned a commendation from Thomas Jefferson. Its 1827 sequel, the blandly titled *America*, was in fact a rapturous take on his nation's glorious beginnings and its ever-increasing prospects. America's "benefactors" were men of boundless energy and monumental purpose. Eyeing the new republics of South America with hope, Everett contemplated the possibility that perhaps Simón Bolivar was another Washington, then caught himself: "The world had been created for six thousand years, before the first or rather the unique Washington," entrusted with power because of his "unspotted hands and blameless heart." His opinion was "decisive with multitudes"; "he was worshipped, as it were like a god."

Everett was similarly effusive about Patrick Henry, remembered at this time as William Wirt depicted him in his clever (if unreliable) 1817 biography. In Everett's view, the Revolution's famed orator may have lacked grace, but he was vintage American: "The language of the simple Virginia farmer melted like honey from his lips, and was alternately endowed with a Ciceronian charm, that captivated all hearts, and pointed with passionate emphasis, that struck down opposition like thunder."[8]

Tapping a more recent memory, Everett held that the coincident deaths of two of the founders, Adams and Jefferson, on the fiftieth Fourth of July, in 1826, could only be seen as "the height and consummation of mortal glory" for the providential nation, the strength of which he ascribed to a natural environment that had long supported a spirit of independence among its worthy settlers. He knew old Adams well: "I have sometimes found my eyes suffused with tears," he remarked, "by the mere emotion of being in his company." He'd not had a comparable encounter with Jefferson but saw sublimity in his "strong taste for contemplative pursuits" and the "lucid current of his language." The auspicious departures of Adams and Jefferson stimulated the author to propose that a site for national pilgrimage be established at George Washington's Mount Vernon, where all the Revolutionary fathers could be remembered together; Mount Vernon's status as a working farm struck him as a "profanation" instead of "consecration" of historical memory. It should be "purchased by the people," Everett said, and converted into a place of meditation.[9]

Everett began practicing this hyper-nationalist script in his early twenties, when he took his first trip abroad as John Quincy Adams's private secretary in St. Petersburg. Well-to-do Russian "ladies" did not equal their American counterparts in "native feeling," he told his diary, and despite well-traveled Europeans' better command of languages, "in cultivation of mind, in the elegant modesty which gives in grace to every action, . . . the beauties of Columbia are far superior." Well before he urged Irving to take up Columbus, then, the diplomat had shown that he was plenty enamored with the story of America.[10]

They'd met in Paris in 1825. Everett was barely settled in Madrid when he invited Irving to move into the neighborhood. Sending a diplomatic passport (for protection along the road), he initially thought Irving should translate a new Spanish work about Columbus rather than compose one of his own. On arrival, the enterprising Irving saw a better opportunity and leaned on Everett to obtain permission from the host government for full access to the "archives of the Indias."[11]

Madrid proved to be more than a detour. Spain's distant past became a calling for Irving, nearly a spiritual commitment. Having previously satirized the colonizing process in *A History of New-York*, he opened to a brighter vision of history that

Everett and he now shared. A young Henry Wadsworth Longfellow visited as Irving was writing *Life and Voyages of Columbus* and recalled the "playful humor" of a man who encouraged
his fellow authors with "an entire absence of all literary jealousy." Longfellow would go on to write the memorable poem
"Paul Revere's Ride" in 1860 and keep alive the virtuous exploits of a patriot hero.

Considering its scope, *Life and Voyages of Columbus* could
only have been written in a passionate sprint. Nervously awaiting the reception of his biography back home, Irving trod in
Columbus's footsteps across southern Spain. From Seville, he
wrote Everett of his visit to Palos, where the discoverer set sail
in 1492, and to the church where Columbus "watched and
prayed all night after his return" in fulfillment of a promise he'd
made to himself during a raging storm at sea. "In short," wrote
the first-time biographer in a romantic pose, "I sought everything that had any connection with him and his history."[12]

Fifteen years and several Spanish-themed volumes later, his
old friend Paulding having just completed a stint as secretary of
the navy, Washington Irving the storyteller-historian assumed the
same ministerial post Everett occupied in the late 1820s. At the
very moment his countrymen were plotting to carve up the North
American territories once known as New Spain, he would be
feasting on the adoration he received from the Spanish people.

In the late 1820s, without any such crystal ball, Everett and
Irving concluded a pact. Each intent on growing their reputations at home, they arranged to help the other in a way that appears ethically problematic through modern eyes. Everett
praised Irving's body of work in the pages of the *North American Review*, getting a jump on any less complimentary critics
who might be waiting in the wings. Irving, in turn, arranged
for John Murray, London's most celebrated publisher, to take
on Everett's book *America* in 1828, the year after its Philadelphia first printing.[13]

The Watershed Years in American Letters

Everett was a biased interpreter of political trends, but he was not a skilled storyteller. Others, like the prolific Cooper and Paulding, took care that American historical themes should enter the literature that was marketed to European readers. They and others joined Irving in reshaping the literary landscape, Cooper most of all. Cooper specialized in vivid descriptions of the literal landscape that he incorporated into his fiction. He knew the forests, undulating hills, waterfalls, and summits of his native New York State. Like Irving, Cooper advanced his career by living for a period of years in Europe, doing much to Americanize the dewy language of poets Wordsworth and Coleridge.

Connections and separations. America needed the Old World to establish itself, to publicize its republic of letters abroad, where it mattered most. Absent true acceptance there, one could not claim to be speaking the language of the ages. The American nation was being punished because it was not imbued with a cultural history of any magnitude. Its land literally bumped up against the savage state of man. To engage with their Old World counterparts, American authors pursued mystery and sublimity—Cooper especially.

Where Irving drew an emotional connection between his larger-than-life Columbus and the father figure Washington, Cooper made the larger-than-life Washington a literal character in his first successful novel, *The Spy* (as noted in chapter 1). As the main action ends, Cooper transports his hero, Harvey Birch, into the future, from 1781 to 1814. In the book's final scene, he dies in battle at Niagara. Chapter 35 connects the two wars, finding its closure in posthumous triumph:

> The body of Washington had long lain moldering in the tomb; but as time was fast obliterating the slight impressions

of political enmity or personal envy, his name was hourly receiving new luster, and his worth and integrity each moment became more visible, not only to his countrymen, but to the world. He was already the acknowledged hero of an age of reason and truth.[14]

American writers felt compelled to recur to the founding narrative as a buffer against the inherited power of the Old World, whose superiority was symbolized by a grandeur they knew they lacked: great libraries and museums, Greek and Roman ruins. Beginning in the 1820s, too, more nonelite Americans began crossing the Atlantic to experience the Grand Tour. If the raw-boned, liberty-obsessed "Brother Jonathan" was starting to outgrow his parochial origins, he was still not seen as John Bull's equal where poetic expression reigned. No one in American publishing felt conflicted about embracing good writing, regardless of its source.[15]

Writers in the Irving-Cooper mold held to traditional forms while performing a kind of cultural shapeshifting. On the other hand, a number of literary critics stateside had begun to decry the profane poetry of the late, lascivious Lord Byron while touting the "native genius" of their high-principled countrymen and women. In 1824, Jared Sparks took over editing tasks from Edward Everett at the *North American Review*, and castigated William Wordsworth for too realistically depicting the poor and thus descending from the high calling of the poet. A new breed of critic was responding to accusations routinely hurled across the pond at the unrefined Americans.[16]

Sparks's rough words for Wordsworth smack of a certain irony. In a footnote to his 1820 review of Irving's *Sketch Book*, the editor of the prestigious *Edinburgh Review*, Francis Jeffrey (later Lord Jeffrey), praises the *North American Review*, describing it as "by far the most promising production of the press of that country that has ever come to our hands. It is written with great spirit, learning, and ability." Then, notably, he adds that "though abundantly patriotic, or rather national, there is nothing offensive or absolutely unreasonable in the tone of its politics."[17]

The "plain" American, in the mode employed by Sparks, was proud of the "vivacity" of his language. (These were well-worn terms.) He did not lapse into a Yankee or a rustic dialect except in the consciously exaggerated reconstruction of those forms in historical novels. Even after Noah Webster had announced the "decline" of British English and actively campaigned for Americans to assume authority over their linguistic future, no American writer was prepared to deny the superiority (or originality) of Addison, Goldsmith, and Sterne, any more than they were prepared to ignore the impact of Isaac Newton on scientific theory or divorce themselves from Shakespeare: they worshipped British-inspired genius in all its forms. Seeking signs of reciprocity, Americans could not but air their grievances, their perception of a seemingly intractable problem with the English-speaking metropolis, namely, London's unwillingness to acknowledge the dignity that flowed from *their* version of the language.

At this moment, New England and New York shared power as separate hubs of literary life. At the center of a select group of men and women who injected their lifeblood into a printing nation stood the highly quotable essayist, lecturer, and truth-seeker Ralph Waldo Emerson (1803–82). "Life is our dictionary," Emerson proclaimed in an 1837 address, "The American Scholar." Reading was a virtuous passion that fed experience, but his philosophy of life privileged living fully over thinking narrowly. "The office of the scholar is to cheer, to raise, and to guide . . . , cataloguing obscure and nebulous stars of the human mind." A scholar had to be "the world's eye[,] . . . the world's heart." He sounded solemn, almost devotional, in his message, presenting his country as the ideal site for a soulful engagement with Nature's gifts. "The better part of every man feels," he said, trusting his audience. "This is my music; this is myself." This was his constant theme, the inherent power possessed by each individual mind.

Building to the conclusion of the address and answering the lament of many good people as to the failings of the social world, he drew on Shakespeare for emotional support. "The time is infected with Hamlet's unhappiness," he acknowledged, "'sicklied o'er with the pale cast of thought.'" But then, to inspire, to elevate the minds of his hearers, he pointed out that "this time, like all times, is a very good one, if we but know what to do with it." Known for his serene appearance, fastidiousness, and idealism, Emerson breathed a liberal-nationalist-individualist mantra; he spoke for the self-created persona that attached to the "new" American. The inflated sense of grandeur, inwardly reflected, would animate (and haunt) Walt Whitman, too.[18]

The "Knickerbocker school" that largely descended on Manhattan from New England owed its initial distinction to the Manhattanite Irving—the original Knickerbocker. But Irving was not their leader, nor was he any kind of public intellectual. He lacked Emersonian self-confidence. Personally modest, he did no more than connect these rising writers, one at a time, with publishers abroad.

The sociable Knickerbockers consciously aimed at shaping a "national literature" that could stand toe-to-toe with Britain's best. They had the so-called American Byron, Fitz-Greene Halleck, who doubled as the private secretary for the tightwad millionaire John Jacob Astor. Another forgotten giant of American letters was the precocious poet ("American Wordsworth") William Cullen Bryant, who became a powerful newspaper editor. The romantic painter and essayist Thomas Cole was also a part of this group. Cooper, occasionally irritable, remarkably prolific, wrote eleven picturesque novels during the decade of the 1820s alone. These men and others who looked promising communed regularly, dined in style, and drank with politicos at the Shakespeare

Tavern. A shift in perceptions occurred: the literati were not second rate; they were not copyists or provincials. The distinctiveness, seriousness, and interesting subjects they took up enabled at least some of them to find a European following.[19]

The 1820s were watershed years in the emergence of a recognizably American culture. A spirit of "improvement" in the form of a rash of building seized the country, as fast-growing Gotham claimed its centrality as a financial and commercial powerhouse, funding progress. The 363-mile-long Erie Canal symbolized engineering genius, connecting the Port of New York to the Great Lakes while giving pride in achievement to a growing citizenry increasingly on the move. American newspaper and magazine editors were quick to pick up on instances where European commentators, ordinarily stingy in their praise of anything American, pointed to an engineering success. A French government official mused in 1822 that, while young as a nation, the United States had "established more communications by water than old Europe in all its states." Such unalloyed tribute rarely went unreported.

Accompanying the rapid development of infrastructure were important changes in American English. An emotional intensity that was not there before appeared in published works. This new lyricism helped bridge the gap between conventional literary emotion and the personal emotions of writers. This same phenomenon appears in familiar letters, with such phrases as "friend of my heart" and "beloved companion" creeping into letter-borne dialogue. Religious and philosophical disquisitions were likewise now framed in a modest (less academic, less wooden) language. Stock phrases were fewer, though letter writers still inserted quotes from great writers and epic poets into the folded pages of letters.[20]

Letter writers did not just tell of personal news but sought to react in language all their own in order to make a more meaningful connection. "Do you remember how I . . . ?" one would write.

"Oh, you would not be so irreverent as to dare tamper with a na-ture like mine." Self-disclosure was okay: inflection—a rhythm, a mood—took the place of artful performance. As a cultural con-cept, conversation now required real evidence of one's humanity; informality assumed value.[21]

The language of affection happily lost itself in the beating heart of history. We see this in the slow transformation of nos-talgia as a concept. From the Greek "return" and "suffering," the word was defined in medical literature dating to the previous century as a weakness, a defect, a "distemper" among those who were emotionally unstable because of their inordinate desire to return to their home country—in French, "mal du pays." Thought to afflict men more than women, it invisibly morphed into a generalized yearning for somewhere, something, that was past and irretrievable.

The word "nostalgia" did not take on its present meaning of sentimental longing until many years later. In the nineteenth century, it gradually lost its sting; the experience of longing, or wistfulness, appeared a perfectly natural aesthetic concept, an emotion that was entirely reasonable. "The longing sailor talked of home," went an amateur poem of 1830. No doubt diary writ-ing with its increasingly personal, emotive content was as popular as it was during the first several decades of the nineteenth century because it captured the satisfaction felt in reliving pleasant sensa-tions and human connections, and spoke to the deeper psycho-logical need to "write away" anxious thoughts. The diary form, a minor mania, was a supplement to education.[22]

Christopher Columbus: Cash Cow

As Irving got to work on Columbus, he was aware of the height-ened sensibility now in vogue, because his own antiquarian fas-cination with yesteryear's productions had significantly contrib-uted to it. In *The Sketch Book* tales that take place in an almost

magical British Library or in the "literary catacomb" of Westminster Abbey ("The Art of Book-Making" and "The Mutabil-
ity of Literature"), his alter ego Geoffrey Crayon, responding to
the touch of precious books and manuscripts, is instantly transported to a world that no longer exists but communicates to
Crayon through an internal dialogue. He senses immortality in
a history that speaks. A significant part of Irving's hold on his
reader is his ability to convey the "touch" of the discoverer, both
the discoverer on the high seas and his awestruck descendant,
the discoverer in the ghostly realm of the archive.

Irving's Columbus is the mystical standard-bearer who "in-
vents" America. We meet an emotional being who does not
speak our language. It becomes clear to the reader by the second volume that any hunger for a heroic, American-style narrative will not be met without certain distinctions having to be
drawn. Irving will not deny his explorer's singular importance,
but disturbing traits are not to be swept entirely under the rug.
An enterprising spirit granted Columbus a proto-American
imagination, yet he remained double sided, purportedly engaged
in a humane project but dangerous when he let his imagination
get the better of him. Of his attempt to ascertain whether he'd
landed in Asia upon encountering the natives of Hispaniola in
1492, Irving remarks that "it is curious to observe how inge-
niously the imagination of Columbus deceived him at every step,
and how he wove every thing into a uniform web of false
conclusions."

We see a similar kind of hesitation in Irving's assessment
of the explorer when he describes how he renegotiated the terms
of his mission with Ferdinand and Isabella:

> The artless manner in which, in his letter to the sovereigns,
> he mingles up the rhapsodies and dreams of his imagination,
> with simple facts, and sound practical observations, pour-
> ing them forth with a kind of scriptural solemnity and po-

etry of language, is one of the most striking illustrations of a character richly compounded of extraordinary and apparently contradictory elements."[23]

And in summing up the explorer's character, Irving is yet again squeezed when he is obliged to embrace the overwrought Columbus he has drawn:

He was decidedly a visionary, but a visionary of an uncommon and successful kind. The manner in which his ardent, imaginative, and mercurial nature was controlled by a powerful judgment and directed by an acute sagacity, is the most extraordinary feature in his character. Thus governed, his imagination, instead of exhausting itself in idle flights, lent aid to his judgment, and enabled him to form conclusions at which common minds could never have arrived.[24]

Irving uses the word "imagination" to characterize the admiral countless times across the Columbus volumes. It's alternately a "heated" imagination, an "ardent" imagination, "vivacity of imagination," "riot of the imagination," "colored by his imagination," or "he was under a spell of the imagination." It is not a word he troubles himself with at all in his equally ambitious *Life of George Washington*, though both of these "great" men were forced to contend with less deserving rivals and gave so much of themselves to their noble causes that they suffered in both body and spirit over time—persisting, as heroes do.[25]

An obvious difficulty that a still-young republic, drawing its moral authority from the example of George Washington, faced in making the historical Columbus relatable, was his deeply held Catholic faith and practice. "Religion mingled with his whole course of thoughts and actions," Irving notes decisively. "His piety was mingled with superstition, and darkened by the bigotry of the age." Reaching a point where "chimerical reveries" commanded his psyche, Columbus went so far as to pen a peevish, self-vindicating letter to a higher authority than Ferdinand and Isabella—the pope—once the Spanish king and queen lost their trust in him.[26]

Despite these failings, Irving's Columbus had to be respected for the "loftiness of spirit" that was his most prominent trait. His "noble pride" regularly caused him to make "dignified demands." He retained throughout his trials an "irrepressible buoyancy of spirit." Not until the twentieth century would the colonizer's tyrannical traits seriously tarnish Irving's largely positive portrait.[27]

One year into his research in Madrid, the author described the process of preparing his Columbus to Brevoort: "I have studied and laboured with a patience and assiduity for which I shall never get the credit." The first-time biographer distrusted the reading public. "I have lost confidence in the favourable disposition of my countrymen and look forward to cold scrutiny & stern criticism." John Murray waited for Robert Southey, England's poet laureate, to pass judgment before proceeding with the first printing. Southey forecast commercial success, although he opined that Irving's manuscript revealed "neither much power of mind nor much knowledge." Despite its cruel-sounding message, Southey's distrust of the imperfect genre of historical biography is well considered.

As things turned out, Irving's fears were misplaced and Murray's reservations unwarranted. Columbus was a cash cow: by the end of the century the multivolume history had been reprinted 175 times, making it the most widely held history in American home libraries. In light of this success, Irving decided to continue milking opportunities in Europe for a few more years so as to guarantee financial comfort adequate to ensure "a moderate independence" back in America. "My dearest affections are entirely centered in my country," he told Brevoort, and it was only the matter of personal finance that kept him away now.[28]

Ultimately, it didn't matter that the hero was flawed: his overreach and extreme religiosity situated him as a man of a different time. The story of Columbus was more important than the politics of an Old World monarchy, because it enthroned the American dream. Prior to Irving's framing of the Columbus story in a way that justified the fantasy of a perfectible America, the explorer had just been a romantic memory that poets played with now and then. All at once, thanks to Irving, Christopher Columbus was a real personality, a proto-American. If Washington was a noble herald of republican strength and judgment, his European precursor, as its first founder, "preunified" the nation by endowing a continent with world historical importance, setting it on a course to rival Europe. That is what the recreators of myth were expected to confer upon culture: a sense of inevitability.

Irving achieved his aim as a transatlantic moderate with a conservative message. "Greatness" arises in men by way of their "mastery over the imperfections of their nature," he says. "Their noblest actions are sometimes struck forth by the collision of their merits and their defects." The *Port-Folio* pointed out that Irving's Columbus confirmed the maxim that "genius always educates itself," a claim also often made in connection with Washington. Despite gaps in formal training, both men had keen powers of observation and profited from hard-won experience.[29]

In *Life of George Washington*, published on the eve of the Civil War, Irving summarizes his subject's character this way: "Prudence, firmness, sagacity, moderation, and overruling judgment, an immovable justice, courage that never faltered." In the case of Columbus, it was "a daring but irregular genius" that led a voyager "to conclusions far beyond the intellectual vision of his contemporaries." Decision marked out a creditable character in this age, but it still needed to be tempered by dispassionate thinking to be socially acceptable. It's what made Washington momentously greater than Columbus.[30]

Paulding's Washington

Great man biography was nothing new, but it reached new heights in the middle decades of the nineteenth century with triumphalist narratives of Columbus, Washington, and associated players from the age of discovery and age of revolutions. Such works were bound to present a comforting view of civilizing progress, a linear expression of history's timeline in which the seeds of a great nation were planted and nurtured by inspired unselfish doers, risk-takers, and imaginers. The ultimate message was always the same: America was the main benefactor of humankind. Like the maudlin historical romances that began pouring from American presses after the War of 1812, historical biographies aimed to offer an irresistible tale, one that urged readers to identify with the moral strength embodied by the hero.[31]

These treatments all drew attention to the subject's humane temperament. While portraiture continued to feature facial expressions barren of emotion, biography was increasingly characterized by a compulsion to inject private elements. James Boswell's groundbreaking *Life of Samuel Johnson* (1791) served as a kind of template; it suggested that such anecdotal elements were of historical interest and thus encouraged writers to include more of them. Nineteenth-century novels were deeply concerned with intimate moments in daily life; biography followed suit, actively attempting to stimulate an interest in human complexity, selling "authenticity" without ignoring the subject's moral character.[32]

John Paulding, who played a lead role in the capture of Major André, was a man of modest means who became a part of Revolutionary lore. He was hailed by General Washington himself for his service to the cause. In 1835, James Kirke Paulding, the honored militiaman's first cousin, kept the nation's love fest going by humanizing Washington in a well-received biography. He cited a family insider "whose authority I cannot doubt," crediting information that came from the lips of "Old Jeremy," an enslaved man still living and "in full possession of his faculties." During their interview, Jeremy reported a juicy vignette, telling Paulding that the first couple's very first meeting was "entirely accidental," that "Massa George" accepted a spontaneous invitation to spend an hour or two at the mansion of a gentleman he ran into on the road at some distance from home. Smitten there by the widow Martha Custis, he delayed his travel extra hours.

Paulding the biographer was proud to have uncovered the private habits of the great man, who breakfasted on "four small corn-cakes, split, buttered, and divided into quarters," enjoyed his tea, and turned in each night at nine o'clock. According to all who served him at home, "he exacted prompt attention and obedience. . . . The eye of the master was everywhere." These few details of ordinariness aside, a founding family's private life could never be on display in a truly revealing way, which the biographer had to admit. "No one ever intruded on his sacred privacy."

This was what readers of the 1830s were limited to, as they did not have access to the sort of report that Benjamin Latrobe's as yet unpublished journal of 1796 made available. While Washington had "something uncommonly majestic and commanding in his walk," Latrobe commented, at meals he "was frequently entirely silent for many minutes, during which time an awkwardness seemed to prevail in everyone present." Not exactly the picture of social gallantry that nineteenth-century Washington biographies required.[33]

Where Irving's Columbus is a superstitious and occasionally misguided man, Paulding's Washington is a portrait of religious rationality inspiring calm action. On the basis of "piety was erected the superstructure of his virtues"; his "noble course" derived from a "manly steadiness of character"; "in times of dismay and suffering, we find him the inspiring soul"; "his untiring industry enabled him to attend to every thing; his sagacity to provide against all emergencies"; he avoided "all the delusions of excess . . . misleading the judgment"; he maintained "a steady and unwavering perseverance in the pursuit of great and good ends." "The courage of Washington," Paulding concludes, "was both morally and physically perfect. It was that of both sentiment and nerve; it was not merely the absence of all fear, but the impulse of a strong, unchangeable, and vigorous feeling, prompting him to exposure and exertion in the cause of his country." The common thread here bespoke a special destiny that embraced manly adventure, a commitment to challenges from which lesser beings shrank, and a steady faith in his own judgment. Columbus and Washington were both "benefactors of mankind," but there could only be one (emotionally undemonstrative yet fascinating) Washington. In his review of Paulding's *Washington*, no less a critic than Edgar Allan Poe detected "forcible, rich, vivid, and comprehensive English," after which, he said, younger writers should model themselves.[34]

Of those whose labors made the decade of the 1830s a real turning point in patriotic biography, Jared Sparks deserves special mention for cementing Washington's position at the center of America's story. He scoured the country collecting Washington correspondence for republication, and in April 1830, when James Madison told him he was unwilling to entrust such documents to the mail, Sparks hopped a steamboat along the Potomac, transferred by stage to Fredericksburg, and rode west from there to Montpelier, where over five days the last of the founding fathers fed him with anecdotes: how Washington, though a regular church-goer, never had much to say about Christianity; how Hamilton had actually disparaged Washington, despite owing him massively for advancing his political career; and finally, from the unchallenged lips of James Madison, an account of the "accident" through which the despised three-fifths compromise was arrived at, which artificially inflated the population of the slaveholding states by allowing human property to be counted for the purpose of securing representation in the House of Representatives.

Sparks spent time among Madison's cache of letters, making copies for what became his twelve-volume *The Life and Writings of George Washington*. He found the octogenarian "busy in arranging his papers," taking pains to recover from the living relatives of former colleagues letters he had written but not made copies of—all for the sake of preservation. Sparks affirmed that Madison was "sprightly, varied, fertile in his topics, and felicitous in his descriptions." He comprehended the national creation story as no one else could, having served in various Congresses and in the executive branch for most of the years between 1780 and 1817. He knew, as Sparks did, that in accumulating valuable texts he was acting on behalf of posterity. Soon, interpreters of the founding archive would assume total control over the narrative, either to paint the past with a fine brush or slap on a thick coat of melodrama. One year, Sparks would attend Harvard commencement with a show-and-tell item for the ages: the "pass" Benedict Arnold had given to Major André and the papers that the doomed spy had hidden in his boots.[35]

Discoveries were being made that adorned the evolving national self-image. At the same time that more and more Americans were swelling with pride at the thought that the United States was a fruited land colonized by an intrepid mariner's imagination, a rival, but no less prideful, story demanded to be heard: "Northmen" (Scandinavians) had discovered America! Prompted by the 1837 publication in English of Danish philologist Carl Christian Rafn's *Antiquitates Americanae*, New Englanders were mesmerized by a new possibility: that a superior people endowed with an abundant energy had preceded Columbus on the North American continent, leaving their traces in Massachusetts and elsewhere.

As twelfth-century Vikings made new waves in the nineteenth, Alexander and Edward Everett published separate pieces attesting to the credible connection between the Northmen of yore and the modern New England identity. It was a history "founded in ancient authorities," according to Alexander, and a tradition involving "Norwegian navigators," according to Edward, who, wanting to have it both ways, added that the Northmen did nothing that diminished the deservedness Irving accorded to the Italian Columbus in reaping the "glory of discovering our continent."

The ancient settlement of "Vinland," supposed a "missionary enterprise" to the Indians, was said to have endured for three centuries, nearly to the time of Columbus, and could now be creatively joined to the story of the Pilgrim fathers in reaffirming the region's unique cultural legacy. Irving's Columbus, Washington's documented life in letters, and the obscure but suggestive Vinland sagas were all puffed-up versions of history that gave greater legitimacy to America's claim to glory.[36]

"An Emanation of the Human Spirit"

Washington Irving returned to the United States in 1832 as an admirer of President Andrew Jackson's storybook career and political instincts. For the remainder of that decade, the legend-maker found new ways to remake America, attributing some of the same qualities he found in Columbus to western heroes of the present. He chronicled their exploits in a pair of books: *A Tour on the Prairies* (1835) and *The Adventures of Captain Bonneville* (1838).

A Tour on the Prairies records how Captain Jesse Bean, a true frontiersman and veteran of General Jackson's New Orleans and

Florida campaigns, kept his army rangers in line while guiding Irving and his party on a months-long adventure through Indian country. Captain Bean, "a thorough woodsman, and a first-rate hunter," looked the part in his "leathern hunting-shirt and leggings, and a leathern foraging cap." His undisciplined men did not inspire much confidence, but the Arkansan officer was himself good natured and demonstrably brave. Like the cast of a good picaresque novel, the men who populate Irving's sprightly travelogue are a motley bunch: a longwinded French Creole from Missouri who serves as cook, a fun-seeking Swiss count who gets separated from the party during a buffalo hunt, the thirty-year-old nephew of the architect Benjamin Henry Latrobe, and the group's putative leader, a self-satisfied Connecticut attorney appointed by the government to scope out resettlement lands for eastern Indians.[37]

The subject of *The Adventures of Captain Bonneville* is Benjamin Bonneville (1796–1878), a West Pointer, who struck Irving's fancy as a romantic figure reminiscent of Sterne's eccentric character Corporal Trim in *Tristram Shandy*. The captain had inherited from his French emigrant father "a happy temperament, festive imagination, and a simplicity of heart." The elder Bonneville was a Shakespeare lover, to boot. But something happened when a civilized man entered the Rocky Mountains for a stretch of time: an emotional shift took place inside his mind that was subsequently reflected in an outward manner. Indian modes and bearing, previously derided as both heartless and out of step with historical progress, seemed completely rational and appropriate. Captain Bonneville's "excitable imagination" made Irving giddy because the mountain West returned a feeling of liberated manhood from a lost past.[38]

As Bonneville prepares for an adventure, the chronicler of his life-in-progress indulges a heart-pumping communion with his all-American subject. It is worth quoting at length:

It is not easy to do justice to the exulting feelings of the worthy captain at finding himself at the head of a stout band of hunters, trappers, and woodmen; fairly launched on the broad prairies, with his face to the boundless West. The tamest inhabitant of cities, the veriest spoiled child of civilization, feels his heart dilate and his pulse beat high on finding himself on horseback in the glorious wilderness; what then must be the excitement of one whose imagination had been stimulated by a residence on the frontier, and to whom the wilderness was a region of romance! His hardy followers partook of his excitement. Most of them had already experienced the wild freedom of savage life, and looked forward to a renewal of past scenes of adventure and exploit.[39]

Bonneville's "band of adventurers" are "animated and joyous" on embarkation, before the roughness of the terrain tests their mettle. It is a story of leadership as well as resilience, and so we get the following refrain: "The idea of risk and hardship, however, only served to stimulate the adventurous spirit of the captain." Amid swirling winds and wintry cold, as horses stumbled on jagged rocks along precipitous paths, the men "felt their hearts quailing under their multiplied hardships." There are place names not yet known by their future associations with US history, like Yellowstone and Bighorn.[40]

From Admiral Columbus to Captain Bonneville, all of Irving's adventurers were meant to be seen as sanitized examples of a masculine spirit that gave the common man of America his uncommonness. As a new but obviously potent genre, the western claimed for itself a distinctly American flavor. In his classic text *Virgin Land*, Henry Nash Smith describes how "yeasty nationalism" converted fur traders and mountain trappers into immodest heroes. As popular literature proliferated, their exploits became ever more exaggerated.[41]

Irving's romance of the Rocky Mountains, visualized from the literary furnace of Manhattan, anticipated the poetic voice of another urbanite, Walt Whitman, whose "Pioneers! O Pioneers!" celebrated the "resistless restless race" of the westward bound, symbolic builders of a new, improved America. "We the youthful sinewy races," Whitman swells, "so impatient, full of action, full of manly pride and friendship." The message was unmistakable: America could never become effete. One had only to experience the vast spaces to know natural abundance. Fear could be conquered out west.[42]

The myth the writers spun seemed inviolable until one left the printed page. Reality was closer to what is related in the unglamorous 1844 diary of a US naval officer stationed in territorial Florida on the eve of statehood. His is a hardboiled story of the instability of ordinary life. It says as much as one can about the world of a mobile, but otherwise average, American.

Edward C. Anderson's mission, if it be called that, was to guard government forest land from poachers. Seminole warriors had only recently been sent packing and non-Indian society stood on a shaky foundation. Aboard a steamer, Anderson, in his thirtieth year, observed his fellow sailors with a critical eye, assessing the pros and cons of each man's character. The commander was "fussy, hard hearted, fond of popularity," yet "amiable to a fault." The purser: "careless in his duties, but respectful," while the quartermaster was "very well educated, Son of a Clergymen," out of his element, "not a seaman." Among the crew were several deemed "a drunkard at times" but otherwise competent. Then there was the prodigal: "an excellent man since he was flogged." Some of Anderson's choice adjectives include "respectful," "sober, steady," and "desperate when drunk."[43]

His was a fatiguing way of life for the most part. As he dodged mosquitos in the vicinity of Jacksonville or foraged for fruit and wild game with minimal success, the diligent diarist recorded the details of days of boredom, punctuating his entries with descriptions of old memories he dredged up to occupy himself. In St. Augustine he writes: "Old associations thick and strong came over me for when I was last here I was upon the point of being married & felt lovesick even unto death." He had a wife at home now; a relative's letter informed him that she was seriously ill. For weeks after, he lingered "in ignorance of whether or not I had a wife to greet me on my return, and my mind was tortured by a thousand surmises of hope & fear." As soon as he had access to a Georgia newspaper, he pored over the obituary notices, afraid to find his wife's name. His happiness daily hung in the balance.[44]

Not surprisingly, he relays combat stories, some with good outcomes, some with tragic endings. Catching sight of someone he recognized while ashore in St. Augustine, Anderson recalls the man as one member of a scouting party that came under fire during the late war with the Seminoles. An officer ordered him to "take a tree," but he refused to take cover, saying, "I am an English Soldier, Lieutenant. I never did such a thing in my life." Strolling on another beach under a bright moon, Anderson reflects on the first wife of a lieutenant who was "killed & scalped by the Indians" a few years before. Throughout the diary he straightforwardly catalogues reminders of dangers faced and lives upended.

The Natives Anderson wrote about were, conventionally, "a villainous looking set, without one redeeming trait about them." In one notable episode, the only individual in the negotiating party who held Anderson's interest was the interpreter, a Black man named Sampson, "the very beau ideal of a handsome fellow"; "his features were perfect & his figure, thin, lithe, graceful." He was "the finest looking man I had ever seen."[45]

Sailing to the Florida Keys and back over two months, Anderson arrived home in Savannah to find his wife restored to health but his beloved sister Georgia dying. "The physician had given her up and the poor girl had been told to prepare herself for death. . . . [I] stood mute & stupefied beside her." With her last breath, he silently cursed God. His siblings cut locks of Georgia's hair to preserve as keepsakes, waiting a full day before laying her to rest to honor her last wish that they not bury her until "a sufficient time had elapsed to convince all" that she was truly gone. They delayed the burial twenty-four hours, when signs of decay became apparent.[46]

Ten days later he had resumed government service and was anchored off Key West when a prisoner was brought onboard, confined in "double irons" and placed below deck. The detainee was an abolitionist who had helped some slaves escape to the West Indies and who was to be tried for his "crime" in Pensacola. By the time they dropped anchor at the gulf port, Anderson wasn't thinking about the abolitionist and his possible fate; his mind was still on his beloved sister's deathbed scene. "I have been very dull of late," he wrote, "and have many sad thoughts connected with my late visit to Savannah." He saw himself sitting on the sofa beside his brother, the two of them cradling Georgia's body in their arms until it was time to proceed with the burial. "Her warm kiss was never to greet me again," he penned from Pensacola, two months after the event he was still struggling to accept as final.[47]

As to the bright scenes of adventure travel promised by Irving and others, Anderson had this self-reflective rejoinder: "I do not object to the woods when within the pale of civilization where one may get his letters [delivered] and the ordinary comforts of life, but to be enclosed in a fresh water Bayou with the miasma assailing one's nerves as the sun goes down & the heat during the night so intolerable . . . is more than my philosophy can bear." At his next birthday, his philosophic jaundice had not improved: "I don't know whether to rejoice or grieve . . . in the flush of health & strength. . . . Who can tell what the future may have in store for me."[48]

His American life is not the American history modern America wants to think about. Nor was this capable navy man exactly a model of patriotism either. After service in the Mexican American War, and creditable work as mayor of Savannah, Edward C. Anderson, a sensitive diarist, went on to conduct a series of assignments in the Confederate Navy.

The Stories We Tell about Ourselves

Insistence on American superiority over the inglorious systems of the Old World led boosters to focus on the need for the United States to overpower Europe's colonizers in the Western Hemisphere. Popular perceptions fed by literary works joined a growing impatience in newsprint. As a British sociologist has recently observed, "There is a tendency—especially among Americans—to think about the United States as if it were an emanation of the human spirit, as if its existence and its constitutional arrangements were a bloodless product of the Enlightenment, John Locke, the genius of the Founding Fathers, and the pure democratic spirit." The nineteenth century did yet not grasp what is better understood today, that US territory was won through a violent "elimination contest," little different from the intermittent wars of the Old World.[49]

The American epic has always been more Washington than Columbus in privileging the hero's moral courage above even his courage in facing the elements. All-American hero worship ultimately combined intrepid action with gallantry in one whose calm inner resolve attested to self-awareness that he stood for good. Credible men aim to do the right thing. They never fall prey to selfish foppery. They are individuals of whom the nation can feel justly proud.

The mythological claims of American exceptionalism and rugged individualism have come under review in the twenty-first century. But in the 1820s and 1830s, that engine was just revving up thanks to the efforts of Sparks, Paulding, Irving, Cooper, and their imitators. With Washington leading the way forward and his thuggish, swaggering bastard child, Andrew Jackson, close behind, the rhetoric of nationalist literature grew apace.

Jackson was the subject of a politically self-serving biography composed in the aftermath of his triumph at the Battle of New Orleans. Nicknamed "the Hero" in popular texts and designated "Old Hickory" after the hardness and toughness of that species of wood, Jackson embraced the legend two of his subordinates in the army constructed for him. It began with his preternatural refusal, at age thirteen, to shine the boots of an imperious British officer, an affair that nearly cost the lad his life. Young and brash and with slight education, the orphan Jackson became that quintessential self-made man of the early republic. Coarse by nature, he could be agreeable—"knightly"— when he wanted. For years he braved uninhabited stretches of the southern frontier, and after defeating the best the British military threw at him, he became the second coming of Washington. In the preface to the first edition of *Life of Andrew Jackson* (1817), its surviving coauthor, John H. Eaton, guaranteed that the Napoleon-like general had no "inducement" to veer from the truth in recounting the events detailed in the biography.[50]

America's destiny was the stuff of toasts and boasts. Each Fourth of July, in every city and town, parades were followed by public oratory that celebrated the Revolution and went to great lengths to characterize the superior worth of the "U. States." In 1798, though it was a moment of deep domestic division, Noah Webster urged anniversary festivals to fortify public spirit, "enkindling the flame of national ardor." In doing so, he pointedly referred to the "debased condition" of the inhabitants of Europe: "If there is a nation on earth which enjoys the same portion of freedom as the people of this country, a knowledge of that nation has never yet reached us." On the Fourth of July 1814, Webster praised his countrymen's rejection of "selfish views of ambition." The best example of that selflessness was, to be sure, "the illustrious" Washington, who never sought votes and "employed no arts to *obtain* the office of President."[51]

On July 4, 1826, in honor of the fiftieth anniversary of the "immortal Declaration," and as yet unaware of the exquisitely times deaths of Adams and Jefferson, Edward Everett spoke in Boston and reminded his hearers that they'd assembled out of love and appreciation, "to pay a filial tribute to the deeds of our fathers." He represented the history of the American Revolution as one of destiny, of inevitability. London had been given a choice between "peaceable separation, or a convulsive rupture"; the patriot leaders responded to threats with a "rapidity of intuition," in "the hope that a new centre of civilization was to be planted on the new continent, at which the social and political institutions of the world may be brought to the standard of reason and truth, after thousands of years of degeneracy." In this neo-Homeric epic, the conqueror was a concept rather than a person.

In Everett's construct, the United States had achieved a "perfect system of government" in its federal and state constitutions. His "beloved country" was unmatched in the extent of its settlements, "in the abundance of the common blessings of life, . . . in public strength and national respectability." Foreshadowing his brother's then-incubating book *America*, he held that fifty years had produced "the equal enjoyment by every citizen of the rights and privileges of the social union." Everett had lived and thrived in Europe as a doctoral student, which gave him the authority to state that other governments gave "great privileges to a small number, and necessarily at the expense of all the rest of the citizens." Good at drawing contrasts, the classically trained orator never rose above this level of vanity and imprecision.

But he did know how to present a case. Everett embraced an American doctrine of "fellow-citizenship" that was given its energy through "charm, veneration, and love, bound up in the name of *country*," a doctrine that proudly rejected British political philosopher Edmund Burke's insistence that "the people" was no more than a legal fiction. The younger Everett brother declared his nation peace loving, extending its influence by "moral force" alone, reserving its right to go to war expressly to "raise the trampled rights of humanity from the dust." The speech, an exercise in faith, helped establish a personal reputation for Edward Everett that continued to build even as North-South comity continued to decay.[52]

In the 1830s, oratory continued to invoke "the faith of our fathers." The speaker for the July 4, 1833, celebration at the First Universalist Church in Providence, Rhode Island, bore the historically significant name Walter Raleigh Danforth. That day, he reenshrined the patriots' courage, sacrifice in battle, and "unconquerable love of freedom." Predictably, he held that of those who lived through the Revolution, no other human could approach Washington's near perfection: "An attempt for me to pronounce his eulogy would be as vain as the effort"—and here Danforth gave way to Shakespeare—"To gild refined gold, to paint the lily / To throw a perfume on the violet" (*King John* [4.2.1738–39]).[53]

At the University of Alabama in Tuscaloosa in 1835, the orator of the day used feeling language that was maudlin even for this annual occasion: "What heart is there that does not this day swell with the most glowing emotions when contemplating his country's wrongs while struggling for freedom?" He recurred to the memory of the fallen: "What eye is there that does not weep at the remembrance of America's martyred heroes?" Lives were given that the underdog colonies might grow from "embryo" republicanism to claim an immense territory. "Knowledge dwells among us, and Plenty empties her full horn into the lap of Tranquility." Here again, while martyrdom dwells in memory, the word of choice is "tranquility," suggesting an arcadian realm where there is a fair chance of overcoming anxious trials and extending life.[54]

Though sectional conflict loomed, the nation as a whole could still be imagined as united and harmonious. Here's a thirty-three-year-old Boston attorney in 1836: "Although majorities elsewhere should be against us, although corruption and licentiousness should prevail all around us, still let *us* maintain the doctrines of Washington." Fourth of July orations globalized the appeal of America's founding greats, "benefactors of the human race, by whose wisdom nations are instructed." It was almost as if, by sidestepping sectionalism, the fatal disconnection could be prayed away.[55]

The question of how popular attitudes spread is among the toughest cultural historians entertain. But patriotic sentiment is one ingredient in mass culture that can be charted. Books and magazine pieces that praised the American character were drawing their evidence from the life stories of statesmen and warriors. Besides the omnipotent Washington, books in this easily reproducible genre lauded a host of once revered figures, now scarcely known. A good example is the 1833 *Memoir of Alexander Macomb, the Major General Commanding the Army of the United States*. Macomb (1782–1841) saw action in the War of 1812 and was appointed to the top command by President John Quincy Adams in 1828. It was Macomb, with roots both in New York and Michigan, who signed the order dispatching Captain Bonneville to the far west.

Like Jackson's first biographers, who joined him in military campaigns, Macomb's biographer, George Richards, served under him as a captain of artillery. He describes his general as an uncannily youthful man. "Often, on an introduction to

strangers, he has been asked if he was the *Son of the old General.*"
Macomb was "finely proportioned . . . having a very pleasant and
yet dignified presence," not to mention "a mild blue eye, radiating
with mind and benevolence—and a mouth and chin indicative of
great decision and firmness." It was as though Lavater's physiognomic guide had been directly consulted to give literal shape to
an able-bodied man of worth whose gift of leadership was written on his face. The possession of sympathetic qualities ("benevolence") was a necessity for subjects in the romantic phase of
American biography (roughly 1830s to 1850s).[56]

Richards fills out the picture, noting that Macomb "is alert
in his motions, and buoyant in his spirits, which are uniformly
in a genial flow" and that "his conversation, too, though marked
with his characteristic good sense and sound learning, is, like
his manners, full of vivacity and fire." In the Washingtonian
mold, he was dignified "in substance," but in a reframing of per-
sonhood that the romantics gave life to, the general would not
be satisfied with mere "etiquette"; he also embraced the new
requirements of sociability: "For himself, he fears no exposure—
is not afraid to be known." *He fears no exposure.* The less penetrating could only see the general's good cheer and sprightliness
with "their *bodily* eyes." Yet Macomb, we are assured, was imbued with something more: he was "fertile and ingenious in
speculation," "prompt, bold, persevering and powerful in action—
with an heroic daring which danger but stimulates." He had
depths.[57]

This complicated description boils down to the claim that
this highest-ranking army officer is all things to all people, the
epitome of military and human virtues. Graced with an almost
magical appearance of youth, he still looked the part of a major
general, exhibited readiness, and moved with alacrity. He was
able to perceive with an eye that was sharper and more penetrating than that of men whose sight was bound to the physical

body. Frontier Michigan's General Alexander Macomb was all bravery and rectitude, a western hero from central casting as much as Irving's Bonneville and Bean, with the added qualities of a wizard-like transcendence.

Romanticism's imagery manifests itself in the urgency and pathos of Fourth of July oratory. Yet most of literary nationalism was oddly unimaginative and closer to the Macomb paradigm. In Macomb there is no mood, no melancholy, no particular cadence but instead a flatness, as though scientific investigation and not intimate knowledge generated the text. What Irving strenuously worked at with Columbus and Paulding managed to do in his Washington treatment, Macomb's biographer did not attempt.[58]

* *

Sailing the high seas, crossing paths in far-flung places, Americans who served as unofficial messengers of the nation formed a cadre of influencers who kept emotional connections to recent history active. Those who wrote affectively for the public or were energetic lecturers self-consciously advanced a conversation with broad cultural implications. A celebration of Washington's birthday serendipitously brought two major influencers together, Edward Everett and Washington Irving. Though both would produce biographies of the first president, they represented two different attitudes as communicators.

Edward Everett took to Irving well before he or his older brother had been introduced to the author. In 1822, writing in the *North American Review*, he praised *Bracebridge Hall*, the collection that followed *The Sketch Book*, as "a book of unwearying pleasantry," "a tissue of merriment and ridicule." In the same journal, in 1835, Alexander Everett wrote (after their Madrid association and with far less objectivity) about the Irving corpus, opening with "we regard Washington Irving as the best living writer of English prose."[59]

The connection between the younger Everett and Irving was not particularly close, however. In 1842, as the US minister to Great Britain, Edward met with the worldly New Yorker when the latter was enroute to Spain to take up his post as US minister. (The substance of their conversation is not known.) Everett returned home three years later to take up the presidency of Harvard, and after that the secretaryship of state, though he tended to make the most news as a public speaker. His steady nationalism led to efforts to moderate the North-South rivalry, which culminated in 1860, when as part of a last-ditch effort to avert war, Everett joined the patriotic bisectional Constitutional Union Party as its candidate for vice president. Interestingly, one who did not praise his oratorical style was a competitor in the field, Ralph Waldo Emerson, who demeaned his "stereotyped phrases" and posturing meant to appeal to mediocre minds. For Emerson, speaking to elevate was what distinguished legitimate efforts to act upon the culture from mere politicking.[60]

Everett persisted. In 1856, he gave a heralded address in Boston at an event in honor of Washington's birthday. Irving was at that moment just finishing the first of his five Washington volumes and Everett was not quite at the starting gate. His Washington oration, which he would deliver many times over, was an extravagant effort, acclaiming the greatest American's unmatched qualities. One critic in attendance reported: "Edward Everett is a man of wood. He is respectability personified. He never rises for a moment from rhetoric to eloquence, from plausibility to TRUTH." Emerson was evidently not alone in his appraisal.

The day's master of ceremonies was the historian George Bancroft, who paused in his laudatory comments about Everett to take note of an audience member. Bancroft beheld the "benevolent countenance" of this cherished figure of American letters, seated in the orchestra section, and spoke his name,

Washington Irving. All at once, "the house resounded with calls for 'Washington Irving.'" The report goes on: "Mr. Irving never speaks. He is as modest as he is beloved." To this critic, at least, American popular culture had its pick between schoolmasterly pomp and serene majesty.[61]

African Colonization.

PROCEEDINGS,

ON THE

FORMATION OF THE NEW-YORK

STATE COLONIZATION SOCIETY;

TOGETHER WITH

AN ADDRESS TO THE PUBLIC,

FROM THE

MANAGERS THEREOF.

ALBANY:
PRINTED BY WEBSTERS AND SKINNERS.

1829.

The title page of *African Colonization*, a pamphlet announcing the formation of the
New York State Colonization Society in 1829. The organizers, as Christians, bemoan
their late arrival to the cause, unanimously agreeing that "the emigration of our blacks"
need not be limited to those already free, convinced as they were that "our southern
slaveholders are as kind hearted and as generous men as we are, and they deplore
the evils of slavery, for which they are no more chargeable than ourselves."

Chapter 6.

Race and Resistance
(Rationalization)

In 1620 the first African slaves were brought
to Virginia. In 1820 the first emancipated
Africans were sent from the United States to
Liberia. If a superior intelligence, while contemplating, from the serene heights of the
mansions of the blessed, the movements, the
tumults, and the aimless activity of the inhabitants of the earth, had observed that one little
ship taking its solitary way across the ocean,
laden with emigrants returning, civilized and
Christianized, to the land which, two centuries
previous, their fathers had left degraded and
idolatrous savages, would he not have thought
that, of all the enterprises then absorbing the
energies and hopes of man, this . . . was the
one which promised to the human race the
largest portion of ultimate good?
   —Sarah Josepha Hale, *Liberia* (1853)

"*What shall we do* with the free people of color?," posed Reverend Robert Finley, a graduate of Princeton and one of the principal founders, in 1816, of the American Colonization Society (ACS). The ACS wholly accepted the Constitution's protection of slavery and each state's right to decide when, if ever, the practice should end. Men of faith and national politicians who joined the ACS regarded themselves as pragmatists as well as philanthropists, claiming to have no less interest in the happiness of Africa-descended as Europe-descended people when they plotted to "draw off" the free Black population. "Anxious solicitude" for the downtrodden, their spokesmen said, merged with a stern recognition that race prejudice was irreversible, leading to the "expediency" of a mass removal effort.[1]

There is no more incisive example of separation or disconnectedness than the Middle Passage, the violent removal of Africans from their native shores and conversion into enslaved men and women in the Western Hemisphere. By the antebellum period, after generations of subjugation, insults, and abuses, having been denied control of their own bodies, slaves (but also free Blacks) lived their whole lives in a state of imposed separateness. Well-developed theories of white superiority normalized the uneasy sensations members of the Anglo-Saxon race felt when placed in physical proximity to the darker skinned. Even Phillis Wheatley, writing in praise of spiritual freedom, bowed to prejudiced language when she speaks of the continent of Africa in a poem: "I left me native Shore / The sable Land of error's darkest night." A few lines later, she repeats, gratified in having been rescued from "the dark abode."[2]

Enlightenment anatomists and philosophes did perhaps more than any other group to harden the system of belief that associated Africanness with medicalized traits: darker blood, sluggishness, poor reasoning ability, hypersexuality, a meaner destiny.[3] Their mass return to West Africa became the idealized objective of a surprising number of white and some Black

Americans who agreed with Sarah Josepha Hale (1788–1879), poet, novelist, and for decades the nation's premier magazine editor, that colonization was a worthy and principled enterprise. Among Hale's achievements as a literary figure was the composition of a popular children's song in 1830, the short saga of a girl named Mary and an affectionate lamb whose fleece was white as snow. "Mary Had a Little Lamb" lives on, though knowledge of Hale's once giant reputation among female readers has faded.

How deep did American racism run? In 1817, after a tour of Virginia, James Kirke Paulding published *Letters from the South*, in which he pronounces that "Negroes are in general a harmless race," "more ignorant than the whites of the poorer classes," "unthinking," "given to petty vices," and likely to "transgress" the law. Commending the musical skills of slaves, he adds that "their laugh is the very echo of thoughtless hilarity. . . . They certainly are exempt from many of the cares that beset their masters." No doubt imagining himself a disinterested observer, Paulding proceeds to credit their legal owners, maintaining that "until they can be freed, without endangering the community[,] . . . it is some comfort to see them well treated by their masters."

Not one of Paulding's statements was founded on personal knowledge. His assumptions were simplistic and banal, his style of argument insensitive and misleading. And none of it would have been regarded as unexpected or particularly offensive in 1817 or decades later. Northern transplants to plantation communities adapted to white southern ways and those enslaved from birth grew up acquiring "affective tactics" (self-suppressive smiles) to avoid physical punishment. Exploiter and exploited "profited" in ways that were unique to each by projecting contentment in an unrelenting, rigidly hierarchical world.[4]

In Baltimore, in 1822, Hezekiah Niles prefaced a long report in his nationally prominent magazine with a personal testament

in support of "just and liberal remarks" he'd consented to publish. The unidentified author of the piece, reared in Britain,
minimized US accountability for the persistence of slavery. He
echoed Jefferson's self-interested charge that England had imposed slavery on its colonies for its own economic gain: thus
America's "misfortune" was the "crime of Britain." The metaphors
compound: "We poured the foul infection into her veins"—an
"otherwise happy country." The writer insisted that he would
"never hold a slave" while at the same time confessing that "the
desire of my heart is to locate myself somewhere in which a black
man is a rarity." He went on to call free Blacks of Baltimore "the
worst persons among us." He decried slavery yet would trust in
the "moral honesty" of an enslaved man—who lived without
hope—over a free Black, who aspired to more and would therefore cut corners to get ahead.[5]

The French Abbé Grégoire (1750–1831) was an early and
outspoken antislavery advocate who exposed unfounded prejudices and described the intellectual merits of Black leaders. In
1826, the *Port-Folio* engaged a surly reviewer to critique a tract
of his bearing the lengthy title "The Nobility of the Skin, or
the Prejudice of the Whites against the Colour of the Africans
and Their Descendants, Whether of Pure or Mixed Blood."
The ill-disposed critic dismissed out of hand Abbé Grégoire's
practical prescription for gradual emancipation, contending that
to prepare the enslaved for freedom "would be about as unprof-
itable an undertaking as teaching an elephant to fly." By way of
explanation, the reviewer added that "the blacks in Philadelphia
and New York, who have been brought to these cities, chiefly by
the influence of mistaken benevolence, are nuisances, although
they have had all the advantages of schools and churches, with
black bishops to boot." The magazine's readers were all expected
to smile knowingly at the critic's final thrust: "Wo betide the land
where 'Black spirits and white, blue spirits and gray / Mingle,
mingle, mingle, as they mingle may.'"[6]

The man who occupied the White House at this time was John Quincy Adams. Not long after his defeat at the polls at the end of a single term, he entered Congress, where he regularly and purposefully got into trouble criticizing slavery, doing all he could to get under the skin of its most virulent defenders among his congressional colleagues. Yet, like millions of others, he was avowedly uncomfortable with an America in which racial mixture was sanctioned. Taking particular aim at Shakespeare's *Othello*, he complained that "the passion of Desdemona for Othello is unnatural, solely and exclusively because of his color." Adams felt no sympathy for one so "deficient in delicacy" and "female modesty." Writing in the *New England Magazine*, he insisted that "black and white blood cannot be intermingled in marriage without a gross outrage upon the law of Nature." Desdemona deserved her fate for transgressing against the reigning definition of social decency. The poet Coleridge agreed: "It would be something monstrous to conceive this beautiful Venetian girl falling in love with a veritable Negro." It should be noted that into the twentieth century, with few exceptions, the role of Othello was performed by white men in blackface.[7]

"The world is full of it," a critical student of history said, referring to the existence of prejudice, so it was not surprising to him that prejudice should feature in any work that professed to tell major truths about a civilization. He was reviewing Alexander Everett's sweeping treatment, *America*, for the *Western Monthly Review* in 1827. "Look even among the calm and thinking men, that you know, and how many of them can you count, that have not their strong and palpable prejudices," he told readers. "In most instances, opinions in morals are settled in the court of self-interest and convenience." This was an unusually astute assessment of the mind's operations.[8]

Beginning with George Washington, no chief magistrate in the early republic saw any productive outcome possible in addressing the slavery issue head on. Even among northern

Federalists, dissenting voices whispered their disgust and pushed only so far. Northern Republicans reached a tacit agreement among themselves by reconciling their ideas about democracy with the continued existence of a known evil. With the Federalist Party's demise, the South's system remained entrenched: this was the only way to promote any North-South political consensus. There would be no interference with slavery where it existed; the issue was how to keep it from advancing west as new states were added. As a cluster of historians have shown, the Missouri crisis of 1819–20 made it perfectly clear that protecting slavery was the price of Union. By then, as colonization gained in appeal, white fears of racial "mixing" were easily exploitable: racial stereotypes were used to expose the "threat" posed by people of questionable morals who sought equal rights in the political community. That Blacks should be accorded greater dignity was meant to be recognized as an indignity to whites.[9]

Physical distinctions framed thoughts of America's future. Widely held assumptions about racial hierarchy "founded on nature" precluded discussion of biracial community. Sex across the color line, a violation of nature's plan, heightened a hysteria that worsened as the United States expanded west and took slavery with it. Before departing Philadelphia for the South, where she would encounter slavery for the first time, the adroit English traveler Harriet Martineau was asked "whether I would not prevent, if I could, the marriage of a white person with a person of colour." She replied that she would never "under any circumstances, try to separate persons who really loved." The questioner, a professedly religious woman, cried, "You are an amalgamationist!" (a person in favor of race mixing) and denounced the Englishwoman for heresy. The common construction of Indians was as a culturally backward people capable of instruction; Blacks, in contrast, were regarded as biologically alien. If "blood" determined race, and race distinctions warned of social decay, this kind of conversation was bound to persist.[10]

The majority's complicated sense of pride was reinforced with the introduction of the much-abused color taxonomy conceived by a German race theorist. It labeled "Caucasian" as an individual with a "white complexion, red cheeks," Afro-American as "more or less black, with black curled hair," and Native American as one with "cinnamon, iron-rust, or tarnished copper" skin. In 1838, Ralph Waldo Emerson used this terminology matter-of-factly in an open letter to President Martin Van Buren when he complained about US treatment of the Cherokees: "We have witnessed with sympathy the painful labors of these red men to redeem their own race from the doom of eternal inferiority" in their seeking to profit from "the arts and customs of the caucasian race."

Simply put, the US government existed for the benefit of whites with land and money. This included mixed-race individuals of means who successfully "passed"—whiteness thus being in the eye of the beholder. In the North as well as the slave South, mainstream opinion held that some state coercion could be brought to bear in defense of such feelings as had been cultivated over two centuries. Importantly, too, the system of racial superiority demanded Black compliance, which saw to it that generations of Blacks inherited the idea of Black inferiority. The ultimate insult to whiteness in much of the literature was the "degrading mixture" that derived from any "taint" of Africanness.[11]

The Wishfulness of Colonization

In November 1825, from Madrid, Alexander Hill Everett fumed at the idea that the Spanish would lose control of their Caribbean possessions before the United States could step in. While he saw

Cuba as "properly an appendage of the Floridas," it seemed quite possible that Mexico, well along in the process of giving up slavery, would intervene there or that a slave insurrection might succeed, as had occurred in Haiti at the start of the century. Spain had just sent troops to Cuba to repel a feared invasion from that Black republic.

Everett's fear was, not surprisingly, racial. The "white population" of the island formed "too small a proportion of the whole number to constitute themselves an independent nation," he wrote. "Africanization" of the inhospitable island was a recipe for trouble that only spelled catastrophe for US security. Washington was abuzz about "Negro insurrection" in Cuba, with free Blacks numbering well over a hundred thousand there; these men were armed and enjoyed rights their US counterparts did not.

When he was secretary of state, Everett's mentor John Quincy Adams had hammered out the treaty with Spain that ceded the whole of Florida to the United States. Spain had lost Mexico; US acquisition of Cuba appeared inevitable. In 1825, at the time Adams became president, Mexico (along with independent Colombia) was making noises about liberating Cuba. Northerners and southerners alike had established sugar plantations there and were importing large numbers of slaves (who had to be regularly replenished, owing to cholera deaths). American slave ships plied Cuban waters. So did American pirates. White Americans worried that Black abolitionists—or the British—would go to Cuba to liberate the island and serve it up to Mexico. That was the scenario Everett painfully imagined. Nothing like this occurred, though, and Spain held onto Cuba until 1898.[12]

In the early 1840s, at a time when Cuba's population was majority Black, Everett paid two long visits. He found that antislavery sentiment was widespread but radical abolitionism was not. A strong proponent of westward expansion, Everett predicted that all former Spanish colonies from the Isthmus of Panama north would come into American hands. He returned from Cuba convinced that the island only awaited US commercial exploitation: "This favored land wants nothing but men to turn its advantages to account and enjoy their results."[13]

Like the majority of his countrymen, Everett basked in the sunshine of Anglo-Saxon superiority. "Nations and races, like individuals, have their day, and seldom have a second," he pronounced. "The blacks had a long and glorious one" over the centuries when ancient Egypt was in the ascendant. Egyptians once led the world morally and intellectually—and in physical beauty. But now, the vagaries of history left few options. The most that white America could do was make Black people, free or enslaved, "as happy as we can," undertaking what was "most expedient" to lift them "by a slow and gradual process." If this process were handled right, a "flourishing and prosperous" Black section of the North American continent would lure more and more free Blacks away from states where whites resented their presence.[14]

In 1816, Sarah Everett (1796–1866), the younger sister of Alexander and Edward Everett and later the author of children's books, married a math teacher. His name was Nathan Hale (1784–1863), a son of Reverend Enoch Hale, the Revolutionary martyr's brother. This Nathan Hale had already founded the *North American Review*, a magazine his Everett brothers-in-law would take turns editing. After being entwined in the early operations of that long-lived periodical, Hale soon branched out, becoming a mainstay of Boston journalism as editor and publisher of the *Boston Daily Advertiser*, where he held forth for the remainder of his life.[15]

The well-connected Everetts and Hales were entirely unrelated to Sarah Josepha Hale, née Buell, the daughter of a tavern owner. She hailed from a small town in New Hampshire and was home taught. In 1813, she married David Hale, an attorney from the next town over. Nine years and five children later, she lost David to pneumonia and never remarried. The widow's first book, *Northwood: Life North and South*, was published in 1827 and sold well. Her stature rose markedly after she took charge of Louis Godey's female-directed magazine, *Godey's Lady's Book*, the first periodical to limit reprintings of British writers while featuring American authors.[16]

By the time Alexander Everett wrote a piece for her magazine in 1840, both of their careers were well established. The two colonization supporters were proponents of Christian morality and Protestant mission. In "The Sabbath," Everett proclaimed that "religion reveals to us the secret of our higher and better nature, lifts us above the common offices of daily life, into communion with the sublime Spirit." He gloried in man's possession of "the germ of a heavenly nature," affirming that religion enlarged the intellect "by familiarizing us with . . . the philosophy of morals and mind." As an elite American Protestant cosmopolitan, he zealously espoused the "civilizing and consolidating influence of Christianity" on "rude barbarians."[17]

Hale included a good amount of pious, doleful Victorian prose and poetry in the pages of her magazine while adopting a series of social causes. Recognizing, for instance, the dangers inherent in a sailor's life, his meager pay, and the impoverished state of dependent women and children left at home for long stretches, she organized the Seamen's Aid Society. It employed women as garment producers at good wages and taught their children trades. She stood up for married women's property rights and fought for female entry into the medical profession. She did nothing half-heartedly.

As a patriot, Hale raised funds to complete the long-unfinished Bunker Hill Monument. She used the sounding board of her magazine to help the Mount Vernon Ladies Association raise funds for the preservation of Washington's home. She felt it incumbent on her to advance the inseverable causes of women's education and female-directed moral persuasion. The women who wrote for *Godey's* were pushing to rewrite the collective autobiography of the United States.[18]

A significant number of regular subscribers to *Godey's Lady's Book* were southern women. While at Louis Godey's insistence the magazine steered clear of sectional politics, Hale's 1853 novel *Liberia* made clear where she stood. Black Americans had "no home" in the United States, she bemoaned, "no position, and no future," because "two races who do not intermarry can never live together as equals." This had been the argument of colonizationists since the turn of the nineteenth century, a position amounting to a pretend form of abolition that recognized ineradicable prejudices and somehow figured a white-directed solution would be seen as charitable, even by Blacks. A proud supporter of the Union, no apologist for southern political interests, Hale embraced Liberia as a better homeland for aggrieved darker-skinned Americans than the land of their birth.[19]

There is no way to sugarcoat the fact that the United States was a deeply racist nation. To enforce belief in white superiority, the law was despotic. It was technically impossible to violate the rights of a noncitizen. Virginia's legislature made it illegal for a free Black to teach another to read: the penalty was thirty-nine lashes. Blacks were deemed fully reasoning *only* when it came to the commission of crimes—crimes as set forth by the master race. Another defense invoked by southern whites was that nature intended the African for menial occupations.[20]

In passing judgment, we need to understand how rationalization operates. Emotional responses to baffling problems require more of the mind, or of a community's stamina, than it is psychically prepared to exert. Even whites who wished to appear enlightened and humane could not conceive of a future in which Black and white schoolchildren learned together and competed for professional advancement. Their sense of the world was not elastic enough to allow them to expect more from the existing order. What psychologists call "ingroup favoritism" operates implicitly, as low-status individuals conform to the dominant group's ideology in spite of its effects. Conflict avoidance tendencies feed the status quo.[21]

Physiognomy and phrenology offered explanations for human differences that dictated behavior. Both insisted that a poorly organized African brain was readable on its surface and that behavior could be predicted on the same basis. Assertive physicians and educators wrote as though such beliefs were empirically proven. Rachel E. Walker, the scholar who has most recently examined the subject, points out that while Black intellectuals thought it possible to capitalize on the popularity of physiognomy and phrenology to depict the "facial eminence" of successful Black Americans and thereby refute the principles that nourished racial prejudice, it was always going to be an uphill climb. Free Blacks were commonly caricatured as "uppity and self-centered dandies attempting to rise above their station," and so, in attempting to promote a positive Black image, those who embraced "the master's tools" served to further demean the innate capacity of lower-class African Americans, reinforcing existing class biases.[22]

Because it was seen to be compatible with Christianity, the colonization movement appeared almost as a *covenant*. While its "radical" critics were able to see through its rationalizations, it was able to parlay the Christian message into an ethical advantage that it retained for a period of years. Colonization painted abolitionism as visionary and impulsive while presenting the munificent removal of Blacks as experimental and practicable. Carefully filtered reports from Liberia were meant to demonstrate the success of colonization. Indeed, that is how rationalization fulfills itself.

Representing the presence of Blacks as an unwelcome "disturbance" in society was an attempt (through language) to deny millions privacy and the freedom to participate in acts of emotional intimacy. Free Black residents in Washington, DC, for example, were subject to nighttime curfews and restricted in the number of people that could attend any gathering that took place in their own homes. The imposed sexualization of women of color translated into the ascription of a hypersexual "nature"; similarly, any congregation of nonwhite men was construed as troublemaking. These dangerous rationalizations were taken up by those who wished for Blacks, free or enslaved, to appear noncompliant with national norms and thereby disqualified from belonging. The life of every nonwhite person was a life under suspicion. From early in the colonial era, whites were taught to look an elder in the eye as a sign of respect, while African Americans who did the same were seen to present a challenge to the other's authority.[23]

The darker skinned were meant to "know their place" and behave with passive accommodation. African American resistance to racist laws tended not to receive publicity outside of antislavery circles. The Black Chicagoan John Jones, a well-known member of a growing community, petitioned the Illinois legislature in writing after its new state constitution declared its intention to prohibit further immigration of free Blacks into the state. He asked for "total repeal of all Laws now existing upon the statute books of this State, whereby discriminations are made among the people on account of complexion." Writing in an abolitionist newspaper, the *Western Citizen*, Jones argued in 1847 that whole regiments of Black men had joined the American Revolution, that more had fought in the War of 1812, and that, as a result, there was no legitimate reason to exclude Black men from all rights of citizenship. In 1848, at a national colored convention held in Cleveland, he joined his comrades in branding the American Colonization Society "deceptive and hypocritical—'clothed with the livery of heaven to serve the devil in.'" As clearheaded as he sounds to our ears, scholars continue to debate how many whites were moved by people like Jones to reconsider their preconceptions and to reason through prejudice.[24]

Uneasy conversations took place in states like Ohio where slavery was prohibited as a result of the 1787 Northwest Ordinance. There were more men like Ulysses S. Grant, born in a nondescript village southeast of Cincinnati in 1822, who tolerated slavery until military exigency ignited the process of breaking it apart four decades later, than there were men like his father, Jesse Root Grant, a farmer and merchant born poor in Pennsylvania in 1794, who came to his antislavery principles early, befriended the archabolitionist John Brown, and refused to socialize with slaveowners.

Like the younger Grant, his fellow Ohioan, fellow West Point graduate, and future comrade-in-arms William T. Sherman did not feel any compunction to overturn slavery in the South. "Two such races," he wrote unambiguously, "cannot live in harmony save as master and slave." The South's hallmark institution was, as practiced, "the mildest and best regulated system of slavery anywhere in the world, now or heretofore." Sherman penned these words from Louisiana on the eve of the Civil War.[25]

At the same time, Ohio contributed a considerable number of voices to the abolition movement. Among those who stood up in Congress, early and often, to register their disgust was Joshua R. Giddings (1795–1864), who, like the elder Grant, was a Pennsylvanian by birth. In a February 13, 1839, speech, he pummeled the southern planter interest with a principled call— obviously going nowhere—to remove the seat of the federal government from the District of Columbia if it remained a slave market: "Northern men will not consent to the continuance of our National Councils where their ears are assailed, while coming to the Capitol, with the voice of the auctioneer, publicly proclaiming the sale of human, of intelligent beings." It would take another full decade before this rank offense to Giddings's sensibilities was removed. And even that, of course, would only serve to delay the coming separation.[26]

The brave men and women who stood before the public and argued for emancipation took their lives in their hands. Passions erupted. Vitriol flowed. If colonizationists took pride in the moral positions they espoused, abolitionists had to use a different kind of speech to "warm up" an audience and avoid being branded "too radical" for the times. A prime example of the latter is the indefatigable Kentucky plantation owner Cassius Marcellus Clay (1810–1903), a cousin of the three-time presidential candidate and Whig Party leader Henry Clay, who delivered his first antislavery speech on the centennial of George Washington's birth in 1832, set up an antislavery newspaper in his home state, and courted reactionary mobs.

Clay's close associate, Presbyterian minister John G. Fee, established the interracial Berea college in 1855 on land given to him by Clay. Of the colonization project, the principled Fee said that "to banish a man from the land of his birth, guilty of no crime, was gross injustice—only adding iniquity to crime." These words were directed at his congregation. He rejected others' description of the more outspoken Clay as a "furious monster" and instead characterized him as a naturally eloquent man who disarmed his hearers on the basis of sound argument. When a protester who embraced the "perpetualism" of American slavery engaged Clay with a barrage of "invective, denunciation, and appeals to passion and prejudice," however, the abolitionist smelled blood. "He waked up the wrong pessenger [sic]," said one audience member who witnessed the skilled tactician respond with colorful anecdotes "until the house echoed with cheers and bursts of laughter." The protester was silenced.

Clay was nothing if not colorful. In 1846, he proclaimed that "the free states build ships and steam cars for the nations of the world; the slave states import the handles for their axes."

In his memoir, published two decades after the Civil War, he insisted that all that had mattered to him was to act on behalf of "those principles which add to human happiness" and that personal power did not concern him otherwise. "[I] use my voice only to intensify my highest thought."

His strength, as Fee explained, and Clay confirmed, lay in his being one of them, a Kentucky planter who could have gone on living in "quietude, ease, and luxury" but instead turned his talent to the plight of "down-trodden humanity." When Clay was criticized for not belonging to a church, his response was that the churches of the South made life too easy for those who would enslave. On the opposite side of the Kentucky spectrum, an unabashedly proslavery newspaper editor in Louisville read the tea leaves in a radically different way, denouncing the colonization project as "deceptive and pernicious and only designed to cover the leading designs of its leading advocates—that of emancipating the slaves."[27]

Kentucky and Ohio: one slave, the other free. The obvious symbolism of the border river in Harriet Beecher Stowe's *Uncle Tom's Cabin* was easily wrought as a dramatic hurdle, a mortal barrier to be crossed if entry to the promised land were to be granted. But even the Ohio River is a problematic symbol. Neither Kentucky nor Ohio communicated a singular ethos. Ideas are unstable and perception is marred by ignorance, which only invites further distortion. Christianity manifests both as pure love (as in the novel) and a tool of oppressors (in the way any religious order can be twisted). Such facts explain why the harmful emotion of prejudice is so difficult to subdue in any age.

Northwood (1827)

Do we get these people yet? Yes and no. We cannot properly comprehend the past while applying our own values to a country whose free population was between 5 and 10 percent of today's US population, whose inhabitants relied on tallow candles and whale oil lamps to read after dark, whose overland commerce moved at seven miles per hour, and whose street life all too often imparted disagreeable odors and uninviting sights. Much of the olfactory offense emanated from animals: populated areas were dotted with livery stables, skin tanning operations, stray dogs, nuisance hogs, and repulsive vermin. Antebellum Americans simply had no choice about these things. The sensory environment that affected their attitudes inevitably extended to the people they were bound to look upon. There's a reason why we say that one can "smell" fear.[28]

Racist science undoubtedly contributed to racist anger. Apprehension over the "amalgamation of the races," the imagined replacement of the white with a mixed breed unappealing to the eye, was fed by well-publicized theories originating in Europe; but it was in the United States that the fear was decidedly felt, owing to the rapid increase in the nonwhite population. Where community norms were well established, long-cultivated prejudices were not about to be recognized all of a sudden as irrational and disprovable. It is not that liberal humanism was failing but that self-protective separation was (and is) a learned response. All human societies have drawn lines and established hierarchies, often unconsciously. One gravitates toward another whose looks and whose habits matches one's own. One recoils at the nearness of another who appears incongruous.

And yet a significant amount of contentious writing in the antebellum period found northern and southern sides each maintaining that they were the less uncomfortable around African Americans. Defenders of slavery pointed out that southern whites were quite accustomed to physical intimacy with Blacks and that hypocritical northerners "possessed of olfactories like the rest of mankind . . . entertain a very wholesome dread" of similar cross-race contact. As Mark M. Smith writes, a slew of amateur anatomists and trained physicians asserted that Blackness brought with it "rank smell" and "morbid sensibilities."[29]

The idea of innate differences between races is invoked in national narratives whenever those in power need "objective" proof to justify their social stature. Yuval Noah Harari writes along these lines that "there is no justice in history" because humans have always "created imagined orders and devised scripts." Preservers of white power refuse to be humiliated (in their minds) by having to witness up close a process of retrenchment, their group's weakening, in the seemingly preventable recoloration of their physical and sensory world. Equal protection under the law (as laid out by the Fourteenth Amendment) has faced pushback in the twenty-first century owing largely to the same concern that underwrote resistance to equality in the nineteenth century, namely, the feeling that the affordance of such protections puts those in power at risk.[30]

Race and class are necessarily intertwined, and the class basis of comfort and discomfort is well documented. The term "well bred" has more than one historical meaning, and its power over the mind is intuitive. Lest we feel superior to our ancestors in every conceivable way, we must recognize that many Americans still view immigrants as "lazy" and "ignorant."

Ordering society so as to "improve" the breed is an impulse as old as the Greeks. When John Adams and Thomas Jefferson corresponded about the theories of the ancient lyric poet Theognis, Jefferson acknowledged that no amount of planning would arrest the "fortuitous concourse of breeders" that resulted from old-fashioned lust. In the early decades of the nineteenth century, as slavery became intractable, breeding theories took on a more stridently racial character. Slave owners deliberately, conscientiously bred their slaves for profit. A century later, Americans were having the same conversation when the frightfully wide embrace among intellectuals of eugenic "science" aimed to rid society of the mentally deficient. The persistence of eugenics shows how many discarded systems of belief only *seem* gone for good.[31]

In the early American republic, claims of white racial superiority were amplified in print with very little pushback. Sarah Josepha Hale's character Lydia Brainard in *Northwood*, a self-indulgent young woman, writes home to New England after arriving in Charleston: "Oh! dear mother, you know how frightened I was at a negro—how I used to run behind your chair when old Sampson came to the door, and always screamed when he offered to step in." Having married a South Carolinian, she was having a hard time accepting her new circumstances. "The negroes are as thick as bees; the streets are full of 'em." The overdramatized sensation of being in a majority-Black environment suited the literature of the day, but northerners often downplayed southerners' reality: when Theodosia Burr Alston was in her first year as the wife of a Charleston-area planter, her father the vice president, in urging that she exercise for her health, wrote from Washington, DC: "You must learn to walk without your husband—alone—or, if you must be in form, with ten negroes at your heels."[32]

While overcharged, the reactions of the fictional Lydia Brainard would have appeared half credible to readers. When a "great black fellow" approaches her husband, Lydia panics. "I trembled all over, for I began to remember the stories I had read of slaves murdering their masters and mistresses." As we have seen, "tremble" and "trembling" were everywhere in sentimental literature, becoming increasingly less common by midcentury as the culture of sensibility receded. Men and women alike "trembled" when their anxiety level rose, and perhaps no example is quite as emblematic as Thomas Jefferson's well-rehearsed and oft-quoted warning in *Notes on Virginia* about the dire consequences America faced if slavery should long persist: "I tremble for my country when I reflect that God is just: that his justice cannot sleep forever."[33]

In this work, Jefferson advances the argument that slavery was doomed, that it damaged the morals of whites, and that the best way to stave off a catastrophic race war was to return African Americans to the continent from which they were stolen. He never wavered in his view that colonization of emancipated slaves was the optimum solution if it could be managed financially. While rejecting slavery as a dehumanizing practice, he took a pass on supplying any sort of remedy. He had a visceral distaste for Blackness, which he voiced in an emblematic 1814 letter to Edward Coles, a Virginian he'd known intimately who had already freed his slaves and established them in Illinois: "The love of justice and the love of country plead equally the cause of these people," Jefferson allowed, but their amalgamation "with the other color produces a degradation which no lover of his country, no lover of excellence in the human character can innocently consent."[34]

Even with her husband's assurance that "Cato" was "one of the best creatures living," Hale's Lydia assumes that the slaves in her presence all carried knives. She confesses to her mother that "I am sure if I had only known this was a negro country I never would have come here." Lydia is adamant about the correctness of her sensations whenever she encounters the house slaves in the absence of her husband: "They hate me, I know they do, yet I tell them every day that I wish they were in Guinea." Nothing short of their banishment would satisfy the frightened white woman.

Lydia's "noble spirited" southern husband was extremely kind to the people he owned, even professing a hatred for slavery. Eager for the institution to disappear, he tried to convince her that it was "the only blot that stained" his section's "character." But her impulsive reaction was all she was capable of, now or ever. Recolonization to Africa, the solution that naturally presented itself to a literary character this vain (and intellectually limited) became the political preference of the book's author

within just a few years. As the most successful US magazine editor of the mid-nineteenth century, Hale committed herself to
the colonization movement in a most public way.[35]

Colonization persuaded Abraham Lincoln, too. While hat-
ing slavery, he supported the Select Committee on Emancipation and Colonization created by Congress in 1862 that dedicated federal funds to the project and encouraged states to
promote voluntary self-deportation. So it should not come as a
surprise that the dominant race, including many would-be benefactors of the underclass, tacitly accepted paternalistic management of the racial order even as abolition societies were
proliferating. Civil laws and customs enforcing social separateness were bound to continue for as long as Black Americans
coinhabited a still sparsely settled continent with the descendants of European colonizers who had problems with their
being around.[36]

Race prejudice did not stop at plantation's end or at the
Mason-Dixon Line. At New York's 1821 constitutional convention, there was a push to disenfranchise free Blacks, whom one
delegate charged were "a peculiar people" uniformly incapable
of "discretion, prudence, or independence." Free people of color
were widely thought "dirty" and prone to idleness, which was
supposed, in turn, to lead to criminality. A racialized policing
authority designed to protect "public morals" made it seem rational to ostensibly well-intentioned white citizens that in their
dismantling of the despised institution of slavery, African
Americans would be best served if they cooperated in their removal instead of imposing new burdens on the state. What
mattered above all else was that whites should be made to feel
comfortable. Referring to Black Americans as "exiled sons of
Africa" helped.[37]

But in order to rationalize their doctrine, colonizationists had to overlook an emergent black *American* identity. Free
Blacks in abundance saw the Declaration of Independence as

a vindication—"all men are created equal" meant just that. They were as fit for civil society as their white counterparts whose ancestors also came from a distant shore. The Declaration may not have been *intended* to invite them to argue for complete social equality, and yet such logic could not be discredited. Their statelessness was of their oppressors' doing. A compulsion to maintain exclusive power had to be why their oppressors designated them as inferior. This was the unabashed message of David Walker's 1829 *Appeal to the Coloured Citizens of the World*. Walker lived in Massachusetts, where eight years earlier the legislature had debated whether to cut off in-migration of free Blacks owing to their purported vices and viciousness as a group. "Do the colonizationists think to send us off without first being reconciled to us?" Walker demanded.[38]

1831–32

The cross-sectional discourse concerning the future of slavery in America took a decided turn in 1831–32. Virginia, the state that would supply six US presidents between 1789 and 1850, all of them slaveholders, was shocked by Nat Turner's bloody rebellion in the summer of 1831. A preacher and prophet, Turner and a company of fellow slaves turned their wrath against their southeastern Virginia neighbors, killing some sixty Southampton County whites—a highly abnormal incident in the generally complacent plantation South.

A month after the rebellion, the *Richmond Enquirer* reported that the charismatic leader had relied on "every means in power to acquire an ascendancy over the minds of slaves," using dark arts to "overawe their minds." A spirit of vengeance rose as the insurrectionists were hanged, which resulted in the murders of many uninvolved Blacks. Yet it was also true that other slaves, in some cases armed, came to the defense of whites threatened by Nat Turner's men.[39]

Shortly thereafter, the Virginia General Assembly had an extended debate over the course the commonwealth should take, contemplating a dramatic shift in dealing with the institution of slavery in what was still the largest of twenty-four states. The idea of compensated emancipation and expulsion of ex-slaves received serious consideration. In the first days of 1832, the third president's grandson and namesake, Thomas Jefferson Randolph, proposed a gradual emancipation plan consistent what had been done in several northern states, meant to eventually remove Blacks "beyond the limits of the United States." The legislators remained hotly divided during the debates, and Randolph's initiative failed but only narrowly.

Shortly before the legislative debate turned heated, Governor John Floyd (1806–63), a former member of the US House of Representatives, officially bemoaned "occurrences of a grave and distressing character" (Nat Turner's rebellion) while wavering over the idea of experimenting with emancipation followed by colonization. Large numbers of Virginians expressed, by petition, their discomfort with "the unhappy and degraded race of Africans, whose presence deforms our land"; they then articulated their desire for the state to gradually purchase and sell off all slaves and to expel free Blacks. A piece in the *Richmond Enquirer* by "A Very Small Slaveholder" confidently asserted that 90 percent wanted free negroes gone, even as he noted that the same percentage had no interest in ending slavery. "Publicola" was no less adamant in stating that the real issue was not how to prevent future insurrections but how to tamp down the excitement caused by state politicians. Had the voices of colonization been heeded "some years ago," and their "principles and designs" acted on, "our free negroes would nearly all, by this time, be out of the country." Emotions engaged, newspapers across the country reported on the "strong sensations" caused by Virginia's abolition quarrels. The genie had escaped the bottle.[40]

In response to developments, Thomas R. Dew, a professor of history and political economy at the College of William and Mary, produced the first, or at least the most stimulating, defense of American slavery. "Abolition of Slavery" was published in September 1832, not in the South but in the Philadelphia-based *American Quarterly Review*. It ran 76 pages in its first version, 130 pages when it appeared in pamphlet form that December. Professor Dew was barely thirty, born within a year or two of the slave Nat Turner. His generation, born in the early years of the nineteenth century, would make up the ranks of pro- and antislavery activists as race and rights became the cause célèbre of a fracturing republic.

Dew's argument boiled down to this: enslaved Africans were "a race of people differing from us in colour and in habits, and vastly inferior in the scale of civilization." Thus, Turner's rebellion was a singular occurrence that did not demand a radical or permanent solution; slave labor was a natural result of property accumulation and the exchange economy, a proper feature of an advancing society formed around plantation agriculture.

A slave, the professor held, was an invaluable investment. Their lives protected, their sustenance provided for, most were accepting of their lot—otherwise world history would not have found so many who had sold themselves into slavery. The costs of emancipation and deportation would be enormous, he calculated; the loss of the demanding climate's labor force would drive up the price of domestic slaves and drive off white population without going far enough to remove the hundreds of thousands already alive and breeding. In short, the internal slave trade was the South's key to future prosperity. While there were local colonization societies in Louisiana and Mississippi, the movement remained strongest in the upper South—Virginia, Maryland, and select areas of Kentucky and Tennessee.[41]

Thomas Smallwood was born a slave in Maryland on Washington's birthday in 1801 and freed at age thirty. From the welcoming arms of Canada, he wrote of his experience after flirting with the American Colonization Society. Initially attracted by its antislavery message, Smallwood came to see that the ACS, "under the mask of philanthropy," was nothing more than a cynical ruse perpetrated by men with "insidious designs" who were prepared to buy off free Blacks like himself with "pecuniary inducements" that served their real aim of ridding the US of free people of color in order to prevent them from encouraging the slave population to seek freedom. "I could have become a merchant in the Liberia trade, backed with the aid and influence of that Society," he wrote. "But I preferred to live in indigent circumstances, and enjoy my morsel with a good conscience, rather than be possessed with wealth and a burning conscience, with a recollection that I had come into possession of these through treachery to my afflicted race."[42]

On January 1, 1831, William Lloyd Garrison's abolitionist newspaper the *Liberator* began publication. Garrison was the no-holds-barred face of abolition as he wrestled with the colonizationists. The input he received directly from African Americans did much to convince him to be "as harsh as truth and as uncompromising as justice," a statement he made in the very first issue of the newspaper. "I never rise to address a colored audience, without feeling ashamed of my own color; ashamed of being identified with a race of men who have done you so much injustice," he began his *Address to the Free People of Color* that same year. "The Colonization Society may plot your removal to a foreign land—to Africa—but they will not succeed."[43]

The next year, Garrison issued his *Thoughts on Colonization*, which tore into the ACS. First, he expressed amazement at its success as an idea: "I saw that eminent statesmen and honorable men were enlisted in the enterprise; the great body of the clergy gave their unqualified support to it; every Fourth of July, the charities of the nation were secured in its behalf; wherever I turned my eye in the free States, I saw nothing but unanimity."

Good people had had the wool pulled over their eyes. It was one thing to wish for the success of the Liberia colony but quite another to believe that the ACS's goal of Christianizing Africa would be an improvement. By tamely representing slavery as an "evil," a "misfortune" that befell American history, the deluded supporters of colonization merely lent their support (and funds) to an organization that was at once "ignorant" and "morally blind," one that refused to label slavery a "crime" and its practitioners criminals, one that failed to make an "earnest appeal to the consciences of men-stealers." Indeed, rather than "disturb the repose . . . of the sinner," it embraced "the expulsion of the free people of color." If the colonizationists truly wanted to help Blacks, why did they not perform their good work *within* the borders of the United States?

His style may have alienated the majority of whites—only war would change enough minds—but Garrison's logic was devastatingly simple. "If I must become a colonizationist, . . . there must be no disagreement between my creed and practice. I must be able to give a reason why all our tall citizens should not conspire to remove their more diminutive brethren, and all the corpulent to remove the lean and lank, and all the strong to remove the weak, . . . as readily as for the removal of those whose skin is 'not colored like my own'; for Nature has sinned as culpably in diversifying the size as the complexion of her progeny." He demanded consistency.

Furthermore, the dictate of whiteness in the United States would have to be matched by pure Blackness in Africa. "I protest against sending any to Africa, in whose blood there is any mixture of our own; for, I repeat it, white blood in Africa would be as repugnant to Nature, as black blood is in this country. Now; most unfortunately for colonizationists, the spirit of amalgamation has been so active for a long series of years,— especially in the slave States,—that there are comparatively few . . . whose blood is not tainted with a foreign ingredient.

Here, then, is a difficulty! What shall be done? All black blood *must* be sent to Africa; but how to collect it is the question." Given the impossible standard that was set, nothing short of an immediate emancipation, absent expulsion, would do.[44]

Black Voices Amplified

Garrison's cause was buoyed by free Blacks. Sarah Forten published her poetry (under a pseudonym) in the *Liberator*, as did her father, the entrepreneurial sailmaker James Forten, who wrote as "A Colored Philadelphian" and declared the ACS to be "the offspring of Prejudice" in a letter to another abolitionist crusader, Carolina-born Angelina Grimké. As a wealthy Black man who employed white people, the elder Forten was a force to be reckoned with who nevertheless allowed his pessimism to tamp down his political activism. Apart from their engagement in Garrisonian pressure politics in shaming southern slave masters, Forten and others like him saw too much ambivalence among free Blacks to do more. A politics of deference seemed to make the most sense in recognition of the power of Negrophobia over the white American mind.[45]

The well-traveled artist Robert Douglass Jr. was another elite Philadelphian who used his native talent to criticize abject racism in the visual culture of the 1830s and 1840s. Despite his family's social status, Douglass was classed with other Black artisans. He fought back in his way, not only writing for the abolitionist press but also producing abolitionist lithographs for sale. Notable among these was a portrait of Garrison. His paintings of Black individuals featured true-to-life faces that put to shame the cartoons of deformed-looking Blacks in white artists' lithographs, then widely sold in the bookstores of northern towns and cities and ostensibly passing as a valid form of satire.

As a champion of education (both classical and vocational), Douglass created the Philadelphia Library Company of Colored

Persons, which included an active debating society. After spending more than a year in Haiti, where he worked on his painting, this staunch opponent of colonization traveled to London and attended the World Anti-Slavery Convention held there in 1840. After his return to the United States, he gave his answer to the colonizationists in verse, asserting that a rising generation of educated Blacks would "successfully disprove/Assertions foul, of those who would remove/The natives hence, to some far distant spot,/Where death from climate soon would be [their] lot."[46]

The emergence of a strong abolitionist element in the early 1830s put the ACS increasingly on the defensive. Abolitionist-funded Lane Seminary in Cincinnati produced scholarly arguments in a religious setting. Theodore Dwight Weld led a student movement in 1834, during which the relative value of gradual colonization versus total abolition ("immediatism") came up for vigorous debate. Firsthand testimony from the African-born James Bradley grabbed the most attention. Enslaved in Kentucky as a young child, Bradley purchased his freedom before coming to Lane. Slaves were accustomed to taking care of their enslavers, he said, and could very well take care of themselves. "Liberty and education" were all they lacked, he emphasized. Africa held no allure.

Another Black voice at this time was that of David Ruggles, a former student of Sarah Josepha Hale's colonizationist friend and literary associate Lydia Sigourney. Ruggles, a New York City–based mariner and grocer in his twenties, wrote for the *Liberator* and published prolifically, founding and editing a journal dedicated to human rights called *Mirror of Liberty*. In one series of pamphlets, he fearlessly attacked a rabid colonizationist, Dr. David M. Reese, who'd written protesting abolitionists' "unnatural elevation of the African race." Belittling Black pride while insisting that abolitionists were themselves solely responsible for white acts of violence against them, Reese would not deign to answer Ruggles, who, not without a sense of humor, dismissed the man's medical credentials as he cast shame on the bigot for his "abuse and falsehood" in rationalizing oppression.[47]

Representative of the ambiguity on slavery's northern border was Baltimorean John Pendleton Kennedy (1795–1870), better known as a novelist than as a politician, though he was both. In 1820, speaking before the state legislature, he rejected the "barbarous system of agriculture" in the Deep South, while at the same time favoring the importation of slaves into Maryland from other states: his sympathetic neighbors could offer an alternative model of benign mastery and save the enslaved from a worse fate ("the tortures which cruelty and covetousness can inflict") elsewhere. Yet he shared the prejudice of those who generalized free Blacks as "dishonest, corrupt, and profligate," and "injurious" to society.

While he did not join the American Colonization Society in Maryland, Kennedy believed in physiognomy and phrenology and in its depiction of African faces as unpromising, their weaker mental attributes detectable at sight. Bridging two worlds, he'd paid a call on Thomas Jefferson at Monticello in 1825 and somewhat later became the intimate friend of Washington Irving. *Swallow Barn* (1832), his best-known novel, was a southern version of Irving's *Bracebridge Hall* (1822) in which he took Irving's effete but entrancing English country patriarch and converted him into a degenerating Virginia planter aristocrat. While the author steered clear of characterizing slavery positively, his resort to Irvingesque satire came at the expense of the Black minor characters. With vintage Jim Crow derision, he contrasted two such characters as they appeared together in the master's parlor: the "rude half-monkey, half-boy" and the mature "waitingman," with "cheeks as black as midnight," who exhibited "old-fashioned negro nobility" but could do no more than ape white conduct and put on airs. Kennedy's caricature was meant to imply that there was only so much progress possible for the African American.[48]

Like Ruggles's nemesis Dr. Reese, a procolonization Fourth of July orator outside of Chillicothe, Ohio, could not decry slavery without making unattractive remarks about free Blacks: "Many of the slaves that have been emancipated, migrate to the free states for protection," he said. "They bring their vices with them, and cannot but produce an unfavorable influence in society within their range. Very few of them are subject to proper restraint, and there is little to hope from the influence of motives upon those minds that are torpid and insensible to the impressions of virtuous emulation." Chillicothe had a vibrant religious community, would shortly become home to Thomas Jefferson's biracial son Eston Hemings, and in time would be active in underground railroad operations.[49]

"*Generations will certainly be needed*"

Those who founded the American Colonization Society in December 1816 were a diverse group of citizens that included House Speaker Henry Clay of Kentucky (who presided at the meeting), Congressman Daniel Webster of Massachusetts, and famed attorney Francis Scott Key of Maryland. The very first president of the ACS was George Washington's nephew, associate justice of the Supreme Court Bushrod Washington, who'd inherited the first president's Mount Vernon estate. The enslaved who lived there under Bushrod and his immediate descendants well understood the issues at hand, and at least one straightforwardly urged visiting members of Congress to cure themselves of the notion that any slaves desired resettlement in Africa. Famed abolitionist Frederick Douglass, himself an escapee from slavery, recognized that the denial of legal standing under the federal Constitution made it entirely possible that forced deportation of free Blacks could eventually result.[50]

The colonization idea was deceitful—it made white people feel better. As we have seen, numerous free Black intellectuals exhibited a pronounced disgust with whites' smug indifference to Blacks' feelings, viewing it as just another form of psychological intimidation. Henry Clay admitted from the outset that the main goal of the ACS was to rid the country of free Blacks. Yet at eighty-two, no less discerning a thinker than James Madison became president of the American Colonization Society, retaining the position from 1833 until his death in 1836. He defended the movement when the Englishwoman Harriet Martineau visited his plantation home in Orange, Virginia ("the negroes must go somewhere"), even as he spoke despairingly of slavery and admitted to her that his own slaves were terrified of the prospect of being shipped out to Liberia.[51]

Because the ACS prioritized relocating free Blacks rather than bringing slavery to an end, it ultimately served the interests of slaveowners. Most of its members judged themselves opponents of slavery, though they maintained human property at home. Garrison was not even the first to question the group's motives. In 1826, an illustrious Virginia congressman made his feelings about the ACS known to the most powerful of American jurists. John Randolph of Roanoke was an oddball, an improvisational orator and unapologetic slaveholder who was famed for his public outbursts and personal insults. His complaint to Chief Justice John Marshall, a Virginian who applauded the organization, was entirely in character for him: "I thought the tendency of [the ACS] bad and mischievous; that a spirit of morbid sensibility, religious fanaticism, vanity and the love of display, were the chief moving causes of that society." Upon Randolph's death in 1833, a long, drawn-out court battle ensued and finally determined that when of sound mind (observers thought him mostly otherwise), he willed more than five hundred slaves their freedom and gave them land in Ohio. His "final wish," if that's what it was, was honored.[52]

The Marshall legacy is as curious. The chief justice, like ex-President Madison, was avidly engaged in ACS activities in the mid-1830s: "I cannot entertain a doubt that Liberia is the best retreat that can be found for our people of colour," he stated unabashedly. He could not imagine anything more "patriotic and philanthropic" than to take part in the colonizationist cause, "an object which ought to be dear to every American bosom." His son Thomas, a slaveowner residing in a part of Virginia where a relatively small fraction of the population was enslaved, was incensed by an institution so "ruinous to the whites," one in which "the master has no capital but what is vested in human flesh." What was more insidious, the inhumanity practiced toward Black people or the degradation of southern society manifest in the fear and loathing of free and enslaved African Americans? Whites' distress was often the main thought.[53]

The iconoclastic Randolph and conflicted Marshall (the younger) aside, self-congratulation prevailed among colonizationists. In 1827, the sitting secretary of state, Henry Clay, pronounced the organization's chief purpose: keeping the Black population from growing and reducing its percentage relative to whites. He couched the argument in terms of a sorrowful acceptance of the fact that Blacks bore minimal responsibility for behaviors that threatened whites. The Virginia legislature appropriated funds to assist the colonization project, while South Carolinians objected to any public discussion that called the institution of slavery into question.

During its first fifteen years, the ACS faced comparatively little pushback, as fewer than two thousand souls made the move to Liberia. In December 1833, that changed. With the active involvement of the abolitionist agitator Garrison, plus leading Quakers and Black and white clergymen, an effective counterweight was born as the American Anti-Slavery Society held its inaugural meeting in Philadelphia. That same year Prudence

Crandall, a Quaker schoolteacher in Connecticut, having been earlier ostracized for admitting a single Black child into her all-white classroom, caused an uproar by announcing a new school devoted to educating Black girls in the fine arts. The blowback was general and extremely emotional: her home was torched, threats were made on her life. Local whites protested that Blacks would now start asking for equality in all aspects of life, and the civil authorities enforced ordinances against "vagrancy" in order to turn away admitted students. A state law took effect requiring out-of-state students, before moving to the state, to obtain "consent in writing" from a majority of Connecticut's government leaders, whose publicly stated fear was of a "great increase of the colored population . . . to the injury of the people."

As Crandall pressed ahead, the school building's windows were smashed and garbage was tossed on the property. An area newspaper printed a searing attack on her support network that was signed "A Friend of the Colonization Cause." Crandall solicited aid from William Lloyd Garrison and other prominent abolitionists while advertising the school in the *Liberator*, but she was thrown into prison and her school was shut down. Twice convicted, she was eventually freed on the basis of "insufficient evidence" in a decision of the state supreme court. Crandall then married a Baptist minister, packed up, and went to Illinois.[54]

The reform landscape grew ever more complex. Under fire from abolitionist groups, the ACS persevered through its publication *African Repository* by featuring regular dispatches from Liberia meant to demonstrate that the movement remained dynamic, principled, and valid. The ACS often (albeit defensively) invoked the "venerable" names of Jefferson, Madison, and Marshall in justifying its principles amid these mounting attacks.

The brilliant, fearless women's rights activist and abolitionist Lucretia Mott (1793–1880) was another who saw through

colonizationist cant. To a Scottish phrenologist with a conciliatory bent, she made plain the utter incompatibility of colonizationists and abolitionists and recommended he look into the
work of the Kentuckian James G. Birney, a Henry Clay ally and
key figure in the ACS in the 1820s who repudiated the organization in the 1830s. For years an ACS agent and attorney in
Alabama and Louisiana, Birney publicly urged his former colleagues to see that in bypassing the true interests of free people
of color, in obtaining "consent . . . by imposition of civil disabili-
ties, disfranchisement, exclusion from sympathy," the colonization principle had become "a solemn farce." For Lucretia Mott,
writing in 1839, "consent" was an obvious lie, colonization "a
false Philosophy and a *falser* Theology." At one time, she allowed, it may have been "actuated by Benevolence," but now
colonization no longer had moral standing: it took perverse
pleasure in an "indifference to the advancement of the free people of color in this—their legitimate home." Black Americans
were Americans.[55]

Gradually, the ACS lost its vigor. By the 1850s, once-
proliferating local branches disappeared, as abolitionism commanded more minds. If contentious southern politicians provoked this shift when they lashed out at northern interference,
changes of heart among reformers were driven by both rational
and emotional factors: clearly, the dual goals of emancipation
and preservation of the Union could not be effected through the
recolonization process and slavery would not die out on its own.
Simply from a logistical perspective, colonization was wholly
impractical.[56]

Liberia's growth was not as impressive as hoped for and new
ideas about how to expand the colony were not forthcoming. Yet
the ACS continued to press its agenda. In 1855, Cincinnati jour-
nalist and ACS agent David Christy published *Cotton Is King*,
in which he simultaneously blasted slaveholding oligarchs and
dismissed abolitionism as doomed to failure. Only Liberia would

do, he insisted. A "diversity of language" and "frequency of its civil wars" ruled out South America. And it was pointless to wait for America to change, because "generations will certainly be needed for the elevation of the Free colored people here." Unloved, they "suffer from inadequate means of improvement." In Liberia alone, the argument went, "all the necessary stimulants to civil, social, intellectual, and moral advancement are within reach of the colored man."[57]

Sarah Josepha Hale is indicative of the movement's longevity and its refusal to budge. In her book *Liberia*, she holds fast to the idea that Africa was the promised land for Black Americans who felt unloved and unable to achieve a position of respect in the United States. Colonization meant an end to their suffering. They would bring the "American" values of honorable industry and Christianity to Africa, breathing an "American" spirit into a continent in need of rescue.

With Liberia declaring itself an independent nation in 1847, Hale applied a familial metaphor to identify the United States as "foster-mother" to the new state, governed by its first president, a biracial free Black from Norfolk, Virginia, Joseph Jenkins Roberts. Revealing its tongue-tied failure to convey respect to persons of color (invariably cast as a "wretched" or "suffering" race), the United States dithered before finally recognizing Liberia, along with Haiti, in October 1862. Prior to that, the Black republic in Haiti was portrayed in much of the US press as a backward, barbarous island.[58]

How much changed, though? From 1800 to 1850, as the US population quadrupled, working spaces received more surveillance and the vigor of bodies came to matter even more. The eighteenth century's emphasis on bloodlines remained current. "Blood" measured purity in the adjudication of racial status, biological capacity, and mental and moral health—the opposite of purity was corruption, defect, contamination. Nat Turner had a chilling effect, too: the chaos and killings he inspired only

262 LONGING for CONNECTION

raised the level of white fear and provoked crackdowns on free Blacks, feeding the fantasy of their expulsion. Blood and bloodletting were unbanishable symbols.[59]

Yet another ardent opponent of the ACS was Martin Robison Delany (1812–85). Son of an enslaved father and free mother, he published *The Condition, Elevation, Emigration, and Destiny of the Colored People of the United States* in 1852. His words sting: "We look upon the American Colonization Society as one of the most arrant enemies of the colored man, ever seeking to discomfit him, and envying him of every privilege that he may enjoy. We believe it to be anti-Christian in its character, and misanthropic in its pretended sympathies." While exposing the "injurious" intentions of the ACS, Delany carefully distinguished between the "arrant hypocrites" and "well wishers" among the whites who honestly believed that colonization could be a means of Black uplift. He himself traveled to West Africa to investigate the suitability of its environment for resettlement.

Delany opens his book with sensitive lines from "The Negro's Complaint" (1788) by the English antislavery poet William Cowper: "Skins may differ, but affections / Dwell in black and white the same." Resisting white America's unthinking reduction of its colored population to objects of "commiseration, sorrow, and contempt," Delany argues that Black Americans should stop passively waiting for those of a "pale complexion" to pave the way for them and instead engage in "self-efforts" to secure their own social elevation. "We are Americans," he exclaims, "having a birthright citizenship—natural claims upon the country—claims common to all others of our fellow citizens—natural rights, which may, by virtue of unjust laws, be obstructed, but never can be annulled." When the Civil War erupted, he recruited African Americans for the military, met with President Lincoln, and entered the war in early 1865 as a Union Army major.[60]

There were others like him. Black newspaper editors and antebellum minister-orators who traveled through the North called out the pipedream of a whites-only future. In 1830, there were already over three hundred thousand free Blacks in the United States, more than half of them in the South. The free-born New Yorker Alexander Crummell (1819–98), an Episcopal minister who spent the years from 1853 to 1872 in Liberia before returning home, was at first a supporter of colonization but then changed his mind and continued to speak out against it long after the end of the Civil War. "The gross and violent intermixing of blood of the southern white man" was not the only measure of racial "amalgamation," he said, qualifying the word most commonly used to describe race mixing in the nineteenth century; "in its exact sense" it meant "the approach of affinities." "Amalgamation," he maintained, had not really occurred before the war, because the sex that happened was properly regarded as "the victimizing of the helpless black woman"—unmarked by affinity.[61]

Ultimately, the abolitionists' language of righteousness and benevolence outdistanced the colonizationists' language of righteousness and benevolence.

"If it is not true, it is well invented"

At nearly every step in Edward Everett's political career—which included ten years in the US House of Representatives, four as Massachusetts governor, and nearly four as US minister to Great Britain as a moderate Whig—his see-saw views on slavery defined him.

His first slavery speech in the House, in 1826, angered many in his section. He crossed a line in attempting to "both sides" the issue, by proclaiming that southerners' fears of slave insurrection were legitimate. Some forms of slavery were understandable, he said, and were not unnecessarily "immoral and irreligious." American slaves were better fed and clothed than the peasants he'd seen in Europe. Here, he echoed the remarks of his brother Alexander, a moderate Democrat, on the state of Europe, the point of which was to highlight America's prospects as a growing "civilized" nation. His brother-in-law, newspaper editor Nathan Hale, commiserated, writing in his paper that the congressman's alarm over "slave insurrection" did not mean he was proslavery. The *Boston Advertiser* would continue to berate Garrisonian abolitionism into the next decade.

In 1830, as President Andrew Jackson was pushing Indian removal, the younger Everett brother differentiated between the "civilized" tribes he championed and the "wild savages of the desert" whom he deplored. It was the compulsory nature of removal that he objected to; he worried about the harm it would cause to America's reputation among the European nations. Yet he saw no contradiction between his partial commitment to Indian rights and his unflinching support for the removal of African Americans. In 1832, in the House of Representatives, he stressed the benevolence of the ACS while saying that "as a class" the free Blacks of his own section of the country were "ignorant and needy" and known for criminal behavior. Unable to convince himself that racial disorder was avoidable, he asked for the federal government to give financial support to the ACS.

In 1839, as he ran for reelection as governor, Everett came out against the addition of new slave states and in favor of abolishing slavery in the District of Columbia. This earned him the support of Garrison's *Liberator*. It also contributed to his brother's signing a public declaration *against* him, which made the difference in a very tight election that went to the Democrat. Though their finances were long intertwined, the brothers' personal relations suffered as the years went by. Misunderstandings enlarged with the slow back-and-forth of letter writing. Alexander, frustrated, once wrote, "Allow me to say how much pleasure it would give me if you would let me see you a little more frequently." In 1847, the elder brother ventured across the Pacific Ocean on a commercial mission to China on behalf of the administration of President James K. Polk. He died of natural causes in the city of Guangzhou not long after he arrived.[62]

As the years went by, regardless of Garrison's endorsement, Edward Everett remained strongly in the colonizationist camp. As US secretary of state in 1853, under the weak Whig president Millard Fillmore, he spoke before the American Colonization Society and bemoaned the "unmerited odium" that had befallen the organization. Everett questioned the logic of free Blacks who resisted exchanging an America that showed them "unfriendly public sentiment" for a land of such giant potential as Liberia that posed no such adversity. He compared these potential Black pioneers to the Puritans who suffered persecution in England and supposed what greater pains they might have suffered if they had convinced themselves "that England belonged to them as much as it did to their oppressors." What if they had stubbornly insisted on remaining where they weren't wanted rather than emigrating to New England?

Long before, Everett had had the distinction of being the first American to receive a PhD. As one of his nation's most accomplished intellectuals, he thought he had it all figured out. It was "a law of human progress," he said, that "the first advances out of barbarism into civilization" should come from overseas. Ancient Egypt brought knowledge to Greece, which contributed its culture to Rome, which in turn helped northern and western Europe advance. America was colonized by Europeans, and it was finally America's turn to supply its spirit of progress to Africa. The idea that the civilizing process was at work, migrating back from the New World as free Blacks revitalized West Africa, struck him as historically just.

Once again, rationalization was easy. Implicitly denying the racist component in his thinking, the cosmopolitan Everett noted that Black Americans had already given ample evidence of ingenuity and intellect despite suffering racial prejudice. Early emigrant Paul Cuffe (1759–1817), his father "a native African slave," his mother belonging to "one of the broken down Indian tribes," successfully "navigated to Liverpool his own vessel, manned by a colored crew." Cuffe, a Massachusetts Quaker and sea captain, built up a thriving shipping business, and was considered the wealthiest biracial man of his era. Before the ACS was even founded, Cuffe had arranged for a number of families to emigrate to the British colony of Freetown, Sierra Leone, where Cuffe himself spent several months.

After invoking the efforts of Paul Cuffe, Everett named African American scholars of Latin from Mississippi, Alabama, and Georgia to make his case that Africa would profit from the infusion of Black American cultural intellect. Civilizing West Africa was an urgent task, and Black America needed to be convinced to send their best. This was Everett's rationalization for a thorough embrace of colonization.

Christian love, "pure, unselfish, manly[,] . . . heavenly love," lay at the heart of his optimistic message. Everett's temperate tone was little different from that which characterized Stowe's *Uncle Tom's Cabin*, the new sensation that Sarah Josepha Hale directly answered with her 1853 novel *Liberia*. One of the main differences between these two novels was that while *Liberia's* Virginia slave-owning protagonist is as mild and salvageable as Stowe's Augustine St. Clare, it features no contrasting character, no one so disreputable and degraded in his attitude toward the enslaved as Stowe's Simon Legree. Yet at the end of Stowe's novel, several of the surviving Black characters find a measure of peace by heading for West Africa, where the character George Harris intends to found a republic. "I want a country, a nation of my own," he says. Stowe came to regret having written this ending.[63]

Everett, a fanatic when it came to patriotic oratory in celebration of the Revolution and George Washington's role in the nation's essential identity, was moderate (if preachy) on most all other political subjects. In his 1853 ACS address, he was appealing to an audience that already agreed with him, and he acknowledged as much as he brought his oration to a close with a short morality tale: when word of California gold reached upper Louisiana, a master brought his slave (Everett uses the milder term "servant") to the West Coast. "They labored together," and though slavery was outlawed in the new state, when the master fell sick and died, the slave buried his "friend" and took their modest earnings back to the man's widow in Louisiana, committed to sharing the wealth and honoring a trust.

Then, Everett confided to his audience that he had no idea whether the story he'd just told them was true. "The Italians have a proverbial saying of a tale like this," he averred, which is "that if it is not true, it is well invented." In antebellum America, a white man's emotional truth—his faith—always outweighed the lived experience of free people of color. It had to if mass exodus was to be kept alive as a viable solution. In the end, of course, colonization was magical thinking, a Band-Aid solution and a mental wall.[64]

"Honor to Washington: A National Ode." The cover page of a song glorifying
the memory of George Washington, dedicated to Edward Everett
and performed in Boston on the Fourth of July 1859.

Courtesy of the Library of Congress.

Conclusion
(The Great Longing)

The international slave trade remained brisk right up to the Civil War, despite uniform disgust for its known viciousness. In 1859, a Portuguese slaver, the *Echo*, left the shores of Angola and headed for Cuba. After eluding British patrols, it was accosted by a US naval vessel before it reached its destination and was rerouted to Charleston, where the Africans were held (at Fort Sumter, of all places) until the federal government ordered their transport to the designated country for recolonized African Americans: Liberia.[1]

The *Echo* reminds us to listen closely when history echoes itself. In W. H. Auden's "The Sea and the Mirror" (1942–44), an extended commentary on *The Tempest* crafted as a combined work of prose and poetry, Prospero tells the bound spirit Ariel that his task as a supplier of magic is to "offer us your echo and your mirror" so that "all we are not stares back at what we are." Auden is saying that we, humankind, can only be rescued from our unwholesome selves by perceiving clearly and that those who falsify history are fated to remain subject to impulse, lost and tormented.[2]

In conducting the introspective exercise Auden demands, students of the past have an obligation to resist glorifying (or reducing) past actors simply to satisfy standards or embrace ideals of the moment. From an unrivaled vantage point, John Adams saw how legends were constructed around Franklin, Washington, Jefferson, and the latest of the illustrious few, General Andrew Jackson. The only one-term president (until his son earned that unenvied distinction), Adams had sincere doubts that future historians would catch what was happening. In his unabashed manner, he asked a Dutch scholar, a regular correspondent, in 1818, "Why Should We not honestly and candidly investigate the Errors and Crimes of our Ancestors, that We may correct, reform and avoid them?"[3]

Fact #1: Lincoln Was a Colonizationist

The dramatis personae of this book must face history's verdict, just as today's Americans will in years to come. Fact #1: Abraham Lincoln argued in 1857 that race mixing was bad for America, that the reason to bar slavery from places where it did not yet exist was to keep the states as white as possible. He cited statistics to argue that "mixing blood" occurred where slavery existed and was extremely rare where it did not. "What colonization needs most is a hearty will," he declared, adding, that "will springs from the two elements of moral sense and self-interest. Let us be brought to believe it is morally right . . . to transfer the African to his native clime." Lincoln's phrasing is strained here: what does it take for one to be "brought to believe," in the absence of moral conviction?

At the same time, as a politician trying to score points, Lincoln distinguished the two national parties in terms of their moral attitudes toward the darker-skinned: "The Republicans inculcate, with whatever of ability they can, that the negro is a man; that his bondage is cruelly wrong, and that the field of his oppression ought not to be enlarged. The Democrats deny his manhood; deny, or dwarf to insignificance, the wrong of his bondage; so far as possible, crush all sympathy for him, and cultivate and excite hatred and disgust against him."[4]

We celebrate Lincoln's humanity on one level while taking in a view of the constituency he represented and the politics he practiced. He formed judgments that ardent abolitionists deplored, and he made statements that became entirely unacceptable within the national narrative once the modern civil rights movement raised awareness and changed political discourse. Since that time, the young have been taught the long history of slavery, how it began on the African coast, how it evolved in low-lying areas where extreme heat and rampant diseases made life tenuous. Words explain, but few will truly sense the anguish of millions, how multiple generations experienced enforced separation. Emotional history doesn't sink in automatically. It is rather the opposite. Between the deliberate distortion of memory and the brain's habit of forgetting, truth must suffer. Choose a metaphor: the journey—the saga—the struggle—the process—is ever ongoing.

The American nation as a whole continues on in dullness of thought, rationalizing the persistence of social injustice and economic inequality. One sees the consequences of history plain as day, yet mainstream culture continually finds it inconvenient, or just difficult, to merge considerations of race and class and gender. That failure, whether willful or not, explains how Americans' most outstanding and habitually recurring assumption about its population is that *skin pigmentation* determines how you feel about yourself and how others judge your social worth.

Hale–Washington–Lincoln–Everett–Hale

Although New Englander Sarah Josepha Hale was ideologically bound to the obnoxious cause of colonization, in other respects, she performed with equanimity as a patriot. Prior to the Civil War, her magazine doubled down on stories and illustrations celebrating Union and the common connection of North and South to George Washington's life and legacy.

No matter what political winds blew, the "first among men" unerringly embodied a unifying ideal. His stoicism and service, his public morality, defined "affectionate attachment"—a mode of conduct he carried out without *affectation*—which was, in turn, how good citizenship was defined. Mrs. Hale stood in an advantageous position herself, as a long-established proponent of female domesticity and Christian propriety who avoided political conflict.

One of her contributions to the nation was her work in institutionalizing Thanksgiving. She first proposed a Thanksgiving holiday in the pages of *Godey's Lady's Book* in 1847, the year Abraham Lincoln entered Congress. At that time it was celebrated in a majority of the states, but on different days with no coordination. The idea continued to consume her for fifteen years. Every president ignored her entreaties. The war inspired her to redouble her efforts, and she finally succeeded in the fall of 1863, at age seventy-four, when a worn President Lincoln responded to her direct appeal and declared Thanksgiving a national holiday.[5] Thanksgivings had been part of colonial-era religious life, and Washington was no stranger to the practice. As commander of the Continental Army and at the behest of Congress, he proclaimed a day of thanksgiving after the Battle of Saratoga turned the tide in the War for Independence. In his first year as president, he designated Thursday, November 26, 1789, as a day of national gratitude to God "for the great degree of tranquillity, Union, and plenty" and to the states themselves, in honor of the newly adopted federal Constitution, brought about in a "peaceable and rational manner."[6]

For Hale, Thanksgiving was an appeal to Americans to find affectionate attachment at home and seek spiritual brotherhood and unity beyond the home. It was to be a twofold expression of religion and patriotism, an ideal Lincoln embraced. He appealed for "humble penitence for our national perverseness and disobedience" and for a demonstration of caring for "all those who have become widows, orphans, mourners or sufferers in the lamentable civil strife in which we are unavoidably engaged." He then prayed for "the Almighty Hand to heal the wounds of the nation and to restore it as soon as may be consistent with the Divine purposes to the full enjoyment of peace, harmony, tranquillity and Union."

Washington Irving's supple prose offers similar exhibitions of a tenacious sentimentalism. In all he wrote after 1815, he sought to connect the emotional threads that bind humanity. His lament for the American Indian ("Humanity shrinks from the cold-blooded detail of indiscriminate butchery") demanded a reaction, namely, condemnation, which no moral person could resist feeling. "They have been dispossessed of their hereditary possessions by mercenary and frequently wanton warfare," he wrote, "and their characters have been traduced by bigoted and interested writers." From the "rude annals" of colonial history, with a historian's forensic eye, he plucked the truth of ethnic slaughter, though it had been "recorded with the coloring of prejudice and bigotry." He believed historical distortions of this kind could not be sustained.[7]

Irving imagined the past by telling stories that brought the dead back to life. A national literature insists that those who are rescued from oblivion or imagined into existence speak to the present as edifying ghosts. Irving acknowledged the most basic truth about cultural memory and cultural hegemony when he wrote of Indian nations wiped out by war and disease that "their very history will be lost to forgetfulness" unless they resurface in "the romantic dreams of the poet." As if to heed Irving's call, Walt Whitman, in "Unnamed Lands," mulled the "nations ten thousand years before these States":

What of liberty and slavery among them,
  what they thought of death and the soul,

Who were witty and wise, who beautiful and poetic,
  who brutish and undevelop'd,
Not a mark, not a record remains—and yet all remains.

O I know that those men and women were not for
  nothing, any more than we are for nothing.[8]

The poet and Whitman scholar Mark Doty writes unequivocally about his subject's oscillations: "The man struggled with attachment, and desire, a profound longing for connection to comfort body and soul and understood that the particular is always perishing, and therefore all the more to be cherished." The language of longing helped Whitman get personal.[9]

Irving was then what Whitman remains today, representative of an essential American energy who united with his readers in self-affirming language, acting out his compulsion to keep the past spiritually alive. When the revered author passed on peacefully in November 1859, at the age of seventy-six, Edward Everett delivered a eulogy in Boston. He did not give examples of Irving's moral condemnation of those who exploited others, highlighting instead the grand biographies of Columbus and Washington. In his tribute, Everett made sure to highlight the role his brother Alexander had played in bringing Irving's Columbus to the world. It took a while, but he did, at last, recall to mind the less earnest side of the author, praising the whimsicality of "Knickerbocker's History" and seating Irving "at the head of American humorists." Only months later, in his single-volume Washington biography, Everett credited Irving's treatment of Washington by designating him the "honored and lamented Nestor of American literature." In Greek mythology, Nestor was witty and outspoken, wise from having traveled.[10]

As an aged statesman, Everett stood at Lincoln's side at the Gettysburg battlefield on Thursday, November 19, 1863, the first national Thanksgiving one week away, and delivered an overlong oration replete with allusions to classical antiquity.

Then Lincoln spoke his immortal 272 words. "I should be glad," Everett wrote Lincoln the next day, "if I could flatter myself that I came as near to the central idea of the occasion, in two hours, as you did in two minutes."[11]

Eleven months later, on the eve of another tense presidential election, Everett spoke at length in favor of Lincoln's handling of "a most causeless and wicked war." He reminded his hearers that Washington came under fire for mismanaging the Revolutionary War, "in terms not unlike those in which Mr. Lincoln's administration is now denounced." In support of the war president's reelection campaign, Everett brought the two greats closer by strategically quoting the father of the country complaining about "the monster of State sovereignty." He argued, as Lincoln had in proposing the Emancipation Proclamation, that the South's rebellion justified a reversal of the prior acceptance of a state's right to determine how and when to end slavery, a system "not being founded on the Law of Nature." The Confederacy was, insisted Everett, little more than the outgrowth of "selfish and ambitious purposes" on the part of a particular group of conspiring men.

The speech, as extracted in Nathan Hale's *Boston Advertiser*, arrived in printed form on Lincoln's desk just days later. And when news was received of Lincoln's victory at the polls, a greatly relieved Everett spoke before his state's electoral college, in florid strains, of "the political storm which had been gathering blackness for a twelve-month." He could breathe easy, now that "the noble fabric of State stands as it stood before the election; not a timber in the frame-work strained, not a stone in the foundation loosened." Everett closed his metaphorically "constructive" address by bidding his hearers "an affectionate farewell."[12]

He died on January 15, 1865, three months to the day before Lincoln's life was taken. The administration's official announcement gave full credit to the orator for his "unsurpassed and disinterested labors of patriotism, at a period of political disorder." A week later, Lincoln wrote of Everett that "his life was a truly great one, and, I think, the greatest part of it was that which crowned its closing years."[13]

We know what came next. In April, after the surrender, an assassin's bullet killed a man and created the indelible image of an unprotected political leader seated in a private box, in a darkened theater. The one-term Illinois congressman, elected president as the Union was being severed, became the paramount symbol of a national melancholy at the moment that Union was entering its presumptive moment of rebirth. Engravings of the slain president's deathbed vigil were strikingly similar to depictions of Washington's final hours at Mount Vernon in 1799. The difference lay in the numbers who were granted access to a quasireligious experience: while Washington's doctor was at the bedside, flanked by women, Lincoln was crowded in by a large number of disciples, engaged in group contemplation of a new, uncertain era.[14]

Lincoln had adored Shakespeare, especially the tragedies *Hamlet* and *Macbeth*. He knew *Richard III* inside out and attended performances of these three plus *Henry IV* and *The Merchant of Venice* within a single year of his presidency. Only days before the assassination he read from *Macbeth* to two senators who were his companions aboard a steamer. The lines he repeated, because he loved how they sounded, were

> Duncan is in his grave;
> Treason has done his worst: no steel, nor poison,
> Malice domestic, foreign levy, nothing
> Can touch him further. (3.2.1194)

It is the humanity of Lincoln that attracts. His pensiveness in photographs taken late in the war reconfirms the almost prophetic manner in which he sometimes spoke of his own fate. Known equally for his gravity and jocularity, he was constantly immersed in literature and poetry, particularly Shakespeare, who by this time had transcended class with his mass appeal among people of varying backgrounds.[15]

As news of the assassination reached the public, Edward Everett's nephew—a Boston clergyman named Hale—wrote bitterly that the act was, if not predictable, oddly appropriate: "The rebellion dies true to itself." He was saying that the violence-prone Confederacy was not *for* anything and that the war brought on by secession pitted "civilization against barbarism." This was, more or less, the same message his uncle delivered the previous October, in one of the last speeches of his life.[16]

The Man without a Country

The nephew, Edward Everett Hale, was the son of newspaperman Nathan Hale and the grandson of Reverend Enoch Hale—thus the grandnephew of the Revolutionary martyr Nathan Hale. It is this Hale who brings us full circle. He authored numerous magazine pieces and one particularly successful work of historical fiction. Over the course of a long life, he had personal encounters with most of the literary and political elite of the nineteenth century. His heavy-handed testament to a privileged life, *Memories of a Hundred Years* (1902), comments on a good number of those whose names are scattered throughout this book: the two presidents Adams, Washington Irving, Jared Sparks, and, naturally, his uncles Alexander Everett and Edward Everett.

In the late 1830s, at Harvard, Edward Everett Hale came to know Jared Sparks as Sparks was compiling Washington's papers—some of which the student's father was engaged by Sparks to print. Through separate letters of introduction from his uncles, young Hale secured a connection with Washington Irving. As he was reading Irving's *Life of Washington* in the mid-1850s, he visited the author's Hudson River–facing home,

Sunnyside. Later, given the distinctive genealogy Hale boasted, he could scarcely avoid making personal connections between the American Revolution and the Civil War he'd lived through and preached on from the pulpit.[17]

Mere months before Sarah Josepha Hale reached out to Abraham Lincoln on the subject of Thanksgiving, Edward Everett Hale published *The Man without a Country*. It began as a story for the *Atlantic*, was published as a novella, and reprinted many times thereafter. In the silent era, it was adapted to film; it was then turned into a radio drama and eventually a made-for-TV movie. *The Man without a Country* seized the imagination of a public ever hungry for gut-wrenching tales of devotion and betrayal, attraction and distraction, love and hate.

The protagonist of Hale's vintage American tale is the regret-filled Philip Nolan, an accomplice to an alleged conspiracy against his country who was sentenced to live out his life as an exile. Nolan declares at trial, "I wish I may never hear of the United States again!" and this causes the judge to banish him from his native shores and to condemn him to remain aboard a navy vessel on the high seas for life, never again to touch US soil. All seamen were forbidden to convey to him any news or knowledge about the country he'd renounced. Being cast adrift was more than a metaphor for the boisterous ocean of politics. It was Nolan's judicially decreed fate.

While the plot is fairly straightforward, the author's path to its creation was labyrinthine, touching on two dramatic episodes in American history: the so-called Burr conspiracy and the Civil War. Once he came up with the idea for *The Man without a Country*, Hale went into the archives, initially to research (as he tells us), "the history of Aaron Burr, and what is called his Plot, winding up with the great Treason Trial at Richmond." Although found not guilty, the war hero, New York senator, and discredited vice president lived in exile in Europe for much of the next decade.

Burr's downfall was gradual. It unfolded over the course of the years from 1805 to 1807, after the Hamilton duel and after he'd been displaced from elective office. Washington Irving visited Burr in his prison cell and penned a sensitive portrait. Jefferson had dismissed Burr, his first-term vice president, in favor of another New Yorker, the older, more pliable Governor George Clinton. As vice president, Burr was not in any way disloyal to Jefferson; most histories, which have villainized him, crib from grossly biased contemporaneous sources—the power of belief is strong—and unlike the families of Hamilton and Jefferson, who either penned or authorized major biographies, Burr's progeny did not survive him. This is yet another reminder that nation-making narratives are intended to simplify and moralize: the story balances the heroic exploits of one against the perverted cause and sinister motives of another. That is how Burr became "bad."[18]

Effectively banished from the Jeffersonian circle after he'd helped elect the Virginian, his political base observably damaged, Burr aimed to reinvent himself in the West, where opportunities abounded. Edward Everett Hale doubted the legality of Burr's plans to encroach upon the Spanish Southwest, but he had strong reservations about Jefferson, too, and considered the circumstances carefully. Jefferson's animosity toward his vice president was clear by his second year in office. Burr was "profuse in his protestations of loyalty"—to no avail, pronounced Hale. Jefferson rebuffed him with a "cold, scornful" bearing. Why had Jefferson turned on Burr "with such intense hatred" that he tried to stage-manage the treason trial of 1807? "Was there not, perhaps, at bottom in Jefferson's heart, a suspicion that Burr would be well out of the way, either if he succeeded in establishing his principality"—leading an assault on Mexican territory—"or if he were killed in battle?"

That is where Nolan comes in. The actual, historical Philip Nolan was a Spanish-speaking, New Orleans–based trader who died in Texas in 1801, in his thirtieth year, years before Burr went west. Hale faulted Jefferson for having "abandoned" Nolan to the Spanish who murdered him. (Nolan had earlier contacted Jefferson about Texas commerce.) Since the mid-1790s, this enterprising young man had been serving the interests, as a "business partner," of the true villain in the matter of Aaron Burr, General James Wilkinson, the man Jefferson put in command of the new Louisiana Territory. Unbeknownst to Jefferson, Wilkinson was in cahoots with the Spanish and tried to save his own skin by turning Burr in and doctoring a letter to make Burr appear guilty. To Hale, Wilkinson's account of himself was "so evidently the falsehood of a traitor and an intriguer that one can only make guesses about what really happened" with Burr. In the course of his profitable historical research, Hale found that US hatred for Spain's rule over Mexico intensified after the Spanish killed Nolan. Public notice of his death highlighted the trader's—no traitor—heroic character. One who knew Nolan wrote for the press: "Few men are better qualified for great and hazardous enterprises than he was." It seems irresistible, at this point, to draw a comparison between Nolan and the Revolution's Nathan Hale himself—cut down when young by a cruel captor. In resurrecting the unlamented Nolan in 1863, Edward Everett Hale converted a forgotten man into the fictional army officer who had one courtroom outburst and paid a steep price for it. "I took the liberty to give [the historical Philip Nolan] a cousin, rather more mythical," he explained years later, "whose adventures should be on the seas."

The Man without a Country was written, Hale later recalled, "in the intensity of feeling" surrounding the Gettysburg campaign and was published soon after Uncle Edward returned from Gettysburg. The author's son, Edward Everett Hale Jr., in a "life and times" biography of his father, underscored the importance of the political backdrop: the treason-targeted parable emerged as northern newspapers were sensationalizing the story of a controversial Ohioan who crossed boundaries in more ways than one.

Clement Vallandigham was a Democratic congressman and the son of a Presbyterian minister who belonged to the American Colonization Society. Early in the war, Vallandigham abandoned the Union cause, viewing it as despotic. He spoke kindly of the rebellious South and was, after trial, escorted across Confederate lines where he was not given a welcome. He eventually sailed to Canada where he fought back politically, campaigning in absentia for the Ohio governorship. At different moments, his activities came close to the common definition of treason: giving aid and comfort to an enemy.[19]

The Man without a Country associates war's momentary clamor with its long-term repercussions on individuals' lives. In the cabin that contains his life at sea, the fictional Philip Nolan momentously surrounds himself with patriotic items, not the least of which is his "shrine" to George Washington. "Here, you see, I have a country," he tells a visitor, his sorrow mixed with pride, at the climax of the tale.

George Washington's Busy Afterlife

The connected worlds of Nathan Hale, the Washingtons and Adamses, Jefferson, Irving, the Everett brothers, and Sarah Josepha Hale all fold neatly into the conceptual world of Edward Everett Hale. Each of these figures either tolerated or directly avowed mythic notions of American identity.

When his father died in 1863, Edward Everett Hale counted up the issues of the *Boston Advertiser* that Nathan Hale had brought to the public over the decades. He concluded that he had printed "more words in that half century than would have been found in all the libraries in the world the day the century came in." Whether or not true, his intentionally bold statement was meant as a reminder that in the course of one century the

United States had gone from an "intellectual desolateness" that had obliged Washington Irving to seek in Europe "advantages, not to say temptations which America could not offer," to a nation of poets and writers in its own right. "It is wholly fair to say there is now a school of American history," he exclaimed.[20]

Cheerleaders for America find it easy to rely on George Washington, whose "firstness" keeps him alive in collective memory and has immunized him from serious questioning in popular literature. It all began with the countless eulogists of 1800, among whom was Edward Everett's minister-father. In his published tribute, Oliver Everett predicted that so refined an example of serene leadership "will probably never be repeated" in American history. Ever since, Washington spoke to posterity through the impassioned oratory of historically informed public men. Edward Everett, we learn from his nephew, possessed an unusually strong memory for facts and never needed notes. On some 125 occasions in cities far and wide, he delivered his George Washington talk, giving all proceeds to the Mount Vernon fund that was so critically important to Sarah Josepha Hale and that encouraged ritual pilgrimage.[21]

Three of the featured players in this book authored full-length Washington biographies: James Kirke Paulding, Washington Irving, and Edward Everett.

Paulding's 1835 *Life of Washington* is a young adult biography, in two volumes. It is stylishly written. Twenty-one years old when George Washington died, Paulding proudly claimed access to living persons possessing insider knowledge of his subject's private life. He met the active owner of Mount Vernon, who by that time was the widow of the nephew of George Washington's nephew—not exactly the most intimate of connections to the great man.[22] Yet in the book's preface, using third-person narration, the author claims that everything in the book is "nothing which he does not believe to be true," which "if necessary," he could produce. And he had a most valuable source in "Old Jeremy," who "delights to talk of Massa George." (It should not be lost on readers that the proslavery Paulding humanized Washington by way of a sensitive Black man.)

Irving's elegant, five-volume Washington, the longest treatment of the antebellum period, published by G. P. Putnam and Company between 1855 and 1859, stresses the hero's self-knowledge and personal dignity. This Washington persuades others of his leadership qualities through his wary manner and acuteness of thought, a sagacious understanding of his environment, and a strong corporeal pose backed up by daring deeds—very much in keeping with Irving's western adventurers. The general's actions are conducted after deliberation, his judgments formed after concentrated study and due consultation with others. He is a man of reason and bringer of good order. In the preface to the first volume, having collected material in the State Department archives and elsewhere, Irving declares that "Washington, in fact, had very little private life, but was eminently a public character," a claim his contemporary readers would have interpreted differently from us. The author's intent is to portray a man who stood above mean urges. Whims and fancies were antithetical to his character.

For Everett, whom his nephew Hale called "a shy man," the American art of persuasion had to be emotional. His 1860 single-volume Washington embraced the memory of a man of flesh and blood, evenhandedly offering a nuanced view of long-accepted anecdotes that pointed to Washington's personal volatility. The great man's understandably human foibles were countered by his self-contained religiosity, "deep, rational, and practical." He was "easy and affable, but not talkative" in small gatherings, given to a "military reserve" in larger assemblies. As a trained warrior, he boldly "seized the opportunity," which would only have appeared "rash" if action had failed. No one would accuse Everett's Washington of hypersensitivity or inappropriate (emotional) reactions.

This multidimensional Washington was as an avatar transcending human form. Neither a man of letters nor a lover of the arts, he was yet "a genius of political and military skill, of social influence, of personal ascendancy; of government;—a genius for practical utility; a moral genius of true heroism, of unselfish patriotism, and of stern public integrity." The qualities Everett assigned were the moral equivalent of "intellect, imagination, and taste, which constitute the poet or the artist." In short, Washington did not need a rhetorical dimension to embody "a consummate manhood." Effectiveness and control was what a fractious society demanded from its foremost benefactor.[23]

Whenever Everett spoke or wrote of Washington, his nephew said, "he brought his audience into sympathy with himself almost as soon as he began and carried them with him as if they were all in the same boat." The power of sympathy protected Washington. While the cherry tree myth that projects young George's impulse to do good in the world gets more press than it deserves, subsequent generations perceived the mature Washington as Everett painted him: as a patriarch who joined the battle without fear or hesitation and who governed with a "love" that could be experienced through faith in his example. His contribution to union (rising above "faction," in the idiom of his time) was his crowning achievement.[24]

In his book on corporeal depictions of Washington, Maurizio Valsania offers a dynamic critique of bestselling twenty-first-century Washington biographies. Without new findings to back up their assertions, several modern authors have gone beyond the superlatives we attach to nineteenth-century treatments. The national father is often described these days as "a superb physical specimen, with a magnificent physique," "powerfully rough-hewn and endowed with matchless strength," "cheek and jaw muscles [that] seemed to ripple right through his skin" and "wide, flaring hips with muscular thighs" that "caused women to swoon." In reality, says Valsania, Washington had a small head in comparison to his trunk, and he was not nearly as tall or as muscular as his legions of admirers would have it. The most one could say about his masculine physique was that the "relatively muscular legs" he developed from a lifetime of horseback riding indicated "military virility." Yet the myths are strong enough to echo throughout Washington biography.[25]

Literally dozens of men named after George Washington have served in Congress. They are more or less equally divided among parties and regions. The first, George Washington Lay (1798–1860), was a Whig born in Catskill, New York, who served two terms in the House. The last, George Washington Blanchard (1884–1964) was a Republican member of the House from Wisconsin during the New Deal. Some of these George Washingtons served in both the US and Confederate congresses. The ambitiously named George Washington Bonaparte Towns (1801–54) spent four years in the House, four more as governor of Georgia. While none of these men underwrote any truly memorable legislation, it could still be argued that the name their parents gave them improved their electoral chances. Republican Nathan Hale of Tennessee (1860–1941) was a businessman before and after his years in politics. He sat in Congress during the presidency of Theodore Roosevelt.[26]

A few publicly active men were named after Edward Everett. One in particular, Edward Everett Brown (b. 1858), distinguished himself as a Boston attorney. In 1885, Brown was denied access to a roller-skating rink by its owner and took the man to court for violating an 1865 state law prohibiting racial segregation in places open to the general public. He won, and further legislation followed. At the end of the century, Brown championed antilynching legislation, lecturing nationally on Constitutional issues such as due process, in support of racial equality. As president of the Crispus Attucks Society and active in several other "Negro organizations" in Massachusetts, Brown directed his eloquence against what he labeled the "lynching mania" of his time, arguing that it "sapp[ed] the life-blood of the republic" by encouraging an anarchic contempt for law and justice. Edward Everett may have come to his antislavery later than others of his place and time, but as a public servant he left behind a reputation for decency.[27]

Fact #2: *Americans Think That Their Illusions Are Who They Truly Are*

Americans grow up believing that essential equality is only achievable under the institutions put in place by our inspired founders. Since the 1820s, when John Quincy Adams introduced the comfortable catchword into his inaugural address, the United States has been denominated a "representative democracy." But is it? The high percentage of "safe districts," gerrymandered congressional districts where "parties choose their voters," and the unconscionable amount of money permitted in "competitive" races, are two rather distinct developments undermining the presumption that the United States of America even fits the proper definition of a republic.

In the twenty-first century, the world has seen the rise of elective autocracies where nationalism has been dangerously manipulated for the purpose of propping up a claimant who nurses a false sense of intimacy while assuming the role of protector. Emotion is goal based, although it happens for the most part unconsciously. For many (and not just fanatics), it is easy to fall for a sham promise, to "drink the Kool-Aid," as it were, and be led to believe that survival is in some way threatened.

History's unseen power is felt. Since the American founding, a vocabulary of enriched feeling has combined with that of justice under the law, the ultimate value in a healthy republic. Optimism is encoded in the concept of the general welfare spelled out in the preamble of the Constitution. It is not theoretical or rhetorical. It demands an adherence to community over private, parochial interests. It is meant to be understood as a collective obligation. It requires an informed citizenry if it is to flourish. One takes solace in such ideas.[28]

Is hope drawn from a nation's beginnings valid? The founders were immersed in Latin and Greek, poetry, ethics, and government as they focused on the accumulated lessons of history. But we have to question whether a retrospective view that assigns prescience to a heroic set of men is historically responsible. It is well known that fairness and justice were put on hold, that the privileged exercised power and the poor languished. Their "kicking the can down the road" allowed the South's "peculiar institution" of chattel slavery to persist. In the annals of emotional history, founder melancholy, concealment, and frustration must share the page with founder splendor.[29]

Fact #2: Americans convince themselves that their illusions are who they truly are. Willful deception can speak high-sounding language. But in a self-proclaimed "land of liberty" that is notably litigious, public safety contends with the battering ram of individual rights and people separate into self-protective subcultures.

Popular mythologies blind. At a certain point in the nineteenth century, southern legislators stopped acknowledging slavery as evil and predicting its peaceful eradication. The abolition movement became the evil that had to be stopped.

Failure of perception is endemic. Belief is powerful.

"One Longing, Lingering Look"

In a society where charitable sentiment is constantly under attack from the unwished-for impulse of unreasoning fear, no government is going to be perfect. "Even among the calm and thinking men [you will find] strong and palpable prejudices," an unnamed magazine contributor exclaimed in 1827. "How many, that have not adopted blind, and yet unchangeable opinions about men, manners, literature, and religion, without being able to give any better reasons for them, than that such are their opinions?" Blind faith, irrational fear, and a herd mentality attach to all times and places.[30]

Emotional states keep history alive and unsettled, while popular fictions corrupt values. It is surprisingly easy to airbrush or whitewash the past. As the historian Peter Fritzsche notes, "Nostalgia yearns for what it cannot possess." Nostalgia leaves memory susceptible to a well-told story. It is part of the human condition to want the impossible.[31]

The longing for connection to a better past is just about as old as the United States. In 1808, Congressman Barent Gardenier of Kinderhook, New York, didn't like the direction the country was heading in. The Federalist, who was also a newspaper editor, despised President Jefferson no less than a more famous son of Kinderhook, Democrat Martin Van Buren, revered him. Gardenier got so worked up about the third president's imposition of a massive embargo on foreign commerce that he fought a duel over it with an equally temperamental colleague from Tennessee, George Washington Campbell. Gardenier sustained a significant wound. In a widely disseminated speech, the recovered duelist denounced the embargo on the grounds that it effected a final, fatal separation from the principles of the founding. Jefferson's usurpation of power, he said, sacrificed "the freedom and happiness of my country."

The warning he sounded was virtually identical to the emotional cries heard from the orators who whipped up a frenzy on the eve of the Revolution. "Shall our liberties be buried under this arbitrary law, and we not permitted to cast our eyes back, and give one longing, lingering look behind us?" Gardenier asked. "Shall we be torn from the embraces of what every American would lay down his life to defend, and not allowed a moment to bid farewell?" The American way of life would never be the same unless an enraged citizenry made a U-turn and restored the founding principles.[32]

He'd lifted the phrase "one longing, lingering look" from Thomas Gray's 1751 poem, "Elegy Written in a Country Churchyard." Gardenier's penetrating (if something less than original) call echoes a known sentiment: the compulsion to paint the past in radiant hues as a time of contentment. In political speech, the past is called into service whenever alarmists bewail degeneration.

Some emotions "feel" universal, while others are clearly time- and environment specific. Of the first type, a fear of boundaries being crossed excites people who imagine the integrity or survival of essential institutions (family, nation) to be under threat. An authoritarian model wants to police boundaries, while a compassionate, more or less democratic desire to "pull down barriers" helps others reason that there are multiple ways to see the world. Both sides claim that only their program equates to a healthy society.

I have sought in these pages to discover in past applications of language a credible way to bring early America closer, a way for us to appreciate a bit better what it felt like to be alive then. Neologies, repeated axioms, common slang, and shifts in the vernacular together exemplify the unrelenting reinvention of an emotional script. Naturally, one can't "teach" emotions to any who weren't alive to experience them. How Pearl Harbor felt "in real time"—let alone Fort Sumter or Lincoln's assassination—is not transmissible. The historian can only do so much.

But we know from dictionaries that new meanings endow old words with multiple lives, often resulting in radical changes. Today, for instance, "discrimination" not only indicates a beneficial ability in discerning, in making small distinctions, a meaning that dates to the seventeenth century, but also refers to race or gender prejudice, a sense it acquired in nineteenth-century America. This is not idle conversation. Emotional implications in language is a significant historical pursuit.[33]

Modern America is divorced from early America in almost every way imaginable. Early Americans experienced restricted sight, the silence of nights beneath starrier skies, the omnipresence of horses and pigs, handheld plows, tall sails and river barges, unidentified diseases, and unreliable doctoring. They mastered a different framework of person-to-person communication. Their lives involved slower-paced physical movement amid greater uncertainty. Vocabulary choices in written correspondence reveal poetic angst as they regularly surrendered loved ones to an early grave.

Remedies prescribed for the diseases that ravaged their world—tuberculosis, pneumonia, scarlet fever, and yellow fever—were as often fatal as curative. For the throat infection that occasioned his final illness, Washington asked to be bled, and his physician most likely hastened, if he did not actually cause, his patient's death. Depletion methods included the ingestion of mercury. Nor did doctors think that operating with dirty hands or previously used instruments was a problem. Charms, omens, and magical cures remained popular in the backcountry. Insanity was considered chiefly a problem of morals. Yet brain science was on the right track in studying the operation of the nerves: their term "sympathetic nervous system" remains in use today.

They recognized emotion as the perception of internal change. They had well-founded ideas about the richness of emotional life; they believed that impressions stimulated body parts and that brain chemistry produced altered states of feeling without which people would be unable to exhibit concern for others. Both moral and medical philosophers analyzed the healthy and unhealthy passions, correlating "affections" with public harmony. They sought to arrest "irritability" by pursuing "salutary" programs of social development. Yet, in the end, it is impossible to measure whether their lives were more stressful than modern lives.[34]

What of the passage of time itself? How did time feel back then? Good scholarship exists on the development of mechanical timepieces and public clocks and what these material objects did to condition people's behavior. Words like "deadline" were not coined until the twentieth century, which bespeaks the slower world of earlier times. Looking "down the road" exclusively referred to glancing in a literal direction. Admittedly, it is difficult to go very far with this kind of analysis, but at least it is suggestive.[35]

For history to be felt, unfamiliar rhythms of life must be recalled in whatever ways are possible. It is a truism that life without complexity is a life without character. Yes, time travel would make doing history easier; but until we can imagine how to explain abstract expressionism to an early American artist, we must accept that we cannot give any more decisive meaning to their reality than the men and women covered in the preceding chapters could conjure today's far busier sensory environment.

Longing and Learning

Everyone wishes to know how *where we came from* relates to *who we are*. This is one reason why metaphors dominate vocabulary. They are the very fabric of creative thought, keeping myths alive and spirits fed. We are estranged from the past, yet it is part of us. Pursuing it, we are like "the man without a country," mariners eternally adrift and hoping to be washed ashore on a land we'll recognize. On the multidimensional map of a past we can only explore in three dimensions, we have no fixed identity. No matter how close we think we're getting to mapping it, we're searching on some level for a world that matches *our* feelings of belonging. Being. Longing.

Some ideas persist. In the *Nicomachean Ethics*, Aristotle examines the passions: "Desire, anger, fear, confidence, envy, joy, friendly affection, hatred, yearning, emulation, pity." He insists that those who act from base passions, who are immune to shame, cannot properly experience the world of sensations. They are neither happy nor free.[36]

Which leads, finally, to the "pursuit of happiness," that metaphysical phrase from Jefferson, by way of Locke, that symbolizes a connection between the Spirit of 1776 and every subsequent moment in the retrospective consciousness Americans indulge. Many have tried to capture its historical meaning, to make its meaning complete, but no political history of the United States has reached anything close to a consensus.

What did the Enlightenment mean by that transcendent phrase? I have always suggested to students that in its proper historical context it refers to that collective happiness without which individual happiness could not be realized, a moral community made possible when a justice-providing government succeeds in maximizing shared interests.

I have a more nuanced appreciation for that quality of happiness, having now written a book that says we cannot detach cultural language from inward sensations or the American exceptionalist narrative from a mimetic engagement with European conventions. America's other is Europe, to which it has compared itself from as far back as its colonial settlements. But the other other is the past itself. Owing to the habitual distortion of memory, the past is a foreign country, as the nearly clichéd but ever valid formulation holds. One communes with it in nearly the same way as one does with an old, favorite song, whose lyrics and melody can stimulate emotion and even retrieve images. (Indeed, there is a phenomenon studied by scholars of music perception known as "music empathy.") Wherever there is that sense of journeying back, there exists the potential of experiencing happiness, though it may not be explainable in ordinary language. Communing with the past has intimacy bred into it.[37]

Charles Darwin regretted having sacrificed the desultory pleasures of music and poetry in favor of an obsessive pursuit of unadulterated scientific investigation. In his *Autobiography*, he remarks that, up to the age of thirty, he had adored Shakespeare's histories and that his turn away from poetry "caused the atrophy of that part of the brain alone, on which the higher tastes depend." To be fully appreciated, life required more that the acquisition of information. "The loss of these tastes," he concludes, "is a loss of happiness, . . . by enfeebling the emotional part of our nature."[38]

Longing for connection is, in a way, the brain's main job. Modern scientists who describe its machinery with empirical precision do not agree on what "the mind" is. In defining mental activity scientifically, such as how a "gut feeling" arises, they struggle to build a bridge from there to the "heart's desire." The brain's limbic system governs memory and emotions. It transmits sensory information and discloses crucial neurobiological linkages. As advanced as brain imagery technology is, science does not claim to know how art (beauty) transmits feelings from one person to the next. The porous boundary between creation and imitation finds its analogue in a historian puzzling through one text's significance over another.

There is something oddly satisfying in the persistence of mystery. Most thought is unconscious; the conscious self recognizes a tiny piece of what happens (and what matters) inside the brain. In evolutionary terms, much of what the brain does on a cellular level is make neural connections that reckon with the past so that one can imagine the future and prepare for it. On a macro level, human societies advance similarly through organization; they establish rules and agreements on what the past authorizes, which is, again, *to make connections.*

Neurobiologist Dean Buonomano details what is happening on the inside: "Our conscious experiences are in essence illusions, convenient running narratives of what the unconscious brain determines are the most relevant events happening in the extracranial world"—outside our heads. His deduction effectively restates the opening premise of this book: whatever history we adhere to is subject to the corruption of memory. We are our stories, whether they are wholly or even partially true, because memory is everything and personality requires it.[39]

The future will judge us as we judge those who rationalized inaction, who knew better but sanctioned race enslavement and allowed selfish, short-sighted urges to extend human suffering. Through the eyes of future historians and social psychologists, the present will likely be seen as an age when a manic preoccupation with inconsequential matters allowed the planet to suffer catastrophic (so-called natural) disasters, known to be caused by human wastefulness and ruinous greed. They'll attempt to explain why so many tamely succumbed to the manipulations of totalitarian corporate consumerism while doing little to ameliorate homelessness and hunger.

They'll conclude that the early twenty-first century failed to address common problems as a conscious community, to pursue happiness as a practical objective.

The cause of history demands little of us beyond honest curiosity, resourcefulness, and decision. Let us keep in mind that memory is assembled and colored by emotion and ultimately composed of longing. The most we can do is to match longing with learning.

Acknowledgments

I have been working at defining emotional history to my own satisfaction for a good many years. In previous books I tackled variations on the theme of historical memory and emotional identity. Two related titles, *The Inner Jefferson* (1995) and *Jefferson's Secrets* (2005), explore epistolary culture and the sensation-driven vocabulary it spawned. Poetry was not Jefferson's medium, but he recognized the importance of lyricism, of cadence, and it allowed him to move hearts and minds.

Sentimental Democracy (1999) shows how a politics of sympathy converted myths into cultural power. Contriving a series of moral justifications, American nationalists translated sentiment into coercive action. In *Lincoln Dreamt He Died* (2013), I unearth the long-hidden dream lore of generations of Americans, recomposing history out of the literal dreams of ordinary and extraordinary eighteenth- and nineteenth-century Americans. The present book's steady engagement with elements of perception is a direct outgrowth of these earlier studies.

I wish to acknowledge the influence of two books whose authors would probably not define their work strictly as emotional history. Carolyn Eastman's *The Strange Genius of Mr. O* (2021) is a richly embroidered study of celebrity making in the early nineteenth century, a subject that cannot be separated from my own "longing for connection" theme. When public lecturer James Ogilvie ("Mr. O") came to town, the local press advertised his presence in exclamatory language. His gestures and voice titillated audiences as he spoke of heartfelt issues that coursed through everyday life. Another inspired work of recent scholarship is Matthew Dennis's *American Relics and the Politics of Public Memory* (2023), which connects material objects and physical remains to the nation's growing pains. From the symbolic "bloody shirt" of war to the haunting void created in the footprints of the vanished Twin Towers in lower Manhattan, grand symbolic efforts record a past meant to be commonly *felt*.

As was true in the case of my earlier book projects, I have consulted many scholars in putting this one together. I make special mention of David Waldstreicher, whose powerful biography of the poet Phillis Wheatley demonstrated for me how one credibly and creatively combines literary and historical analysis. Alexis McCrossen, Amy Greenberg, Matthew Dennis, Gregory May, Maurizio Valsania, and Joseph Ellis have all engaged at length with this study at various stages of production. I value, too, instructive conversations with Anna Baldwin May, Aaron Sheehan-Dean, John Bardes, Scott Casper, Frank Cogliano, Andrew O'Shaughnessy, the late Annette Kolodny, Mary Furth, Martin Kolton, Spencer McBride, Shakeel Harris, Rosemarie Zagarri, Rosemary James, the late Joe DeSalvo, Keith Howells, and Steve Kluger.

At Johns Hopkins University Press, Laura Davulis and Ezra Rodriguez have made the process of bringing a manuscript to life entirely satisfying and largely trouble free. Juliana McCarthy and Hilary Jacqmin kept production on track. The unsung heroes of book publishing are the careful copyeditors who ought to leave every author in a state of awe, and MJ Devaney is an excellent example of the mastery and professionalism I have come to count on over the years.

My persevering literary agent, Laura Gross, has been a stable source of wisdom and encouragement. Nancy Isenberg, my partner, professional colleague, and frequent coauthor, accepts that I will never be the equal of either Roger Federer or Fred Astaire, which is big of her.

Notes

Introduction

1. To catch a glimpse of life as lived in this period, one must appreciate how poetry was read (quietly and out loud) and how private matters were committed to paper. Books that take up this subject include Paul Giles, *Transatlantic Insurrections: British Culture and the Formation of American Literature, 1730–1860* (Philadelphia: University of Pennsylvania Press, 2001), and Abigail Williams, *The Social Life of Books: Reading Together in the Eighteenth-Century Home* (New Haven, CT: Yale University Press, 2017).

2. Mather Byles's letter of 1727 to Pope was reprinted in *(Boston) Massachusetts Mercury*, Oct. 27, 1797, and in *Eastern Herald and Gazette of Maine*, Nov. 6, 1797. Byles's and Pope's influence on Wheatley is established by David Waldstreicher in *The Odyssey of Phillis Wheatley: A Poet's Journeys through American Slavery and Independence* (New York: Farrar, Straus and Giroux, 2023), who notes that Wheatley relied heavily on Pope's translations of Homer. On her 1773 visit to England, Wheatley met with Lord Dartmouth, who gave her five guineas so that she might "get the whole of Mr. Pope's Works." She carried the eighteen-volume set home to Boston. "Like Pope," writes Waldstreicher, "Wheatley aims to please a broad audience looking for a middle way: religious but not doctrinaire, moral but not judgmental of any particular social stratum, playful but not fanciful, feminine but not easily dismissed as uneducated or unworldly" (see chapters 15 and 16.)

3. John Adams diary 11, Dec. 18–29, 1765, Massachusetts Historical Society, Boston.

4. Alexander Pope, *Essay on Man* (Hartford, CT: Silas Andrus, 1824), 23. Pope contrasts the "mix'd and softened" passion with the "lazy

apathy" of stoics, whose icy virtue is of little use: "strength of mind is exercise, not rest."

5. Samuel Johnson, *Lives of the English Poets*, 3 vols., ed. George Birbeck Hill (Oxford: Oxford University Press, 1905), 3:233; Benjamin Waterhouse to Thomas Jefferson, Dec. 14, 1815, Founders Online, founders.archives.gov (henceforth FOL).

6. *Village Messenger* (Amherst, NH), Sept. 2, 1797.

7. "Alexander Pope," *New York Weekly Museum*, Feb. 3, 1816.

8. William Scott, *Lessons in Elocution; or, a Selection of Pieces in Prose and Verse, for the Improvement of Youth* (Philadelphia: William Young, 1801), 215–16; *Prospect; or, View of the Moral World*, Dec. 31, 1803, 25–26; *Western Monthly Review* 3 (Oct. 1829): 205ff.; Van Wyck Brooks, *The Flowering of New England* (New York: E. P. Dutton, 1936), 355; "Address before the Wisconsin State Agricultural Society, Milwaukee," Sept. 30, 1859; Matthew Stewart, *Nature's God: The Heretical Origins of the American Republic* (New York: Norton, 2014), 64–65.

9. Anonymous to Thomas Jefferson, Feb. 26, 1802, in *The Papers of Thomas Jefferson*, ed. Julian P. Boyd et al., 47 vols. to date (Princeton, NJ: Princeton University Press, 1950–), 36:641; William Shakespeare, *Henry VIII*, in *Complete Works*, ed. Richard Proudfoot, Ann Thompson, David Scott Kastan, and H. R. Woudhuysen (London: Bloomsbury, 2020), 706.

10. I draw a distinction between the study of *longing* and that of *desire*, the latter of which, ever since Aristotle, has been cast as a potentially disruptive force, or as Spinoza defines it, "appetite with a consciousness of itself" (*Ethics*, vol. 3 [London: Dent, 1948], 92). In recent scholarly literature, desire (beyond mere sexual need) is often attached to discussions of rights and entitlements. By contrast, expressions of longing carry a heartening element of expectancy with the ultimate aim of binding, of bringing people closer, and combining individual emotions with larger unifying forces. The two terms are used interchangeably when the human condition is viewed as a composite of longing and desire for a world that is better than the one that exists, longings thus being directed backward as nostalgia and also glowingly projected forward in time.

11. Robert Morris to George Washington, Feb. 4, 1792, FOL; William Shakespeare, *King Lear*, in *Complete Works*, 764.

12. Rachael Scarborough King, *Writing to the World: Letters and the Origins of Modern Print Culture* (Baltimore: Johns Hopkins University

Press, 2018); Bruce Redford, *The Converse of the Pen: Acts of Intimacy in the Eighteenth-Century Familiar Letter* (Chicago: University of Chicago Press, 1986).

13. Samuel Johnson, quoted in King, *Writing to the World*, 117–18.

14. Julia Shaw, *The Memory Illusion: Remembering Forgetting, and the Science of False Memory* (New York: Random House, 2016); Tali Sharot, *The Optimism Bias: A Tour of the Irrationally Positive Brain* (New York: Pantheon, 2011).

15. Mark M. Smith, *A Sensory History Manifesto* (University Park, PA: Pennsylvania State University Press, 2021), 43. Smith extensively discusses historiography in "Producing Sense, Consuming Sense, Making Sense: Perils and Prospects for Sensory History," *Journal of Social History* 40, no. 4 (2007): 841–58. See also Peter Charles Hoffer, *Sensory Worlds in Early America* (Baltimore: Johns Hopkins University Press, 2003); A. Roger Ekirch, *At Day's Close: Night in Times Past* (New York: Norton, 2005), Richard Cullen Rath, *How Early America Sounded* (Ithaca, NY: Cornell University Press, 2003), and Carolyn Purnell, *The Sensational Past: How the Enlightenment Changed the Way We Use Our Senses* (New York: Norton, 2017).

16. Paul Connerton, *How Modernity Forgets* (Cambridge: Cambridge University Press, 2009), 89; Paul Ricoeur, *Memory, History, Forgetting* (Chicago: University of Chicago Press, 2004).

17. Paul Ricoeur, *The Rule of Metaphor* (Toronto: University of Toronto Press, 1975), 9–43, 120; Sean Silver, *The Mind Is a Collection: Case Studies in Eighteenth-Century Thought* (Philadelphia: University of Pennsylvania Press, 2015), 23–31; Hans Lindquist and Magnus Levin, *Corpus Linguistics and the Description of English* (Edinburgh: Edinburgh University Press, 2009), chap. 6; Zoltán Kövecses, *Metaphor: A Practical Introduction* (New York: Oxford University Press, 2010); Jeanne Gaakeer, *Judging from Experience: Law, Praxis, Humanities* (Edinburgh: University of Edinburgh Press, 2019), chap. 7.

18. I intentionally isolate the body as the site of expressive metaphorical constructions that have stood the test of time: we see with the naked eye, roll our eyes at a big mouth who won't shut up, feast our eyes on a delightful something, etc. The eye is metaphorically connected to an emotional core and to the heart of who we are. Language experts George Lakoff and Mark Johnson exhort that "metaphor is one of our most important tools for trying to comprehend partially what cannot be comprehended totally: our feelings, aesthetic experiences, moral

practices, and spiritual awareness" (*Metaphors We Live By* [Chicago: University of Chicago Press, 1980], 193).

19. Peter N. Stearns, "Emotionology: Clarifying the History of Emotions and Emotional Standards," *American Historical Review* 90, no. 4 (1985): 813–36; Peter N. Stearns and Jan Lewis, eds., *An Emotional History of the United States* (New York: New York University Press, 1998); Susan J. Matt and Peter N. Stearns, eds., *Doing Emotions History* (Urbana: University of Illinois Press, 2014); Keith Oatley, *Best Laid Schemes: The Psychology of the Emotions* (New York: Cambridge University Press, 1992). On early America specifically, see Nicole Eustace, *Passion Is the Gale: Emotion, Power, and the Coming of the American Revolution* (Chapel Hill: University of North Carolina Press, 2008), Nicole Eustace, *1812: War and the Passions of Patriotism* (Philadelphia: University of Pennsylvania Press, 2012), Michael E. Woods, *Emotional and Sectional Conflict in the Antebellum United States* (Cambridge University Press, 2014), and Michael Woods, "Interdisciplinary Studies of the Civil War Era: Recent Trends and Future Prospects," *Journal of American Studies* 51, no. 2 (2017): 349–83 (which focuses on scholarly literature regarding the emotions surrounding slavery and North-South conflict).

In an early essay on the interdisciplinary formula, Burton Raffel defines emotional history as reconstructing "inner existences from firsthand evidence," noting that "the overwhelming concern is to re-enter a vanished emotional world." However, while emotional history is multidisciplinary in coverage, its account of emotional states does not rely on psychological theory ("Emotional History: An Exploratory Essay," *Biography* 7, no. 4 [1984]: 352–62). I am equally intrigued by scholarship that explores culture and impulse together, which includes Roy Porter's work on philosophical medicine, the cultural studies of G. J. Barker-Benfield, and the cognitive science of Dean Buonomano, Antonio Damasio, and David Eagleman. For conceptual guidance, I have also drawn on Paul Ekman and Richard J. Davidson, eds., *The Nature of Emotion: Fundamental Questions* (New York: Oxford University Press, 1994), Aleida Assmann, "Transformations between History and Memory," *Social Research* 75, no. 1 (2008): 49–72, Stephen R. Leighton, "Modern Theories of Emotion," *Journal of Speculative Philosophy* 2, no. 3 (1988): 206–24, and Katherine Tullmann and Leslie Buckwalter, "Does the Paradox of

Fiction Exist?" *Erkenntnis* 79, no. 4 (2014): 779–96 (on feeling empathy for fictional characters).

20. Ezra Stiles, *The United States Elevated to Glory and Honour* (New Haven, CT: Thomas and Samuel Green, 1783), 8, 14; Stewart, *Nature's God*, 67.

21. Reinhold Niebuhr, *The Irony of American History* (New York: Charles Scribner's Sons, 1952), 24–26.

22. Free Blacks during the period 1775 to 1865 embraced genteel culture, as seen in the material objects they owned, their artistic production, and their reading habits. An example of Black women as eager consumers of print culture is the prevalence of decorative scrapbooks (so-called friendship albums) at home, prominently placed on a parlor table, welcoming visitors. These sentimental keepsakes, ornately bound in calf, contained a considerable amount of poetry, connecting literate women to the powerful language of feeling from the 1820s forward. See Jasmine Nichole Cobb, "'Forget Me Not': Free Black Women and Sentimentality," *MELUS* 40, no. 3 (2015): 28–46, and Mary Kelley, "'Talents Committed to Your Care': Reading and Writing Radical Abolitionism in Antebellum America," *New England Quarterly* 88, no. 1 (2015): 42–44.

23. Houston A. Baker Jr., "Balancing the Perspective: A Look at Early Black American Literary Artistry," *African American Review* 50, no. 4 (2017): 513–18. In the view of Raymond Williams, literary expression involves "structures of feeling" (less individualistic than cultural), shared symbols, and collective memories, which explains why educated Americans loved elite classic poetic forms but believed these forms could reach beyond their class and create a new American sensibility (*The Long Revolution* [New York: Columbia University Press, 1961], 64–65). As Jackson Lears similarly notes, the experiences of dominant groups are "validated in public discourse"; the line between dominant and subordinate cultures remains "a permeable membrane, not an impenetrable barrier" ("The Concept of Cultural Hegemony: Problems and Possibilities," *American Historical Review* 90, no. 3 [1983]: 567–93, esp. 574).

Chapter 1. Memorable Words

1. Edward Clodd, *Myths and Dreams* (1885; repr. London: Chatto and Windus, 1891), 115.

2. See, for example, John Kingston's *Life of General George Washington* (Baltimore: J. Kingston, 1813), which opens with the declaration that "nothing can ever tarnish, or destroy, his glory" (v). This "sober, thoughtful, honest man" (vi) exceeded all his peers: "*Washington*, the great, the virtuous *Washington*" (208), and Anna C. Reed's *Life of George Washington, Written for the American Sunday-School Union* (Philadelphia: American Sunday-School Union, 1829), which notes that "his history is as a shining light upon the path of virtue" (17). and that he exhibited "patient virtue" (196), "stern virtue" (137), "unyielding virtue" (99). and, repeatedly, "wisdom and virtue" (220, 230, 263). In Mason Weems's oft-mocked classic *Life of George Washington* (1808; repr. Philadelphia: Joseph Allen, 1825), published soon after Washington's death and containing the cherry tree legend, Washington is "the temperate and virtuous Washington" (219) "the best of men" (203, 209), "born to teach his countrymen what sweet peace and harmony might for ever smile in the habitations of men" (207).

3. David Waldstreicher, *In the Midst of Perpetual Fetes: The Making of American Nationalism, 1776–1820* (Chapel Hill: University of North Carolina Press, 1997), 122–23.

4. Benjamin Henry Latrobe, *The Journal of Latrobe: Being the Notes and Sketches of an Architect, Naturalist, and Traveler in the United States from 1796 to 1820* (New York: Appleton, 1905), 50–63. Maurizio Valsania gets us as close as we can get to Washington's enjoyment of the domestic scene and his easy capacity to laugh at jokes in *First Among Men: George Washington and the Myth of American Masculinity* (Baltimore: Johns Hopkins University Press, 2022), esp. 199–203.

5. George Washington to Martha Custis Washington, June 18 and 23, 1775, *The Papers of George Washington*, Revolutionary War series (henceforth *PGW*-RW), vol. 1, ed. Philander D. Chase (Charlottesville: University Press of Virginia, 1985), 3–6, 27–28. Valsania details another episode, this one in 1797, when a friend of the Washingtons found a cache of their intimate correspondence left in the drawer of a writing desk she'd bought from them; see *First Among Men*, 149–51.

6. George Washington to Marquis de Lafayette, Dec. 31, 1777, in *PGW*-RW, vol. 13, ed. Edward G. Lengel (Charlottesville: University of Virginia Press, 2003), 83. Biographies of Washington often fail to point out that he demonstrated a need to be held in esteem by younger men, who shied from ever challenging his judgment. His "affection" was in that way conditional.

7. Richard M. Ketchum, *The Battle for Bunker Hill* (Garden City, NY: Doubleday, 1962); "Extract of a Letter from Norwich," *Pennsylvania Evening Post*, June 22, 1775; *Pennsylvania Ledger*, June 24, 1775. The first complete account (extant) was printed in the *Pennsylvania Packet*, June 26, 1775, and was elaborated on by the *Pennsylvania Evening Post*, June 27, 1775. Washington would not have known of the numbers dead and wounded—450 American casualties and over a thousand British—until he was in or beyond New York City.

8. George Washington to Martha Custis Washington, June 18 and 23, 1775, in *PGW*-RW, 1:3–6, 27–28; Martha Custis Washington to Elizabeth Ramsay, Dec. 30, 1775, in Joseph E. Fields, comp. *"Worthy Partner": The Papers of Martha Washington* (Westport, CT: Greenwood Press, 1994), 164. Today, the symmetrical Georgian home is a national landmark. In the 1840s, it housed Edward Everett during his tenure as president of Harvard. The poet Henry Wadsworth Longfellow rented rooms there in 1837 and died under its roof in 1882, as its owner.

9. See especially Antoine Lilti, *The Invention of Celebrity* (Malden, MA: Polity, 2017), 193–203.

10. The legends surrounding Putnam are manifest in William Cutter, *Life of Israel Putnam, Major-General in the Army of the American Revolution* (New York: G. F. Cooledge and Brother, 1847). The episode describing his capture and torture by Indians ("inhuman tormentors") appears in chapter 7.

11. These were the words of Yale-educated Humphreys: Putnam's courage was "attended with a serenity of soul, a clearness of conception, a degree of self-possession . . . , entirely distinct from any thing that can be achieved by ferment of blood" (*An Essay on the Life of the Honorable Major General Israel Putnam* [1788; repr. Boston: Samuel Avery, 1818], 96–97, 180ff., appendix.

12. George Washington to Josiah Quincy, Mar. 24, 1776, *PGW*-RW, vol. 3, ed. Philander D. Chase (Charlottesville: University Press of Virginia, 1988), 528–29.

13. Humphreys, *An Essay on Life of the Honorable Major General Israel Putnam*, 115–18.

14. Isaac William Stuart, *Life of Captain Nathan Hale* (Hartford, CT: F. A. Brown, 1856), chap. 2; Henry Phelps Johnston, *Nathan Hale: Biography and Memorials* (New York: privately printed, 1901), chap. 5; Frances Manwaring Caulkins, *History of New London, Connecticut*

(New London, CT: self-published, 1852), chaps. 30 and 32. The best recent treatment that includes details of the martyr's upbringing is Virginia DeJohn Anderson, *The Martyr and the Traitor: Nathan Hale, Moses Dunbar, and the American Revolution* (New York: Oxford University Press, 2017).

15. Nathan Hale to Enoch Hale, May 30, 1776, in the possession of Edward Everett Hale, reprinted in Johnston, *Nathan Hale*, 141–43.

16. Ashbel Woodward, *Memoir of Col. Thomas Knowlton of Ashford, Connecticut* (Boston: Henry W. Dutton, 1861), 5–7.

17. Johnston, *Nathan Hale*, 98–105.

18. On Knowlton's tragic end, see Joseph J. Ellis, *The Cause: The American Revolution and Its Discontents, 1773–1783* (New York: Liveright, 2021), 142–43.

19. Mary Beth Baker, "Nathan Hale: Icon of Innocence," *Connecticut History Review* 45, no. 1 (2006): 1–30. For the claim that Samuel Hale betrayed him, see *Freeman's Journal* (Portsmouth, NH), Feb. 18, 1777.

20. Maria Campbell, *Revolutionary Services and Civil Life of General William Hull; Prepared from His Manuscripts* (New York: Appleton,1848), iii–iv, 38; Samuel C. Clarke, *Memoir of Gen. William Hull* (Boston: David Clapp and Son, 1893), 4–5. The only difference between Hull's version and the version as it is typically rendered is the comma after "regret" in Hull's (commas were often used before restrictive clauses in eighteenth- and nineteenth-century English). Hull may be the one responsible for having transmitted to Boston's *Independent Chronicle* a more cumbersome version of Hale's "last words," obviously paraphrased, in 1781; see Phelps, *Nathan Hale*, 192. See also Jean Christie Root, *Nathan Hale* (New York: Macmillan, 1915), 129–33.

21. Hannah Adams, *A Summary History of New-England* (Dedham, MA: H. Mann and J. H. Adams, 1799), 358–61. In her later memoir, Adams admits taking her military history from the South Carolinian Dr. David Ramsay, a respected army surgeon, whose 1789 history of the Revolution was the first full-length record of the events of 1775–83 (*Memoir of Miss Hannah Adams* [Boston: Gray and Bowen, 1832], 26). Her recording of Hull's information about Hale is also remarked on in another popular work, Jedidiah Morse's *Annals of the American Revolution* (Hartford, CT: n.p., 1824); see 259–60. On the Hale-Hull friendship, see M. William Phelps, *Nathan Hale: The Life and Death of America's First Spy* (New York: St. Martin's, 2008),

91–97, 125. The "dying observation," like the deathbed confession that becomes a trope in detective stories, carries a special weight. It provides a way for the noble victim of an armed conflict to grant himself spiritual ease at the end. It is next up to posterity to decide the posthumous fate of individuals who are said to have made such dying observations.

22. Frederick Mackenzie, *Diary of Frederick Mackenzie Giving a Daily Narrative of His Military Service [. . .]*, 2 vols. (Cambridge, MA: Harvard University Press, 1930), 1:62.

23. For an account of the career and character of Montresor (1736–1799), see *The Dictionary of Canadian Biography*, vol. 4, ed. Francis G. Halpenny (Toronto: University of Toronto Press, 1979), 552–53. While in New York, Montresor purchased an island that he gave his name (it was later renamed Randall's Island).

24. Peter Smithers, *The Life of Joseph Addison* (New York: Oxford University Press, 1968); John E. Ferling, *The First of Men: A Life of George Washington* (Knoxville: University of Tennessee Press, 1988), 6, 56, 516n. Hale's familiarity with Addison's *Cato* is substantiated by Frederic M. Litto, "Addison's *Cato* in the Colonies," *William and Mary Quarterly* 23, no. 3 (1966): 445–47. An alternative source, even earlier, is the Leveler John Lilburne; see F. K. Donnelly, "A Possible Source for Nathan Hale's Dying Words," *William and Mary Quarterly* 42, no. 3 (1985): 394–96.

25. See especially Roger Kaplan, "The Hidden War: British Intelligence Operations during the American Revolution," *William and Mary Quarterly* 47, no. 1 (1990): 115–28.

26. Kenneth Daigler, *Spies, Patriots, and Traitors: American Intelligence in the Revolutionary War* (Washington, DC: Georgetown University Press, 2014), chaps. 5 and 7; Michael J. Sulick, *Spying in America: Espionage from the Revolutionary War to the Cold War* (Washington, DC: Georgetown University Press, 2012), 15–20. Hannah Adams's recording in 1799 of Hull's prescient warning to Hale has been repeated by many others since, and in chapter 5 of his book, Daigler provides contextualization, arguing why he believes Hale was unsuited to spying. Jay, as it happens, was a friend to James Fenimore Cooper and a source of information for that emerging author's foray into this very subject in novel form. It was tactical intelligence that enabled Washington to stage his attacks on Trenton and Princeton at the end of 1776.

27. Andrew Burstein and Nancy Isenberg, *Madison and Jefferson* (New York: Random House, 2010), 513; Milo Quaife, "William Hull and His Critics," *Ohio Archaeological and Historical Quarterly* 47, no. 2 (1938): 168–84; Campbell, *Revolutionary Services and Civil Life of General William Hull*; James Freeman Clarke, *William Hull and the Surrender of Detroit* (Boston: George H. Ellis, 1912). James Freeman Clarke, a minister in Boston, was Hull's grandson, son of his daughter Rebecca and her husband, Samuel Clarke.

28. In 1901, four hundred copies of *Nathan Hale, 1776: Biography and Memorials* were printed (Johnston obituary, *Proceedings of the American Antiquarian Society* 36 [Oct. 1926], 177–78).

29. Johnston, *Nathan Hale*, 108–26,198–200; [James Stanton Babcock], *Memoir of Nathan Hale* (New Haven, CT: S. Babcock, 1844), 16; Josiah C. Pumpelly, "Nathan Hale: Yale's Martyr Patriot," *Americana* (July 1911): 753–59. The prolific popular historian John Frost, a Philadelphian, echoes Babcock in *Heroes of the Revolution* (New York: Saxton and Miles, 1844): "Hale has remained unnoticed, and it is scarcely known that such a character existed. . . . To the memory of Hale, not a stone has been erected, nor an inscription to preserve his ashes from insult." (176–78). Root sees Third Avenue at 66th Street as the likelier spot (*Nathan Hale*, 99). A plaque recently placed on a building at Third Avenue and 64th Street is devoted to the "legendary 21-year old hero"; it makes note of the unsettled controversy over possible execution sites between the UN-area and 66th Street but then states that the hanging "probably" occurred "within 100 yards" of the plaque. A third suggestion, based on a Montresor document at the New-York Historical Society, is East 77th Street. I thank investigator Matthew Dennis for tracking down this historical marker.

30. Edwin Wildman, *The Founders of America in the Day of the Revolution* (Boston: L. C. Page, 1924); the comparison dates are derived from Google ngram and not guaranteed to be precise.

31. James Kirby Martin, *Benedict Arnold, Revolutionary Hero: An American Warrior Reconsidered* (New York: New York University Press, 1997). On the fascination with Arnold and André, see also Michael Kammen, *A Season of Youth: The American Revolution and the Historical Imagination* (Ithaca, NY: Cornell University Press, 1978).

32. There are multiple examples in Benson J. Lossing, *The Two Spies: Nathan Hale and John André* (New York: Appleton, 1903). "The equal of André" is a phrase from an oration delivered in 1853 in Tarrytown, New York, near where André was captured. See also [Babcock], *Memoir of Nathan Hale*, 14–16, Frost, *Heroes of the Revolution*, 177, Stuart, *Life of Captain Nathan Hale*, and Root, *Nathan Hale*.

33. Nancy Isenberg and Andrew Burstein, *The Problem of Democracy: The Presidents Adams Confront the Cult of Personality* (New York: Viking, 2019), 17–18.

34. Trumbull painted the signers from life in his most famous canvas, the twelve-foot-tall *Declaration of Independence*, which has been hanging in the Capitol Rotunda since 1826. It was Jefferson who suggested to Trumbull that he compose the *Declaration of Independence* (William Howard Adams, *The Paris Years of Thomas Jefferson* [New Haven, CT: Yale University Press, 1997], 92–94). Note as well that in the Bunker Hill canvas, Trumbull also conspicuously positioned Washington's highly valued spymaster, the doomed Colonel Thomas Knowlton, musket in hand.

35. Washington iconography was, and remains to this day, in a class by itself. The first to honor him with a grand statue was the Virginia Assembly, in 1784. The two US diplomats in Paris at the time, Benjamin Franklin and Thomas Jefferson, were called upon by Richmond to make the arrangements. Jefferson selected Jean Antoine Houdon, whose bust of Voltaire was admired. The only problem was one of logistics. Jefferson wrote Washington: "I find that a Monsr. Houdon of this place possesses the reputation of being the first statuary in the world. . . . [He] offers to go himself to America for the purpose of forming your bust from the life, leaving all his business here in the mean time." So great was Washington's reputation abroad that Houdon jumped at the assignment. Rather than wait the months it would have taken for the general to agree, he sailed to America, studied the man's proportions up close, spending the weeks he needed at Mount Vernon. He then returned to France with plaster casts made from life and got to work. Jefferson gave Washington his rationale in dispatching the sculptor so quickly: "I trust that having given to your country so much of your time heretofore, you will add the short space which this operation will require to enable them to transmit to posterity the form of the person whose actions will be delivered to them by History" (Thomas Jefferson to George Washington, Dec. 10,

1784, in *The Papers of Thomas Jefferson*, ed. Julian P. Boyd et al., 47 vols. to date [Princeton, NJ: Princeton University Press, 1950–], 7:566–67). Houdon's statue of Washington, the most famous and most copied, arrived in the Virginia State Capitol in 1796.

36. Alexander H. Everett, "Joseph Warren," in Jared Sparks, *The Library of American Biography*, vol. 10 (New York: Harper and Brothers, 1845), 181; "A Lady of Boston," *Stories about General Warren in Relation to the Fifth of March Massacre and the Battle of Bunker Hill* (Boston: James Loring, 1835).

37. *Orations Delivered at the Request of the Inhabitants of the Town of Boston to Commemorate the Evening of the Fifth of March, 1770* (Boston: Peter Edes, 1785).

38. [James Allen], *The Poem Which the Committee of the Town of Boston Had Voted Unanimously to Be Published with the Late Oration* (Boston: E. Russell, 1772). This was reprinted in 1788 in Mathew Carey's Philadelphia-based literary magazine *American Museum*.

39. *Massachusetts Spy*, May 8, 1783; *Independent Gazetteer* (Philadelphia), Jan. 24, 1784.

40. "On the Memory of Capt. Nathan Hale, a Revolutionary War Officer, Who Hazarded His Life for His Country," *Connecticut Mirror*, Aug. 28, 1820. Another Hartford paper had a short time earlier printed the toasts given at a dinner honoring Revolutionary veterans. The order of toasts was a measure of significance to the occasion: the first toast was to "The American Revolution"; third, "General George Washington"; fifth, "General Joseph Warren"; sixth, "General Israel Putnam—neither Danger nor Treason dared look him in the face"; ninth, "Captain Nathan Hale—the blood of such martyrs is the seed of liberty and independence." General Montgomery was overlooked ("A Revolutionary Martyr," *Times*, Aug. 8, 1820).

41. Johnston, *Nathan Hale*, 162–63; Timothy Dwight, *The Conquest of Canaan* (Hartford, CT: Elisha Babcock, 1785), 3. In a footnote, Dwight notes that "as it was impossible to pay this little tribute of respect to all the deserving characters, who have fallen in defence of American liberty," he "determined to desist after the first attempt. The lines on Major Andre are an exception."

42. Ferling, *First of Men*, 284–86. André was hanged nine days after his capture. On October 2, 1780, Alexander Hamilton wrote to his wife about his refusal to offer André a way out through the presumptive exchange for Arnold: "As a man of honor he could not but reject it

and I would not for the world have proposed to him a thing, which must have placed me in the unamiable light of supposing him capable of a meanness, or of not feeling myself the impropriety of the measure. I confess to you I had the weakness to value the esteem of a *dying* man; because I reverenced his merit." In a second letter dated October 11, 1780, he sent his wife a copy of his letter to close comrade Lieutenant Colonel John Laurens with more detailed praise of André (*The Papers of Alexander Hamilton* (henceforth *PAH*), vol. 2, ed. Harold C. Syrett [New York: Columbia University Press, 1961], 448–50, 460–70).

43. Benjamin Tallmadge to Samuel Webb, Sept. 30, 1780, in *Memoir of Colonel Benjamin Tallmadge*, ed. Henry Phelps Johnston (New York: Gilliss Press, 1904), 132; Thomas P. Robinson, "Some Notes on Major-General Richard Montgomery," *New York History* 37, no. 4 (1956): 388–98. On the Tallmadge-Hale friendship, see James Bishop, "'A Different Kind of Tie': The Personal and Political Affinities of America's Leadership Class, 1765–1820" (PhD diss., Louisiana State University, 2022). Arnold was a key figure in the Canada invasion, though he and André did not meet then.

44. The subtitle of Cooper's novel, "A Tale of the Neutral Ground," refers to the area in Westchester County, New York, where André was captured. "Neutral ground" was considered ambiguous in terms of the applicability of military law. "The law of the neutral ground is the law of the strongest" (*The Spy*, vol. 1 [1821; repr. New York: Stringer and Townsend], 1852), 240). Cooper expresses the feeling that prevailed, as Tallmadge says he told Hale before his mission that an operative was less honorable than a soldier in uniform who fought his enemy without disguise: "A soldier, Captain Wharton, should never meet his enemy but openly, and with arms in his hands. . . . Never did I approach a foe, unless under the light of the sun, and with honest notice that an enemy was nigh" (147).

45. Washington Irving, *Life of George Washington*, 4 vols. (New York: Thomas Y. Crowell, 1855), 3–4:274–90, Hale footnote at 276–77. Undertaking what was an almost obligatory task for romantic writers of biography, Irving injected the emotional history Hale and André were said to have shared. André had "formed a romantic attachment to a beautiful girl, Honora Sneyd, by whom his passion was returned." Hale "contracted an engagement of marriage; not unlike Andre in this respect, who wooed his 'Honora' at eighteen." In addition, there was

the faithful attendant of Hale's waning days, one Asher Wright, who lived to be ninety but was "never the same again" from the moment he learned the captain's fate. Finally, Hale had a dastardly foe in Cunningham, the man in charge of the captured spy on his final night, who insulted him to his face and buried his memory by preventing a dramatic catharsis. Typical of the depictions of Cunningham—purportedly based on testimony of living persons familiar with his character—is Stuart's. After recounting Hale's last words (which are set in Old English bold type), the author unloads: "Maddened to hear a sentiment so sublime burst from the lips of the sufferer, and to witness visible signs of sympathy from the crowd, Cunningham instantly shouted for the catastrophe to close—'Swing the rebel off!'" (*Life of Captain Nathan Hale*, 142). See also Phelps, *Nathan Hale*, chap. 19, and Root, *Nathan Hale*, 136–37.

46. Alexander Hamilton to Elizabeth Hamilton, Oct. 2, 1780, in *PAH*, 448.

47. James Thacher, *Military Journal of the American Revolution* (Hartford, CT: Hurlbut, Williams, 1862), 226–33, quote at 227. Washington drew the ultimate distinction, writing contemporaneously that "André has met his fate with that fortitude which is to be expected from an accomplished man & gallant Officer—but I am mistaken if Arnold is suffering at *this* time the torments of a mental Hell—He wants feeling." André, in Washington's view, was just doing his job as a military intelligence officer; see George Washington to John Laurens, Oct. 13, 1780, Library of Congress.

48. Michael Meranze, "Major André's Exhumation," in *Mortal Remains: Death in Early America*, ed. Nancy Isenberg and Andrew Burstein (Philadelphia: University of Pennsylvania Press, 2003), 123–35. The Continental Congress authorized a monument to Montgomery in January 1776, the first national memorial so conceived. It was designed and executed in France and placed at St. Paul's Chapel in 1788.

49. Edward Everett, *The Life of George Washington* (New York: Sheldon, 1860), 144–46. We do not in fact know that Washington struggled with his feelings, but to be the storied Washington, he had to.

50. Stuart, *Life of Captain Nathan Hale*; Johnston, *Nathan Hale, 1776*, 194–95; Robert E. Cray Jr., "The Revolutionary Spy as Hero: Nathan Hale in the Public Memory, 1776–1846," *Connecticut History Review* 38, no. 2 (1999): 96–98.

51. Alfred F. Young, *The Shoemaker and the Tea Party* (Boston: Beacon Press, 1999), 7, 10–13, 42–44, 58, 64, 87–88.

52. Barry Schwartz, "Social Change and Collective Memory: The Democratization of George Washington," *American Sociological Review* 56, no. 2 (1991): 221–36; Everett, *Life of George Washington*, 142, 269.

53. Scott E. Casper, *Constructing American Lives: Biography and Culture in Nineteenth-Century America* (Chapel Hill: University of North Carolina Press, 1999), chap. 1 and 138–53; Cutter, *Life of Israel Putnam*, 91–95.

54. Levi Woodbury, *A Lecture on the Uncertainties of History* (Washington, DC: J. & G. S. Gideon, 1843), 5–6.

55. Cooper's spy is Harvey Birch, a double agent assigned the job of infiltrating British territory by none other than General Washington, who appears in disguise as well. The plot involves characters whose loyalties are uncertain. Harvey, captured by Continentals who believe him a *British* spy, does not reveal his identity as Washington's trusted, even though he could be hanged; at one point, under sentence of death from a Virginia officer, he destroys the only evidence (Washington's pen) that exonerates him and escapes in order to continue his mission. As war winds down, Washington tries to reward his spy with money, but the patriot refuses to accept it. Harvey lives out his life content in the knowledge of his special service, retaining a personal message of thanks on his person, signed by Washington.

56. Burstein and Isenberg, *Madison and Jefferson*, 347–48. Washington's carefully orchestrated, unquestionably moving, nine-page address neutralizing conspiratorial officers in Newburgh, New York, on March 15, 1783, is a critical exception to his otherwise unmemorable writing style.

57. Hugh Blair, *Lectures on Rhetoric and Belles Lettres* (1783; repr. Philadelphia: Troutman and Hayes, 1852), lectures 4, 13.

58. On the relationship between Jefferson and Henry, see Peter S. Onuf, *Jefferson and the Virginians: Democracy, Constitutions, and Empire* (Baton Rouge: Louisiana State University Press, 2018), chap. 2.

59. William Wirt, *The Life of Patrick Henry*, vol. 4 (Hartford, CT: Silas Andrus, 1817), 129–31.

60. Wirt, *The Life of Patrick Henry*, 141–42. For a wise assessment of Henry's influences and the authenticity of Wirt's recounting, see Charles L. Cohen, "The 'Liberty or Death' Speech: A Note on

Religion and Revolutionary Rhetoric," *William and Mary Quarterly* 38, no. 4 (1981): 702–17. For a breakdown of what Wirt actually knew of Henry's actual words, see David A. McCants, "The Authenticity of William Wirt's Version of Patrick Henry's 'Liberty or Death' Speech," *Virginia Magazine of History and Biography* 87, no. 4 (1979): 387–402. McCants only deems credible the *effect* of Henry's speech on the minds of auditors.

61. Phelps, *Nathan Hale*, 152. The author cites Hempstead's recollection, as published in the *Missouri Republican* on January 18, 1827.

62. *PGW*-RW, vol. 5, ed. Philander D. Chase (Charlottesville: University Press of Virginia, 1993), 1–3. General Washington had direct dealings with men who engaged in espionage activities. For the interesting case of a successful double agent Washington met with, whose character was spoken for by John Jay and who had contacts with John André in 1779, see Elijah Hunter to George Washington, Dec. 9, 1789, with extensive notes, in *The Papers of George Washington*, presidential series, vol. 4, ed. Dorothy Twohig (Charlottesville: University Press of Virginia, 1993), 377–83.

63. Frank Moore, *Songs and Ballads of the American Revolution* (New York: Appleton, 1856), 130–34. Moore explains that his version of Hale's story comes from Hannah Adams.

64. For the Epaminondas quip, see "That Our Happiness Must Not Be Judged until after Our Death," in *The Complete Essays of Montaigne*, ed. Donald M. Frame (Stanford, CA: Stanford University Press, 1965), 54–55.

Chapter 2. Great Distances

1. Martha Custis Washington to Abigail Adams, July 19, 1794, in *The Papers of John Adams*, vols. 9–10, ed. Gregg Lint et al. (Cambridge, MA: Harvard University Press, 1996), 10:214–15; John Quincy Adams diary, July 18–19, 1794, Massachusetts Historical Society.

2. John Quincy Adams to Abigail Adams, Oct. 24, 1794;, and Abigail Adams to John Quincy Adams, Nov. 26, 1794, in *Adams Family Correspondence* (henceforth *AFC*), 15 vols. to date, eds. L. H. Butterfield, et al. (Cambridge, MA: Belknap Press, 1963–), 15 vols. to date (henceforth *AFC*), 10:239, 274.

3. Abigail Adams to John Quincy Adams, Feb. 29, 1796, and Apr. 21, 1798, in *AFC*, 11:194–96, 12:516.

4. Susan J. Matt, *Homesickness: An American History* (New York: Oxford University Press, 2011), 31–33. Matt notes that the word "nostalgia" entered the vocabulary in the late seventeenth century and "home-sickness" in the mid-eighteenth, in both cases in connection with a medical phenomenon (26–27).

5. Abigail Adams to John Adams, July 16, 1775, and Mercy Warren to Abigail Adams, Apr. 17, 1776, in *AFC*, 1:245–47, 385–86; Warren, *History of the Rise, Progress, and Termination of the American Revolution* (Boston: Manning and Loring, 1805), 1:195. For Washington's views on education, see Paul K. Longmore, *The Invention of George Washington* (Berkeley: University of California Press, 1988), 213–26.

6. G. J. Barker-Benfield, *Horrors of the Half-Known Life: Male Attitudes toward Women and Sexuality in Nineteenth-Century America* (New York: Harper and Row, 1976); Abigail Adams to Mary Smith Cranch, July 12, 1789, in *AFC*, 8:388–89.

7. The best extended treatment is Maurizio Valsania, *First Among Men: George Washington and the Myth of American Masculinity* (Baltimore: Johns Hopkins University Press, 2022). Valsania takes careful note of the lengths to which Washington went to embody civility: he points out how the master was punctual at meals so as not to inconvenience his enslaved household laborers; in 1796, he cared enough to query Benjamin Henry Latrobe's servant as to whether he had had breakfast (166–67). For further discussion, see Richard L. Bushman, *The Refinement of America: Persons, House, Cities* (New York: Knopf, 1992).

8. Alexander Pope, "Eloisa and Abelard," in *Works* (London: W. Boyer, 1717), 415. "I Tremble at the consequences that this defeat may have," writes the young officer George Washington to Governor Robert Dinwiddie, from the backcountry (July 18, 1755, Founders Online, founders.archives.gov [henceforth FOL]). "I tremble to paint the consequences," states Benjamin Franklin (Oct. 30, 1772, FOL). "I open all your letters with trembling, lest I should find some horrid circumstance," writes Louisa Catherine Adams to John Quincy Adams (Sept. 10, 1814, FOL).

9. Alexander Pope, "Eloisa and Abelard," 417; "Letters," *Scioto Gazette* (Chillicothe, OH), Nov. 20, 1809.

10. Samuel F. B. Morse to Edward Morse, Mar. 15, 1805, Samuel Finley Breese Morse Papers, Library of Congress.

11. Sally Coles Stevenson to Dolley Madison, July 19, 1813, *Papers of Dolley Madison, Digital Edition*; Elizabeth Smith Shaw to Abigail Adams, December 29, 1793, *AFC*, 9:487–89.

12. Martha Custis Washington to Abigail Adams, May 30, 1791, and Abigail Adams to Martha Washington, June 25, 1791, FOL.

13. See for example, *Commercial Register* (Norfolk, VA), Nov. 22, 1802. Typically, multiple newspapers carried reports of sensation-producing events.

14. For the account of Arnold's wife, which is attributed to Alexander Hamilton, see Egbert Benson, *Vindication of the Captors of Major Andre* (New York: Kirk and Mercein, 1817), 66–67.

15. Louisa Catherine Johnson to John Quincy Adams, Dec. 30, 1796, in *AFC*, 11:470–72.

16. John Quincy Adams to Louisa Catherine Adams, Jan. 6 and 14, 1807, and Louisa Catherine Adams to John Quincy Adams, Jan. 21, 1807, FOL.

17. Sensible people acknowledged the link between bodily sympathies (without nerves to the brain, the stomach would not know hunger) and social sympathy. For astute accounts of the nervous origins of eighteenth-century culture, see George Makari, *Soul Machine: The Invention of the Modern Mind* (New York: Norton, 2015), chap. 8, Roy Porter, *Flesh in the Age of Reason: The Modern Foundations of Body and Soul* (New York: Norton, 2003), Barker-Benfield, *Horrors of the Half-Known Life*, G. J. Barker-Benfield, *The Culture of Sensibility: Sex and Society in Eighteenth-Century Britain* (Chicago: University of Chicago Press, 1992), G. J. Barker-Benfield, *Abigail and John Adams: The Americanization of Sensibility* (Chicago: University of Chicago Press, 2010), Sarah Knott, *Sensibility and the American Revolution* (Chapel Hill: University of North Carolina Press, 2009), and John Adams to Hezekiah Niles, Feb. 13, 1818, FOL.

18. From the *Autobiography of Charles Caldwell, M.D.*, cited in David Waldstreicher, *In the Midst of Perpetual Fetes: The Making of American Nationalism, 1776–1820* (Chapel Hill: University of North Carolina Press, 1997), 117–24.

19. Oliver Everett, *An Eulogy on General George Washington* (Charlestown, MA: Samuel Etheridge, 1800), 8.

20. Constance Classen, *The Deepest Sense: A Cultural History of Touch* (Urbana: University of Illinois Press, 2012), 160–64; Brad Pasanek,

Metaphors of Mind: An Eighteenth-Century Dictionary (Baltimore: Johns Hopkins University Press, 2015), 137–58.

21. Antonio Damasio, *Looking for Spinoza: Joy, Sorrow, and the Feeling Brain* (New York: Harcourt, 2003), 88–92, 155–56; Antonio Damasio, *The Strange Order of Things: Life, Feeling, and the Making of Cultures* (New York: Pantheon, 2018).

22. Rebecca Shrum, *In the Looking Glass: Mirrors and Identity in Early America* (Baltimore: Johns Hopkins University Press, 2017), esp. chap. 4. According to Shrum, men used mirrors to inspect themselves as well but appeared to have less care as to how they looked than women did.

23. Michael McKeon, *The Secret History of Domesticity: Public, Private, and the Division of Knowledge* (Baltimore: Johns Hopkins University Press, 2005), chap. 5; Pasanek, *Metaphors of Mind*, 207–10.

24. Andrew M. Stauffer, *Book Traces: Nineteenth-Century Readers and the Future of the Library* (Philadelphia: University of Pennsylvania Press, 2021).

25. Patricia Meyer Spacks, *Privacy: Concealing the Eighteenth-Century Self* (Chicago: University of Chicago Press, 2003), esp. chaps. 2 and 3; Abigail Williams, *The Social Life of Books: Reading Together in the Eighteenth-Century Home* (New Haven, CT: Yale University Press, 2017), chap. 7; Edward Young, *The Complaint, or Night-Thoughts on Life, Death, and Immortality* (1742–45; repr.; Glasgow: R. Allen, 1798), 40.

26. I am distinguishing desire in its modern incarnation (as ego-invested, with a certain unboundedness or wildness attached) from the longing that letter writing promoted in the past.

27. Hugh Blair, *Lectures on Rhetoric and Belles Lettres* (Philadelphia: Troutman and Hayes, 1849), 159.

28. Blair, *Lectures on Rhetoric and Belles Lettres*, 157, emphasis added; Classen, *The Deepest Sense*; Pasanek, *Metaphors of Mind*, 137–48 (the work Pasanek mentions is the erotic English novel *Fanny Hill* [1748]); George Lakoff and Mark Johnson, *Metaphors We Live By* (Chicago: University of Chicago Press, 1980), 193; Zoltán Kövecses, *Metaphor and Emotion: Language, Culture, and Body in Human Feeling* (New York: Oxford University Press, 2010), 232–38.

29. Elizabeth Larsen, "Re-Inventing Invention: Alexander Gerard and *An Essay on Genius*," *Rhetorica* 11, no. 2 (1993): 181–97; Waldstreicher,

The Odyssey of Phillis Wheatley: A Poet's Journeys through American Slavery and Independence (New York: Farrar Straus and Giroux, 2023), chap. 16. Waldstreicher also observes that "a hallmark of Horace's writing is his ironic wit about the fate and feelings of people like himself: masters in a slave society where some slaves became free." In one Horatian ode, there is even the mention of a slave named Phillis.

30. Margaretta V. Faugeres, *The Posthumous Works of Ann Eliza Bleecker in Prose and Verse* (New York: T. and J. Swords, 1793), 107, 166, 359; Margaretta V. Faugeres, *The Ghost of John Young the Homicide* (New York: n.p., 1797); "Died," *Weekly Museum* (New York), Jan. 17, 1801.

31. "To Mitio, My Friend, an Epistle," in *The Poetical Works of Isaac Watts*, vol. 6 (Edinburgh: Apollo Press, 1782), 88–92. The poem opens with "life's a long tragedy."

32. Andrew Burstein, *The Inner Jefferson: Portrait of a Grieving Optimist* (Charlottesville: University Press of Virginia, 1995), 60–62.

33. Laurence Sterne, *The Beauties of Sterne; Including Many of His Letters and Sermons, All His Pathetic Tales, Humorous Descriptions, and Most Distinguished Observations on Life* (London: G. Kearsley, et al, 1799), v–viii. Sterne was an original and a sensualist, as Lord Byron was among the romantics. Their respective genius was captured in the free-flowing use of language that distinguished each in his lifetime.

34. As a modifier, "morbid" referred to a physical disease but could also denote an affliction perceived present in the body politic, where, perversely, a "nervous" man was defined as strong and a "nervous" woman as weak. See relevant entries in Robley Dunglison, *Medical Lexicon: A Dictionary of Medical Science* (1833; repr., Philadelphia: Blanchard and Lea, 1860).

35. Even if they did not openly espouse the radical ideas of Mary Wollstonecraft, author of the 1792 *Vindication of the Rights of Women*, not all women agreed to the binary determinations dictated by medical science or moral convention. Abigail Adams, Mercy Warren, and Margaretta Faugeres are just a few examples of strong, outspoken women. Yet others whose bearing was deemed overly assertive and unbecoming were termed "repulsive" to men because they had "unsexed" themselves.

36. Hester Chapone, *Letters on the Improvement of the Mind* (Philadelphia: David Hogan, 1823), 90.

37. Charles Brockden Brown, *Wieland; or, The Transformation: An American Tale* (1798; repr. Philadelphia: M. Polock, 1857), 63; William

Godwin, *The Adventures of Caleb Williams* (1798; repr., New York: Greenberg, 1926), 20, 57, 20, 10.

38. Frances Webster to Lucien Bonaparte Webster, Sept. 7, 1840, in *The Websters: Letters of an Army Family in Peace and War, 1836–1853* (Kent, OH: Kent State University Press, 2000), 7–9.

39. "I am really hurt at the stile of your last letter which appears to insinuate that it is owing to my negligence," she wrote in one. "Believe me when I tell you I have written four or five different times and I can no way account for the loss of my letters" (Louisa Catherine Adams to John Quincy Adams, Dec. 24, 1806, FOL).

40. Hannah Nicholson Gallatin to Dolley Madison, Aug. 15, 1813, in *The Papers of Dolley Madison*, digital edition (henceforth *PDM*), ed. Holly C. Shulman (Charlottesville: University of Virginia Press, 2008). Absences intensified the "tortures that suspense and anxiety could inflict," wrote another of Mrs. Madison's correspondents, Sally Coles Stevenson (July 19, 1813, in *PDM*).

41. William W. Story, *Life and Letters of Joseph Story* (Boston: Charles C. Little and James Brown, 1851), 104–5, 113–14.

42. Abigail Adams to John Quincy Adams, Sept. 13, 1813, FOL. The self-described epicurean Thomas Jefferson aimed for "tranquil permanent felicity." When, as Washington's secretary of state, he was charged with having opposed the federal Constitution, he wrote to the president in his own defense, concluding by noting that "it is essential to my tranquillity not to be mis-known to you. I hope it is the last time I shall feel a necessity of asking your attention to a disagreeable subject, being with sincere wishes for your tranquility & happiness, & with perfect respect, Sir your most obedt & most humble servt." (Oct. 17, 1792, in *PTJ*, 24:494–96). The phrase "tranquil permanent felicity" also appears in Jefferson's letter to Charles Bellini dated September 30, 1785 (*PTJ*, 8:568–70). The shared meaning of the term "tranquility" for this generation crystalizes in the philosophy of Adam Smith, who associates it with the effect of companionship and sympathetic communion, pastoral retirement, a composed mind, and confidence in one's good judgment (*Theory of Moral Sentiments* [1759; repr. Amherst, NY: Prometheus Books, 2000], 24, 40, 49, 67, 180–81).

43. Catharine Maria Sedgwick to Robert Sedgwick, June 2, 1821, and Catharine Maria Sedgwick to K. M. Sedgwick Minot, Feb. 2, 1831, in *Life and Letters of Catharine M. Sedgwick* (New York: Harper and Brothers, 1871), 120, 222–23.

44. There has been a considerable amount of scholarship on mourning rituals, material culture, and practices surrounding death in early America. See especially Gary Laderman, *The Sacred Remains: American Attitudes toward Death, 1799–1883* (New Haven, CT: Yale University Press, 1996), Robert V. Wells, *Facing the "King of Terrors": Death and Society in an Early American Community, 1750–1990* (New York: Cambridge University Press, 2000), Susan M. Stabile, *Memory's Daughters: The Material Culture of Remembrance in Eighteenth-Century America* (Ithaca, NY: Cornell University Press, 2004), and Nancy Isenberg and Andrew Burstein, eds., *Mortal Remains: Death in Early America* (Philadelphia: University of Pennsylvania Press, 2002). Monticello acquired the watch-winding key in 2021.
45. As a prime example, see Laurel Thatcher Ulrich, *The Age of Homespun: Objects and Stories in the Creation of an American Myth* (New York: Knopf, 2001).
46. Eliza Pinckney to Daniel [Charles L. Pinckney] Horry, Feb. 6, 1787, and Eliza Pinckney to Thomas Lucas, [1743], in *The Papers of Eliza Lucas Pinckney and Harriott Pinckney Horry*, digital edition, ed. Constance Schulz (Charlottesville: University of Virginia Press, 2012).
47. Phoebe Pemberton Morris to Dolley Madison, May 6, 1811, in *PDM*.
48. [Alexander Mackenzie], *Alexander Mackenzie's Voyage to the Pacific Ocean in 1793* (Chicago: Lakeside Press, 1931), 25–29, and passim.
49. "Josiah Quincy's Opening for the Defense," Nov. 20, 1770, in *Legal Papers of John Adams*, vol. 3, ed. L. Kinvin Wroth and Hiller B. Zobel (Cambridge, MA: Belknap Press, 1965) 158–59; Abigail Adams to John Quincy Adams, Mar. 20, 1780, in *AFC*, 3:310–12; Nancy Isenberg and Andrew Burstein, *The Problem of Democracy: The Presidents Adams Confront the Cult of Personality* (New York: Viking, 2019), 387; Elijah Griffiths to Thomas Jefferson, Apr. 7, 1820, FOL.
50. Alexander Pope, *An Essay on Man* (1733; repr., Hartford, CT: Silas Andrus, 1824), 23. See also Nicole Eustace, *Passion Is the Gale: Emotion, Power, and the Coming of the American Revolution* (Chapel Hill: University of North Carolina Press, 2008), and Ritchie Robertson, *The Enlightenment: The Pursuit of Happiness, 1680–1790* (New York: Norton, 2021), 35. The "card" of reason refers to a compass card used in navigation. In epistle 1 of the same poem, Pope attests that

> better for us, perhaps, it might appear,
> Were there all harmony, all virtue here;
> That never air or ocean felt the wind;
> That never passion discompos'd the mind.
> But ALL subsists by elemental strife;
> And passions are the elements of life (15).

51. Elijah Griffiths to Thomas Jefferson, Apr. 7, 1820, FOL.
52. Abigail Adams to John Adams, May 18, 1778, in *AFC*, 1:277–78.
53. John to Abigail Adams, Nov. 15, 1779, in *AFC*, 3:237–38; Isenberg and Burstein, *The Problem of Democracy*, 43–47, 56–57.
54. Médéric Louis Elie Moreau de Saint-Méry, *Moreau de St. Méry's American Journey*, ed. Kenneth Roberts and Anna M. Roberts (Garden City, NY: Doubleday, 1947), 11–40.
55. Harriot W. Warner, ed., *Autobiography of Charles Caldwell, M.D.* (1855; repr. New York: Da Capo Press, 1968), 394–95.
56. Warner, *Autobiography of Charles Caldwell, M.D*, 395–97.
57. John Davis, *Travels of Four Years and a Half in the United State of America* (London: R. Edwards, 1803), 9–11.
58. Theodosia Burr Alston to Aaron Burr, July 12 and Aug. 12, 1812, in *Correspondence of Aaron Burr and His Daughter Theodosia* (New York: S. A. Jacobs, 1929), 339–40.
59. Joseph Alston to Aaron Burr, July 26, 1812, and Joseph Alston to Theodosia Burr Alston, Jan. 15, 1813, in *Correspondence of Aaron Burr and His Daughter Theodosia*, 343–45; Nancy Isenberg, *Fallen Founder: The Life of Aaron Burr* (New York: Viking, 2007).
60. Joseph Alston to Theodosia Burr Alston, Jan. 19, 1813, and Joseph Alston to Aaron Burr, Jan. 19, 1813, in *Correspondence of Aaron Burr and His Daughter Theodosia*, 345–46.
61. Joseph Alston to Aaron Burr, Feb. 25, 1813, in *Correspondence of Aaron Burr and His Daughter Theodosia*, 349.
62. Isenberg, *Fallen Founder*, 394.
63. Ramsay MacMullen, *Sisters of the Brush: Their Family, Art, Life, and Letters, 1797–1833* (New Haven, CT: PastTimes Press, 1997), 90–92.
64. Stephen R. Berry, *A Path in the Mighty Waters: Shipboard Life and Atlantic Crossings to the New World* (New Haven, CT: Yale University Press, 2015), esp. chap. 1. Pulmonary diseases were the number one killer in early America.

65. Paul Gilje, *To Swear Like a Sailor: Maritime Culture in America, 1750–1850* (New York: Cambridge University Press, 2016), 171; Gilje, *Liberty on the Waterfront: American Maritime Culture in the Age of Revolution* (Philadelphia: University of Pennsylvania Press, 2004).

66. George Gordon Byron, *Childe Harold's Pilgrimage, Canto the Third* (London: John Murray, 1816), 4.

67. Abigail Adams to Catherine Johnson, May 9, 1800, FOL. When he was in Europe, John Adams pondered the "ship of state" metaphor: "A Ship has frequently been used as the Emblem of an Empire, and the metaphor is very applicable here. When the Serenity of the ocean is ruffled by a moderate gale, the vessel pursues its course steadily, and is in perfect Security; but a total Calm, is almost always the forerunner of an outrageous tempest" (John Adams diary, July 6, 1786, Massachusetts Historical Society).

68. Barbara A. Mowat, "*The Tempest*: A Modern Perspective," in *The Tempest*, ed. Barbara A. Mowat and Paul Werstine (New York: Simon and Schuster, 2015), 185–99.

69. Philip Weinstein, "Less," *Hedgehog Review* 24, no. 2 (2022): 100–105.

Chapter 3. Shakespearean Recitals

1. "Poetry," in George Gregory, *A Dictionary of Arts and Sciences*, 2nd ed., vol. 3 (New York: W. T. Robinson, 1822).

2. Thomas Jefferson to Abigail Adams, Aug. 12, 1813, and Abigail Adams to Thomas Jefferson, Sept. 20, 1813, in *The Adams-Jefferson Letters: The Complete Correspondence between Thomas Jefferson and Abigail and John Adams* (henceforth *AJL*), ed. Lester J. Cappon (Chapel Hill: University of North Carolina Press, 1959), 366–67, 377–78; Abigail Adams to William Cranch, Dec. 3, 1797, in *Adams Family Correspondence* (henceforth *AFC*), 12:318–19; William Shakespeare, *A Comedy of Errors*, in *Complete Works*, ed. Richard Proudfoot, Ann Thompson, David Scott Kastan, and H. R. Woudhuysen (London: Bloomsbury, 2020), 211; William Shakespeare, *Measure for Measure*, in *Complete Works*, 936. In a twist of political fate, or perhaps in a show of bipartisanship, Jefferson, as president, named Abigail's nephew Cranch chief judge of the US District Court for the District of Columbia.

3. Abigail Adams to John Adams, April 7–11, 1776, in *AFC*, 15 vols. to date, ed. L. H. Butterfield et al. (Cambridge, MA: Belknap Press,

1963–), 1:374–76; William Shakespeare, *Julius Caesar*, in *Complete Works*, 438.

4. Abigail Adams to Mary Cranch Smith, July 4, 1786, in *AFC*, 7:234–40; William Shakespeare, *Two Gentleman of Verona*, in *Complete Works*, 1387.

5. Abigail Adams to John Quincy Adams, Feb. 16, 1786, in *AFC*, 7:62–70; Thomas Jefferson to John Wayles Eppes, Nov. 6, 1813, *The Papers of Thomas Jefferson*, retirement series, vol. 6, ed. J. Jefferson Looney (Princeton, NJ: Princeton University Press, 2010), 592; George Washington to Henry Laurens, Oct. 3, 1778, in *The Papers of George Washington*, Revolutionary War series, ed. Philander D. Chase (Charlottesville: University of Virginia Press), 17:237–38; George Washington to Elizabeth Willing Powel, Apr. 23, 1792, in *The Papers of George Washington*, presidential series, vol. 10, ed. Robert F. Haggard and Mark A. Mastromarino (Charlottesville: University of Virginia Press, 2002), 313; James Wilkinson, *Memoirs of My Own Times* (Philadelphia: Abraham Small, 1816), 2:424; Kevin J. Hayes, *Shakespeare and the Making of America* (Gloucestershire, UK: Amberley, 2020), 206–7; William Shakespeare, *Two Gentlemen of Verona*, 1375; William Shakespeare, *The Tempest*, in *Complete Works*, 1232. At this moment in the play, Prospero is explaining the melting away of spirits he has called upon to cast a spell on Ferdinand, who is in love with Prospero's daughter, Miranda. In the same speech he utters the famous line (4.1.1887–88), "We are such stuff / As dreams are made of" (276). Evidencing his familiarity with the same play, in a letter to John Marshall, John Adams responded sarcastically to the prospect of politically objectionable schoolmasters being imported into the United States: "I had rather countenance the introduction of Ariel & Caliban, with a troop of Spirits the most mischievous from Fairy land" (Aug. 11, 1800, Founders Online, founders.archives.gov [henceforth FOL]). In *The Tempest*, Ariel is a troublemaking spirit, and Caliban a slave prone to acts of evil.

6. Abigail Adams to John Adams, May 10, 1794, in *AFC*, 10:169; Shakespeare, *Julius Caesar*, 427.

7. Dec. 1758 entry, in *Diary and Autobiography of John Adams*, 4 vols., ed. L. H. Butterfield (Cambridge, MA: Harvard University Press, 1961), 1:101–3, 2:53–54; John Adams to John Quincy Adams, Jan. 20, 1805, FOL; Kim C. Sturgess, *Shakespeare and the American Nation* (New York: Cambridge University Press, 2004), 124; Philip Hone

diary, cited in Gilman M. Ostrander, *Republic of Letters: The American Intellectual Community, 1776–1865* (Madison, WI: Madison House, 1999), 87. Good examples of Abigail Adams's Shakespeare allusions or quotes in letters to John Adams, are to be found in those dated April 10, 1776, September 20, 1783, January 15, 1797 in *AFC*.

8. Lloyd J. Matthews, "Patrick Henry's 'Liberty or Death' Speech and Cassius's Speech in Shakespeare's *Julius Caesar*," *Virginia Magazine of History and Biography* 86, no. 3 (1978): 299–305.

9. Joseph Alston to Aaron Burr, Feb. 25, 1813, in *Correspondence of Aaron Burr and His Daughter Theodosia* (New York: S. A. Jacobs, 1929), 349.

10. Aaron Burr to Theodosia Burr, Dec, 9, 1803, and May 26, 1804, in *Correspondence of Aaron Burr and His Daughter Theodosia*, 140, 162. On Theodosia's education and for details on Burr's relationship with Alston, see Nancy Isenberg, *Fallen Founder: The Life of Aaron Burr* (New York: Viking, 2007), 81–83, 159–60, 216, 387.

11. *Jefferson's Literary Commonplace Book*, ed. Douglas L. Wilson (Princeton, NJ: Princeton University Press, 1989), 106–10, 180–82; *Jefferson's Memorandum Books*, vol. 1, ed., James A. Bear Jr. and Lucia C. Stanton (Princeton, NJ: Princeton University Press, 1997), 619, 622.

12. *Catalogue of the Library of Thomas Jefferson*, vol. 4, comp. E. Millicent Sowerby (Washington, DC: Library of Congress, 1952–59), 535–36; Thomas Jefferson to Robert Skipwith, Aug. 3, 1771, in *Papers of Thomas Jefferson*, ed. Julian P. Boyd et al., 47 vols. to date (Princeton, NJ: Princeton University Press, 1950–),1:78–81.

13. Hayes, *Shakespeare and the Making of America*, chap. 3; David Johnson, *John Randolph of Roanoke* (Baton Rouge: Louisiana State University Press, 2012), 25.

14. William Shakespeare, *Hamlet*, in *Complete Works*, 406; William Shakespeare, *Henry IV, Part II*, in *Complete Works*, 538.

15. William Shakespeare, *Henry IV, Part I*, in *Complete Works*, 481; Shakespeare, *The Tempest*, 1232; Shakespeare, *Hamlet*, 360. John Hanson Thomas, *Oration Delivered in the Presbyterian Meeting House, on Saturday the Fourth of July, 1807* (Alexandria, VA: S. Snowden, 1807); Among other Shakespearean quotes, he included one from the soliloquy in *Hamlet* (2.2.333–63) concerning vengeance and from *Henry IV, Part II* (1.3.697): "He that buildeth on the vulgar heart" (518).

16. William Shakespeare, *Romeo and Juliet*, in *Complete Works*, 1136; Shakespeare, *All's Well that Ends Well*, in *Complete Works*, 175; William Shakespeare, *Cymbeline*, in *Complete Works*, 359; William Shakespeare, *Richard II*, in *Complete Works*, 797.
17. Shakespeare, *Henry VI, Part 2*, 621; *National Intelligencer*, Nov. 6, 1807, and Dec. 10, 1813.
18. Alfred Van Rensselaer Westfall, *American Shakespearean Criticism, 1607–1865* (New York: Benjamin Blom, 1968), 34–61; Lawrence Levine, *Highbrow/Lowbrow: The Emergence of Cultural Hierarchy in America* (Cambridge, MA: Harvard University Press, 1988), 16; *Diaries of George Washington*, vol. 5, ed., Donald Jackson and Dorothy Twohig (Charlottesville: University Press of Virginia, 1979), 175–76. According to Westfall, the greatest number of performances took place in Philadelphia, followed by New York, Charleston, South Carolina, and Annapolis, Maryland. Outrage over the rowdy behavior of audience members and presence of prostitutes dogged the development of legitimate theater in America. There is disagreement among scholars as to the extent of Washington's commitment to poetry and literature, but he unmistakably adored attending performances of Shakespeare; see Paul K. Longmore, *The Invention of George Washington* (Charlottesville: University Press of Virginia, 1999), 213–26.
19. Sturgess, *Shakespeare and the American Nation*, 55–57; Hayes, *Shakespeare and the Making of America*, 75.
20. Sturgess, *Shakespeare and the American Nation*, 19–20, 64–65, 78. Through the 1850s, a remarkable twenty-nine separate editions of the works of Shakespeare were published in the United States.
21. [Herman Mann], *The Female Review; or, Memoirs of an American Young Lady* (Dedham, MA: Nathaniel and Benjamin Heaton, 1797). On cross-dressing, see also Daniel A. Cohen, ed., *The Female Marine and Related Works: Narratives of Cross-Dressing and Urban Vice in America's Early Republic* (Amherst: University of Massachusetts Press, 1997).
22. Note that Abigail Adams, who adopted the pen name "Portia" before the Revolution, took it from Brutus's wife in *Julius Caesar*, not from the character in *Merchant of Venice*.
23. William Shakespeare, *All's Well That Ends Well*, 103; William Shakespeare, *Coriolanus*, in *Complete Works*, 249; William Shakespeare, *Henry V*, in *Complete Works*, 568; William Shakespeare, *Henry VI, Part 1*, in *Complete Works*, 585; William Shakespeare, *Henry VIII*, in

Complete Works, 702, 706, 715, 697; Shakespeare, *Julius Caesar*, 434, 441.

24. Tobias Smollett, *The Adventures of Peregrine Pickle*, in *The Miscellaneous Works of Tobias Smollett*, vol. 2 (Edinburgh: C. Elliot, 1809), 221. Smollett's character Matthew Bramble in *The Expedition of Humphry Clinker* and Oliver Goldsmith's Drybone, the man in black, in *The Citizen of the World* are two prime examples of the odd, compassionate misanthrope, while Joseph Addison's emotionally neutral adopted persona Mr. Spectator stood apart and brilliantly espied men's souls. American readers appreciated complex characters who exuded feeling. See Michael McKeon, *The Secret History of Domesticity: Public, Private, and the Division of Knowledge* (Baltimore: Johns Hopkins University Press, 2005), 229–31, and Thomas R. Preston, "Smollett and the Benevolent Misanthrope Type," *PMLA* 79, no. 1 (1964): 51–57.

25. "An Unfortunate Mother's Advice to Her Daughters" (1807), quoted in Patricia Spacks, *Privacy: Concealing the Eighteenth-Century Self* (Chicago: University of Chicago Press, 2003), 89–90.

26. Benjamin Waterhouse to John Adams, Dec. 13, 1817, FOL.

27. John Adams to Benjamin Waterhouse, Dec. 19, 1817, FOL. Though her year of birth is not indicated on her grave marker, the woman in question was likely Louisa Lee (d. 1863), whom Dr. Waterhouse married in 1819.

28. William Shakespeare, *Much Ado about Nothing*, in *Complete Works*, 1048; Harold Bloom, *Shakespeare: The Invention of the Human* (New York: Riverhead, 1998), 200.

29. William Shakespeare, sonnet 24, in *Complete Works*, 22.

30. Rachel E. Walker, *Beauty and the Brain: The Science of Human Nature in Early America* (Chicago: University of Chicago Press, 2023), 24–25. The author quotes Peale assuring that his artful presentation was "a very certain means of studying Characters, to define the measure of Intulects [*sic*] as well as disposition." Walker notes, however, that it became apparent over time that unscientific believers in physiognomy were making snap judgments that proved wrong; in 1822, Louisa Catherine Adams quipped: "Poor Lavater little knew the mischief he was to do" (22–23).

31. Henry Mackenzie, *The Man of Feeling* (London: The Strand, 1771), 86.

32. Christopher Lukasik, *Discerning Characters: The Culture of Appearance in Early America* (Philadelphia: University of Pennsylvania Press, 2011),

esp. 132–35; Johann Caspar Lavater, *The Pocket Lavater, or, the Science of Physiognomy* (New York: C. Wiley and Co., 1818), 9. In light of this new cultural phenomenon, painters, sculptors, and engravers, beginning in the 1790s, tried to capture the character of George Washington by way of physiognomy; see Lavater, *The Pocket Lavater,* 9.

33. Benjamin Reiss, "Bardology in Bedlam: Shakespeare, Psychiatry, and Cultural Authority in Nineteenth-Century America," *ELH* 72, no. 4 (2005): 769–97; Paul S. Conklin, *A History of "Hamlet" Criticism, 1601–1821* (New York; King's Crown, 1947), 70–71.

34. Shakespeare, *Hamlet,* 391, 403; William Shakespeare, *Twelfth Night,* in *Complete Works,* 1357; William Shakespeare, *King Lear,* in *Complete Works,* 781.

35. *Claypoole's American Daily Advertiser* (Philadelphia), Jan. 1, Jan. 4, and Jan. 5, 1799; *Weekly Magazine* (Philadelphia), May 25, 1799), 219.

36. William Wordsworth, *William Wordsworth: Selected Poems* (New York: Penguin, 2004), 159; Samuel Taylor Coleridge, quoted in Walter Jackson Bate, *Coleridge* (New York: Macmillan, 1968), 152. As a young man, the poet-critic had a fantastic idea for a colony in Pennsylvania, where "equal government for all" would be maintained, and which was to be called a "pantisocracy"—the neologism itself attributed to Coleridge. (15–16)

37. The *Monthly Magazine* referenced the earliest coinage of the word "neologism" itself to the 1726 *Dictionaire neologique.* Another who employed the word "neology" early on was Sir Brooke Boothby, linguist and translator. In his 1792 tract *Observations on the Appeal from the New to the Old Whigs,* Boothby criticizes mobs for using "a sort of neology of their own, to confound ideas of right and wrong" (London: John Stockdale, 1792), 265–67. His worry was that words could be turned into instruments of upheaval.

　　Unlike the English, the French gave neology a mostly positive valuation, much as Jefferson would do in America. The French "néologie" and "néologisme" are generally dated to between 1726 and 1731. In the mid-1790s, however, after the French Revolution reached its most violent and disruptive stage, the words were cast in negative terms, "néologisme" being described as "the injudicious introduction of new words and phrases into a language." See William Dupré, *Lexicographica Neologica-Gallica, the Neological French Dictionary; Containing Words of New Creation Not to Be Found in Any French or English Vocabulary Hitherto Published* (London:

Thomas Baylis, 1801), 200. Dupré open his preface with the observation that "languages, like the people who use them, are in a continual state of fluctuation, which nothing is able to prevent."

38. *(London) Times*, Jan. 26, 1826.

39. Festive singing begun in Revolutionary times grew with annual Fourth of July celebration and contributed to democratizing nationalism in public spaces. See David Waldstreicher, *In the Midst of Perpetual Fetes: The Making of American Nationalism, 1776–1820* (Chapel Hill: University of North Carolina Press, 1997).

40. Thomas Jefferson to John Waldo, Aug. 6, 1813, and July 1, 1814, in *PTJ-R*, 6:402–407, 7:449; Thomas Jefferson to John Adams, Aug. 15, 1820, in *AJL*, 565–67; John Bristed, *America and Her Resources* (London: Henry Colburn, 1818), 359; the "Neologist" appeared in the *New-York Daily Advertiser*.

41. Edward Everett to John Adams, Sept. 16, 1820, FOL. The article in question begins on page 115 of the January 1820 issue of the *North American Review*, and the critique of neologism appears on page 125. On the early years and personnel involved in the magazine, see Gregory Paine, "Cooper and the *North American Review*," *Studies in Philology* 28, no. 4 (1931): 799–809. Everett patterned an original poem, "American Pilgrimage," on Byron's *Childe Harold's Pilgrimage*. Regarding his meeting with the poet, see Mark Peterson, *The City-State of Boston: The Rise and Fall of an Atlantic Power, 1630–1865* (Princeton, NJ: Princeton University Press, 2019), chap. 10.

42. Henry E. Shepherd, "Thomas Jefferson as a Philologist," *American Journal of Philology* 3, no. 10 (1882): 211–14; Henry E. Shepherd, *The History of the English Language from the Teutonic Invasion of Britain to the Close of the Georgian Era* (New York: E. J. Hale and Son, 1874), 177.

43. Peter Martin, *The Dictionary Wars: The American Fight over the English Language* (Princeton, NJ: Princeton University Press, 2019), chaps. 1 and 2; Cynthia S. Jordan, "'Old Words' in 'New Circumstances': Language and Leadership in Post-Revolutionary America," *American Quarterly* 40, no. 4 (1988): 491–513.

44. Thomas Jefferson, *Notes on the State of Virginia*, ed. Robert Pierce Forbes (New Haven, CT: Yale University Press, 2022), query 6, 107, emphasis added. With nationalist pride, a principal New York City paper celebrated the First Congress of the United States by sneering at those "whose envy at our growing greatness, and increasing

happiness, can find no rest but in venting itself in lies and defamation—and in attempts to *belittle* the free and independent citizens of this glorious country." The italicization in the original points to the fact that "belittle" was as yet an unusual word (*Gazette of the United States*, Mar. 6, 1790).

45. Thomas Jefferson to Joseph Milligan, April 6, 1816, FOL; Dumas Malone, *Jefferson and His Time. The Sage of Monticello* (Boston: Little Brown, 1980), 208–10; in general, see David Simpson, *The Politics of American English, 1776–1850* (New York: Oxford University Press, 1986). The timing of a piece printed in an upstate New York newspaper appears coincidental. In 1817, it explained a series of words that caused confusion among the reading public. Included was the following: "*Neology* is the invention and use of words not before in the language and [in distinction from neologism] such as sound criticism will warrant. *Neologism* is the abuse of neology—the affectation of coining new words or using old words in an entirely new sense" (*Northern Whig* [Hudson, NY], July 29, 1817). The insistence on the distinction between the two—the bracketed words are in the original—appears unnecessary and is even at odds with Jefferson's and all earlier accounts, which maintained that "neology" and "neologism" are effectively the same. See also Malone, *Jefferson and His Time*, 208–12, 305–7.

46. On neology and sound symbolism as applied here, see Steven Pinker, *The Stuff of Thought: Language as a Window into Human Nature* (New York: Viking Penguin, 2007), esp. 296–304.

47. Thomas Jefferson to Edward Everett, Feb. 24, 1823, and Thomas Jefferson to John Pickering, Feb. 20, 1825, FOL; Peter Thompson, "'Judicious Neology': The Imperative of Paternalism in Thomas Jefferson's Linguistic Studies," *Early American Studies* 1, no. 2 (2003): 187–224.

48. "On Americanisms, with a Fragment of a Trans-Atlantic Pastoral," *Athenian and Literary Gazette* (Boston), April 15, 1821, 1.

49. Lawrence W. Levine, *Highbrow/Lowbrow: The Emergence of Cultural Hierarchy in America* (Cambridge, MA: Harvard University Press, 1988), 45.

50. John Adams diary, Dec. [5], 1758, Massachusetts Historical Society. The entire thought is as follows: "Let me search for the Clue, which Led great Shakespeare into the Labyrinth of mental Nature! Let me

examine how men think. Shakespeare had never seen in real Life
Persons under the Influence of all those Scenes of Pleasure and
distress, which he has described in his Works, but he imagined how a
Person of such a Character would behave in such Circumstances, by
analogy from the Behaviour of others that were most like that
Character in nearly similar Circumstances."

51. "The Genius of Shakespeare and Milton Compared," *National
Intelligencer*, May 11, 1807; "Fidelity of Shakespeare," in *Alexandria
Gazette*, reprinted in *National Intelligencer*, Sept. 7, 1818; "Shakespeare's Hamlet," *National Intelligencer*, Sept. 3, 1817, reprinted from
the *National Advocate*; *Raleigh Register*, May 4, 1827.

52. Adam Smith, *The Theory of Moral Sentiments* (1759; repr. Amherst,
NY: Prometheus Books, 2000), 44.

53. Examples from Shakespeare's works include "perfidiously he has
betray'd your business" (*Coriolanus* [5.6.3930–31], 253), "that a brother
should be so perfidious!–he whom next thyself of all the world I loved"
(*The Tempest* [1.2.66–67], 1222), and "a most perfidious and drunken
monster!" (*The Tempest* [2.2.1237–38], 1232). In a letter to John
Robinson dated May 30, 1757, George Washington writes, "Hence
they accuse us of perfidy and deceit! I cou'd recapitulate a great
number of their reproachful complaints" (FOL), while in a letter
dated June 23, 1821, to his grandson George Washington Adams,
John Adams cautions: "Among the good, are activity, exertion,
industry, hard study, hard labor, benevolence, friendship, patience
prudence, temperance, justice, fortitude, in short, every virtue, and
every good quality in human life; on the contrary among the bad are
simulation, and dissimulation, deceit, fraud, perfidy, hypocrisy,
violence, jealously, envy, malice, hatred, revenge, cruelty, Slander,
libels, in short every hateful vice and vilainy, every infernal quality of
which human life is susceptible, or human nature capable" (FOL).

54. William Shakespeare, *Venus and Adonis*, in *Complete Works*, 54;
Shakespeare, *Comedy of Errors*, 198; Shakespeare, *Coriolanus*, 228.

55. Shakespeare, *All's Well That Ends Well*, 93; Shakespeare, *Comedy of
Errors*, 207; Shakespeare, *King Lear*, 770; William Shakespeare, *Antony
and Cleopatra*, in *Complete Works*, 127; Shakespeare, *Hamlet*, 366.

56. Sturgess, *Shakespeare and the American Nation*, 181–91.

57. *Long Island (NY) Weekly Intelligencer*, Jan. 1, 1807; William Shakespeare,
Othello, in *Complete Works*, 1079.

Chapter 4. Explosive Satire

1. James Madison to Thomas Jefferson, Oct. 14, 1812, in *The Papers of Thomas Jefferson*, retirement series (henceforth *PTJ-R*), vol. 5, ed. J. Jefferson Looney (Princeton, NJ: Princeton University Press, 2009), 396–97.

2. The word "salmagundi" was not original with the New Yorkers, even in its satirical use. The British satirical poet George Huddesford (1749–1809) published a collection in 1791 titled *Salmagundi*; at least as early as 1801, American newspapers reprinted doggerel verse from England in which "salmagundi" rhymed with "Sunday." On the Calliopean Society, see Amos Herold, *James Kirke Paulding: Versatile American* (New York: 1926; repr. AMC Press, 1966), 20–21, Stanley T. Williams, *The Life of Washington Irving* (New York: Oxford University Press, 1935), 1:16. On the communication between the younger Paulding and Irving, see Wayne R. Kime, *Pierre M. Irving and Washington Irving: A Collaboration in Life and Letters* (Waterloo, Ont.: Wilfrid Laurier University Press, 1977), 249–51.

3. Washington Irving, *The Sketch Book of Geoffrey Crayon, Gent.*, ed. Haskell Springer (Boston: Twayne, 1978), 106, 209–10, 91–99.

4. [James Kirke Paulding], *The Diverting History of John Bull and Brother Jonathan* (Philadelphia: Carey, 1819), 6, 7, 8.

5. Constance Rourke, *American Humor: A Study of the National Character* (New York: Harcourt Brace, 1931), 12–16; *Independent Gazetteer* (Worcester, MA), Feb. 11, 1800; *The American Jester, or, The Seamen and Landsmen's Funny Companion* (New England: Printed for the Booksellers, 1807), 8–9.

6. [Paulding], *The Diverting History of John Bull and Brother Jonathan*, 61, 54, 58, 60, 141.

7. Thomas Jefferson to Elizabeth Trist, May 10, 1813, in *PTJ-R*, vol. 6, ed. J. Jefferson Looney (Princeton, NJ: Princeton University Press, 2010), 110–11. Adding an apostrophe to the possessive "its" was a quirky choice Jefferson made throughout his life of writing.

8. [James Kirke Paulding], *The United States and England* (Philadelphia: Bradford and Inskeep, 1815), 94, 103–4; William Irving to James Madison, Jan. 2, 1815, Founders Online, founders.archives.gov.

9. Ralph L. Ketcham, "An Unpublished Sketch of James Madison by James K. Paulding," *Virginia Magazine of History and Biography* 67, no. 4 (1959): 432–37.

330 NOTES TO PAGES 153-157

10. Washington Irving to [Mary Fairlie?], July 7, 1807, in *Letters*, 4 vols., ed., Ralph M. Aderman, Herbert L. Kleinfield, and Jenifer S. Banks (Boston: Twayne, 1978), 1:243.

11. Washington Irving to Mary Fairlie, May 2 and May 13, 1807, in *Letters*, 1:231, 234–36; *Salmagundi* (Philadelphia: J. B. Lippincott, 1871), June 2, 1807, 233.

12. Irving to "Andrew Quoz" (possibly a nickname for Paulding at this time), Jan. 5, 1805, *Letters*, 1:165–69; the same letter contains a quote from *Othello*. On Irving's representation of localities and the burlesque form, see Paul Giles, *Transatlantic Insurrections: British Culture and the Formation of American Literature, 1730–1860* (Philadelphia: University of Pennsylvania Press, 2001), chap. 6.

13. [Francis Hopkinson], *A Pretty Story Written in the Year of Our Lord 1774* (Philadelphia: John Dunlap, 1774).

14. Robert Secor, "Ethnic Humor in Early American Jest Books," in *A Mixed Race: Ethnicity in Early America*, ed. Frank Shuffelton (New York: Oxford University Press, 1993), 163–93. In another example of Indian cleverness, an Indian who was brought before a judge on charges of stealing a Spaniard's horse placed a covering over the mare's eyes and demanded that the Spaniard, who claimed he'd raised the horse from birth, identify which of the animal's eyes was sightless. Having a fifty–fifty chance, the thief promptly answered, "the right," and the Indian revealed that his horse had perfect vision, thus winning the case. See *A New Book of Oddities, and Literary Olio . . . Interspersed with Ludicrous & Facetious Poetry* (Philadelphia: Solomon Wieatt, 1803), 137–38. On the forty-year-old woman, see *The American Jester*, 31–32.

15. "Pun," *Weekly Visitor and Ladies Museum* (New York), June 28, 1823; *Rutland (VT) Herald*, June 14, 1815, 4; *New-York Mirror*, Feb. 28, 1824, 3; *Ladies Literary Museum* (Philadelphia), Feb. 9, 1818, 71.

16. "Money in the Bank" and "Eulogy on Punning," *New England Farmer* (Boston), Dec. 27, 1823; "Pun," *Weekly Visitor and Ladies Museum*, June 7, 1823; "The Country Carpenter," *Boston Intelligencer*, July 22, 1820; *Juvenile Port-Folio* (Boston), Feb. 3, 1816. Lawyer/judge jokes remained popular for years: in another, a creditor who was stiffed was asked by his attorney what the man who owed him had said when reminded of his debt. "He told me to go to the devil." "And what did you do then?" "Why I came to you" (*Boston Cultivator*, July 13, 1844).

17. *Salmagundi*, Aug. 14, 1807, 301–2.
18. *Sentinel of Freedom* (Newark, NJ), June 13, 1809, 4.
19. "Wit or Humor," in the *North American*, Apr. 13, 1842; *Atlas* (Boston), Dec. 26, 1845; *Boston Investigator*, Jan. 12, 1848; *(Hudson) Ohio Observer*, Feb. 14, 1849; "Wit and Humor," *Placer Times* (Sacramento, CA), June 5, 1850; "Yankee Humor," *Fayetteville (NC) Observer*, May 3, 1855.
20. *Miscellaneous Cabinet* (Schenectady, NY), Sept. 13, 1823, 80.
21. "Relics of the Revolution," *Niles' Weekly Register*, Oct. 6, 1832, cited in Edward Tang, "Writing the American Revolution: War Veterans in the Nineteenth-Century Cultural Memory," *Journal of American Studies* 32, no. 1 (1998): 69.
22. "Conjurors," *New-York Mirror*, Nov. 22, 1823.
23. Washington Irving to Gouverneur Kemble, May 26, 1806, in *Letters*, 1:219–20.
24. For speculation on the identities of the pseudonymous authors, see Pierre M. Irving, *The Life and Letters of Washington Irving*, 4 vols. (New York: G. P. Putnam, 1862), 1:164–79, Herold, *James Kirke Paulding*, chap. 3, Mary Weatherspoon Bowden, "Cocklofts and Slang-Whangers: The Historical Sources of Washington Irving's 'Salmagundi,'" *New York History* 61, no. 2 (1980): 133–60, and Andrew Burstein, *The Original Knickerbocker: The Life of Washington Irving* (New York: Basic Books, 2007), chap. 3. Will Wizard may have been William Irving.
25. *Salmagundi*, Nov. 11, 1807, 392–93. This particular satire was written at the height of the Irving-Paulding collaboration and may well be a joint production.
26. *Salmagundi*, Apr. 18, 1807, 173–81.
27. *Salmagundi*, Mar. 20, 1807, 123–25; Bowden, "Cocklofts and Slang-Whangers."
28. [John Rodman], *Fragment of a Journal of a Sentimental Philosopher* (New York: E. Sargent, 1809), 13; Andrew Burstein, *Sentimental Democracy: The Evolution of America's Romantic Self-Image* (New York: Hill and Wang, 1999), 308–9; "On Style," *Salmagundi*, Apr. 18, 1807; Carolyn Eastman, *The Strange Genius of Mr. O: The World of the United States' First Forgotten Celebrity* (Chapel Hill: University of North Carolina Press, 2021), chap. 6. Eastman refers to the Boston Public Library copy of *Fragment of a Journal of a Sentimental Philosopher*, which contains Rodman's notation that names Irving as a thinly

disguised character in his takedown of Ogilvie (106–8). Coming from a family of modest clergymen, Ogilvie proved his erudition first, then managed his own public relations with a deftness akin to young Benjamin Franklin in the previous century. The Scotsman's eloquence and graceful manner were widely touted and his lectures attended by both women and men. He was given total access to Jefferson's Monticello library, then welcomed into the parlor of John Quincy and Louisa Catherine Adams and the salons of Washington society. He was showered with praise and at the height of his celebrity received the ultimate compliment: "In the expression of every passion by words, SHAKESPEARE was nature's masterpiece. In the display of passion by action GARRICK [the British stage actor] was her son." Nature "join'd the former two" to make Ogilvie (Eastman, *The Strange Genius of Mr. O*, 132). The itinerant orator received his introduction to Irving by way of the author's onetime European traveling companion, Joseph Cabell, a Virginia neighbor and protégé of Jefferson's. Irving and Ogilvie became good friends, sympathizing with one another in times of financial reversal or critical condemnation (Irving, *The Life and Letters of Washington Irving*, 1:369–70).

29. *Salmagundi*, Apr. 4, 1807, 146–53; David Simpson, *The Politics of American English, 1776–1850* (New York: Oxford University Press, 1986), 112.
30. *Salmagundi*, Mar. 20, 1807, 136–45; *Salmagundi*, Apr. 18, 1807, 173–75.
31. James Kirke Paulding, "The Azure Hose," in *Chronicles of the City of Gotham* (New York: G. and C. and H. Carvill, 1830).
32. The example is from "Literary Intelligence," *Guardian* (Albany, NY), Nov. 21, 1807.
33. *Salmagundi*, Apr. 4, 1807, 157. On the real-life New York visitor "Mustaffa," captain of the "Ketch *Abdullah*," see *Salmagundi*, ed. Bruce I. Granger and Martha Hartzog (Boston: Twayne, 1977), 343n.
34. *Salmagundi*, Mar. 7, 1807, 99–111.
35. Herold, *James Kirke Paulding*, 35; Burstein, *The Original Knickerbocker*, 64; *Salmagundi* (London: Thomas Tegg, 1839), vii.
36. Advertisement for the *Observer*, Jan. 6, 1807, in the *Republican Star* (Easton, MD); review of *The Miseries of Life*, in *The People's Friend*, Apr. 27, 1807; *Evening Post* (New York, NY), May 12, 1807; *City Gazette* (Charleston, SC), June 12, 1807.

37. *The People's Friend*, Jan. 31, 1807; *Aurora*, Sept. 3, 1807; *Tickler*, Sept. 23, 1807; *New-Bedford (MA) Mercury*, Nov. 13, 1807.

38. Washington Irving to Henry Brevoort, Jan. 13, 1811, and Washington Irving to William Irving, Jr., Feb. 20, 1811, in *Letters*, 1:295–300, 305–6. Irving's tart reference is apparently an allusion to a bit of banter in Shakespeare's *Henry IV, Part 2* (2.4.1227–28) at the Eastcheap tavern that centered on the applejohn: "What the devil hast thou brought there—apple-john? / Thou knowest Sir John cannot endure an apple-john" (*Complete Works*, ed. Richard Proudfoot, Ann Thompson, David Scott Kastan, and H. R. Woudhuysen [London: Bloomsbury, 2020], 523). In his *Dictionarium Botanicum* (London: T. Woodward, 1728), Richard Bradley offers the following definition: "The Deuxann or Apple John, is a delicate fine Fruit, well relished when it beginneth to be fit to be eaten, and endureth good longer than any other apple." The applejohn appears to have had no place in eighteenth-century America, according to Robert Nares, *A Glossary, or Collection of Words, Phrases, Names, and Allusions to Customs, Proverbs, Etc.* (1822; repr. London: John Russell Smith, 1859), who describes them as "dry, round, old, withered" objects, a species of apple once known for its keeping property (some two years). In France, they were known as "deux ans."

39. Burstein, *The Original Knickerbocker*, 71–72.

40. Washington Irving, *A History of New York* (1809; repr. London: George Routledge, 1850), 21.

41. Irving, *A History of New York*, 109, 108.

42. Burstein, *The Original Knickerbocker*, 121.

43. Burstein, *Sentimental Democracy*, 210–11.

44. Joseph Dennie, *The Lay Preacher* (1796; repr., Philadelphia: Harrison Hall, 1817). A good example of Dennie's wordplay is "An EPI-GRAM should be—if right, / Short, simple, pointed, keen and bright, / A lively little thing! / Like wasp, with taper body—bound/ By lines—not many, neat and round, All ending in a sting" (*Port-Folio*, July 11, 1801, 224.)

45. *Port-Folio*, Jan. 23, 1802, 24; William Shakespeare, *Henry VI, Part 3*, in *Complete Works*, 668; Nancy Isenberg, *Fallen Founder: The Life of Aaron Burr* (New York: Viking, 2007), 348. The brother to whom Washington Irving was closest over the course of his life, Peter, had edited New York's Burrite newspaper, the *Morning Chronicle* (for which Paulding

also wrote). Irving, trained in the law though he never practiced it, took a break from *Salmagundi* to attend Burr's trial, proffering aid to the defendant. Privately, he did not agree with some of Burr's political positions, but he sympathized with the publicly abused man he'd known for years, writing with compassionate attachment about the spectacle he watched unfold in court. This was a preview of sentimental tales to follow, when the author eased his way from satire to broken hearts, drowsy scenes, endearing bachelors, and time-bending visions.

46. Carolyn Eastman, "Reading Aloud: Editorial Societies and Orality in Magazines of the Early American Republic," *Early American Literature* 54, no. 1 (2019): 163–88; Albert H. Smyth, *The Philadelphia Magazines and Their Contributors, 1741–1850* (Philadelphia: Robert M. Lindsay, 1892), 181–86, 241; *Port-Folio*, Jan. 23, 1802; "Strictures on Satire," *The Cynick*, Nov. 2, 1811.

47. H. H. Brackenridge, *Modern Chivalry, or, The Adventures of Captain Farrago and Teague O'Regan* (Philadelphia: T. B. Peterson, 1856), 181.

48. John Engell, "Brackenridge, 'Modern Chivalry,' and American Humor," *Early American Literature* 22, no. 1 (1987): 43–62.

49. Vic Gatrell, *City of Laughter: Sex and Satire in Eighteenth-Century London* (New York: Walker, 2006), 173. Notable among T. J. Mathias's publications is his long satirical poem, *The Shade of Alexander Pope, on the Banks of the Thames* (Philadelphia: H. Maxwell, 1800).

50. William Hedges, *Washington Irving: An American Study, 1802–1832* (Baltimore: Johns Hopkins University Press, 1965), 21–24.

51. Washington Irving, *Oliver Goldsmith: A Biography* (London: George Routledge, 1850), 1.

52. Peter Smithers, *The Life of Joseph Addison* (New York: Oxford University Press, 1968), 225–26.

53. Herold, *James Kirke Paulding*, 98–99.

54. *National Intelligencer*, Apr. 7, 1843; *New Orleans Chronicle*, Aug. 25, 1819.

55. *New-York Organ*, June 12, 1847, and Nov. 10, 1849.

56. *Port-Folio*, Oct. 24, 1801, 337; *Port-Folio*, Mar. 13, 1802, 76; William Shakespeare, *Measure for Measure*, in *Complete Works*, 932.

57. Article 3, letter 2, *Port-Folio*, Dec. 1821, 306.

58. "Criticism," *Port-Folio*, Aug. 1819, 129–32; D. Graham Burnett, *Trying Leviathan: The Nineteenth-Century New York Court Case That Put the Whale on Trial and Challenged the Order of Nature* (Princeton, NJ: Princeton University Press, 2007).

59. "National Pride," *Port-Folio*, Oct. 1827, 317–18; Burstein, *Sentimental Democracy*, 283–84; *Biographical Encyclopaedia of Ohio* (Cincinnati: Galaxy Publishing, 1876).

60. "Practical Satire," *Niles' Weekly Register*, Apr. 1, 1837, 69.

61. "Jonathan Bull and Mary Bull," *Southern Literary Messenger*, Mar. 1835, 342–47; Robert J. Allison, "'From the Covenant of Peace, a Simile of Sorrow': James Madison's American Allegory," *Virginia Magazine of History and Biography* 99, no. 3 (1991): 327–50; Andrew Burstein and Nancy Isenberg, *Madison and Jefferson* (New York: Random House, 2010), 578–80. "Jonathan Bull and Mary Bull" was introduced as "copy of a Manuscript written, but not published at the period of the Missouri Question, 1821" (342).

62. "Madison and the Allegory of Jonathan and Mary Bull—an Editorial Note," *Papers of James Madison—Retirement Series*, ed. David B. Mattern, J. C. A. Stagg, et al. (Charlottesville: University of Virginia Press, 2013), 2:444–45.

Chapter 5. Historical Sensibilities

1. J. Fenimore Cooper, *England, with Sketches of Society in the Metropolis* (Paris: Baudry's European Library, 1837), letters 6, 22, and 28. The book was published in the United States in the same year as *Gleanings in Europe: England* by Carey, Lea, and Blanchard of Philadelphia.

2. Michael Chevalier, *Society, Manners, and Politics in the United States*, ed. John William Ward (1836; repr. Garden City, NY: Doubleday, 1961), 414–17. Chevalier was in the United States for two years, from 1833 to 1835, considerably longer than Tocqueville.

3. Harriet Martineau, *Retrospect of Western Travel* (New York: Harper and Brothers, 1838), 1:143–49.

4. John Bristed, *An Oration on the Utility of Literary Establishments* (New York: Eastburn, Kirk, 1814), 7, 9; Bristed, *America and Her Resources* (London: Henry Colburn, 1818), 236, 244. His son, Charles Astor Bristed, with transatlantic degrees from Yale and Cambridge, became an admired writer of occasional pieces on society life; he in turn married the daughter of Dutch American Henry Brevoort, Washington Irving's longtime confidant. (Bristed and Brevoort family histories can be found in *Appleton's Cyclopaedia of American Biography*.)

5. Washington Irving to Henry Brevoort, Mar. 10, 1821, *Letters*, 4 vols., ed., Ralph M. Aderman, Herbert L. Kleinfield, and Jenifer S. Banks (Boston: Twayne, 1978), 1:614.

6. Washington Irving to John Constable, Aug. 19, 1825, *Letters*, 2:126–27.

7. For a survey of the promotion of Columbus and Columbia in the first years of the republic, see especially Michael D. Hattem, *Past and Prologue: Politics and Memory in the American Revolution* (New Haven, CT: Yale University Press, 2020), 212–22.

8. Alexander Hill Everett, *America: or a General Survey of the Political Situation of the Several Powers of the Western Continent by a Citizen of the United States* (Philadelphia: Carey and Lea, 1827), 118, 120, 181–83, 188. Those with even a rudimentary education knew that Cicero was the greatest statesman of the Roman republic, a seasoned philosopher and orator par excellence. His writings cover subjects ranging from the art of politics to the art of living and even contain touches of satire. Henry was no Cicero, but owing to the patriotic fiction newly taking hold, a popular champion might leave no permanent record of his critical thought (a slang-whanging logocrat, in *Salmagundian* terminology) yet lose no part of his luster.

9. Everett, *America*, 300, 312–14, 325–27; Edward Everett to Thomas Jefferson, Feb. 9, 1823, Founders Online, founders.archives.gov.

10. Alexander Everett journal, Jan. 10, 1810, Everett-Noble Papers, Massachusetts Historical Society. Jennifer R. Mercieca attests that the second generation "clothed America's republican fiction in the unquestionable divine-right narrative of the old monarchical fiction"; see *Founding Fictions* (Tuscaloosa: University of Alabama Press, 2010), 206.

11. Pierre M. Irving, *The Life and Letters of Washington Irving*, 4 vols. (New York: G. P. Putnam, 1862), 2:245–49; Lindsay DiCuirci, *Colonial Revivals: The Nineteenth-Century Lives of Early American Books* (Philadelphia: University of Pennsylvania Press, 2019), 171–72. DiCuirci incisively states that in the United States, "Columbus's story seemed to be the literary inheritance of the United States and not Spain; Irving had accessed the long-sealed vault, the unopened book."

12. Irving, *The Life and Letters of Washington Irving*, 2:265–66. When he embarked on his biography, Irving was staying at the Madrid home of US consul Obadiah Rich, which had an immense library of some

four thousand volumes, many of which pertained to the life and times of Columbus.

13. Irving, *The Life and Letters of Washington Irving*, 2:312–16, 335–39; Washington Irving to Alexander Hill Everett, Aug. 20, 1828, in *The Life and Letters of Washington Irving*, 338–39.

14. James Fenimore Cooper, *The Spy*, vol. 2 (1821; repr. New York: Wiley, 1824), 278.

15. Michelle Sizemore, "Rites and Times of the Grand Tour," in *Rip Van Winkle's Republic: Washington Irving in History and Memory*, ed. Andrew Burstein and Nancy Isenberg (Baton Rouge: Louisiana State University Press, 2022), 19–41; Sarah Goldsmith, *Masculinity and Danger on the Eighteenth-Century Grand Tour* (London: University of London Press, 2021).

16. Karen L. Kilcup, "Feeling American in the Poetic Republic," *Nineteenth-Century Literature* 70, no. 3 (2015): 299–335, esp. 306–10, 315. Edward Everett assumed editorship of the *North American Review* in January 1820, having returned home from Europe the previous October. Jared Sparks succeeded him in 1824, and Everett took charge again for a period when Sparks took a trip to Europe. Alexander Everett bought the magazine in 1830. While Edward Everett was editor, both his older brother and his brother-in-law Nathan Hale wrote for it.

17. Edward Everett Hale, "The Semi-Centenary of the *North American Review*," *North American Review* 100 (Jan. 1865): 320.

18. "The American Scholar," in Ralph Waldo Emerson, *Nature; Addresses and Lectures* (Boston: James Munroe, 1849); Rob Wilson, "Literary Vocation as Occupational Idealism: The Example of Emerson's 'American Scholar,'" *Cultural Critique* 15 (Spring 1990): 83–114. For information on Emerson's touring of Ohio and Indiana and his contemporaneous impact on audiences, see Mary Kupiec Cayton, "The Making of an American Prophet: Emerson, His Audiences, and the Rise of the Culture Industry in Nineteenth-Century America," *American Historical Review* 92, no. 3 (1987): 597–620. On Emerson's engagement with Shakespeare from the perspective of a young critic attending his lectures, see Robert A. Gross, *The Transcendentalists and Their World* (New York: Farrar, Straus and Giroux, 2021), 418–19.

19. Charles Henry Brown, *William Cullen Bryant* (New York: Charles Scribner's Sons, 1971); John W. M. Hallock, *The American Byron:*

Homosexuality and the Fall of Fitz-Greene Halleck (Madison: University of Wisconsin Press, 2000); Andrew Burstein, *The Original Knickerbocker: The Life of Washington Irving* (New York: Basic Books, 2007), chap. 11.

20. David Simpson, *The Politics of American English, 1776–1850* (New York: Oxford University Press, 1986), chaps. 2–5; Paul Giles, *Transatlantic Insurrections: British Culture and the Formation of American Literature, 1730–1860* (Philadelphia: University of Pennsylvania Press, 2001); Thomas Gustafson, *Representative Words: Politics, Literature, and the American Language, 1776–1865* (New York; Cambridge University Press, 1992), 310–317; "Canals," *Niles' Weekly Register,* Sept. 7, 1822, 3.

21. Karen Lystra, *Searching the Heart: Women, Men, and Romantic Love in the Nineteenth Century* (New York: Oxford University Press, 1989); William Merrill Decker, *Epistolary Practices: Letter Writing in America before Telecommunications* (Chapel Hill: University of North Carolina Press, 1998); Elizabeth Hewitt, *Correspondence and American Literature, 1770–1865* (New York: Cambridge University Press, 2004). Further examples of self-disclosure can be found in John Matteson, *The Lives of Margaret Fuller: A Biography* (New York: Norton, 2012), and Rachel Hope Cleves, *Charity and Sylvia: A Same-Sex Marriage in Early America* (New York: Oxford University Press, 2014).

22. Robley Dunglison, *Dunglison's Medical Dictionary* (Philadelphia: Blanchard and Lea, 1860), 637; Kevis Goodman, "'Uncertain Disease': Nostalgia, Pathologies of Motion, Practices of Reading," *Studies in Romanticism* 49, no. 2 (2010): 197–227; *Republican Star* (Baltimore), Feb. 9, 1830; "Home-Sickness, or Mal-du-Pays," *Penny Magazine,* Nov. 14, 1840. Lindsay DiCuirci meticulously treats antiquarian fascination in the United States, along with the revivification of old books and Irving's experience in Spanish archives, in *Colonial Revivals,* chap. 5.

23. Washington Irving, *The Life and Voyages of Christopher Columbus,* in *Life and Works of Washington Irving* (1828; repr., New York: Crowell, 1883), 201.

24. Irving, *The Life and Voyages of Christopher Columbus,* 230.

25. Irving, *The Life and Voyages of Christopher Columbus,* 204, 108, 83, 47, 46, 44.

26. Irving, *The Life and Voyages of Christopher Columbus,* 230, 142.

27. Burstein, *The Original Knickerbocker*, 203–4; Irving, *The Life and Voyages of Christopher Columbus*, 31, 242. Irving waffles on the delicate subject of the enslavement of Indians, not entirely excusing Columbus but assigning greatest responsibility to Spanish acceptance of the practice; the only person who comes across as humane in this regard is Queen Isabella. "Let it remain a blot on his illustrious name," Irving concludes, "and let others derive a lesson from it" (230), although Irving himself did not take a public position on American slavery. Columbus-related misconceptions are also discussed in Grace Marmor Spruch, "The Legend of Christopher Columbus," *American Scholar* 71, no. 4 (2002): 61–68.

28. Washington Irving to Henry Brevoort, Apr. 4, 1827, and May 23, 1829, in *The Letters of Washington Irving to Henry Brevoort*, 2 vols., ed. George S. Hellman (New York: Putnam, 1915), 2:197–98, 218; Burstein, *The Original Knickerbocker*, 195–96.

29. Irving, *The Life and Voyages of Christopher Columbus*, 228; *Port-Folio*, Nov. 1, 1827.

30. Washington Irving, *Life of George Washington*, vol. 5 (Leipzig: Tauchnitz, 1859), 282; Irving, *The Life and Voyages of Christopher Columbus*, 229.

31. Scott E. Casper, *Constructing American Lives: Biography and Culture in Nineteenth-Century America* (Chapel Hill: University of North Carolina Press, 1999), chap. 1; Lloyd Pratt, *Archives of American Time: Literature and Modernity in the Nineteenth Century* (Philadelphia: University of Pennsylvania Press, 2010), chap. 2.

32. Antoine Lilti, *The Invention of Celebrity, 1750–1850* (Cambridge, UK: Polity, 2017), 74–82; Casper, *Constructing American Lives*, 33–35.

33. James Kirke Paulding, *A Life of Washington*, 2 vols. (New York: Harper and Brothers, 1835), 1:106, 108, 110, 111; 2:190; Benjamin Henry Latrobe, *The Journal of Latrobe* (New York: Appleton, 1905), 62.

34. Paulding, *A Life of Washington*, 2:210, 211, 213, 219, 220, 215; Amos L. Herold, *James Kirke Paulding, Versatile American* (1926; repr., New York: AMC Press, 1966), 115–17.

35. [Mary Lucile Proctor], "After-Dinner Anecdotes of James Madison: Excerpt from Jared Sparks' Journal for 1829–31," *Virginia Magazine of History and Biography* 60, no. 2 (1952): 255–65, quotes at 264–65. For Sparks's extensive contacts with Washington's heirs, Madison, Irving, and the Everetts, see Herbert B. Adams, *The Life and Writings*

of Jared Sparks, 2 vols. (Boston: Houghton Mifflin, 1893), and Harriet Martineau, 3 vols., *Retrospect of Western Travel* (New York: Harper and Brothers, 1838), 2:103.

36. Annette Kolodny, *In Search of First Contact: The Vikings of Vinland, the Peoples of the Dawnland, and the Anglo-American Discovery of America* (Durham, NC: Duke University Press, 2012), 105–20, 132–4, 343n6, quotes at 115–16. One of the arguments put forward during these years was that Columbus had visited Iceland in 1477 and was inspired to widen his fact-finding voyages after learning of the Scandinavian settlement (Kolodny, *In Search of First Contact*, 108). The Everetts, along with such notables as Daniel Webster and Henry Wadsworth Longfellow, belonged to the American branch of Rafn's Royal Nordic Society of Northern Antiquaries.

37. *A Tour on the Prairies*, ed. John Francis McDermott (Norman: University of Oklahoma Press, 1956), 48. Alexander Everett's glowing review of the book is in the *North American Review* 41 (July 1835): 1–28. "It is not a romance," he states, "for it is all true. It is a sort of sentimental journey" (5). He was even more complimentary about the man: "Washington Irving possesses, in the highest degree, the gift of the poet" (11–12).

38. Washington Irving, *The Adventures of Captain Bonneville*, ed. Robert A. Rees and Alan Sandy (Boston: Twayne, 1977), 3; Jimmy L. Bryan Jr., *The American Elsewhere: Adventure and Manliness in the Age of Expansion* (Lawrence: University Press of Kansas, 2017), chap. 3. In this study of literary treatments of the West, Bryan compellingly demonstrates how these treatments match a soulful sentimentalism with muscular adventuring.

39. Irving, *The Adventures of Captain Bonneville*, 14. Thomas J. Lyon notes Irving's emphasis on the "spiritual exaltation that accompanies the physical exhilaration of the wilderness life" in his reading of *Captain Bonneville* ("Washington Irving's Wilderness," *Western American Literature* 1, no. 3 (1966): 170).

40. Irving, *The Adventures of Captain Bonneville*, 14, 159, 168.

41. Henry Nash Smith, *Virgin Land: The American West as Symbol and Myth* (Cambridge, MA: Harvard University Press, 1950), 84. Smith develops a critical argument about the agrarian utopia myth that flourished in literature but failed on the ground.

42. Walt Whitman, "Pioneers! O Pioneers!," in *Leaves of Grass* (1892; repr. New York: Bantam, 1983), 185–88.

43. Edward Anderson, *Florida Territory in 1844: The Diary of Master Edward Clifford Anderson, USN*, ed. W. Stanley Hoole (Tuscaloosa: University of Alabama Press, 2009), 13–14.

44. Anderson, *Florida Territory in 1844*, 23, 58.

45. Anderson, *Florida Territory in 1844*, 30, 16, 31.

46. Anderson, *Florida Territory in 1844*, 42, 43.

47. Anderson, *Florida Territory in 1844*, 45, 48, 50.

48. Anderson, *Florida Territory in 1844*, 46, 59. The abolitionist was found guilty and branded "S.S." for "slave stealer" on his hand.

49. Stephen Mennell, "Power, Individualism, and Collective Self Perception in the USA," *Historical Social Research* 45, no. 1 (2020): 314. Mennell cites Norbert Elias's witticism that "to some extent the same is true of the French kings and their representatives as was once said of the American pioneer: 'He didn't want all the land; he just wanted the land next to his.'" Mennell contends that "when Americans boast of their 'individualism' and 'the freedom of the individual,' they mean what the rest of us call 'selfishness'" (320).

50. Andrew Burstein, *The Passions of Andrew Jackson* (New York: Knopf, 2003); John Reid and John Henry Eaton, *The Life of Andrew Jackson, Major General* (Philadelphia: Carey and Son, 1817), 3. Reid and Eaton's book was widely republished and redistributed after 1827.

51. Noah Webster Jr., *An Oration Pronounced before the Citizens of New-Haven, on the Anniversary of the Independence of the United States* (New Haven, CT: T. and S. Green, 1798), 11; Noah Webster Jr., *An Oration Pronounced before the Knox and Warren Branches of the Washington Benevolent Society at Amherst: On the Celebration of the Anniversary of the Declaration of Independence, July 4, 1814* (Northampton, MA: William Butler, 1814), 3–4.

    "Illustrious," in Shakespeare, alluded to social rank: "this high illustrious prince" (4.3.3283) (*King Lear*, in *Complete Works*, ed. Richard Proudfoot, Ann Thompson, David Scott Kastan, and H. R. Woudhuysen [London: Bloomsbury, 2020], 785) or, more colorfully to "a most illustrious wight / a man of fire-new words, fashion's own knight" (1.1.182) (*Love's Labour Lost*, in *Complete Works*, 866).

52. Edward Everett, *An Oration Delivered at Cambridge on the Fiftieth Anniversary of the Declaration of the Independence of the United States of America* (Boston: Cummings, Hillard, 1826), 4–7, 29–32, 46–48.

53. Walter R. Danforth, *An Oration Pronounced in the Universalist Chapel on Thursday, July 4, 1833* (Providence, RI: J. Hutchens, 1833), 14; William Shakespeare, *King John*, in *Complete Works*, 739.

54. *Alabama Intelligencer*, July 18, 1835.

55. Henry Willis Kinsman, *An Oration, Pronounced before the Inhabitants of Boston, July the Fourth, 1836* (Boston: J. H. Eastburn, 1836), 22–23.

56. George H. Richards, *Memoir of Alexander Macomb, the Major General Commanding the Army of the United States* (New York: M'Elrath, Bangs, 1833), 136–37.

57. Richards, *Memoir of Alexander Macomb*, 127–29.

58. The most authoritative treatment of American biography of this period is Casper, *Constructing American Lives*.

59. The occasion was the issuance of *A Tour on the Prairies*, but the fulsome review encompassed all that had preceded it. See "Bracebridge Hall," *North American Review* 15 (July1822): 204–23, and "A Tour on the Prairies," *North American Review* 41 (July 1835): 2–27.

60. Gross, *The Transcendentalists and Their World*, 391.

61. "Everett upon Washington," *Life Illustrated* (New York), reprinted in *Liberator*, Mar. 21, 1856.

Chapter 6. Race and Resistance

1. Robert Finley, "Thoughts on the Colonization of Free Blacks" (Washington, DC., 1816); Isaac Van Arsdale Brown, *Biography of the Rev. Robert Finley, D. D.* (Philadelphia: John W. Moore, 1857), esp. chap. 5. There was, according to ACS members' logic, "a moral fitness, in restoring them to the land of their fathers," since free Blacks existed in "a state of degradation" and could never enjoy the "inalienable rights" assigned to whites (from Elias Caldwell's speech at the ACS founding meeting, quoted in Jesse Torrey, "A Picture of Africa at Home," in *A Portraiture of Domestic Slavery, in the United States* [Philadelphia: Jesse Torrey, 1817], 88). Finley's biographer, like Finley, led a congregation in New Jersey. After helping organize the ACS, Finley was named president of the University of Georgia and died months later in Athens, GA. See also Christopher Castiglia, "Pedagogical Discipline and the Creation of White Citizenship: John Witherspoon, Robert Finley, and the Colonization Society," *Early American Literature* 33, no. 2 (1998): 192–214.

2. Phillis Wheatley, *Memoirs and Poems* (Boston: George Light, 1834), 42. See, relatedly, Nicholas Guyatt, "'The Outskirts of Our Happiness': Race and the Lure of Colonization in the Early Republic," *Journal of American History* 95, no. 4 (2009): 986–1011, Nicholas Guyatt, *Bind Us Apart: How Enlightened Americans Invented Racial Segregation* (New York: Basic Books, 2016), James Brewer Stewart, "Modernizing 'Difference': The Political Meanings of Color in the Free States, 1776–1840," *Journal of the Early Republic* 19, no. 4 (1999): 691–712, and David Waldstreicher, *The Odyssey of Phillis Wheatley: A Poet's Journeys through American Slavery and Independence* (New York: Farrar, Straus and Giroux, 2023), chap. 5. Some interpreters of the poem see subtle mockery of whites in her language. Indeed, Waldstreicher notes that Wheatley's voice can legitimately be read as "satirical" in places where her words sound "beseeching" (7).

3. See esp. Andrew S. Curran, *The Anatomy of Blackness: Science and Slavery in the Age of Enlightenment* (Baltimore: Johns Hopkins University Press, 2011).

4. James K. Paulding, *Letters from the South*, vol. 1 (New York: Harper and Brothers, 1835), 117, 117–18, 118, 120. Paulding's racism intensified as the years went by, as he courted South Carolina nullifiers and urged on the most radical of South Carolinians in the 1850s, embracing the state's "rights and honor" and supporting the move toward secession as early as 1851; in a letter dated September 6, 1851 to his friends in the Southern Rights Association, he wrote that "those who cannot live together in peace, must not part in peace" (*The Letters of James Kirke Paulding*, ed. Ralph M. Aderman [Madison: University of Wisconsin Press, 1962], 523). On the pathological atmosphere marked by a mutual distrust felt between the enslaved and their enslavers and the manner of maintaining appearances, see Erin Austin Dwyer, *Mastering Emotions: Feelings, Power, and Slavery in the United States* (Philadelphia: University of Pennsylvania Press, 2021).

5. *Niles' Weekly Register*, Sept. 14, 1822, 17–18.

6. "Literary and Miscellaneous Intelligence," *Port-Folio*, Sept. 1826, 262–63; David Brion Davis, *The Problem of Slavery in the Age of Emancipation* (New York: Knopf, 2014), 67–68; William Shakespeare, *Macbeth*, in *Complete Works*, ed. Richard Proudfoot, Ann Thompson, David Scott Kastan, and H. R. Woudhuysen (London: Bloomsbury, 2020), 909. "Black spirits and white" references a song that the mistress of the witches in Shakespeare's *Macbeth* is indicated

to sing in act 4, scene 1, only by the stage direction "'Black spirits,' &cc" but has been assumed by scholars to be the song that appears in Thomas Middleton's later *The Witch* (which the reviewer here quotes imperfectly).

7. James Shapiro, *Shakespeare in a Divided America: What His Plays Tell Us about our Past and Future* (New York: Penguin, 2020), chap. 12; Paula Marantz Cohen, *Of Human Kindness: What Shakespeare Teaches Us about Empathy* (New Haven, CT: Yale University Press, 2021), 143–44. Adams, as a rule, did not affiliate with activists, even when he was in general agreement with their positions; he stated as a congressman that an adherence to the federal Constitution was his only determined affiliation.

8. "Thoughts upon Prejudice," *Western Monthly Review* 1 (Aug. 1827): 202.

9. On the Republicans' tacit understanding, see especially Padraig Riley, *Slavery and the Democratic Conscience: Political Life in Jeffersonian America* (Philadelphia: University of Pennsylvania Press, 2016). Despite what most observers saw happening in 1820, Jefferson, in retirement, saw a Federalist resurgence in the effort of northern "restrictionists" to make the disallowing of slavery in Missouri the price to be paid for entrance into the Union.

10. Harriet Martineau, *Retrospect of Western Travel*, 3 vols. (New York: Harper and Brothers, 1838), 1:139–41.

11. The earliest newspaper story I have encountered that features the familiar racial taxonomy associated with the naturalist-anthropologist Johann Friedrich Blumenbach (1752–1840) is titled "Classification of Mankind," published in the *Concord (NH) Observer*, Sept. 11, 1820; Ralph Waldo Emerson to Martin Van Buren, dated Apr. 13, 1838, in *New-Bedford (MA) Mercury*, May 25, 1838. Blumenbach, who built his race theory on a 1775 essay by Immanuel Kant, actually decried slavery and praised Phillis Wheatley along with several Blacks who had been educated in Europe and had scholarly achievements; see Ritchie Robertson, *The Enlightenment: The Pursuit of Happiness, 1680–1790* (New York: Norton, 2021), 313–16. Robert A. Gross notes that Emerson had no issue with racial intermarriage and that sentiments in Massachusetts differed to a degree from those elsewhere in the North, as a number of those who sided with the ACS simultaneously recognized free Blacks' long history in New England, appreciated their opposition to

colonization, and looked favorably on Black education and the extension of other social advantages; see Gross, *The Transcendentalists and Their World* (New York: Farrar, Straus and Giroux, 2021), 333–38. More generally, see Elise Lemire, *"Miscegenation": Making Race in America* (Philadelphia: University of Pennsylvania Press, 2002).

12. Alexander Hill Everett, quoted in Gerald Horne, *Race to Revolution: The U.S. and Cuba during Slavery and Jim Crow* (New York: Monthly Review Press, 2014), 45. For evidence that Mexican slavery had been in steep decline since the seventeenth century, see Dennis N. Valdés, "The Decline of Slavery in Mexico," *Americas* 44, no. (1987): 167–94.

13. Robert L. Paquette, "The Everett-Del Monte Connection: A Study in the International Politics of Slavery," *Diplomatic History* 11, no. 1 (1987): 1–21. While in Cuba, Everett learned that American literature, including works by Irving and Cooper, had found adherents among the elites; copies of the *North American Review* (which he edited from 1830 to 1836) were on hand and well thumbed through.

14. Alexander Hill Everett, *America, or a General Survey of the Political Situation of the Several Powers of the Western Continent* (Philadelphia: Carey and Lea, 1827), 217–25.

15. Edward Everett Hale, *Memories of a Hundred Years*, 2 vols. (New York: Macmillan, 1902), 1:108–11. A history of the magazine founded by Nathan Hale was composed for its centennial; see Julius H. Ward, "The North American Review," *North American Review* 201 (Jan. 1915): 123–34. Alexander and Edward Everett edited and wrote for the *Review* on and off until 1835.

16. "Literary Women of America: Sarah Josepha Hale," *Ladies' Repository* 15 (Apr. 1855): 193–97. As yet another indication of Shakespeare's hold, this tavern keeper's home-taught daughter received a complete set of the works at age fifteen.

17. Alexander Everett, "The Sabbath," *Godey's Lady's Book* 20 (Apr. 1840): 145–46.

18. Ruth E. Finley, *The Lady of Godey's: Sarah Josepha Hale* (Philadelphia: Lippincott, 1938), esp. chaps. 2, 4, 7, and 11. While keeping the Bunker Hill commemoration in the public eye, Mrs. Hale was buoyed by the efforts of Edward Everett in Washington.

19. Finley, *The Lady of Godey's*, 176.

20. Lacy K. Ford, *Deliver Us from Evil: The Slavery Question in the Old South* (New York: Oxford University Press, 2009), 337.

21. For a good synthesis of research on this subject, see John T. Jost, Mahzarin R. Banaji, and Brian A. Nosek, "A Decade of System Justification Theory: Accumulated Evidence of Conscious and Unconscious Bolstering of the Status Quo," *Political Psychology* 25, no. 6 (2004): 881–919. The article explains how power dynamics operate within unequal societies, supporting rationalization. The "Uncle Tom syndrome" describes which low-status individuals come to abide another group's dominance. "Research shows that dominants and subordinates are highly averse to conflict and antagonism and generally develop within the context of dramatically inegalitarian institutions such as slavery" (883).

22. Susan Branson, "Phrenology and the Science of Race in Antebellum America," *Early American Studies* 15, no. 1 (2017): 164–93; Christopher J. Lukasik, *Discerning Characters: The Culture of Appearance in Early America* (Philadelphia: University of Pennsylvania Press, 2011); Rachel E. Walker, *Beauty and the Brain: The Science of Human Nature in Early America* (Chicago: University of Chicago Press, 2023), 167–70; Walker notes that the abolitionist author Harriet Beecher Stowe used the language of physiognomy in her positive portrayal of Uncle Tom, whose "expression of grave and steady good sense" partook of his "truly African features" (173).

23. An abundance of literature exists on these subjects. For a range of perspectives, see Jenny Davidson, *Breeding: A Partial History of the Eighteenth Century* (New York: Columbia University Press, 2009), chap. 5, Andrew N. Wegmann, *An American Color: Race and Identity in New Orleans and the Atlantic World* (Athens: University of Georgia Press, 2022), chap. 5, Christa Dierksheide, *Amelioration and Empire: Progress and Slavery in the Plantation Americas, 1770–1840* (Charlottesville: University of Virginia Press, 2014), Mark M. Smith, *How Race Is Made: Slavery, Segregation, and the Senses* (Chapel Hill: University of North Carolina Press, 2006), Matthew Mason, *Slavery and Politics in the Early American Republic* (Chapel Hill: University of North Carolina Press, 2006), John Wood Sweet, *Bodies Politic: Negotiating Race in the American North, 1730–1830* (Baltimore: John Hopkins University Press, 2003), Peter Charles Hoffer, *Sensory Worlds in Early America* (Baltimore: Johns Hopkins University Press, 2003), chap. 3, Lemire, *"Miscegenation,"* Mia Bay, *The White Image in the Black Mind: African-American Ideas about White People, 1830–1925* (New York: Oxford University Press, 2000), esp. chaps. 1 and 2, Saidiya V.

Hartman, *Scenes of Subjection: Terror, Slavery, and Self-Making in Nineteenth-Century America* (New York: Oxford University Press, 1997), Alexander Boulton, "The American Paradox: Jeffersonian Equality and Racial Science," *American Quarterly* 47, no. 3 (1995): 467–92, James Oakes, *The Ruling Race: A History of American Slaveholders* (New York: Knopf, 1982), and David Brion Davis, *The Problem of Slavery in the Age of Revolution, 1770–1823* (Ithaca, NY: Cornell University Press, 1975).

24. Roger D. Bridges, "Antebellum Struggle for Citizenship," *Journal of the Illinois State Historical Society* 108, nos. 3–4 (2015): 296–321.

25. Brooks D. Simpson, *Ulysses S. Grant: Triumph over Adversity, 1822–1865* (Boston: Houghton Mifflin, 2000); Nicholas W. Sacco, "'I Was Never an Abolitionist': Ulysses S. Grant and Slavery, 1854–1863," *Journal of the Civil War Era* 9, no. 3 (2019): 410–37; Brian Holden Reid, *The Scourge of War: The Life of William Tecumseh Sherman* (New York: Oxford University Press, 2020), 69. Prior to the Civil War, Grant was in the position of appraising the monetary value of slaves on a neighbor's estate (Sacco, "'I Was Never an Abolitionist,'" 416–17).

26. "Remarks of Mr. Giddings," *(New York) Emancipator*, Mar. 7, 1839.

27. [John G. Fee], *Autobiography of John G. Fee, Berea, Kentucky* (Chicago: National Christian Association, 1891), 29; "Emancipation in Kentucky," *National Era* (Washington, DC), June 28, 1849; "Cassius M. Clay and John G. Fee," *Journal of Negro History* 42 no. 3 (1957): 201–13; Cassius Marcellus Clay, *The Life of Cassius Marcellus Clay: Memoir, Writings, and Speeches* (Cincinnati: J. Fletcher Brennan, 1886), iv, 57, 88; Jeffrey Brooke Allen, "Did Southern Colonizationists Oppose Slavery? Kentucky 1816–1850 as a Test Case," *Register of the Kentucky Historical Society* 75, no. 2 (1977): 92–111.

28. The disease environment in New York is painstakingly outlined in Catherine McNeur, *Taming Manhattan: Environmental Battles in the Antebellum City* (Cambridge, MA: Harvard University Press 2014). She states, for example, that a horse left behind as much as forty pounds of manure a day, a considerable amount of which lay on streets where pedestrians moved about (101). Obviously, rural and urban conditions differed, though medium-sized towns faced some of the same problems as both. Outbreaks of horrible diseases were far more common than they are now, and the causes of illness remained pure guesswork.

29. Lemire, *"Miscegenation,"* chap. 4; Smith, *How Race Is Made*, chaps. 1 and 2. The tactile resonated in commentary no less than the olfactory: enslaved boys and girls were permitted to fondly touch their mistresses in the plantation South. As a symbolic show of equality, later preserved in a well-known work of art, the martyr John Brown kissed a Black child as he headed to the gallows.

30. Yuval Noah Harari, *Sapiens: A Brief History of Humankind* (New York: HarperCollins, 2015), 133.

31. Andrew Burstein, *Jefferson's Secrets: Death and Desire at Monticello* (New York: Basic Books, 2005), 160–69. On class-inflected biases over time, and the eugenics factor in US history, see Nancy Isenberg, *White Trash: The 400–Year Untold History of Class in America* (New York: Viking, 2016), esp. chap 8.

32. Aaron Burr to Theodosia Burr Alston, Jan. 16, 1802, in *Correspondence of Aaron Burr and His Daughter Theodosia* (New York: S. A. Jacobs, 1929), 78.

33. Jefferson, *Notes on Virginia*, query 18. Similarly, blushing, another stock image for a physical sensation with an emotional register in the eighteenth century, is resorted to in literature less frequently as the nineteenth century moves on. A Google ngram test for "tremble" and "blush" show almost identical wave patterns after 1800.

34. Thomas Jefferson, quoted in Burstein, *Jefferson's Secrets*, 137, and in Peter S. Onuf, *Jefferson's Empire: The Language of American Nationalism* (Charlottesville: University of Virginia Press, 2000), 182. Virginia's leading thinkers continued to debate whether areas of the West unsettled by whites might suit postemancipation colonization; a common assumption was that Blacks were "either by nature or long habit" a degraded race that should be banned from owning deadly arms and barred from US citizenship; see especially Guyatt, *Bind Us Apart*, 215–24. For a sound explanation of how modern scholars ought to evaluate past generations' search for a practical solution to slavery, see Davis, *The Problem of Slavery in the Age of Revolution, 1770–1823*, chap. 4.

35. Mrs. S. J. Hale, *Northwood: A Tale of New England*, 2 vols. (Boston: Bowles and Dearborn, 1827), 1:25–26, 30.

36. Michael Vorenberg, "Abraham Lincoln and the Politics of Black Colonization," *Journal of the Abraham Lincoln Association* 14, no. 2 (1993): 22–45; James D. Lockett, "Abraham Lincoln and Colonization: An Episode That Ends in Tragedy at L'ille a Vache, Haiti,

1863–1864," *Journal of Black Studies* 21, no. 4 (1991): 428–44. Lincoln likewise rejected southern arguments that the enslaved did not suffer indignity and also made a mockery of the inherent contradiction in slaveowners' logic about skin pigmentation, saying that if color determined right and superiority, then a lighter-skinned white could justly enslave a slightly darker skinned white. See, for example, Ronald C. White, *Lincoln in Private* (New York: Random House, 2021), chap. 3.

37. Hartman, *Scenes of Subjection*, chaps. 2 and 3; Mason, *Slavery and Politics in the Early American Republic*, 210.

38. This argument is neatly made in Peter Thompson, "David Walker's Nationalism—and Thomas Jefferson's," *Journal of the Early Republic* 37, no. 1 (2017): 47–80.

39. Patrick H. Breen, *The Land Shall Be Deluged in Blood: A New History of the Nat Turner Revolt* (New York: Oxford University Press, 2016); David F. Allmendinger, *Nat Turner and the Rising in Southampton County* (Baltimore: Johns Hopkins University Press, 2014); Kenneth S. Greenberg, ed., *Nat Turner: A Slave Rebellion in History and Memory* (New York: Oxford University Press, 2003); *Richmond Enquirer*, quoted in Patrick H. Breen, "A Prophet in His Own Land: Support for Nat Turner and His Rebellion within Southampton's Black Community," in *Nat Turner*, 104.

40. Christopher Tomlins, *In the Matter of Nat Turner: A Speculative History* (Princeton, NJ: Princeton University Press, 2020), 165–81. Tomlins notes that T. J. Randolph's proposal was quiet on the question of compensation for masters whose slaves were freed (the quote concerning Virginia petitions is cited in Tomlins [172] and is drawn from Eva Sheppard Wolf, *Race and Liberty in the New Nation: Emancipation in Virginia from the Revolution to Nat Turner's Rebellion* [Baton Rouge: Louisiana State University Press, 2006], 245); "A Very Small Slaveholder" and "Publicola," *Richmond Enquirer*, Jan. 21, 1832; "Slavery," *Connecticut Courant*, Jan. 31, 1832.

41. Tomlins, *In the Matter of Nat Turner*, 184–201; Timothy F. Reilly, "The Louisiana Colonization Society and the Protestant Missionary, 1830–1860," *Louisiana History* 43, no. 4 (2002): 433–77.

42. Thomas Smallwood, *A Narrative of Thomas Smallwood, Coloured Man* (Toronto: James Stephens, 1851), 15.

43. William Lloyd Garrison, *An Address Delivered before the Free People of Color, in Philadelphia, New-York, and Other Cities* (Boston: Stephen

Foster, 1831); Manisha Sinha, *The Slave's Cause: A History of Abolition* (New Haven, CT: Yale University Press, 2016), 214–21.

44. William Lloyd Garrison, *Thoughts on African Colonization* (Boston: Garrison and Knapp, 1832), 120–21.

45. Mary Kelley, "'Talents Committed to Your Care': Reading and Writing Radical Abolitionism in Antebellum America," *New England Quarterly* 88, no. 1 (2015): 37–72; Van Gosse, *The First Reconstruction: Black Politics in America from the Revolution to the Civil War* (Chapel Hill: University of North Carolina Press, 2021), 71–86.

46. Aston Gonzalez, "The Art of Racial Politics: The Work of Robert Douglass, Jr., 1833–1846," *Pennsylvania Magazine of History and Biography* 138, no. 1 (2014): 5–37.

47. Sinha, *The Slave's Cause*, 241–46.

48. Andrew R. Black, *John Pendleton Kennedy: Early American Novelist, Whig Statesman, and Ardent Nationalist* (Baton Rouge: Louisiana State University Press, 2016), 45–48, 99–105. The physiognomic calculus can hardly be overestimated in mid-nineteenth-century speculations; even the prolific feminist-abolitionist writer Lydia Maria Child bought into the relevance of such thinking, writing in 1843 that "facial angle and shape of the head . . . are the effects of spiritual influences operating on character" (Mary Cathryn Cain, "The Art and Politics of Looking White: Beauty Practice among White Women in Antebellum America," *Winterthur Portfolio* 42, no. 1 [2008]: 30–31). Whiteness in a woman's face was associated with an aesthetic that defined her delicacy and natural removal from labor; blackness offered no such immunity.

49. E. Deming, "An Oration, Delivered in Oldtown, Ross County," *Scioto Gazette* (Chillicothe, OH), July 26, 1827.

50. Scott Casper, *Sarah Johnson's Mount Vernon: The Forgotten History of an American Shrine* (New York: Hill and Wang, 2008), 29, 34–35; William G. Thomas III, *A Question of Freedom: The Families Who Challenged Slavery from the Nation's Founding to the Civil War* (New Haven, CT: Yale University Press, 2020), 199–207.

51. Davis, *The Problem of Slavery in the Age of Emancipation*, chap. 8; Drew R. McCoy, *The Last of the Fathers: James Madison and the Republican Legacy* (New York: Cambridge University Press, 1989), 5–6, 279–86.

52. John Randolph to Dr. John Brockenbrough, Feb. 20, 1826, in *Collected Letters of John Randolph of Roanoke to Dr. John Brockenbrough,*

1812–1833, ed. Kenneth Shorey (New Brunswick, NJ: Transaction books, 1988), 67; David Johnson, *John Randolph of Roanoke* (Baton Rouge: Louisiana State University Press, 2012). The definitive work is Gregory May, *A Madman's Will: John Randolph, Four Hundred Slaves, and the Mirage of Freedom* (New York: Liveright, 2023); see also John M. Grammer, *Pastoral and Politics in the Old South* (Baton Rouge: Louisiana State University Press, 1996), chap. 2.

53. *African Repository* (Mar. 1835): 94; Leonard Baker, *John Marshall: A Life in Law* (New York: Macmillan, 1974), 718–24; R. Kent Newmyer, *John Marshall and the Heroic Age of the Supreme Court* (Baton Rouge: Louisiana State University Press, 2002), 416. On Marshall's long and problematic engagement with slavery, see especially Paul Finkelman, *Supreme Injustice: Slavery in the Nation's Highest Court* (Cambridge, MA: Harvard University Press, 2018).

54. P. J. Staudenraus, *The African Colonization Movement, 1816–1865* (New York: Columbia University Press, 1961); Benjamin Quarles, *Black Abolitionists* (New York: Oxford University Press, 1969); David S. Heidler and Jeanne T. Heidler, *Henry Clay: The Essential American* (New York: Random House, 2010), 131–32; Edwin W. and Miriam R. Small, "Prudence Crandall: Champion of Negro Education," *New England Quarterly* 17, no. 4 (1944): 506–29; Bruce Rosen, "Abolition and Colonization, the Years of Conflict, 1832–1834," *Phylon* 33, no. 2 (1972): 177–92; Richard D. Brown, *Self-Evident Truths: Contesting Equal Rights from the Revolution to the Civil War* (New Haven, CT: Yale University Press, 2017), 159–67. In a strange twist, Prudence Crandall's brother, a physician who opposed her efforts, was arrested in Washington, DC, and prosecuted by ACS stalwart Francis Scott Key for allegedly distributing abolitionist literature to "excite a discontented or insurrectionary spirit." He was found not guilty; see Neil S. Kramer, "The Trial of Reuben Crandall," *Records of the Columbia Historical Society, Washington, D.C.* 50 (1980): 123–29.

55. James G. Birney, *Letter on Colonization* (New York: Anti-Slavery Reporter, 1834), 7; Lucretia Mott to George Combe, June 13, 1839, in *Selected Letters of Lucretia Coffin Mott*, ed., Beverly Wilson Palmer (Urbana: University of Illinois Press, 2002), 51.

56. The long-running *African Repository* fed subscribers' bright hopes, month after month, year after year beginning in 1825. Typical is an 1844 report to the secretary of the navy from Commodore Matthew C. Perry after he returned home in which he assured all concerned that

the colonial settlement in Liberia sponsored by Maryland was thriving: "It is gratifying to witness the comforts that most of these people have gathered about them; many are familiar with the luxuries which were unknown to the early settlers of North America. . . . Roads throughout the settlement are excellent, surprisingly so when we consider the recent establishment of the colony and the limited means of the settlers. . . . The morals of the people are good, and the houses of religion are well attended." Their political leaders, more-over, were "intelligent and estimable men, executing their functions with wisdom and dignity" (June 1844, 168–69).

For a good roundup of scholarly literature on the shifting fortunes of the ACS, see Karen Fisher Younger, "Philadelphia's Ladies' Liberia School Association and the Rise and Decline of Female Colonization Support," *Pennsylvania Magazine of History and Biography* 134, no. 3 (2010): 235–61. Philadelphia was the center of Quaker-led abolitionism and home to large numbers of free Blacks who decried colonization; the city saw some of the most notorious episodes of antiabolitionist violence in the 1830s and 1840s.

57. David Christy, *Cotton Is King* (Cincinnati: Moore, Wilstach, Keys, 1855), 161–62.

58. On Hale's language choices and interpretive elements, see Etsuko Taketani, "Postcolonial Liberia: Sarah Josepha Hale's Africa," *American Literary History* 14, no. 3 (2002): 479–504. Taketani argues that *Liberia*, while racist and paternalistic, has little good to say about a US government that took credit for the colony's health but ignored its sensible request for formal diplomatic acknowledgment.

59. Matters of blood merged with the heightened importance of thoughts about guarding the racial-sexual boundary. See Michel Foucault, *Right of Death and Power over Life*, vol. 5 of *The History of Sexuality* (New York: Random House, 1978), Peter W. Bardaglio, *Reconstructing the Household: Families, Sex, and the Law in the Nineteenth-Century South* (Chapel Hill: University of North Carolina Press, 1995), and Joshua D. Rothman, *Notorious in the Neighborhood: Sex and Families across the Color Line in Virginia, 1787–1861* (Charlottesville: University of Virginia Press, 2003).

60. Martin Robison Delany, *The Condition, Elevation, Emigration, and Destiny of the Colored People of the United States* (Philadelphia: the author, 1852), Project Gutenberg, chaps. 3–6.

61. Alexander Crummell, *The Race-Problem in America* (Washington, DC: William R. Morrison, 1889). See also Davis, *The Problem of Slavery in the Age of Emancipation*, chap. 4. Free Black population statistics come from www.ncpedia.org/sites/default/files/census_stats_ 1790–1860.

62. "Slavery," *Salem Gazette*, Apr. 14, 1826; Matthew Mason, *Apostle of Union. A Political Biography of Edward Everett* (Chapel Hill: University of North Carolina Press, 2016), chap. 3; Paul Revere Frothingham, *Edward Everett: Orator and Statesman* (Boston: Houghton Mifflin, 1925), 107–8, 149–55; Alexander Everett to Edward Everett, July 8, 1835, in Mary B. Ellis, "The Hale Family Papers," *Quarterly Journal of Current Acquisitions* 12, no. 3 (1955): 106–11.

63. Josephine Donovan, "A Source for Stowe's Idea on Race in *Uncle Tom's Cabin*," *NWSA Journal* 7, no. 3 (1995): 24–34; Susan M. Ryan, "Errand into Africa: Colonization and Nation Building in Sarah J. Hale's Liberia," *New England Quarterly* 68, no. 4 (1995): 558–83; Lamont D. Thomas, *Rise to Be a People: A Biography of Paul Cuffe* (Urbana: University of Illinois Press, 1986); "Captain Paul Cuffe, Colonizationist and Philanthropist," *Negro History Bulletin* 1, no. 4 (1938). For an analysis of the lives of free Black mariners in the early republic, see W. Jeffrey Bolster, "'To Feel Like a Man': Black Seamen in the Northern States, 1800–1860," *Journal of American History* 76, no. 4 (1990): 1173–99. On the comparison of Hale and Stowe, see also Beverly Peterson, "Mrs. Hale on Mrs. Stowe and Slavery," *American Periodicals* 8 (1998): 30–44.

64. Edward Everett, *Address of the Hon. Edward Everett at the Anniversary of the American Colonization Society, January, 18, 1853* (Boston: Massachusetts Colonization Society, 1853).

Conclusion

1. Jonathan Daniel Wells, *The Kidnapping Club: Wall Street, Slavery, and Resistance on the Eve of the Civil War* (New York: Bold Type Books, 2020), 238–42.

2. W. H. Auden, "The Sea and the Mirror: A Commentary on Shakespeare's *The Tempest*," in *W. H. Auden: Collected Poems* (New York: Modern Library, 2007), 426. Auden was writing in the midst of World War II, hoping to find signs of life, of renewal, through an engagement with the bard.

3. John Adams to François Adriaan Van Der Kemp, Aug. 22, 1818, Founders Online, founders.archives.gov (henceforth FOL).

4. Abraham Lincoln, "Speech at Springfield, Illinois," June 26, 1857, in *Collected Works of Abraham Lincoln*, 8 vols., ed. Roy P. Basler et al. (New Brunswick, NJ: Rutgers University Press, 1953–55), 2:408–10. Similarly, in Peoria, Illinois, on October 16, 1854, and in the first Lincoln-Douglas debate, August 21, 1858, he stated that "my first impulse would be to free all the slaves, and send them to Liberia—to their own native land. But a moment's reflection would convince me that . . . its sudden execution is impossible. . . . What next? Free them, and make them politically and socially our equals? My own feelings will not admit of this; and if mine would, we well know that those of the great mass of white people will not" (*Collected Works of Abraham Lincoln*, 2:255–56, 3:15). Lincoln consistently recognized contradictions in proslavery rhetoric, the theological dimension of which is emphasized most recently in Ronald C. White, *Lincoln in Private* (New York: Random House, 2021), chaps. 7 and 10. Lincoln's dramatic shift in favor of full emancipation is masterfully told in James Oakes, *The Radical and the Republican: Frederick Douglass, Abraham Lincoln, and the Triumph of Antislavery Politics* (New York: Norton, 2007).

5. The story has been told many times, most recently in David S. Reynolds, *Abe: Abraham Lincoln in His Times* (New York: Penguin, 2020), 726–28; also see Matthew Dennis, *Red, White, and Blue Letter Days: An American Calendar* (Ithaca, NY: Cornell University Press, 2002), 88–90; and Ruth E. Finley, *The Lady of Godey's: Sarah Josepha Hale* (Philadelphia: Lippincott, 1938), 183–90, and chap. 12, and "Proclamation of Thanksgiving," Oct. 3, 1863, in *Collected Works of Abraham Lincoln*, 6:496–97. The first time Hale lovingly described the Thanksgiving holiday in her prose was in *Northwood* (2 vols. [Boston: Bowles and Dearborn, 1827], 1:46, 69, 82, 107–9. As the date approached again in 1864, Hale wrote to Secretary of State William Seward, asking that he remind the president to again honor Thanksgiving in November.

6. "General Orders," Dec. 22, 1778; "Thanksgiving Proclamation," Oct. 3, 1789, FOL; Benjamin E. Park, *American Nationalisms: Imagining Union in the Age of Revolutions, 1783–1833* (New York: Cambridge University Press, 2018), chap. 2; in *Pulpit and Nation: Clergymen and the Politics of Revolutionary America* (Charlottesville:

University of Virginia Press, 2016), Spencer W. McBride traces the ritual pronouncements of fast days and their providential implications in the context of concurrent and later invocations of thanksgiving in sermons and other modes.

7. Washington Irving, "Traits of Indian Character," in *The Sketch Book of Geoffrey Crayon, Gent.*, ed. Haskell Springer (Boston: Twayne, 1978), 225, 231.

8. Irving, "Traits of Indian Character," 233; Walt Whitman, "Unnamed Lands," in *The Works of Walt Whitman* (Ware, UK: Wordsworth, 1995), 340.

9. Mark Doty, *What Is the Grass: Walt Whitman in My Life* (New York: Norton, 2020), 52.

10. Edward Everett, *A Tribute to the Memory of Washington Irving* (New York: H. H. Lloyd, 1860), 234; Edward Everett, *The Life of George Washington* (New York: Sheldon, 1860), 27–28.

11. Edward Everett, *An Address Delivered at Charlestown August 1, 1826, in Commemoration of John Adams and Thomas Jefferson* (Boston: William L. Lewis, 1826), 16; Edward Everett to Abraham Lincoln, Nov. 20, 1863, in *Collected Works of Abraham Lincoln*, 7:24–25.

12. "Address by Hon. Edward Everett, Delivered in Faneuil Hall, October 19, 1864" (Boston: New England Loyal Publication Society, 1864), 2, 3, 6, 10, 13; Abraham Lincoln to S. Austin Allibone, Oct. 29, 1864, in *Collected Works of Abraham, Lincoln*, 8:80; "Speech of Hon. Edward Everett," *The Liberator*, Dec. 23, 1864.

13. "Lincoln to Philadelphia delegation," Jan. 24, 1865, in *Collected Works of Abraham Lincoln*, 8:236; *New York Times*, Jan. 16, 1865.

14. The pathos of the deathbed scene was a familiar subject for the people of early America. The art that was produced in this vein for select public figures served the obvious purpose of encouraging widespread devotion to the idea of the nation. As evidenced by the character of those at their respective bedsides, Washington's final moments were without political character, Lincoln's intensely political.

15. William Shakespeare, *Macbeth*, in *Complete Works*, ed. Richard Proudfoot, Ann Thompson, David Scott Kastan, and H. R. Woud-huysen (London: Bloomsbury, 2020), 905; Alfred Van Rensselaer Westfall, *American Shakespeare Criticism, 1607–1865* (New York: Benjamin Blom, 1939), 227–29; Andrew Burstein, *Lincoln Dreamt He Died* (New York: Palgrave, 2013); Reynolds, *Abe*, 741–43. According to Reynolds, a prolific literary scholar and biographer specializing in

the nineteenth century, Shakespeare had ceased to be an elite passion by midcentury.

16. Edward Everett Hale Jr., *The Life and Letters of Edward Everett Hale*, 2 vols. (Boston: Little, Brown, 1917), 1:382.

17. Edward Everett Hale Jr., *Memories of a Hundred Years*, 2 vols. (New York: Macmillan, 1902), 2:51–52, 74–75.

18. Nancy Isenberg, *Fallen Founder: The Life of Aaron Burr* (New York: Viking, 2007), esp. chap. 9.

19. Hale, *Life and Letters of Edward Everett Hale*, 1:346, 1:357–59, 2:256–57; Hale, *Memories of a Hundred Years*, 1:86–100. For the characterization of the historical Philip Nolan, see *(New York) Commercial Advertiser* and *(Baltimore) Federal Gazette*, June 30, 1801, and *Massachusetts Mercury* (Boston), July 7, 1801. For Lincoln's stated position on Vallandigham, see his response of June 12, 1863, to Democratic meeting held in Albany, NY, in *President Lincoln's Views* (Philadelphia: King and Baird, 1863). See also Frank L. Klement, "Clement L. Vallandigham's Exile in the Confederacy," *Journal of Southern History* 31, no. 2 (1965): 149–63. Lincoln chose to banish the ostensible traitor from the Union rather than imprison him.

20. Hale, *Life and Letters of Edward Everett Hale*, 2:224–29.

21. Edward Everett Hale, *Sketches of the Lives of the Brothers Everett* (Boston: Little, Brown, 1878), 6–7; Oliver Everett, *An Eulogy on General George Washington* (Charlestown, MA: Samuel Etheridge, 1800), 13. As early as 1818, an English-born immigrant with significant social connections noted that "the force of public opinion and sentiment, attached to [Washington's] person throughout the whole of the United States, bore a striking resemblance to that kind of magical power and illusion, which many most distinguished political writers attribute to the pervading influences of monarchy, under the name of loyalty to the reigning sovereign." He predicted that none of Washington's successors would ever be able to replicate such quasiroyal feelings of attachment (John Bristed, *America and Her Resources* [London: Henry Colburn, 1818], 381).

22. James Kirke Paulding, *A Life of Washington*, 2 vols. (New York: Harper and Brothers, 1835), 1:62. The owner of Mount Vernon in 1835 was Jane Charlotte Blackburn Washington.

23. Hale, *Memories of a Hundred Years*, 2:12; Everett, *Life of George Washington*, 260–61, 267–71. Everett's biography contains appendices that provide a medical expert's blow-by-blow analysis of the subject's

final illness and treatment and all items contained in Washington's
estate at the time of his death, including some five hundred volumes,
the majority of which were of a practical nature.

24. Hale, *Memories of a Hundred Years*, 2:23.

25. Maurizio Valsania, *First Among Men: George Washington and the Myth
of American Masculinity* (Baltimore. John Hopkins University Press,
2022), esp. chap. 1; see also Andrew M. Schocket, *Fighting over the
Founders: How We Remember the American Revolution* (New York:
New York University Press, 2015), and Heinz Tschachler, *George
Washington and Political Fatherhood: The Endurance of a National Myth*
(Jefferson, NC: McFarland, 2020).

26. *Biographical Directory of the American Congress, 1774–1949* (Washington, DC: US Government Printing Office, 1950), 858, 1250, 1444,
1927.

27. Millington W. Bergeson-Lockwood, "'We Do Not Care Particularly
about the Skating Rinks': African American Challenges to Racial
Discrimination in Places of Public Amusement in Nineteenth-
Century Boston, Massachusetts," *Journal of the Civil Rights Era* 5,
no. 2 (2015): 254–88; "Duty of the Government," *The Colored
American* (Washington, DC), Nov. 25, 1899.

28. Peter Charles Hoffer, *For Ourselves and Our Posterity: The Preamble to
the Federal Constitution in American History* (New York: Oxford
University Press, 2013), 72–73, 92–93; Richard D. Brown, *The
Strength of a People: The Idea of an Informed Citizenry in America,
1650–1870* (Chapel Hill: University of North Carolina Press, 1996).

29. Case in point: the so-called father of the Constitution, James
Madison, was *displeased* by the results of the Constitutional Convention and said so. He did not get what he wanted. The unheralded
Roger Sherman of Connecticut was *at least* as influential as Madison
during those grueling months in Philadelphia. Madison had more
faith in an elite class of men to ensure the public good than he was
invested in the popular voice on any important issue. Initially, he did
not support a bill of rights either, and he judged at this time that
"humane masters" were making trouble by emancipating slaves: color
was an "insuperable" barrier to a healthy polity, and society would be
adversely affected by "freedmen who retain the vices and habits of
slaves" unless they were adequately managed. Add to these circumstances the fact that Alexander Hamilton deserted the Constitutional
Convention, calling his further attendance a waste of his time. Instead

of arguing for a position, he returned at the end of the convention, describing the final text as "better than nothing" as he affixed his signature. Yet as "Publius," coauthors of the *Federalist Papers*, no two men are more closely associated with the strength of the document and their personal commitment to its provisions. Of course, a nuanced exposition is not the narrative students of history receive, because history's father figures cannot be rendered too complicated or emotionally torn. See Andrew Burstein and Nancy Isenberg, *Madison and Jefferson* (New York: Random House, 2010), 149–53, 172–74, 196, 200; see also Jennifer R. Mercieca, *Founding Fictions* (Tuscaloosa: University of Alabama Press, 2010).

30. "Thoughts upon Prejudice," *Western Monthly Review* 1 (Aug. 1827), 202.

31. Peter Fritzsche, *Stranded in the Present: Modern Time and the Melancholy of History* (Cambridge, MA: Harvard University Press, 2004), 65.

32. "Mr. Gardenier's Speech," *Albany Gazette*, Mar. 3, 1808; *(New York) Public Advertiser*, Mar. 3, 1808; *New-York Gazette*, Mar. 7, 1808, and *(New York) Public Advertiser* (report on the Gardenier-Campbell duel in Bladensburg), Mar. 7, 1808; *Boston Gazette*, Jan. 2, 1809 (excerpts of Gardenier speech, Dec. 22, 1808); *Northern Whig* (Hudson, NY), Jan. 3, 1809; Myra L. Spaulding, "Dueling in the District of Columbia," *Records of the Columbia Historical Society, Washington, D.C.* 29–30 (1928): 123. Jefferson pursued the embargo as "peaceable coercion" in an effort to punish Great Britain without resorting to war. George Washington Campbell was born in Scotland in 1769 and could not have been named after the first president; he later served as a secretary of the treasury under President Madison. The proximate cause of the duel was Gardenier's allusion to the "invisible influence" of Napoleon on Jefferson's policy; *Albany Register*, Mar. 8, 1808.

33. Paul Ricoeur, *The Rule of Metaphor* (Toronto: University of Toronto Press, 1977). Ricoeur examines the phenomenon of polysemy (how words acquire multiple meanings) through "association by resemblance" and "a psychologizing semantics." We can readily grasp how expressions like "a *warm* color" and "a *clear* voice" satisfy the logic of metaphor building and therefore have gained social acceptance. "The synaesthetics constitute a case of spontaneous perception of resemblances. . . . Sensorial correspondences harmonize" (118–20). Words don't always make logical sense: one "sits" in the "stands" at a ball game. One can occupy a position in physical space (resident

on a plot of land, ten meters north), hold a position within an organization (assistant to the president), or adopt a position in the form of an opinion. See also Steven Pinker, *The Stuff of Thought: Language as a Window into Human Nature* (New York: Viking Penguin, 2007), chap. 5. New words frequently enter vocabulary in response to emotional developments. In 2020, the editor of the *Oxford English Dictionary* saw fit to update the definition of "social distancing," first used in 1957 to mean "an aloofness or a deliberate attempt to distance oneself from others socially." The global pandemic gave new life to a little-used term, now primarily defined as "keeping a physical distance between ourselves and others to avoid infection" (Bernadette Paton, executive editor of the *OED*, quoted in the *Guardian*, Apr. 8, 2020).

34. Elaine G. Breslaw, *Lotions, Potions, Pills, and Magic: Health Care in Early America* (New York: New York University Press, 2012); Andrew Burstein, *Jefferson's Secrets: Death and Desire at Monticello* (New York: Basic Books, 2005), chap. 2; Roy Porter, *Flesh in the Age of Reason* (New York: Norton, 2003).

35. Alexis McCrossen covers the entire nineteenth century in *Marking Modern Times: A History of Clocks, Watches, and Other Timekeepers in American Life* (Chicago: University of Chicago Press, 2013).

36. Aristotle, *Aristotle's Nicomachean Ethics*, trans. Robert C. Bartlett and Susan D. Collins (Chicago: University of Chicago Press, 2011), 32, 229–30.

37. Sandra Garrido and Emery Schubert, "Individual Differences in the Enjoyment of Negative Emotion in Music: A Literature Review and Experiment," *Music Perception: An Interdisciplinary Journal* 28, no. 3 (2011): 279–96. "The past is a foreign country" was coined by novelist L. P. Hartley in 1953 (it is the opening line of his book *The Go-Between*). In a letter to August von Hennings dated June 25, 1782, German Jewish moral philosopher Moses Mendelssohn (1729–1786) offers another way to understand Jefferson's "pursuit," defining pursuit as process: "Human happiness lies more in man's struggling and striving than in the consumption of the fruits of his labor" (*Moses Mendelssohn: Selections from His Writings*, ed. Eva Jospe [New York: Viking, 1975], 169). The most recent book to deal comprehensively with the intellectual character of the Enlightenment uses the phrase in its subtitle. Ritchie Robertson refers to "pursuit of happiness" as the "governing idea" of the movement; he treats emotional nature in the production

of empathy in combination with literary enthusiasm, a classically
driven aesthetic appreciation, and charitable activity, i.e., "practical
humanity" (*The Enlightenment: The Pursuit of Happiness, 1680–1790*
[New York: Harper, 2021]).

38. Charles Darwin cited in Marina Van Zuylen, *The Plenitude of Distraction* (New York: Sequence Press, 2017), 6, 10, quote at 7. Van Zuylen
notes that this condition, clinically known as "anhedonia," an inability
to experience pleasure, is the equivalent of that suffered by modern
workaholics.

39. Dean Buonomano, *Your Brain Is a Time Machine: The Neuroscience and
Physics of Time* (New York: Norton, 2017), 72. Another contemporary
authority in the science of emotions puts a positive spin on automatic
processes: "Culture works most smoothly if we believe in our own
mental creations, such as money and laws, without realizing that
we're doing so. We don't suspect the involvement of our own hand (or
neurons, as it were) in these constructions, so we just treat them as
reality" (Lisa Feldman Barrett, *How Emotions Are Made: The Secret
Life of the Brain* [Boston: Houghton Mifflin Harcourt, 2017], 286).

Index

abolitionists. *See* antislavery
  advocates
absence and separation: as experienced in the eighteenth and
  nineteenth centuries, 12–13, 18,
  88–93; letters as solace during,
  88–93; and memory, 91–93
Adams, Abigail, 11, 42; correspondence of, 72–73, 317n42; and
  Thomas Jefferson, 108, 109; sea
  metaphor as used by, 94, 95–96,
  103; on separation from family,
  66–68; Shakespeare as quoted in
  letters of, 108–12; and Elizabeth
  Smith Shaw, 72–73, 84–85; on
  George Washington, 69, 70; and
  Martha Washington, 66, 69, 73,
  108
Adams, Hannah, 305n26; *A Summary History of New-England*,
  36–37
Adams, John, 11, 28, 66–67; on
  affection and sentiment, 77; and
  correspondence with Benjamin
  Waterhouse, 122–25; death of,
  194–95; on imagination, 87–88;
  and Thomas Jefferson, 109, 132,

244; on history, 270; on neology,
  132; and Alexander Pope, 4, 5, 6;
  on Shakespeare, 107, 112, 132;
  on Shakespeare's characters, 112;
  sea travel as experienced by, 96
Adams, John Quincy, 6, 221, 286;
  absences of, 66, 67, 74–75; and
  Louisa Catherine Adams, 74–75,
  88–89; on America as a "representative democracy," 181; on
  ceding of Florida to the US, 234;
  as minister to the Netherlands,
  66; on mixing of races, 231; poem
  by, 75–76; as reader of Shakespeare, 112–13; as president, 194;
  sea metaphor as used by, 94; sea
  travel as experienced by, 96
Adams, Louisa Catherine Johnson,
  317n39; on her husband's absence,
  74–75, 88–89; on her husband's
  poem for her sister, 75–76
Adams, Samuel, 62
Adams family: as admirers of
  Shakespeare, 108–13, 114;
  papers and correspondence of,
  66–68; separations experienced
  by, 12–13, 66–69, 88–89

Ohio: slavery prohibited in, 240
Oliver, John W., 180
Oxford English Dictionary: "neology" and "neologism" as defined in, 129–30

painting: as metaphor in letters, 81–82, 91–92; as metaphor in Shakespeare, 125–26
past, the: and the distortion of memory, 292–93; nostalgia for, 9, 16, 171, 202, 288, 292–93; as reimagined in literature, 273–74. *See also* emotional connections
patriotic biography: and the national creation story, 53–56; during the Revolutionary era, 52
Paulding, James Kirke, 13, 145, 196; "The Azure Hose," 165; background of, 148; biography of Washington by, 207–8, 282–83; *Chronicles of the City of Gotham*, 147; *The Diverting History of John Bull and Brother Jonathan*, 146, 149–50, 154, 184; *Letters from the South*, 229; *Lion of the West*, 179; on "Negroes," 229; "On Style," 162, 164; as publisher of *Salmagundi*, 146–47, 161; racism of, 343n4; on Shakespeare, 152; *The United States and England*, 151–52
Paulding, John, 146, 207
Paulding, William, 147
Paulding, William Irving, 147
Peale, Charles Willson, 126, 324n30
People's Friend, 167
Perry, Commodore Matthew C., 351–52n56

Philadelphia Library Company of Colored Persons, 253–54
physiognomy: as basis for racial prejudice, 238, 255; as guide to human character, 126–27, 346n22, 346n24, 350n48; of Alexander Pope, 4, 6
Pinckney, Eliza, 92
poetry: as alluded to in letters, 84–85; Black women and, 4, 83, 253, 301n22, 344n11; Darwin's regrets about, 293; hate mail in the form of, 8–9; and the imagination, 83; as the language of emotion, 3, 7–8; reading of, as source of pleasure, 80, 301n23. *See also* metaphors; *names of individual poets*
Polk, James K., 265
Pope, Alexander, 84; as adapted for satire of Homer, 159; *Dunciad*, 177; "Eloisa and Abelard," 71–72; "Epistle to Dr. Arbuthnot," 173; *Essay on Man*, 3, 4–5, 19; on letters as an expression of emotion, 71–72; letters of, 15; on perception, 5; physical appearance of, 4, 6; popularity of, 3–4, 6–7; as quoted by Abigail Adams, 67–68; sea metaphor as used by, 94; and Shakespeare, 7; as source of emotional sustenance, 4–5; translation of the *Iliad* by, 177
Port-Folio, 171, 173, 180–81, 206; on emancipation of slaves, 230
prejudices: rationalizations for, 231, 232–33, 242. *See also* races, mixing of; racial prejudice
Prescott, William, 57